D0927853

SPENSER'S PROVERB LORE

With Special Reference to His Use of the *Sententiae* of Leonard Culman and Publilius Syrus

Spenser's Proverb Lore

With Special Reference to His Use of the *Sententiae* of Leonard Culman and Publilius Syrus

CHARLES G. SMITH

HARVARD UNIVERSITY PRESS
Cambridge, Massachusetts
1970

Distributed in Great Britain by Oxford University Press, London
Library of Congress Catalog Card Number 78–85078
SBN 674–83200–0
Made and printed in Great Britain by
William Clowes and Sons, Limited, London and Beccles

To my wife
Cornelia Marschall Smith
Sine qua non

PREFACE

In this adventurous project I am breaking new ground. Never before have Spenser's proverbs been given serious study. The present endeavor is to make a complete collection of Spenser's proverbs. The background, Elizabethan and classical, of each proverb is given.

Many important items have been turned up: the most significant of these are the two hundred and thirty Leonard Culman and the two hundred forty-five Publilius Syrus parallels.

I have been studying Spenser's proverbs for more than thirty years. In the beginning the principal aim was to find and to authenticate his proverbs and to seek out as many Elizabethan and classical parallels as possible. In the course of all this, the Latin and Greek parallels became evident and meaningful: Leonard Culman and Publilius Syrus came alive.

In 1950 Tilley's monumental collection, *A Dictionary of the Proverbs in England in the Sixteenth and Seventeenth Centuries*, was published. Hundreds of the parallels which I had collected over the years he had in his dictionary. Hence it became necessary for me to revise my collection: in doing this I discarded many Elizabethan parallels. Tilley's *Dictionary* contained some forty-five Spenser proverbs I had not authenticated. In this collection, therefore, many proverbs are presented without parallels. Tilley's and other collections which contained parallels are cited; however, I have included Elizabethan parallels which Tilley's and other collections do not have.

To colleagues and students I owe kindnesses far too many to enumerate. Above all others I am indebted to Dr. E. Hudson Long, Chairman of the Department of English, Baylor University, for assistance and encouragement. I am indebted to Dr. Roy F. Butler, Dr. Richard Cutter, and Professor Elmer Fisher for assistance in translating many of the Greek and Latin proverbs. To the Baylor University Library staff, in particular to Estaline Cox, Lulu Stine, and Lucy Sue Williams; to the University of Michigan Library for the use of its copy of the *Sentences* of Publilius Syrus edited by Jules Chenu, printed in Paris in 1835; to John B. Stetson University Library for the use of Bickford-Smith's 1895 edition of Publilius Syrus; and to Miss Fannie Ratchford, Curator of the Research Center at the University of Texas, for her many favors over a period of several years, I wish to express my gratitude. For assistance in the preparation of this material for publication I owe thanks to Eunice Webber, Lois Thacker, Tama Dell Porter, Helen Jo Nelson, Katherine Bond, Sandra Mitchell, Paula-Kay Lyall, Linda Cruser, Marsha Whitlow, and Linda Stamps. For preparing the copy of this book for the press I am indebted to my wife, Cornelia Marschall Smith, without whose help and cooperation the book could never have been published.

POST PREFACE

This book was finished by my late husband, except for the writing of the Introduction for which he had assembled some sixty handwritten pages of notes, when death overtook him. The President of the University and the members of the faculty of the Department of English immediately came to my assistance with assurances and encouragement and made it possible for me to remain in Mr. Smith's office to finish his book. I nonetheless undertook the writing of the Introduction with trepidation. My sister, Irene Marschall King, and a former student of Mr. Smith's, Robert

Grant Burns, by their constructive suggestions and criticism contributed significantly to the writing of the Introduction. I also am grateful to Professor Richard Cutter for his critical reading of the manuscript and to Professor James L. Shepherd for reading the proof.

The author, Charles G. Smith, son of Janette Paschal and Robert Daniel Smith, was born June 6, 1891, near Siler City, Chatham County, North Carolina, where he received his elementary education. From the Siler Latin Grammar School he entered Wake Forest College, where he earned the B.A., *magna cum laude*, Phi Beta Kappa, and the M.A., and where later he was awarded the Litt.D. degree. He also earned master's degrees from the University of Pennsylvania and from the University of North Carolina, and the Ph.D. from Johns Hopkins. In 1929 he was elected to membership in the Tudor and Stuart Club. He was a student under Professor Edwin Greenlaw, eminent Spenser scholar, at North Carolina and at Hopkins. Once the author's interest in Renaissance literature was awakened, it never waned. In the years to come he published studies on *Spenser's Theory of Friendship* (Johns Hopkins Press, 1935) and *Shakespeare's Proverb Lore* (Harvard University Press, 1963).

Except for two years at Goucher College and five at Stetson University, most of his college teaching was done at Baylor University, where he was named Distinguished Professor in 1961. "And gladly wolde he lerne and gladly teche."

CORNELIA M. SMITH

Waco, Texas
1969

CONTENTS

SPENSER'S PROVERB LORE

With Special Reference to His Use of the
Sententiae of Leonard Culman and Publilius Syrus

INTRODUCTION

In the English Renaissance the interest in proverbs climbed to an astonishing height: the Elizabethans were truly proverb conscious; they were steeped in proverbs; they loved moral maxims or *sententiae*.[1] They knew that "when we deal with proverbs we are close to man and often near to wisdom." Francis Bacon asserted that the genius, wit, and spirit of a nation are discovered in its proverbs. The Elizabethans made no distinction between proverbs and *sententiae*; hence no distinction is made between them in this study. Such a distinction, rigidly enforced on this Spenser material, would break down.[2]

Proverbs in the Elizabethan period were so popular that many collections were made. Queen Elizabeth evidently had considerable interest in proverb lore, for, according to tradition, when John Heywood presented her with a copy of his collection, the first collection of English proverbs,[3] she promptly challenged him, saying that she would wager that he had omitted some. The unique proverb she had in mind, "Bate me an ace, quoth Bolton," was not in his collection.

The Elizabethan estimate of the validity of proverbs is similar to Aristotle's, who tested his dicta by the moral judgment of his

[1] B. J. Whiting, Francis W. Bradley, Richard Jente, Archer Taylor, and M. P. Tilley, "The Study of Proverbs," *Modern Language Forum*, vol. XXIV, no. 2 (June 1939), p. 83.

[2] For a further consideration of proverb definition see Mary Kemendo Sendón, "Spenser's Use of Proverbs" (unpublished master's thesis, Dept. of English, Baylor University, 1932) and Gustav Cornelius Adams, "Proverb Lore in Spenser's Minor Poems and in "A View of the Present State of Ireland" (unpublished master's thesis, Dept. of English, John B. Stetson University, 1936).

[3] W. G. Smith, *The Oxford Dictionary of English Proverbs* (Oxford: Clarendon Press, 1935), Introduction, p. xx, and John Heywood, *Dialogue of the Effectual Proverbs in the English Tongue Concerning Marriage* (London: Gibbings and Co., 1906).

age and country as evidenced by proverbs and *sententiae*. In dealing with proverbs it must be remembered that Spenser's use of them illustrates a diffused humanism.[4]

With the Latin proverb, "*In medio superest via gurgite*" (see "List of Proverbs,"[5] no. 523), Spenser expresses his philosophy of the golden mean in a letter to Harvey. This, moreover, is the theme both of the *Shepheardes Calender* and of the *Faerie Queene*.[6] At another time in writing to Spenser, Harvey cites Spenser's motto, a proverb: "Your oulde Autenticall Rule, that you were wunt to saye you learned first of ower Master Rydge, *Cautela superabundans non nocet*" (One can never be too cautious; no. 90).

The connection of Elizabethan proverb lore with the many emblem books of the period emphasizes the importance of proverbs to the Elizabethans. The theory generally was accepted that poetry should teach; consistently poetry and philosophy were associated.[7] In such a literary environment Spenser, who wished to "moralize his song," inevitably made use of proverb lore. The emblems in the *Shepheardes Calender* attest to this belief, for of the thirty-one emblems in the *Shepheardes Calender*, twelve contain proverbs. Of these twelve, nine emblems are stated as proverbs and each of three additional long emblems includes a proverb; in these twelve, furthermore, Spenser uses the Greek version in one, and the Latin in five. His use of Greek and Latin is not surprising, for he was a diligent student of the classics, and he frequently used Greek and Latin insets in his poems.

Although the proverbs found in Spenser have a timeless quality about them, a few are purely contemporary, for example, "Scottes and Redd-shankes" (see no. 642). The Elizabethans, in their fond-

[4] Charles G. Smith, *Shakespeare's Proverb Lore* (Cambridge, Massachusetts: Harvard University Press, 1963), pp. 13–14.

[5] The 892 exhibited in this book. Succeeding references are by number only.

[6] Emile Legouis, *Spenser* (New York: E. P. Dutton and Co., 1926), p. 17, and H. S. V. Jones, *A Spenser Handbook* (New York: Appleton-Century-Crofts, 1930), p. 50.

[7] B. E. C. Davis, *Edmund Spenser* (Cambridge: Cambridge University Press, 1933), p. 210.

ness for *sententiae*, often expressed platitudes (trite or commonplace remarks), for example, "all men must die" (no. 179) and "all things change" (no. 95), or maxims (rules of conduct), for example, "avoid shame and disgrace" (no. 31) and "one can never be too cautious" (no. 90) in proverbs. A concise inlaid maxim or emblem, a well-known phrase or sententious saying gleaned from Erasmus or others, delighted their ears.[8]

In school, Spenser was taught to devise pithy aphorisms.[9] Like other schoolboys, he had to study and even memorize proverbs. He probably memorized the school collection of *sententiae* of Publilius Syrus[10] compiled by Erasmus[11] and the *Sententiae*

[8] Gabriel Harvey, for example, wrote Spenser: "You know the Greek proverb πορφύρα περὶ πορφύραν διακριτέα" (purple is more easily judged when compared with purple). See Gabriel Harvey, *Works*, vol. I, ed. Alexander B. Grosart (London: Printed for private circulation only, 1884–1885), pp. 18–19.

When Professor Henry Trantham, Chairman of the Department of Classics at Baylor, was asked to translate this proverb to show the latitude permitted in stating a proverbial truth, he gave several versions:

Literal: 1. Purple must be judged in relation to purple.
Very free: 2. In the glory of the King lesser lights grow dim.
Other: 3. There are various shades of purple.
4. Purple differeth from purple in glory.
5. You must know your purple (colloquial).
6. There's purple and purple (colloquial).

[9] W. L. Renwick, *Edmund Spenser* (London: Edward Arnold & Co., 1925), p. 124.

[10] Publilius Syrus belonged to the age of Julius Caesar. Of Syrian origin, he came to Rome probably from Antioch. For some time he was a slave in Rome. His talents and virtues gaining for him his freedom, he began to write plays called *mimes*. His great success attracted the attention of Julius Caesar, who called him to Rome and showered honors upon him. His plays have all been lost. Only his moral maxims—his pithy *sententiae*—have survived.

[11] An account of the origin and use of Culman's *Sententiae Pueriles* and of Publilius Syrus' *Sentences* and his *Sententiae* is set forth in Charles G. Smith's *Shakespeare's Proverb Lore*, pp. 5–9 and 17. He shows that it is highly probable that these collections of *sententiae* were used as textbooks by the Elizabethan schoolboy and that Culman compiled his collections from numerous sources and edited it *circa* 1540, whereas the original Publilius Syrus collection was made perhaps in the first century A.D. Later, additional proverbs were foisted into the Publilian collection. The two collections used in this study are: *Sentences* of Publilius Syrus edited by Jules Chenu, 1835, and *Sententiae* of Publilius Syrus edited by J. Wight Duff and Arnold M. Duff, 1934. In the "List of Proverbs" of the present study, an asterisk marks the *sententiae* of Publilius Syrus found in the Elizabethan school collection and included in the *Catonis Disticha* prepared by Erasmus.

Pueriles compiled by Leonard Culman,[12] and it is not at all unlikely that he was required to keep in his commonplace book a collection of proverbs drawn from his reading.

> The new [Elizabethan] poets were scholars, and proud of it. They wrote for scholars who would understand and appreciate the neat insetting of a well-known phrase to enrich the content of a passage by the reader's memory of its origin, and still more, perhaps, of a "sentence," the sententious saying which that age so loved and studied in the classics and in the collections of Erasmus [and others].[13]

Spenser takes the stiffness and rigidity out of proverbs; he seldom quotes them as such. If he does quote, he shows a tendency to admire their dexterity of ingenious word play. When Spenser chooses, he weaves a complete stanza or a whole sonnet entirely out of one proverb; in other words, a proverb becomes the *thema* of that composition. Six times he weaves the entire stanza of nine lines; four times he weaves eight lines, seven lines, and six lines; and eleven times he weaves five lines from single proverbs.[14] Harvey considered this "the hall-mark of elegant learning."[15]

[12] Leonard Culman [Leonhardus Culmannus] was born in Crailsheim, Germany, on February 22, 1497 or 1498. His pre-university schooling was in Halle, Dinkelsbühl, Nürnberg, and Saalfeld. He studied later at Erfurt and Leipzig. He served as a schoolmaster in Bamberg, Ansbach, and Nürnberg. Finally, he became an evangelical clergyman. In 1558 he took a pastorate in Bernstatt near the capital city of Ulm. In this region in 1562 he died. For further information concerning him consult *Allgemeine Deutsche Biographie*, Leipzig, 1876.

[13] Renwick, *Edmund Spenser*, p. 124.

[14] The following is a list of proverbs used to make 5–9 lines of a stanza, that is, the *thema* of the stanza.

"List of Proverbs," no.	Number of lines
146, 293, 370, 423, 475, 502, 600, 608, 654, 732, 798	5
21, 86, 186, 437	6
197, 535, 659, 816	7
215, 362, 508, 885	8
111, 214, 350, 391, 565, 725	9

[15] Gabriel Harvey, *Ciceronianus*, trans. by Clarence A. Forbes, and ed. with an Introduction and Notes by Harold S. Wilson and Clarence A. Forbes, *University of Nebraska Studies* ("Studies in the Humanities," no. 4 [November 1945], p. 30).

Spenser never uses *sententiae* as mere copybook tags. Only one proverbial phrase (see no. 408), "in hugger-mugger," is identified as slang;[16] on occasion, however, Spenser uses a proverb as a gnomic tag,[17] for example, "A dram of sweet is worth a pound of sour" (no. 743) or "Acorns were good till bread was found" (no. 5). It is to be questioned whether he coined a single new maxim bearing the personal mark.[18]

In many instances the context of Spenser's verse calls for a proverb: the words, as it were, compel a response with a particular proverb.

The distribution of proverbs used by Spenser to cap off, that is, to begin or end, a stanza in the *Faerie Queene* and other poems is not without interest. Spenser uses the principle of repetition or epic variation: he expresses an idea and then reinforces it by capping it with a proverb. Although no proverbs are used in this manner in *Epithalamion*, *The Fowre Hymnes*, *Prothalamion*, *Astrophel*, or in *Colin Clouts Come Home Againe*, one is used in *Daphnaïda*, eleven in *Complaints*, sixteen in *Amoretti*, and 419 in the *Faerie Queene*.[19] To tabulate the number of proverbs in each book of the *Faerie Queene*, the number of proverbs in each book used to cap, and then to corrolate this information with the subject matter treated in each book, the chart at the top of page 6 is set up. It is interesting to note that the largest number of proverbs used to cap a stanza is found in Book IV, which deals with friendship,[20] and that Book I, which treats of "holinesse," contains the second largest group. Worthy of special mention is the fact that, of the total 190

[16] F. O. Matthiessen, *Translation: An Elizabethan Art* (Cambridge, Massachusetts: Harvard University Press, 1931), p. 83.

[17] Davis, *Edmund Spenser*, p. 145.

[18] Legouis, *Spenser*, p. 44.

[19] R. E. Neil Dodge, ed., *The Complete Poetical Works of Spenser* (Boston: Houghton Mifflin Co., 1936 [Cambridge Edition]) is the text used when tabulations are made and recorded in this research.

[20] The Fourth Book of the *Faerie Queene* in its observations on friendship is essentially sententious. Spenser was eclectic in selecting his material to picture his ideas about friendship. See Charles G. Smith, *Spenser's Theory of Friendship* (Baltimore: Johns Hopkins Press, 1935), pp. 27–42.

"Capping" in the *Faerie Queene*

Book	Total number of proverbs	Number of proverbs used to cap	Subject matter
I	234	77	Holinesse
II	196	70	Temperaunce
III	181	75	Chastity
IV	190	104	Friendship
V	145	30	Justice
VI	155	55	Courtesie
VII	24	8	Mutabilitie

proverbs found in Book IV, 104 either begin or end a stanza, whereas, of the 234 found in Book I, only 77 are used to begin or end a stanza.

Spenser, furthermore, often uses the same proverb more than once to cap stanzas in the *Faerie Queene*.[21] In fact eighty-one

[21] Repetitive use of certain proverbs to cap stanzas in the *Faerie Queene*: "b" indicates that a proverb begins and "e" that a proverb ends a stanza or stanzas.

"List of Proverbs," no.	Reference in *Faerie Queene*	Key	"List of Proverbs," no.	Reference in *Faerie Queene*	Key
4	V, iv, 28, 1–3	b	105	VI, vii, 4, 1–2	b
	VI, ix, 29, 1–2	b	128	III, vii, 26, 9	e
14	III, xi, 16, 1	b		IV, iii, 8, 9	e
	17, 9	e	151	I, x, 42, 8–9	e
24	VI, ix, 29, 9	e		II, viii, 29, 6–9	e
	30, 9	e	153	I, ix, 47, 9	e
	31, 1–2	b		III, ii, 39, 9	e
41	III, i, 22, 1	b	157	III, v, 45, 8–9	e
	VI, v, 19, 1	b		ix, 14, 8–9	e
	vii, 47, 1	b		V, iv, 32, 8–9	e
43	III, vii, 29, 8–9	e		xi, 55, 9	e
	IV, xi, 45, 9	e	163	II, i, 36, 6–9	e
52	I, x, 6, 1	b		IV, viii, 16, 9	e
	III, ii, 36, 9	e	167	I, ix, 2, 8–9	e
60	I, v, 20, 8–9	e		III, xi, 9, 8–9	e
	vii, 37, 9	e	178	III, i, 37, 9	e
88	V, viii, 7, 9	e		iv, 27, 1–2	b
	VI, ii, 23, 7–9	e		36, 9	e
105	II, vii, 45, 9	e	191	V, viii, 7, 1	b

"List of Proverbs," no.	Reference in *Faerie Queene*	Key	"List of Proverbs," no.	Reference in *Faerie Queene*	Key
191	VI, xi, 17, 1–4	b	359	VI, i, 41, 9	e
193	IV, iv, 27, 1–2	b	391	II, iii, 40, 9	e
	V, ii, 42, 1	b		IV, ii, 27, 8–9	e
198	III, xii, 33, 9	e		xi, 22, 8–9	e
	IV, v, 9, 9	e		VI, ii, 2, 9	e
	VI, ii, 13, 8–9	e		ix, 2, 1–9	be
200	II, viii, 4, 1	b	407	II, ix, 52, 9	e
	III, i, 23, 1	b		IV, vi, 2, 1	b
201	II, i, 31, 1	b		V, xi, 14, 9	e
	vi, 23, 9	e	415	III, i, 54, 8–9	e
214	I, iv, 32, 1–9	be		IV, x, 49, 9	e
	V, xii, 31, 1–3	b	427	I, viii, 44, 9	e
215	I, iv, 30, 1–5	b		V, iii, 9, 1	b
	V, xii, 31, 1–8	b	441	II, xi, 25, 9	e
220	II, viii, 28, 9	e		III, i, 32, 1–2	b
	29, 1–2	b	476	I, i, 30, 1	b
230	I, iii, 9, 9	e		III, x, 23, 9	e
	VII, vi, 28, 9	e		37, 9	e
235	III, xii, 28, 1–2	b		V, iii, 34, 9	e
	V, v, 49, 9	e	481	III, i, 29, 8–9	e
247	III, vi, 54, 9	e		VI, ix, 37, 9	e
	II, iv, 32, 1	b	484	II, iv, 24, 9	e
	III, vii, 26, 9	e		III, iv, 9, 6–9	e
260	II, xi, 32, 1–5	b	486	III, vii, 20, 9	e
	V, v, 53, 7–9	e		V, vi, 3, 9	e
281	I, ix, 11, 1–3	b	490	III, i, 49, 8–9	e
	III, x, 10, 1–2	b		iii, 1, 4–9	e
290	I, ix, 6, 8–9	e	493	I, v, 18, 7–9	e
	III, v, 27, 1	b		IV, vii, 10, 9	e
	x, 3, 1–2	b		VI, iii, 12, 1–3	b
	V, iv, 27, 9	e	494	I, vi, 3, 8–9	e
300	I, xii, 22, 1	b		IV, v, 25, 9	e
	IV, x, 37, 9	e	523	II, i, 58, 1–2	b
303	IV, ii, 18, 8–9	e		ii, 38, 1–4	b
	ix, 27, 7–9	e	557	II, vii, 12, 1–2	b
309	I, x, 62, 9	e		III, x, 31, 8–9	e
	IV, iv, 1, 8–9	e	585	III, xi, 30, 9	e
311	IV, ii, 29, 9	e		IV, x, 42, 9	e
	vi, 46, 8–9	e	593	II, x, 14, 9	e
312	IV, vi, 31, 6–9	e		III, x, 28, 9	e
	x, 27, 7–9	e	597	I, x, 23, 7–9	e
316	I, v, 25, 9	e		28, 8–9	e
	V, xii, 32, 8–9	e		xi, 38, 9	e
351	I, vii, 41, 1–2	b	614	III, xi, 16, 1–2	b
	51, 9	e		V, viii, 41, 9	e
359	III, vi, 21, 9	e		VI, ii, 10, 9	e

proverbs are used in this manner and these eighty-one are distributed as shown in the accompanying chart.

The number of times and where, beginning and/or end, a particular proverb is repeated is as follows ("b" indicates that a proverb begins and "e" that a proverb ends a stanza or stanzas):

two	*three*	*four*	*five*	*six*
9—bb	2—bbb	2—bbee	1—bbeee	1—beeeee
19—be	3—bbe	1—beee		
35—ee	6—bee			
	3—eee			

"List of Proverbs," no.	Reference in *Faerie Queene*	Key	"List of Proverbs," no.	Reference in *Faerie Queene*	Key
635	I, v, 33, 7–9	e	772	IV, ii, 33, 1–2	b
	II, viii, 45, 7–9	e		V, iv, 8, 1	b
637	I, vii, 29, 9	e	780	VI, i, 8, 8–9	e
	viii, 50, 9	e		vi, 12, 2–9	e
640	II, ii, 11, 1	b	782	II, i, 5, 9	e
	IV, v, 24, 9	e		III, xii, 12, 1	b
648	I, vi, 47, 1–4	b	811	II, vii, 59, 1	b
	IV, ix, 34, 9	e		61, 9	e
661	II, ii, 29, 8–9	e		III, x, 39, 9	e
	V, viii, 30, 9	e		VI, iv, 9, 1	b
681	IV, vi, 6, 1	b	824	IV, iii, 28, 1–2	b
	VI, 1, 25, 9	e		ix, 24, 8–9	e
696	II, v, 30, 8–9	e		V, ii, 17, 1	b
	VI, viii, 36, 9	e	825	I, vii, 1, 1	b
704	II, v, 34, 1	b		II, vi, 26, 1	b
	III, xi, 28, 8–9	e		IV, i, 17, 9	e
731	II, iv, 11, 9	e	828	I, viii, 43, 1	b
	III, vii, 34, 1–3	b		V, vi, 23, 9	e
738	IV, vii, 7, 9	e	838	II, ix, 19, 1	b
	VI, iv, 36, 7–9	e		I, x, 13, 1	b
	VII, vi, 6, 9	e	840	I, i, 4, 9	e
761	I, vii, 40, 9	e		IV, xi, 49, 9	e
	II, i, 46, 9	e	853	I, xii, 1, 9	e
762	II, iv, 33, 8–9	e		II, xi, 4, 7–8	e
	xi, 2, 9	e	858	II, v, 21, 6–9	e
765	III, iv, 46, 1–3	b		VI, i, 30, 7–9	e
	vii, 23, 1–2	b	879	IV, viii, 26, 9	e
	VI, vii, 44, 1–2	b		VI, vii, 49, 9	e

This compilation shows that when Spenser wishes to stress an idea, he clothes it in a proverb and places the proverb at the beginning and/or end of a stanza; the compilation further shows that, in such instances, Spenser prefers using the end over the beginning (26 to 15 times). This technique of repetitive capping is an arresting example of how Spenser makes certain ideas or truths prevail in his poetry. In the repetition of these eighty-one proverbs, the compilation also shows that 63 are repeated twice, 14 three, 3 four, 1 five, and 1 six times: another illustration of how Spenser through repetition submits proverbs to the shaping power of his imagination.

It is apropos to exemplify Spenser's use of double proverb construction, *FQ*, III, xi, 16–17. The speaker here begins his complaint with a proverb, and, after two stanzas, ends his complaint with the same proverb. To take another example: *FQ*, VI, vi, 14, 1–2 ("The best . . . that I can you advise, Is to avoide the occasion of the ill:") and *FQ*, VI, vi, 14, 3–4 ("when the cause, whence evill doth arize, Removed is, th' effect surceaseth . . .") In the first instance Spenser uses the same proverb, in the second, different proverbs.

Grouping proverbs in clusters is a strategem which Spenser also employed. He manifests dexterity in his interplay of proverb upon proverb to carry and emphasize the central theme. The number of proverbs in a cluster varies from three to as many as ten. The distribution of proverb clusters [22] in Spenser's poems is as follows:

[22] Proverb Clusters

Reference	Proverbs in cluster
Faerie Queene:	
I, i, 12	146, 263, 539, 639, 820
I, ii, 26–27	145, 304, 373, 473, 511
I, iv, 29–30	135, 175, 209, 214, 215, 361, 559, 619
I, vii, 40–41	123, 351, 653, 761, 848
I, viii, 44, 2–9	249, 427, 653, 825
I, ix, 42–43	53, 68, 155, 160, 179, 240, 472, 570
II, vi, 23, 2–9	201, 622, 678, 827
III, ix, 6–7, 7–4	25, 250, 872, 874

Faerie Queene, 35; *Shepheardes Calender*, 10; *Complaints*, 8; *Amoretti*, 5; *Colin Clouts Come Home Againe*, 2; *Astrophel*, 1; and *Daphnaïda*, 1. A further examination of these proverb clusters reveals 42 uses of a three-proverb cluster; 11 uses of a four-proverb cluster; 3 uses of a five-proverb cluster; 2 uses of a six- and of an eight-proverb cluster; 1 use of a seven- and of a ten-proverb cluster: all clusters occur within a few lines, and at most, within two stanzas; for example, *FQ*, I, iv, 29, 1–5 has five proverbs in five lines, and *FQ*, VI, ix, 29–30 has ten proverbs in two stanzas.

Spenser repeats a chosen proverb in certain books of the *Faerie Queene* as often as three times or sometimes even more frequently; and he usually confines the repetition of the chosen proverb to a particular book. For instance, in Book I he repeats "To bite upon the bridle" (see no. 60) five times, and in Book IV he uses "A false friend is a dangerous enemy" (see no. 303) three times; thereafter he makes no further use of these proverbs in the *Faerie Queene*. When he uses a chosen proverb several times, and in that book only, the inference is that he wrote the book as a unit and

---

Reference	Proverbs in cluster
Faerie Queene	
III, x, 3, 1–6	250, 290, 598, 826
V, xi, 55–56, 9–7	157, 231, 791, 891
VI, iii, 41–42, 5–3	267, 286, 359, 520, 527, 601
VI, vi, 14, 1–7	2, 77, 89, 221, 256, 257
VI, ix, 29–30	4, 24, 24, 120, 172, 275, 536, 559, 831, 857
Amoretti:	
LVIII, 3–12	79, 267, 386, 447, 582, 679, 772
Shepheardes Calender:	
Sept., 12–18	107, 349, 663, 761
Nov., 153–157	91, 91, 518, 519
Virgils Gnat:	
355–366	159, 572, 586, 614
Mother H., 903–910	87, 203, 505, 552
Muiopotmos, 217–227	234, 447, 513, 847
Visions of B., I, 3–14	11, 113, 328, 693

with a dominant idea in mind. Certain proverbs appear three times each in Book I (nos. 69 and 653), Book II (no. 523), Book III (no. 247), and Book V (no. 248). "Music eases the troubled mind" (no. 564) contains an idea that was popular with Spenser's contemporaries; hence, it is not surprising that he uses that proverb four times in a single book, Book I. The following maxims are repeated four times each in the book named: "To be wary and wise" (no. 825) in Book II, "At the door of death," (no. 159) in Book I, "The doom of destiny cannot be avoided" (no. 178) in Book III. A sense of coherence is given to the book and an image fixed in the reader's mind by this repetition.

Spenser uses parentheses to enclose proverbs seventeen times; he uses brackets only once.[23] The seventeen parentheses are distributed in his poems as follows: *Faerie Queene*, 8; *Shepheardes Calender*, 4; *Complaints*, 4; and *Astrophel*, 1.

The frequent placing of a colon after the second line of the stanzas in *Colin Clouts Come Home Againe* justifies the assertion that the use of the colon may be called "a trademark of *Colin*."[24] The *Faerie Queene* likewise elicits a special designation for the repeated use of a colon, in this instance, immediately preceding a proverb; in Spenser's poems a total of 324 colons is employed in this manner: Book I has 44; II, 46; III, 43; IV, 45; V, 31; VI, 29; VII, 6; *Complaints*, 30 (17 are in *Mother Hubberd's Tale*); *Shepheardes Calender*, 23; *Amoretti*, 12; *Colin Clouts Come Home Againe*, 7; *Fowre Hymnes*, 4; *Daphnaïda*, 2; *Astrophel*, 1; and *Epithalamion* 1.

Except for two visits to England, Spenser spent the last eighteen years[25] of his life in Ireland. Here he came under the direct influence of the Irish view of proverbs, crystallized in the saying, "Nothing can beat a proverb."[26] An examination of the proverbs

[23] *Shep. Cal.*, Dec., 158.

[24] H. S. V. Jones, *A Spenser Handbook* (New York: Appleton-Century-Crofts, Inc., 1930), p. 333.

[25] W. Renwick, *Spenser* (Oxford: Clarendon Press, 1923), pp. xiv–xv.

[26] Thomas F. O'Rahilly, *A Miscellany of Irish Proverbs* (Dublin: Talbot Press, Ltd., 1922), Preface.

in the "List of Proverbs" of this monograph reveals that Spenser probably came by several proverbs from the Irish.[27]

In his passion for books Spenser showed a particular interest in the English chronicles and in Irish manuscripts and sayings. As Thomas F. O'Rahilly states in *A Miscellany of Irish Proverbs*: ". . . every fluent native-speaker of Irish possesses a repertory of proverbs on which he delights to draw in order to clench an argument or drive home an opinion."[28] When the backdrop against which Spenser wrote is surveyed, his proclivity for the use of a proverb to prove a point is readily understood. Further study of this tendency reveals that Spenser, more than 100 times, presents his premise followed by a proverb introduced by the word "for." The *Faerie Queene* alone contains eighty-one such instances: 14 in Book I, 5 in Book II, 14 in Book III, 21 in Book IV, 9 in Book V, 16 in Book VI, and 2 in Book VII. In addition, 16 are found in *Complaints* (9 are in *Mother Hubberd's Tale*), 11 in *Shepheardes Calender*, 7 in *Colin Clouts Come Home Againe*, 6 in *Amoretti*, 5 in *Fowre Hymnes*, and 2 in *Daphnaïda*.

The interest of Renaissance scholars in proverbs is an aspect of their love of rhetoric. Spenser was in all probability a close student of rhetorical manuals, such as Wilson's; he, therefore, presumably was influenced by his and other rhetoricians' emphasis on proverbs. Following the example of Quintilian, Wilson in his *Arte of Rhetorique*, among other items, emphasizes the use of proverbs for amplification, and Lyly is extravagant in his use of "figures," one type of which is proverbs and pithy sayings.[29]

[27] See "List of Proverbs," nos. 9, 23, 106, 107, 108, 150, 155, 157, 168, 169, 205, 220, 226, 233, 238, 272, 305, 314, 326, 349, 367, 375, 400, 445, 484, 487, 517, 532, 549, 568, 596, 597, 623, 624, 630, 648, 695, 701, 734, 761, 795, 802, 822, 830, 863, and 871.

James Hardiman, *Irish Minstrelsy, or Bardic Remains of Ireland with English Poetic Translations* (London: Joseph Robins, 1831), II, 397–408 (over 200 proverbs in Irish, alphabetically arranged).

John O'Daly, *The Irish Language Miscellany: Being a Selection of Poems by the Munster Bards of the Last Century* (Dublin: O'Daly, 1876), pp. 89–98 (190 proverbs in Irish in alphabetical order).

[28] O'Rahilly, Preface.

[29] Morris Palmer Tilley, *Elizabethan Proverb Lore in Lyly's Euphues and in Pettie's Petite Pallace* (New York: The Macmillan Company, 1926), p. 22.

Since eighteen of the proverbs found in Spenser are also found in Lyly it is not at all unlikely that Spenser was subject to the same influences that prevailed upon Lyly.

Unlike Lyly, Spenser does not use proverbs to ornament his style; as revealed by this study, he uses them to enforce his ideas, to illustrate, to illuminate, and to focus, as with a lens or prism, on a particular thought. Spenser's poetry may be characterized justly by "pithiness." His style is not marked by an opulence of proverbial material thrown in to secure ornamental effects, as in Lyly's *Euphues*. Spenser does not use proverbs to raise a laugh, or to heighten his character drawing, but chiefly to make what he says more poignant. Although this study reveals that Spenser's poetry fairly bristles with proverbs, they are embedded in the material to such a degree that they are at times hardly recognizable.

The present study shows that of the total of 892 proverbs found in Spenser, 245 have Publilius Syrus parallels:[30] 200 appear once; 39, twice; 3, three times; 2, four times; and 1, five times. These add up to a total of 300 uses. Of these 245 Spenser proverbs with Publilius Syrus parallels, 56 have no other good parallels; 57 have parallels both in Publilius Syrus and in Culman; 68 are in Erasmus' school collection.

In the *Shepheardes Calender* Februarie Glosse 13–15, E. K. quotes a proverb found in Publilius Syrus (1934), 331: "*Improbe Neptunum accusat qui itorum naufragium facit*" (It is an outrage in a man twice shipwrecked to blame Neptune).

Although Spenser usually agrees with Publilius Syrus (for example, his Latin motto cited above has a quality which definitely reflects Publilius Syrus), in a few instances he does not agree. Spenser states in *Visions of the Worlds Vanitie*, xii, 12: "Forget not what you be" (see no. 280); Publilius Syrus (1934), 179, on the other hand, states "*Etiam oblivisci quid sis interdum expedit*" (Sometimes it is fitting even to forget what you are).

Publilius Syrus' "*Parium cum paribus facilis congregatio est*" (Easy

[30] For footnote see following page.

[30] At Johns Hopkins (1928) I [Charles G. Smith] was studying the Fourth Book of the *Faerie Queene* and at the same time I was taking two courses in philosophy under Professor George Boaz. I told him I was working on the Fourth Book. He went through it hurriedly, reading a little here and there. He said it looks "as if Spenser studied Publilius Syrus. I see statements here which smack of Publilius Syrus." The next day he handed me a list of Publilius Syrus' *sententiae* concerning friendship.

Parallels in Publilius Syrus are shown in "List of Proverbs," nos.:

4	(154)	−257^{2}	364^{2}	*492	*597^{2}	−739
−13	−156	261	365	493	*600	(755)
*(14)^{2}	(157)^{2}	263	380	*494	608	*756^{2}
(15)	*163	*273	382	495	*613	757
(18)	165^{2}	274	*383^{2}	*496^{2}	*614	758
−19	167	−275	*385	498	615	761
−22	*(170)	*280	(391)	−501	618^{2}	767
24^{2}	(172)	(282)	*393^{2}	*502	*623	771
(33)	174^{2}	*284	*395^{2}	506	*627	−794
*34	(175)^{2}	*286	−405^{2}	*508	631	−795
*35	*179^{2}	−287	(413)	520	(632)	797^{2}
43	−184	289	−415	(523)	(638)	(802)^{2}
(44)	*185	(290)^{2}	418	−538	(640)	*806^{2}
*45	198	−291	−425	539	645	−812
(66)	207	293	*427	*541	*646	816
−67	210	294	(434)	*543^{2}	*(647)^{3}	820
−74	−211	*(296)	435	544	*(649)^{3}	*826^{4}
90	(212)^{2}	302	−446	−547	651	(831)
(96)	*215	303	*449	*549	653	(835)^{2}
*104^{2}	−218	−305	453	−550	*654	(844)
105	(219)	307	*455^{2}	(551)	655	848
(108)	*222	312	*(456)	(553)	*668	−858^{2}
(112)	*(223)	*(316)	461	(556)	−678	860
−115	225	324	462	−558	(679)	(862)
116^{2}	226	325^{2}	*463	559^{2}	*(682)	*865
117	(228)	−333	−464	−560	*688	*866
120	235	*339	(466)	567^{2}	691	*874
(123)	*(238)^{5}	341	468	−569	694^{2}	(878)
124	(244)	342	(472)	(570)^{4}	(701)	*885
128^{2}	246^{2}	349	475	*572	708	−886
129^{3}	−248	−353	478	*573	711^{2}	887
*137	−249	359	482	(579)	712	888
*146	*250	−361^{2}	*483	581	(715)	*890
−148	251^{2}	*362	(485)	591	−721	*(891)
*(153)^{2}	*252	363^{2}	486	(596)	733	−892

Key to symbols

* in Erasmus' school collection (*Catonis Disticha*)
— only in Publilius Syrus
( ) in Publilius Syrus and in Culman
exponent $^{2, 3, 4,}$ or ^{5} indicates the number of times, above one, parallel is used

is the intercourse of equals with equals) and "*Simulans amicum inimicus inimicissimus*" (A false friend is the most dangerous of enemies) are the *themata* of Book IV.[31] These proverbs exemplify the probable source of these concepts in Spenser's thought.[32]

This collection shows that 230 of Spenser's proverbs have Culman parallels:[33] 161 have one only, 53 have two, 11 have three,

[31] Smith, *Spenser's Theory of Friendship*. [32] *Ibid.*, p. 25.

[33] Parallels in Leonard Culman are shown in the "List of Proverbs," nos.:

2	118	−217	−330[2]	(466)[2]	−616	−762
6[2]	(123)	(219)[3]	331[2]	(472)[3]	617[2]	769
9[3]	131[2]	220	332[2]	481	624[2]	770
10	132	*(223)[3]	334[2]	(485)[2]	625	772
*(14)	133	224	−335[2]	487	(632)	773[3]
(15)	134[2]	(228)[5]	340	504	634	−780
−16	−135	−229	344	505[2]	−635	785
(18)	*(153)	236	350[2]	−509	637	792
20	(154)	237	366	513	(638)	796
−21	(157)	*(238)	371[2]	515	−639[2]	798[2]
−27	158	239	−384[2]	(523)[4]	(640)	(802)
−31	−160	(244)	−390	−525	*(647)	804
(33)[2]	161	245	(391)[3]	535[2]	*(649)[3]	819
(44)	162	254	396	542[2]	650	821[3]
52	*(170)	272	398	546	657[2]	−823
54	−171	276	400	(551)	−659	824[2]
(66)[2]	(172)	277	411[2]	−552	660	(831)
77[2]	(175)[5]	−278	412	(553)	662	(835)[2]
79	178	(282)	(413)[4]	555[2]	667[2]	(844)
84	181[2]	283[2]	−423	(556)[3]	−667	846
87	182[3]	288	426	557[2]	(679)	850
91[2]	183	(290)	428[2]	−565[2]	*(682)	856
94	−186	*(296)	432	566[2]	689	857[2]
95[2]	−188	−298	(434)	(570)	−692	(862)[2]
(96)[2]	193	308	436	578[2]	695	863[2]
−97[2]	197	*(316)	439	(579)[3]	700	864
98	−204	320[2]	440[2]	−582	(701)[4]	872[2]
102	206[2]	322	447	−585	713	876
(108)	−208	323	450[2]	−586	(715)	(878)[2]
110	209	−326[2]	452	593	728	879
−111	(212)	−327[2]	454	(596)	732	881
(112)	213	328	*(456)[2]	599	754	*(891)[2]
−113	214	329	465	−607	(755)	

Key to symbols

— only in Culman
( ) in Culman and Publilius Syrus
* in Erasmus' school collection (*Catonis Disticha*)
exponent [2, 3, 4,] or [5] indicates the number of times, above one, parallel is used

3 have four, and 2 have five Culman parallels. This makes a total of 322 parallels. The fact that there are fifty-seven proverbs common to Publilius Syrus and Culman, as previously cited, adds weight to the hypothesis that Spenser committed to memory the *sententiae* of Publilius Syrus and of Culman.

Forty-two of Spenser's proverbs, for the first time cited in this monograph, have no other good parallels except those found in Culman. The identification of forty-two Spenser proverbs with only Culman parallels and fifty-six Spenser proverbs with only Publilius Syrus parallels is noteworthy. A cogent deduction is that Spenser obtained some of his proverbial wisdom from Culman and from Publilius Syrus.

Of the 474 Spenser proverbs with Tilley references [34] exhibited in this monograph, Tilley shows 120 to have Spenser parallels (two of which have two Spenser parallels, cf. nos. 272 and 777); this investigation establishes an additional 354 proverbs exhibited in Tilley which also have Spenser parallels. The present study points out that thirty-seven of these have Publilius Syrus parallels; Tilley exhibits none with Publilius Syrus parallels. For the proverb, "True friendship (love) is based on virtue" (see no. 311), Tilley quotes two parallels, one of which is in Spenser's poems; here are added another from Spenser and thirteen from the works of classical and contemporary writers.

A tabulation of Spenser's proverbs with parallels in Erasmus and in Cato reveals that Spenser wove 128 proverbs with Erasmus parallels and 34 with Cato parallels into his poetry. Five parallels (see nos. 244, 424, 452, 551, and 695) are found both in Erasmus and Cato.

Two hundred and two of Spenser's proverbs have parallels in W. G. Smith's *Oxford Dictionary of English Proverbs*, while 181 have parallels in Apperson's *English Proverbs and Proverbial Phrases*.

[34] Tilley, *Elizabethan Proverb Lore in Lyly's Euphues and in Pettie's Petite Pallace*; see also, *A Dictionary of the Proverbs in England in the Sixteenth and Seventeenth Centuries* (Ann Arbor: University of Michigan Press, 1950).

W. G. Smith, however, attributes only thirty to Spenser and Apperson attributes only twenty-nine to Spenser. This investigation brings to light 172 additional Spenser proverbs with parallels in W. G. Smith and 152 additional Spenser proverbs with parallels in Apperson.

The author sought but never found a parallel in any of the various proverb collections for: "Correction should begin at the howse of God" (see no. 122). However, it has a close parallel in the Bible,[35] apparently not until now observed. It is not annotated in the Johns Hopkins *Variorum*. Todd's *Variorum* and the Johns Hopkins *Variorum*, in fact, recognize only a few proverbs.[36] "The driest wood is soonest burnt to dust" (see no. 875) is another example of a proverb in this collection which has not been listed as a proverb in any other collection known to this investigator. This proverb has been arrived at inductively: this is, as it were, breaking new ground. Twenty-eight proverbs were established by this method.[37]

Additional parallels for a proverb, in many instances, may easily be had by checking the various references cited in connection with the parallels. In this collection, no effort is made to cite a multiplicity of parallels, and, as a rule, parallels that date past the early seventeenth century are omitted. A few noteworthy exceptions can be found, among them the proverb, "The many fail, the few succeed" (see no. 232), which is absent from the collections of proverbs known to the author, but is present in Tennyson's poem, *The Day Dream*: *The Arrival*.

Although it is difficult to prove that Spenser took a proverb from any specific writer, a good example of such a hypothetical infusion is no. 201: "So can he turn his earnest unto game,"

[35] Compare *I Peter*, iv, 17.

[36] Todd's annotates thirty-two; the Johns Hopkins *Variorum* recognizes seventy-eight.

[37] Proverbs arrived at inductively include "List of Proverbs," nos.: 72, 122, 127, 130, 138, 143, 177, 232, 264, 420, 473, 474, 499, 521, 524, 589, 590, 643, 661, 722, 774, 793, 803, 807, 808, 809, 836, and 880.

Faerie Queen, II, i, 31, 1. This is so similar in phrasing to a line in Chaucer that one might easily believe that Spenser echoes Chaucer. The Chaucer line is: "So kanst turnen ernest into game," Chaucer, *Manciple's P.*, 100. This investigation helps to establish seventy-nine Spenser proverbs with parallels in Chaucer, twenty-one which echo Virgil, and thirteen which reflect Horace. The frequent use of echo phrases evidences the interest of people of the Renaissance in clichés.[38]

It is not to be deduced that all the material quoted from Spenser as proverbial is used by him in proverb form. Such is not the case. It is used by him to suit his purposes. The material presented in this study does demonstrate that proverbs are commonplace; but in a great many instances the material serves as a corrective for ascribing passages in Spenser to a definite source. Hence, the folly of definite source ascription becomes apparent. H. S. V. Jones[39] nevertheless has fallen into such an error: he misuses parallels which are nothing but proverbial stuff to prove or reflect kinship between the *Shepheardes Calender* and *Mother Hubberd's Tale*. In like manner, Patch,[40] who because Chaucer's Diomede and Criseyde each happen to use the same proverb, makes the statement: "This is one more of the astonishing parallels in the poem." Familiarity with the provenience and pervasiveness of proverbs should keep a writer from making such an assumption.

In a discussion of stanza connection in the *Faerie Queene*, R. J. Shoeck[41] concludes by aptly stating: "There remains for further study the larger problem of Spenser's employment of this and other stanza-linking devices to develop themes and ideas over the space of a number of stanzas: as a 'kind of sweet undertone' it is still one of the secrets of his melody." Spenser's subtle, skillful

[38] George Arms, "Clichés, Extended and Otherwise," *The Saturday Review of Literature*, vol. CCXIX, no. 3 (November 30, 1946), p. 9.

[39] Jones, *A Spenser Handbook*, p. 100.

[40] Howard R. Patch, *On Rereading Chaucer* (Cambridge, Massachusetts: Harvard University Press, 1939), p. 76.

[41] "Alliteration as a Means of Stanza Connection in *The Faerie Queene*," *Modern Language Notes*, LXIV (1949), p. 90–93.

use of proverbs and proverb lore, as elaborated in this monograph, helps further, it is hoped, to illuminate and to reveal the secrets of his melody.

In the academic game of derivations and influences, the importance and relevance of the *sententiae* of Leonard Culman and Publilius Syrus become apparent. It also is shown that of the 892 proverbs exhibited in the "List of Proverbs" in this book, 743 are recognized for the first time as proverbs in Spenser's poems. Furthermore, it becomes evident that it is unwise to ascribe a definite source to a proverb; they are commonplace. Proverbial wisdom is vital to Spenser's thought—a deeply diffused humanism.

LIST OF PROVERBS

LIST OF PROVERBS

This is a complete list of Spenser's authenticated proverbs. The arrangement of the proverbs under each numbered boldface heading, alphabetized according to a more or less arbitrarily selected catchword, is as follows: 1. The proverbial material from Spenser, taken, except when otherwise indicated, from *The Complete Poetical Works of Spenser* (Cambridge edition) edited by R. E. Neil Dodge and from *A View of the Present State of Ireland* in *The Works of Edmund Spenser* (Globe edition) edited by R. Morris. As far as possible the material is arranged chronologically. 2. All the parallels that have been found in Leonard Culman's *Sententiae Pueriles* and Publilius Syrus' *Sententiae*. The 1685 edition of Culman is used; two collections of Publilius Syrus are used: the collection edited by Jules Chenu, 1835, and the collection edited by J. Wight Duff and Arnold M. Duff, 1934. The *sententiae* of Publilius Syrus marked by an asterisk were in the Elizabethan school collection included in *Catonis Disticha* prepared by Erasmus. 3. Parallels from Greek and Latin authors and from Erasmus. (Nearly all of the sententious material cited from Latin and Greek authors is taken from the Loeb Classical Library editions.) Many parallels are also cited from early or contemporary English literature. 4. References, primarily to modern collections of proverbs.

1 ALL **ABROAD** AND NOTHING AT HOME

Shep. Cal., Sept., 28: In forrein costes, men sayd, was plentye. ¶ *Mother Hub.*, 101: Abroad, where change is, good may gotten bee.

Marvell, *Rehearsal Transpos'd* (1673), II, 105: All abroad and nothing is at home.

Cf. W. G. Smith, 7.

2 **ABSTAIN** FROM IDLE PLEASURE

FQ, II, ii, 45, 4: Learne from Pleasures poyson to abstaine. ¶ *Ibid.*, VI, vi, 14, 5: Abstaine from pleasure.

Culman, 2: Ludos fuge (Avoid idle pastimes).

Cf. Tilley, V71.

3 THE BEST THINGS MAY BE **ABUSED**

Hymne in Honour of B., 157–158: Nothing so good, but that through guilty shame May be corrupt, and wrested unto will.

Northbrooke, *Treatise agst. Dicing*, 46–47: *Cuius rei est vsus, eiusdem est et abusus*: there is nothing vsed but that also maye be abused. ¶ Harvey, *Marginalia*, 103: It is an easy matter to abuse the greatest things of all. ¶ Nashe, *Pierce P.*, *Works*, I, 154: There is nothing that if a man list he may not wrest or peruert.

Cf. Bacon, *Promus*, 1072; W. G. Smith, 36; Tilley, N317.

4 **ACCUSING** FORTUNE IS ONLY EXCUSING OURSELVES

FQ, V, iv, 28, 1–3: Faulty men use oftentimes To attribute their folly unto fate, And lay on heaven the guilt of their owne crimes. ¶ *Ibid.*, VI, ix, 29, 1–2: In vaine . . . doe men The heavens of their fortunes fault accuse. ¶ *View*, 609: It is the manner of men, that when they are fallen into any absurditye, or theyr actions succeede not as they would, they are ready allwayes to impute the blame therof unto the heavens, soe to excuse their owne follyes and imperfectiones.

Publilius Syrus (1934), 667: Stultum est queri de adversis, ubi culpa est tua (It is silly to grumble about misfortune when the fault's your own).

Homer, *Odyssey*, i, 32: *Ὢ πόποι, οἷον δή νυ θεοὺς βροτοὶ αἰτιόωνται* (Look you now, how ready mortals are to blame the gods). ¶ Aristotle, *N. Ethics*, III, i, 11: *τῶν μὲν καλῶν ἑαυτόν, τῶν δ' αἰσχρῶν τὰ ἡδέα.* (It is absurd to blame external things, instead of blaming ourselves). ¶ Quintilian, *Inst. Orat.*, vi, Pref., 13: Frustra mala omnia ad crimen fortunae relegamus (It is in vain that we impute all our ills to fortune). ¶ Plutarch, *Moralia*: *Tranq. of the Mind*, 471D: *μειζόνων ἐφιεμένους ταῖς ἐλπίσιν εἶτ' ἀποτυγχάνοντας αἰτιᾶσθαι δαίμονα καὶ τύχην ἀλλὰ μὴ τὴν αὑτῶν ἀβελτερίαν.* (When we fail, we blame our destiny and our fortune instead of our own folly). ¶ Sidney, *Arcadia*, *Works*, I, 156: You blame your fortune very wrongfully, since the fault is not in Fortune, but in you that cannot frame your selfe to your fortune.

Cf. Tilley, F101; C. G. Smith, 1.

5 **ACORNS** WERE GOOD TILL BREAD WAS FOUND

Teares of the M., 589–591: Borne of salvage brood, And having beene with acorns alwaies fed, Can no whit savour this celestiall food. ¶ *Virgils Gnat*, 206–207: Acornes were our foode, before That Ceres seede of mortall men were knowne.

Cf. Erasmus, *Adagia*, 151E; Tilley, A21.

6 BEAR **ADVERSITIES** WITH PATIENCE

FQ, I, viii, 45, 2: Maister . . . mishaps with patient might.

Culman, 7: Malum patientia tollitur (An evil thing is borne by patience). ¶ *Ibid.*, 17: Adversa aequo animo sunt toleranda (Adversities are to be borne with a patient mind).

Shakespeare, *Rom. & Jul.*, V, iii, 220–221: Forbear, And let mischance be slave to patience.

7 **AFRICA** IS ALWAYS PRODUCING SOMETHING NEW

Ruines of R., xxix, 10: All that which Afrike ever brought forth strange.

Cf. Tilley, A56.

8 **AGE** BREEDS ACHES

Shep. Cal., Feb., 90: Age, the hoste of greevaunce.

Cf. Apperson, 4; Tilley, A66.

9 WE ARE MADE WISER BY **AGE**

FQ, II, vi, 48, 5: Weake handes, but counsell is most strong in age. ¶ *Ibid.*, ix, 55, 9: Weake body well is chang'd for minds redoubled forse.

Culman, 5: Aetate prudentiores reddimur (We are made wiser by age). ¶ *Ibid.*, 10: Ante annos prudentia nulla (There is no discretion before years). ¶ *Ibid.*, 15: Praestantiores sunt senum sententiae (Old men's opinions are the best).

Euripides, *Phoen. Maidens*, 529–530: ἡμπειρία ἔχει τι λέξαι τῶν νέων σοφώτερον (Experience can plead more wisely than the lips of youth). ¶ Terence, *Adelphoe*, 832: Aetate sapimus rectius (We get wiser as we grow older). ¶ Cicero, *De Sen.*, xix, 67: Mens enim et ratio et consilium in senibus est (It is in old men that reason and good judgment are found). ¶ Lucian, *Heracles*, 4: τὸ δὲ γῆρας ἔχει τι λέξαι τῶν νέων σοφώτερον (Old age has wiser words to say than youth). ¶ Erasmus, *Adagia*, 929D: Aetate prudentiores reddimur (We are made wiser by age). ¶ Sidney, *Arcadia*, *Works*, I, 149: Old age is wise and full of constant truth.

Cf. C. G. Smith, 6.

10 WHEN **AGE** IS IN, WIT IS OUT

Shep. Cal., Feb., 53–54: I deeme thy braine emperished bee Through rusty elde, that hath rotted thee. ¶ *FQ*, II, iii, 16, 2–4: Through many yeares thy wits thee faile, And . . . weake eld hath left thee nothing wise, Els never should thy judgement be so frayle.

Culman, 17: Ad omnem disciplinam tardior est senectus (Old age is slower to all kinds of learning).

Vergil, *Eclog.*, ix, 51: Omnia fert aetas, animum quoque (Age steals away all things, even the mind). ¶ Shakespeare, *Much Ado*, III, v, 37: As they say, "When the age is in, the wit is out."

Cf. Stevenson, 39:2.

11 **ALL** IS VANITY

Ruines of T., 583: All is vanitie. ¶ *Visions of B.*, i, 11: All is nought but flying vanitee!

Cf. Stevenson, 2415:3; Tilley, A152.

12 **ALL** THINGS COME TO AN END

Cf. no. 53: Whatever has a beginning has an end; no. 447: On earth nothing is long lasting

Shep. Cal., Dec., 158: *Vivitur ingenio: caetera mortis erunt.* ¶ *Ibid.*, Glosse, 105–106: All thinges perish and come to theyr last end. ¶ *Ruines of T.*, 55–56: Sith all that in this world is great or gaie Doth as a vapour vanish, and decaie. ¶ *Ruines of R.*, xx, 14: All in th' end to nought shall fade. ¶ *Visions of P.*, v, 7–8: Each thing at last we see Doth passe away. ¶ *FQ*, III, vi, 40, 9: All things decay in time, and to their end doe draw.

Chaucer, *Troilus*, III, 615: Every thyng hath ende; cf. *Leg. Good Women*, 651. ¶ Chaucer, *Knight's T.*, 3026: Thanne may ye se that al this thyng hath ende. ¶ Greene, *Mourning Garment*, *Works*, IX, 181: All things must haue an end. ¶ Lodge, *Robert, Sec. Duke of Normandy*, *Works*, II, 54: All things are ordained to an end. ¶ Sidney, *Poems* (1593), *Works*, II, 228: Yet sure an end, to each thing time doth give. ¶ Nashe, *Strange Newes*, *Works*, I, 281: Euery thing hath an end.

Cf. Apperson, 8; W. G. Smith, 180; Stevenson, 677:5; Tilley, T177.

13 ONE WHO IS **ALLOWED** MORE THAN IS RIGHT WANTS MORE THAN IS ALLOWED

FQ, VI, xi, 7, 5–6: She saw, through that small favours gaine, That further then she willing was he prest.

Publilius Syrus (1934), 145: Cui plus licet quam par est plus vult quam licet (One who is allowed more than is right wants more than is allowed).

14 WHAT CANNOT BE **ALTERED** MUST BE BORNE, NOT BLAMED (LAMENTED)

Cf. no. 44: Bear willingly that which must needs be

Shep. Cal., Feb., 21–22: Ne ever was to fortune foeman, But gently tooke that ungently came. ¶ *FQ*, I, iv, 49, 5: Helplesse hap it booteth not to mone. ¶ *Ibid.*, II, iii, 3, 3–4: Helplesse what may it boot To frett for anger, or for griefe to mone? ¶ *Ibid.*, III, xi, 16, 1: What boots it plaine that cannot be redrest. ¶ *Ibid.*, 17, 9: What boots it then to plaine that cannot be redrest?

Culman, 24: Patienter ferenda quae mutari non possunt (Those things which cannot be altered are to be patiently borne). ¶* Publilius Syrus (1934), 206: Feras non culpes quod mutari non potest (What can't be changed you should bear, not blame). ¶ *Ibid.*, 479: Necessitatem ferre non flere addecet (It is fitting to bear and not bemoan necessity).

Erasmus, *Adagia*, 117D: Feras non culpes, quod vitari non potest (What can't be avoided you should bear, not blame).

Cf. Tilley, A231; C. G. Smith, 7.

15 **ANGER** IS A HARD THING TO CURB

Shep. Cal., Maye, 136–137: When choler is inflamed with rage, Wanting revenge, is hard to asswage. ¶ *FQ*, IV, v, 31, 9: Nought but dire revenge his anger mote defray.

Culman, 6: Iram compescere arduum (It is a hard thing to bridle anger). ¶ Publilius Syrus (1934), 638: Respicere nihil consuevit iracundia (Anger's way is to regard nothing).

Aristotle, *Politics*, v, 9, 18: *Ἡράκλειτος εἶπε, χαλεπὸν φάσκων εἶναι θυμῷ μάχεσθαι, ψυχῆς γὰρ ὠνεῖσθαι* (Heraclitus said that anger is hard to combat because it is willing to buy revenge with life).

Cf. Stevenson, 68:7.

16 **ANGER** IS OFTEN PROVOKED BY LIGHT CAUSES

Muiopotmos, 7–8: From small jarre Their wraths at length broke into open warre.

Culman, 26: Saepe de levissimis causis existit ira (Often anger arises from very light causes).

17 **ANGER** IS THE WHETSTONE OF VALOR

FQ, II, i, 57, 4–8: Raging passion . . . with bold furie armes the weakest hart.

Cato, *Collectio Monos.*, 23: Quemlibet ignavum facit indignatio fortem (Wrath forces any coward to be brave). ¶ Ovid, *Amores*, I, vii, 66: Quamlibet infirmas adiuvat ira manus (However weak the hand, ire gives it strength). ¶ Clarke, 178: Ira cos est fortudinis (Anger edgeth valor).

Cf. Stevenson, 67:8.

18 **ANGER** TORMENTS ITSELF

FQ, II, v, 16, 3–6: Outrageous anger, and woe working jarre, Direfull impatience, and hartmurdring love . . . thee to endlesse bale captived lead. ¶ *Amoretti*, lxxxv, 8–14: Coles of yre . . . Consume thee quite, . . . and mischiefe thy reward, Due to thy selfe, that it for me prepared.

Culman, 6: Ira tormentum sui ipsius (Anger is the torment of itself). ¶ Publilius Syrus (1835), 1025: Expetit poenas iratus ab alio; a se ipso exigit (Anger would inflict punishment on another; meanwhile, it tortures itself).

Erasmus, *Similia*, 588C: Iracundia sibi nocet saepenumero, cum aliis nocere studet (Anger often injures itself, when it strives to injure others). ¶ Shakespeare, *Coriol.*, IV, ii, 50–51: Anger's my meat. I sup upon myself, And so shall starve with feeding.

Cf. Stevenson, 71:2; Tilley, A247; C. G. Smith, 8.

19 **ANGER** USUALLY FORGETS THE LAW

FQ, V, viii, 41, 1–4: Such was the furie of these head-strong steeds . . . That all obedience both to words and deeds They quite forgot, and scornd all former law.

Publilius Syrus (1934), 345: Legem solet obliviscier iracundia (Anger usually forgets the law).

20 MODERATE YOUR **ANGER**

FQ, I, v, 14, 5: Quench the flame of furious despight. ¶ *Ibid.*, II, v, 18, 5: Quench thy whott emboyling wrath.

Culman, 2: Iracundiam tempera (Moderate your anger).

Cato, *Collectio Dis. Vulg.*, 45: Iracundiam rege (Control your anger). ¶ Juvenal, *Sat.*, viii, 88: Pone irae frena modumque (Set a curb and a limit to your passion).

Cf. C. G. Smith, 10.

21 RASH **ANGER** CAUSES MANY EVILS

FQ, I, iv, 35, 1–6: Full many mischiefes follow cruell Wrath; . . . bloodshed . . . strife . . . murder . . . scath . . . despight . . . griefe . . . and many evils moe haunt Ire.

Culman, 24: Praeceps ira multorum malorum author (Rash anger is the cause of many evils).

22 WHEN AN **ANGRY** MAN RETURNS TO HIS SENSES, HE IS ANGRY WITH HIMSELF

FQ, I, iv, 34, 6–7: When the furious fitt was overpast, His cruell facts he often would repent.

Publilius Syrus (1934), 311: Iratus cum ad se rediit sibi tum irascitur (When the angry man returns to his senses, he is angry with himself).

23 A SOFT **ANSWER** TURNS AWAY WRATH

FQ, II, vi, 36, 3–5: At her speach their rages gan relent, And calme the sea of their tempestuous spight: Such powre have pleasing wordes. ¶ *Ibid.*, viii, 26, 7–8: Words well dispost Have secrete powre t' appease inflamed rage. ¶ *Ibid.*, III, ii, 15, 5–6: For pleasing wordes are like to magick art, That doth the charmed snake in slomber lay. ¶ *Ibid.*, IV, ii, 2, 5–6: Such musicke is wise words with time concented, To moderate stiffe mindes, disposed to strive. ¶ *Ibid.*, ix, 14, 6–7: He with good thewes and speaches well applyde Did mollifie, and calme her raging heat. ¶ *Ibid.*, VI, v, 30, 6–8: With such faire words she did their heate asswage, And the strong course of their displeasure breake, That they to pitty turnd their former rage.

Old Testament: Proverbs, xv, 1: A soft answer turneth away wrath. ¶ Breton, *Crossing of Prov.*, *Works*, II, *e*, 5: Faire words pacifie wrath.

Cf. Henderson, 134; W. G. Smith, 602; Stevenson, 2610: 2; Tilley, W822.

24 A MAN IS THE **ARCHITECT** OF HIS OWN FORTUNE

FQ, I, viii, 28, 3: Your fortune maister eke with governing. ¶ *Ibid.*, VI, ix, 29, 9: Each hath his fortune in his brest. ¶ *Ibid.*, 30, 9: Each unto himselfe his life may fortunize. ¶ *Ibid.*, 31, 1–2: In each mans self . . . It is, to fashion his owne lyfes estate. ¶ *Hymne in Honour of L.*, 224: His faith, his fortune, in his breast he beares. ¶ *View*, 673: Everye man standeth uppon himselfe, and buildeth his fortunes upon his owne fayth and firme assuraunce.

Publilius Syrus (1835), 209: Dona ingeni et fortunae proposita omnibus (The rewards of talent and fortune are offered to all). ¶ *Ibid.*, 286: Fortunam cuique mores confingunt sui (His own character is the arbiter of everyone's fortune).

Plautus, *Trinummus*, 363: Nam sapiens quidem pol ipsus fingit fortunam sibi (For I tell you, a man, a wise man, molds his own destiny). ¶ Sallust, *Ad Caesarem De Rep.*, i, 2: In carminibus Appius ait, fabrum esse suae quemque fortunae (Appius says in his verses that every man is the architect of his own fortune). ¶ Erasmus, *Adagia*, 532E: Sui cuique mores fingunt fortunam (His own character shapes each man's fortune). ¶ Nashe, *Terrors of the Night*, *Works*, I, 377: There is an olde philosophicall common Prouerbe, *Vnusquisque fingit fortunam sibi*, Euerie one shapes hys owne fortune as he lists. ¶ Bacon, *Adv. of Learn.*, II, xxiii, 10: It grew to an adage, *Faber quisque fortunae propriae*.

Cf. Tilley, M126; C. G. Smith, 11.

25 AS FULL OF EYES AS **ARGUS**

Shep. Cal., July, 154: Well eyed as Argus was. ¶ *Ibid.*, Sept., 203: Roffy is wise, and as Argus eyed. ¶ *Ibid.*, Oct., 32: Bright Argus blazing eye. ¶ *FQ*, I, iv, 17, 9: Full of Argus eyes. ¶ *Ibid.*, III, ix, 7, 3–4: Argus . . . hundred eyes.

Ovid, *Metam.*, i, 625: Centum luminibus cinctum caput Argus habebat (Argus' head was set about with a hundred eyes). ¶ Claudian, *De Consulatu Stilichonis*, i, 312: Argum fama canit centeno lumine cinctum (Fame tells how Argus girt with a hundred eyes). ¶ Chaucer, *Troilus*, IV, 1459: Youre fader is in sleght as Argus eyed. ¶ Chaucer, *Merch. T.*, E2111: Argus . . . hadde an hondred yen. ¶ Chaucer, *Wife of Bath's Prol.*, 358: Thogh thou preye Argus with his hundred yen. ¶ Pettie, *Petite P.*, 204: Argus with his two hundred eies. ¶ Greene, *Planetomachia*, *Works*, V, 49: As full of Eyes as *Argus*. ¶ Greene, *Never Too Late*, *Works*, VIII, 37: As watchfull as *Argus* with all his eyes. ¶ Lodge, *Rosalynde*, *Works*, I, 111: Argus with an hundred eies. ¶ Sidney, *Astro. and S. Works*, II, 301: Lest that *Argus* eyes perceive you. ¶ Harvey, *Pierces Super.*, *Works*, II, 259: The hondred-eyed Argus. ¶ Greene, *Frier Bacon*, 1661, *Works*, XIII, 77: Argos . . . had his hundred eyes. ¶ Harvey, *Trimming of Thomas Nashe*, *Works*, III, 30: Argus that had an hundred eyes.

Cf. W. G. Smith, 184; Tilley, E254.

26 **ART** IMPROVES NATURE

FQ, IV, x, 21, 8–9: All that Nature did omit, Art, playing second Natures part, supplyed it.

Shakespeare, *Winter's T.*, IV, iv, 95–96: Art . . . does mend nature. ¶ Jonson, *Discoveries*, 2503, *Works*, VIII, 639: Without Art, Nature can ne'er bee perfect.

Cf. Apperson, 16; W. G. Smith, 14; Stevenson, 98:4.

27 **ART** OFTEN EXCELS NATURE

FQ, II, v, 29, 1–2: Art, stryving to compayre [rival] With Nature. ¶ *Muiopotmos*, 163–166: Lavish Nature, in her best attire . . . And Arte, with her contending, doth aspire T' excell the naturall with made delights. ¶ *Hymne in Honour of B.*, 83–84: Oftimes we Nature see of Art Exceld.

Culman, 5: Ars vincit naturam (Art overmatches nature).

28 AS PALE AS **ASHES**

FQ, I, iv, 33, 7: As ashes pale of hew. ¶ *Ibid.*, II, xi, 22, 1: As pale and wan as ashes. ¶ *Ibid.*, III, xii, 12, 6: As ashes pale of hew. ¶ *Ibid.*, VI, vii, 17, 8: Like ashes deadly pale.

Cf. Apperson, 482; Stevenson, 1741:3; Tilley, A339.

29 TO TREMBLE LIKE AN **ASPEN** LEAF

FQ, I, ix, 51, 4: Tremble like a leafe of aspin greene.

Lodge, *Wits Mis.*, *Works*, IV, 65: He trembles like an aspen leafe.

Cf. Apperson, 18; W. G. Smith, 15; Stevenson, 788: 11; Tilley, L140.

30 AN **ASS** IS KNOWN BY HIS EARS

Colin Clouts, 711–712: Mans worth is measured by his weed, As . . . asses by their eares.

Cf. Tilley, A355.

31 **AVOID** SHAME AND DISGRACE

FQ, I, vi, 18, 7: Fly away for feare of fowle disgrace. ¶ *Ibid.*, III, v, 45, 8: Fayre death it is, to shonne more shame, to dy.

Culman, 3: Probrum fugito (Avoid a disgrace).

32 TO BEAR ONE ON YOUR **BACK**

Muiopotmos, 278: On his backe Her through the sea did beare. ¶ *FQ*, VI, ii, 47, 8: To beare this burden [a man] on your dainty backe. ¶ *Ibid.*, iii, 32, 4: Beare her on thy backe.

Cf. Apperson, 30; W. G. Smith, 26; Stevenson, 113:8; Tilley, B14.

33 DO NOT **BACKBITE**

Mother Hub., 717–720: The brave courtier, in whose beauteous thought Regard of honor harbours more than ought, Doth loath such base condition, to backbite Anies good name for envie or despite.

Culman, 1: Calumniam oderis (Hate slandering). ¶ *Ibid.*, 8: Ne cui obtrectato (Do not backbite anyone). ¶ Publilius Syrus (1934), 322: Ingenuus animus non fert vocis verbera (A noble mind has no ear for unjust reproaches).

Ben Sira, *Book of Wisdom*: *Ecclesiasticus*, v, 14: Slander not with thy tongue. ¶ *Apocrypha: The Wisdom of Solomon*, i, 11: Refrain your tongue from backbiting. ¶ Shakespeare, *Rich. III*, I, iv, 246: Do not slander him. ¶ Shakespeare, *1 Hen. IV*, IV, iii, 8: Do me no slander.

34 EVERY **BAD** NATURE HAS ITS PATRON

View, 641: There is none soe badd . . . but shall finde some to favoure his doinges.

* Publilius Syrus (1934), 369: Malae naturae numquam doctore indigent (Bad natures never lack an instructor).

Jonson, *Discoveries*, 543–544, *Works*, VIII, 580: It is strange, there should be no vice without his patronage.

Cf. Tilley, V42; C. G. Smith, 13.

35 EVERYTHING GOES FROM **BAD** TO WORSE

Shep. Cal., Feb., 11–12: Must not the world wend in his commun course, From good to badd, and from badde to worse. ¶ *FQ*, V, Prol., 1, 7–9: The world . . . growes daily wourse and wourse. ¶ *Ibid.*, VII, vi, 6, 6: All this world is woxen daily worse. ¶ *Ibid.*, vii, 19, 4–6: And men themselves doe change continually, From youth to eld, from wealth to poverty, From good to bad, from bad to worst of all.

* Publilius Syrus (1934), 119: Cotidie est deterior posterior dies (Daily the following day is worse).

Quintilian, *Inst. Orat.*, i, 1, 5: Nam bona facile mutantur in peius (What is good readily changes for the worse).

Ch. Stevenson, 2636:2; Tilley, B27, T168.

36 THE **BAD** IS THE BEST

Shep. Cal., Sept., 105: Badde is the best.

Erasmus, *Adagia*, 1008D: Malum est bonum (The bad is the best).

Cf. Apperson, 22; W. G. Smith, 19; Stevenson, 115:2; Tilley, B316.

37 THE **BAIT** HIDES THE HOOK

FQ, I, i, 49, 6: Under blacke stole hyding her bayted hooke. ¶ *Ibid.*, III, ii, 38, 9: Unwares the hidden hooke with baite I swallowed. ¶ *Amoretti*, xlvii, 3–4: Lyke but unto golden hookes, That from the foolish fish theyr bayts do hyde.

Greene, *Royal Exch.*, *Works*, VII, 252: Vice . . . hideth her impoysoned hookes with a sugered bayte.

Cf. Apperson, 23; W. G. Smith, 20; Tilley, B50.

38 TO SELL ONE A **BARGAIN**

Mother Hub., 871–872: Then would he seeme a farmer, that would sell Bargaines of woods.

Cf. Tilley, B80.

39 **BARNABY** BRIGHT, THE LONGEST DAY AND THE SHORTEST NIGHT

Epithalamion, 265–272: This day the sunne is in his chiefest hight, With Barnaby the bright, . . . the longest day in all the yeare, And shortest night.

Cf. Apperson, 27; W. G. Smith, 23; Stevenson, 493:10; Tilley, B92.

40 THE **BASILISK'S** EYE IS FATAL

FQ, IV, viii, 39, 7–9: The basiliske . . . From powerfull eyes close venim doth convay Into the lookers hart, and killeth farre away.

Cf. Tilley, B99.

41 AT A **BAY**

FQ, III, i, 22, 1: Having at a bay The salvage beast. ¶ *Ibid.*, IV, vi, 41, 3: Unto a bay he brought her. ¶ *Ibid.*, viii, 48, 5: He her brought Unto his bay. ¶ *Ibid.*, VI, v, 19, 1: Like a wylde bull . . . being at a bay. ¶ *Ibid.*, vii, 47, 1: Having at a bay a salvage bull.

Cf. Tilley, B109.

42 LET **BE**, AS MAY BE

Shep. Cal., March, 58: Let be, as may be.

Cf. Tilley, B65.

43 TO **BE** RATHER THAN TO SEEM

FQ, III, vii, 29, 8–9: Rather joyd to bee then seemen sich: For both to be and seeme to him was labor lich. ¶ *Ibid.*, IV, xi, 45, 9: It was no mortall worke, that seem'd and yet was not.

Publilius Syrus (1835), 800: Quid ipse sis, non quid habearis, interest (It matters not what you are thought to be, but what you are).

Aeschylus, *Seven agst. Thebes*, 592: οὐ γὰρ δοκεῖν ἄριστος, ἀλλ' εἶναι θέλει (His resolve is not to seem the bravest, but to be); cf. Plato, *Republic*, ii, 361B; Plutarch, *Moralia*: *Sayings of Kings and Commanders*, 186B. ¶ Cicero, *De Offic.*, II, 12, 43: Praeclare Socrates hanc viam ad gloriam proximam et quasi compendiariam dicebat esse, si quis id ageret, ut, qualis haberi vellet, talis esset (Socrates used to express it so admirably: "The nearest way to glory—a short cut, as it were—is to strive to be what you wish to be thought to be"); cf. *De Amicitia*, xxvi, 98. ¶ Sallust, *Catilina*, liv, 6: Esse quam videri bonus malebat (He preferred to be, rather than to seem, virtuous). ¶ Ovid, *Tristia*, v, 13, 26: Quod non es, ne videare, cave (Beware of seeming what you are not). ¶ Erasmus, *Adagia*, 990A: Cura esse, quod audis (Take care to be what you are reported to be). ¶ Ascham, *Scholemaster*, *Eng. Works* (Wright), 185: To seeme, and not to bee. ¶ Gascoigne, *Grief of Joye*, *Works*, II, 535: They strive to seeme, but never care to be. ¶ *Paradise of D. Dev.*, 35: Euery man should be in deede, that he desires to seeme.

Cf. Bacon, *Promus*, 509; Tilley, S214; C. G. Smith, 14.

44 **BEAR** WILLINGLY THAT WHICH MUST NEEDS BE

Cf. no. 14: What cannot be altered must be borne, not blamed (lamented)

Shep. Cal., Sept., 137–139: Better it were a little to feyne, And cleanly cover that cannot be cured: Such il as is forced mought nedes be endured. ¶ *Teares of the M.*, 128–130: Man . . . Fortunes freakes, is wisely taught to beare. ¶ *FQ*, V, v, 38, 1–3: To a courage great It is no lesse beseeming well, to beare The storme of Fortunes frowne, or Heavens threat.

Culman, 13: Libenter feras quod necesse est (Bear willingly that which must needs be). ¶ Publilius Syrus (1934), 411: Mutare quod non possis, ut natum est, feras (What you cannot change, you should bear as it comes).

Seneca, *Epist.*, cvii, 9: Optimum est pati, quod emendare non possis (That which you cannot reform, it is best to endure). ¶ Shakespeare, *Othello*, IV, i, 63: Bear your fortune like a man.

Cf. Apperson, 129; Tilley, C922; C. G. Smith, 47.

45 HE CAN **BEAR** THE EASY WHO HAS BORNE THE HARD

FQ, I, vi, 37, 9: The lesser pangs can beare, who hath endur'd the chief. ¶ *Ibid.*, vii, 25, 5: Who hath endur'd the whole, can beare ech part.

* Publilius Syrus (1835), 262: Fer difficilia, facilia levius feres (Endure the heavy burdens, and you will the more easily carry the lighter).

Aristotle, *Rhetoric*, ii, 19, 3–4: *εἰ τὸ χαλεπώτερον δυνατόν, καὶ τὸ ῥᾷον* (If the harder of two things is possible, so also is the easier).

46 LIKE A **BEAR** TO A HONEYPOT

FQ, III, x, 53, 4: Like as a beare, That creeping close, amongst the hives to reare An hony combe.

Cf. W. G. Smith, 26; Tilley, B130.

47 TO GO LIKE A **BEAR** TO THE STAKE

Shep. Cal., Oct., 48: The white beare to the stake did bring.

Harvey, *Foure Lett.*, *Works*, I, 222: With such an alacrity of courage, as the sorry beare goeth to the stake.

Cf. Apperson, 30; W. G. Smith, 26; Tilley, B127.

48 **BEAUTY** IS INVINCIBLE

FQ, I, iii, 6, 4: How can beautie maister the most strong! ¶ *Ibid.*, V, v, 13, 5–6: No hand so cruell, nor no hart so hard, But ruth of beautie will it mollifie. ¶ *Ibid.*, viii, 1, 1–3: Nought under heaven so strongly doth allure The sence of man, and all his minde possesse, As beauties lovely baite. ¶ *Ibid.*, VI, vii, 31, 6–8: Her beautie had such soveraine might, That with the onely twinckle of her eye, She could or save or spill. ¶ *Ibid.*, VII, vi, 31, 2–4: Faire beames of beauty . . . could the greatest wrath soone turne to grace (Such sway doth beauty even in heaven beare).

Sidney, *Arcadia*, *Works*, I, 161: Know, what power heavenly beauty hath. ¶ *Ibid.*, 404: A faire woman shall not onely commaund without authoritie, but perswade without speaking. ¶ *Ibid.*, IV, 48: There was no harte so base, nor weapon so feeble, but, that the force of her beuty was well able, to enable them for the performance of great matters. ¶ Shakespeare, *Pericles*, I, ii, 34–35: Beauty hath his power and will, which can as well inflame as it can kill.

Cf. Tilley, B166.

49 **BEAUTY** WITHOUT VIRTUE IS A CURSE

FQ, III, i, 48, 9: Shamelesse beauty soone becomes a loathly sight.

Cf. Erasmus, *Adagia*, 123D; Fuller, 957; Henderson, 435; Tilley, B175.

50 IT IS EASIER TO **BEGIN** SOMETHING THAN IT IS TO END IT

FQ, IV, i, 20, 9: Harder is to end then to begin. ¶ *Ibid.*, x, 3, 4: Harder may be ended, then begonne. ¶ *Colin Clouts*, 590–591: More eath . . . it is in such a case How to begin, then know how to have donne.

Plautus, *Poenulus*, 974: Incipere multost quam impetrare facilius (It is much easier to begin than to finish). ¶ Cicero, *Pro Lege Manilia*, i, 3: Difficilius est exitum quam principium invenere (It is harder to end than to begin). ¶ Sidney, *Arcadia*, *Works*, IV, 125: But how to end yt . . . they knew not: So muche easyer yt ys to enflame then to quenche, to tye, then to loose knottes.

Cf. Henderson, 174; Stevenson, 155:4.

51 A GOOD **BEGINNING** MAKES A GOOD ENDING

FQ, I, viii, 28, 4: Well begonne end all so well. ¶ *Ibid.*, VII, vi, 23, 9: Good on-set boads good end.

Plato, *Laws*, vi, 753E: ἀρχὴ γὰρ λέγεται μὲν ἥμισυ παντὸς [ἐν ταῖς παροιμίαις] ἔργου (As the proverb says, "a good beginning is half the business"); cf. Aristotle, *Politics*, v, 3, 2. ¶ Horace, *Epist.*, i, 2, 40: Dimidium facti qui coepit habet (Well begun is half done). ¶ Gower, *Conf. Aman.*, Prol., 86–88: But in proverbe I have herd seye That who that wel his werk begynneth The rather a good ende he wynneth.

Cf. Apperson, 257; Henderson, 41; W. G. Smith, 250; Stevenson, 136:3; Tilley, B259.

52 EVERY **BEGINNING** IS HARD

FQ, I, x, 6, 1: Each goodly thing is hardest to begin. ¶ *Ibid.*, III, ii, 36, 9: Things ofte impossible . . . seeme ere begonne. ¶ *Ibid.*, iii, 21, 7–8: Let no whit thee dismay The hard beginne that meetes thee.

Culman, 8: Omne principium grave (Every beginning is troublesome).

Ovid, *Rem. Amoris*, 120: Difficiles aditus impetus omnis habet (Impetuous force is ever hard to face). ¶ *Ibid.*, 234: Et labor est unus tempora prima pati (And your only labor will be to endure the first beginning). ¶ Painter, *Palace of P.*, III, 64: The first assayes be harde, and the minde doubtfull. ¶ *Fedele and Fortunio* (Malone S.), 1050: Beginnings are harde, this prouerbe is olde.

Cf. Apperson, 187; Stevenson, 152:2; Tilley, B256.

53 WHATEVER HAS A **BEGINNING** HAS AN END

Cf. no. 150: The longest day has an end; no. 12: All things come to an end

FQ, I, ix, 42, 3: All ends, that was begonne. ¶ *Mother Hub.*, 126–127: Everie thing that is begun with reason Will come by readie meanes unto his end.

Sallust, *Ad Caesarem*, v, 2: Orta omnia intereunt (All beginnings must have an end). ¶ Seneca, *Ad Polybium de Con.*, i, 1: Quicquid coepit et desinit (Whatever has a beginning has also an end). ¶ Wilson, *Arte of Rhet.*, 72: Whatsoeuer hath a beginning, the same hath also an ending. ¶ Barnfield, *Aff. Shep.*, 23: All must end that ever was begunne.

Cf. Stevenson, 156:1.

54 DO NOT **BELIEVE** RASHLY

FQ, I, iv, 1, 3–6: Beware of fraud, beware of ficklenesse . . . Least thou of her believe too lightly blame, And rash misweening doe thy hart remove.

Culman, 7: Nihil temere credideris (Believe nothing rashly).

Cato, *Collectio Dis. Vulg.*, 24: Nihil temere credideris (Believe nothing rashly). ¶ Ovid, *Artis Amat.*, iii, 685: Nec cito credideris: quantum cito credere laedat (Do not believe hastily: what harm quick belief can do).

55 TO BEAR THE **BELL**

FQ, IV, iv, 25, 9: So Satyrane that day was judg'd to beare the bell. ¶ *Ibid.*, v, 13, 6: She should surely beare the bell away. ¶ *Ibid.*, VI, x, 26, 4: Above all other lasses beare the bell.

Ascham, *Scholemaster*, *Eng. Works* (Wright), 256: Amongest all fooles the bell may beare. ¶ Greene, *Mamillia*, *Works*, II, 217: He was the man that bare the bell for courtly bringing vp. ¶ Barnfield, *Aff. Shep.*, 24: For pure white the Lilly beares the bell. ¶ Nashe, *Have with You*, *Works*, III, 15: Hath long borne the bell.

Cf. Tilley, B275.

56 TO TAKE OFF YOUR **BELLS** AND LET YOU FLY

FQ, VI, iv, 19, 6–9: He felt himselfe so light, That like an hauke, which feeling her selfe freed From bels and jesses, which did let her flight, Him seem'd his feet did fly.

Cf. Tilley, B282.

57 **BEWARE** OF HAD I WIST

Cf. n. 862: There is no wisdom in being wise too late

Mother Hub., 892–893: Most miserable man, whom wicked fate Hath brought to court, to sue for had ywist.

Greene, *Mamillia*, *Works*, II, 238: Least had I wist come too late. ¶ Greene, *Arbasto*, *Works*, III, 186: Take (had I wist) for an excuse. ¶ Greene, *Card of F.*, *Works*, IV, 110: Had I wist now comes to late; cf. IV, 130. ¶ Harvey, *Marginalia*, 99: Had I wist, cummith too late. ¶ Lodge, *Rosalynde*, *Works*, I, 106: There is no follie in Loue to had I wist.

Cf. W. G. Smith, 270; Stevenson, 1946:14; Tilley, H8.

58 TO **BITE** NEAR

FQ, II, ii, 23, 3: And suffred not their blowes to byte him nere. ¶ *Mother Hub.*, 424: Spite bites neare. ¶ *FQ*, V, xi, 64, 2: Rebuke, that bit her neare.

Cf. Tilley, B426.

59 TO **BITE** THE DUST

Cf. no. 438: To kiss the ground

FQ, III, v, 22, 1–2: With gnashing teeth did bite The bitter earth. ¶ *Ibid.*, V, ii, 18, 6: It bit the earth. ¶ *Ibid.*, xi, 14, 7: Byting th' earth.

Homer, *Iliad*, ii, 418: πρηνέες ἐν κονίῃσιν ὀδὰξ λαζοίατο γαῖαν (Fall headlong in the dust and bite the earth). ¶ Vergil, *Aeneid*, xi, 418: Humum semel ore momordit (Once for all he has bitten the dust).

¶ *Ibid.*, 668: Sanguinis ille vomens rivos cadit (He bites the gory dust). ¶ Erasmus, *Moriae Encomium*, 435D: Terram ore momordit (He lies biting the earth).

Cf. Stevenson, 647:3.

60 TO **BITE** UPON THE BRIDLE

FQ, I, i, 1, 6: His angry steede did chide his foming bitt. ¶ *Ibid.*, iii, 33, 3–5: On a courser free, That . . . the sharpe yron did for anger eat. ¶ *Ibid.*, v, 20, 8–9: Coleblacke steedes . . . on their rusty bits did champ. ¶ *Ibid.*, v, 28, 8: Then foming tarre, their bridles they would champ. ¶ *Ibid.*, vii, 37, 9: The yron rowels into frothy fome he bitt.

Vergil, *Aeneid*, iv, 134–135: Ostroque insignis et auro stat sonipes ac frena ferox spumantia mandit (Her prancing steed stands brilliant in purple and gold, and proudly champs the foaming bit). ¶ Ovid, *Artis Amat.*, i, 20: Frenaque magnanimi dente teruntur equi (And the high-mettled steed champs the bridle with his teeth). ¶ Statius, *Thebaidos*, iii, 268: Spumantem . . . mandunt adamanta iugales (The horses champ the foaming steel). ¶ Erasmus, *Adagia*, 156E: Mordere frenum (To bite the bridle). ¶ Greene, *Menaphon*, *Works*, VI, 111: Had sufficiently bitten on the bridle. ¶ Greene, *Scot. Hist. of James the Fourth*, 563, *Works*, XIII, 228: Euer chewing on the bridle. ¶ Shakespeare, *Venus & A.*, 269: The iron bit he crusheth 'tween his teeth.

Cf. Apperson, 68; W. G. Smith, 46; Stevenson, 245:7; Tilley, B670.

61 **BLACK** BEST SETS FORTH WHITE

FQ, III, ix, 2, 2–4: Good, by paragone Of evill, may more notably be rad, As white seemes fayrer, macht with blacke.

Chaucer, *Troilus*, I, 642–643: Eke whit by blak, by shame ek worthinesse, Ech set by other, more for other semeth. ¶ Lydgate, *Temple of Glass*, 1250–1251: For white is whitter, if it be set bi blak, And swete is swettir eftir bitternes. ¶ Hawes, *Past. Pleas.*, 56: Whyte by blacke doth shyne more clerely.

Cf. Tilley, B435.

62 AS **BLACK** (DARK) AS HELL

FQ, I, viii, 39, 8: As darke as hell.

Chaucer, *Duchess*, 170–171: This cave was also as derk As helle-pit.

Cf. Apperson, 51; Tilley, H397.

63 AS **BLACK** AS INK

FQ, I, i, 22, 7: Deformed monsters, fowle, and blacke as inke.

Lyly, *Euph. and His Eng.*, *Works*, II, 18: As blacke as incke.

Cf. Apperson, 51; W. G. Smith, 47; Tilley, I73

64 AS **BLACK** AS JET

FQ, II, vii, 28, 9: Clouds more black than jett.

Cf. Stevenson, 192:9; Tilley, J49.

65 AS **BLACK** (DARK) AS PITCH

Shep. Cal., June, 23: More black then pitche. ¶ *FQ*, I, v, 20, 1–3: Night . . . in a foule blacke pitchy mantle clad. ¶ *Ibid.*, 28, 4: Blacke as pitch. ¶ *Ibid.*, VI, vii, 43, 7: As blacke as pitchy night.

Chaucer, *Miller's T.*, 3731: Derk was the nyght as pich. ¶ Foxe, *Acts and Mon.*, II, 420: As black as pitch; cf. IV, 616, 688. ¶ Deloney, *Jack Newb.*, *Works*, 37: As black as pitch.

Cf. W. G. Smith, 47; Stevenson, 192:8; Tilley, P357.

66 DO NOT **BLAME** RASHLY

Cf. no. 112: Do not condemn ignorantly

Colin Clouts, 925–926: Beware . . . How rashly blame of Rosalind ye raise. ¶ *Amoretti*, lxi, 3–4: Dare not . . . rashly blame for ought.

Culman, 12: Damnare facile neminem debemus (We ought to condemn no one rashly). ¶ *Ibid.*, 30: Damnandum temere nihil est (We must blame nothing rashly). ¶ Publilius Syrus (1835), 1058: Neminem nec accusaveris, nec laudaveris cito (Do not be too hasty in accusing, or approving, anyone).

67 **BLOOD** IS NO BLEMISH

FQ, VI, i, 26, 4: Bloud is no blemish.

Publilius Syrus (1934), 313: Iucunda macula est ex inimici sanguine (Pleasant to see is the stain from the blood of an enemy).

68 **BLOOD** WILL HAVE BLOOD

FQ, I, v, 26, 3–4: He . . . Shall with his owne blood price that he hath spilt. ¶ *Ibid.*, ix, 37, 9: With thine owne blood to price his blood. ¶ *Ibid.*, 43, 6: For life must life, and blood must blood repay.

Euripides, *Suppliants*, 614–615: δίκα δίκαν δ' ἐκάλεσε καὶ φόνος φόνον (Yet justice aloud unto justice calls, and blood calls for blood). ¶ Lydgate, *Fall of P.*, I, 7049: Blood shad for blood is fynal recompence. ¶ *Ibid.*, III, 883–886: Blood will vengid be . . . Blood shad for blood. ¶ Foxe, *Acts and Mon.*, I, 341: Blood commonly requireth blood again. ¶ Lodge, *Robert, Sec. Duke of Normandy*, *Works*, II, 27: It is bloud that must requite bloud.

Cf. W. G. Smith, 52; Stevenson, 202:6; Tilley, B458.

69 TO **BLUSH** RED

FQ, I, xi, 51, 4: With rosy cheekes, for shame as blushing red. ¶ *Ibid.*, II, ix, 41, 3–4: With rosy red The bashfull blood her snowy cheekes did dye.

Cf. Stevenson, 207:14.

70 A **BOLD** BAD MAN

FQ, I, i, 37, 7: A bold bad man.

Shakespeare, *Hen. VIII*, II, ii, 44: This bold bad man. ¶ Massinger, *A New Way*, IV, i, 161: This bold bad man. ¶ Fletcher, *Loyal Subject*,

IV, v, 91: Bold bad men. ¶ Wordsworth, *Prelude* (1805), VII, 322: A bold bad man.

71 BE NOT TOO **BOLD**

FQ, III, xi, 54, 8: *Be not too bold* ¶ *Ibid.*, IV, x, 54, 2–3: Being over bold . . . was to knight unseemely shame.

Skelton, *Magnyf.* (E.E.T.S.), 1405: Be not to bolde. ¶ Tusser, *Husb.* (E.D.S.), 109: Be not too bold. ¶ Golding, *Ovid*, x, 630: Forbeare too bold too bee. ¶ Ascham, *Scholemaster*, *Eng. Works* (Wright), 260: A man ought to beware, to be ouer bold. ¶ Lodge, *Rosalynde*, *Works*, I, 69: Be not too bolde. ¶ Shakespeare, *Rom. & Jul.*, II, ii, 14: I am too bold.

Cf. Apperson, 59.

72 **BOLDNESS** IS A MASK FOR FEAR

FQ, V, iii, 15, 5: Courage lent a cloke to cowardise.

Lucan, *De Bello Civili*, iv, 702: Audendo magnus tegitur timor (Great fear is hidden by a bluster of daring).

73 **BOLDNESS** IS BLIND

Teares of the M., 266: Blind is bold. ¶ *Colin Clouts*, 348: Base shepheard bold and blind.

Cf. Tilley, B507.

74 THE SEMBLANCE OF **BOLDNESS** HELPS ONE TO WIN

Cf. no. 129: In great danger courage is everything

FQ, IV, x, 16, 8–9: With the terrour of his countenance bold Full many did affray, that else faine enter would.

Publilius Syrus (1934), 717: Virtutis vultus partem habet victoriae (The countenance of bravery has a share in the victory).

75 TO **BOLT** TO THE BRAN

FQ, II, iv, 24, 2: Saying, he now had boulted all the floure.

Chaucer, *Nun's Priest's T.*, 4430: But I ne kan nat bulte it to the bren. ¶ Draxe, 380, 672 (*s. v.* Fancie): Fancie may so long boult branne, that at length it may turne to floure.

Cf. *FQ* (Variorum), II, 229–230.

76 AS YOU **BREW**, SO MUST YOU DRINK

Shep. Cal., Sept., 101: As they han brewed, so let hem beare blame.

Cf. Taverner, 46; Apperson, 67; W. G. Smith, 64; Tilley, B654.

77 **BRIDLE** YOUR DELIGHTS

FQ, VI, vi, 14, 6: Bridle loose delight.

Culman, 3: Voluptatem tempera (Moderate your pleasure). ¶ *Ibid.*, 24: Ponere modum irae & voluptati, bonum est (It is good to keep measure in anger and pleasure).

Shakespeare, *Merch. of V.*, III, ii, 111–112: Be moderate; allay thy ecstasy; In measure rain thy joy.

78 AS **BRIGHT** AS DAY

FQ, I, iv, 8, 2: As bright as sunny day. ¶ *Ibid.*, V, ix, 24, 2: In armour bright as day.

Cf. Apperson, 68; Stevenson, 246:1; Tilley, D55.

79 MAN IS BUT A **BUBBLE**

Shep. Cal., Feb., 87: Youngth is a bubble blown up with breath. ¶ *Ruines of T.*, 50: Flesh, a bubble glas of breath. ¶ *Amoretti*, lviii, 5–6: All flesh is frayle, . . . Like a vaine bubble blowen up with ayre.

Culman, 28: Vita nostra similis bullae in aqua (Our life is like a bubble on the water).

Varro, *De Re Rustica*, i, l, 1: Ut dicitur, si est homo bulla (If man is a bubble, as the proverb has it). ¶ Erasmus, *Adagia*, 500A: Homo bulla (Man is a bubble).

Cf. Taverner, 33; Stevenson, 1509:6; Tilley, M246; C. G. Smith, 191.

80 **BUGS** TO SCARE BABES

FQ, II, xii, 25, 7–8: For all, that here on earth we dreadfull hold, Be but as bugs to fearen babes withall.

Jewel, *Defense of an Apologie* (1565), 285: A bug meet only to fray Children. ¶ Shakespeare, *3 Hen. VI*, V, ii, 2: Warwick was a bug that fear'd us all. ¶ Shakespeare, *T. of Shrew*, I, ii, 211: Tush, tush! Fear boys with bugs! ¶ Shakespeare, *Winter's T.*, III, ii, 93: The bug which you would fright me with I seek.

Cf. Stevenson, 251:5; Tilley, B703.

81 TO **BURN** LIKE FIRE

Amoretti, lv, 6: Her love doth burne like fyre.

Chaucer, *Troilus*, III, 425: As the fir he brende. ¶ Chaucer, *Leg. Good Women*, 1751: In his herte brende as any fyr.

Cf. Stevenson, 808:11.

82 ONE BEATS THE **BUSH**, ANOTHER CATCHES THE BIRD

Cf. no. 710: One man sows, another man reaps

Shep. Cal., Oct., 17: I beate the bush, the byrds to them doe flye.

Cf. Stevenson, 259:4; Tilley, B740.

83 TO **BUY** TOO DEAR

Shep. Cal., Julye, 148: Love he bought to deare. ¶ *Ibid.*, Aug., 108: You may buye gold to deare. ¶ *FQ*, I, ii, 31, 7: O too deare love, love bought with death too deare! ¶ *Ibid.*, II, i, 53, 8–9: So deare thee, babe, I bought; Yet nought to dear I deemd.

Erasmus, *Adagia*, 38E: Non emo tanti poenitere (Do not buy repentance too dear).

Cf. Apperson, 75; W. G. Smith, 73; Stevenson, 988:10; Tilley, M257, R81–2.

84 EVERY **CALAMITY** IS A PUNISHMENT OF SIN

Cf. no. 188: Diseases are caused by sin

FQ, IV, i, 20, 2–3: Plagues and harmes . . . punish wicked men, that walke amisse.

Culman, 30: Calamitas omnis peccatorum poena est (Every calamity is a punishment of sin).

85 NEVER GOOD **CAPTAIN** THAT NEVER WAS SOLDIER

View, 661: Any one, before he come to be a captayne, should have bene a souldiour.

Thomas Starkey, *England in the Reign of Henry VIII* (1538), I, 1: Common saying, "He was . . . never good captain that never was soldier."

Cf. Stevenson, 382:3.

86 WHERE **CARE** LODGES SLEEP WILL NEVER LIE

FQ, I, i, 40, 5–6; Care . . . oft is wont to trouble gentle Sleepe. ¶ *Ibid.*, II, vii, 25, 1–6: Before the dore sat selfe-consuming Care, Day and night keeping wary watch and ward, . . . Ne would he suffer Sleepe once thetherward Approch. ¶ *Ibid.*, IV, v, arg.: Scudamour, comming to Cares house, Doth sleepe from him expell.

Theocritus, *Idyls*, xxi, 28: ἁ φροντὶς κόπτοισα μακρὰν τὰν νύκτα ποιεῖ τιν (Care makes your night long by disturbing your slumber). ¶ Tibullus, *Elegies*, iii, 4, 20: Somnus sollicitas deficit ante domos (Sleep vanishes before the house of care). ¶ Shakespeare, *Rom. & Jul.*, II, iii, 35: Where care lodges sleep will never lie. ¶ Shakespeare, *2 Hen. IV*, IV, v, 23: Golden care! That keep'st the ports of slumber open wide.

Cf. Stevenson, 289:1; 2137:1.

87 DO NOT TORMENT YOUR MIND WITH **CARES**

Mother Hub., 903: To fret thy soule with crosses and with cares.

Culman, 22: Ne curis tuum ipsius animum excrucies (Do not torment your mind with cares).

Cf. C. G. Smith, 21.

88 **CAUGHT** IN ONE'S OWN TRAP

Cf. no. 352: The guiler himself shall be beguiled; no. 410: He that hurts another hurts himself

FQ, III, v, 25, 8: So mischief fel upon the meaners crowne. ¶ *Ibid.*, V, viii, 7, 9: So mischiefe overmatcht the wronger. ¶ *Ibid.*, VI, ii, 23, 7–9: Who ever thinkes through confidence of might, Or through support of count'nance proud and hault. To wrong the weaker, oft falles in his owne assault.

Erasmus, *Adagia*, 49B: Suo ipsius laqueo captus est (He is caught in his own snare). ¶ Foxe, *Acts and Mon.*, V, 466: "He that layeth a snare for another man," saith Solomon, "shall be taken in it himself"; cf. *Old Testament: Psalms*, vii, 16; *Proverbs*, xxvi, 27. ¶ Pettie, *Petite P.*, 95: Shee may bee taken in the net which shee layeth to intangle other[s]. ¶ Sidney, *Arcadia*, *Works*, I, 438: Thy wicked wiles have caught thy selfe in thine owne nette. ¶ Greene, *Conny-Catching*, *Works*, X, 101: He that maketh a trap falleth into the snare him selfe.

Cf. Stevenson, 1969:6; Tilley, F626.

89 THE **CAUSE** TAKEN AWAY, THE EFFECT VANISHES

FQ, VI, vi, 14, 3–4: When the cause, whence evill doth arize, Removed is, th' effect surceaseth.

Aristotle, *Rhetoric*, ii, 23, 25: *ἄν τε ὑπάρχῃ, ὅτι ἔστι, κἂν μὴ ὑπάρχῃ, ὅτι οὐκ ἔστιν* (If the cause exists, the effect exists; if the cause does not exist, the effect does not exist). ¶ Chaucer, *Troilus*, II, 483: Cesse cause, ay cesseth maladie. ¶ Greene, *Carde of F.*, *Works*, IV, 157: If the cause be taken awaie the effect faileth. ¶ Greene, *Alcida*, *Works*, IX, 105: He thought by taking away the cause, to raze out the effects. ¶ Sidney, *Arcadia*, *Works*, II, 165: The cause being taken away, the effect followes.

Cf. Stevenson, 305:4; Tilley, C202.

90 ONE CAN NEVER BE TOO **CAUTIOUS**

Cf. no. 572: Neglect a danger, and it will take you by surprise; no. 826: Good watch prevents misfortune

Spenser's motto: Cautela superabundans non nocet (One can never be too cautious); cf. Harvey, *Works*, I, 133.

Publilius Syrus (1934), 102: Cavendi nulla est dimittenda occasio (No opportunity for caution should be let slip).

Cf. Harvey, *Letter-Book*, 75; Legouis, *Spenser* (1926), 17.

91 ON EARTH NOTHING IS **CERTAIN**

Shep. Cal., Nov., 153: O trustlesse state of earthly things. ¶ *Ibid.*, 157: Nys on earth assuraunce to be sought. ¶ *FQ*, I, ix, 11, 5: Nothing is sure that growes on earthly grownd. ¶ *Ibid.*, II, ix, 21, 9: No earthly thing is sure. ¶ *Ibid.*, xi, 30, 3–5: So feeble is mans state, and life unsound, That in assuraunce it may never stand, Till it dissolved be from earthly band. ¶ *Ibid.*, VI, iii, 5, 2: So tickle is the state of earthly things.

Culman, 5: Dubius rerum eventus (The issue of things is doubtful). ¶ *Ibid.*, 6: Incertus rerum exitus (The end of things is uncertain).

Ovid, *Tristia*, v, 5, 27: Nil homini certum est (Naught is certain for man). ¶ Seneca, *Ad Polybium de Con.*, ix, 9: Nihil ne in totum quidem diem certi est (We can be sure of nothing—not even for the whole of one day). ¶ Foxe, *Acts and Mon.*, III, 745: There is nothing in this mutable world firm and stable. ¶ Painter, *Palace of P.*, I, 284: There is nothing vnder the heauens that is stable and sure. ¶ Sidney, *Arcadia*,

Works, I, 26: There is nothing so certaine, as our continual uncertaintie. ¶ Greene, *Groatsworth of Wit*, *Works*, XII, 104: No certaintie can be founde in this vncertaine world.

92 THE **CHAMELEON** CAN CHANGE TO ALL COLORS SAVE WHITE

FQ, IV, i, 18, 4–5: As ever could cameleon colours new; So could she forge all colors, save the trew.

Erasmus, *Similia*, 565A: Chamaeleon omnem imitatur colorem praeterquam album (The chameleon imitates every color except white).

Cf. Tilley, C222.

93 ALL **CHANCE** IS UNSOUND

Cf. no 94: Change is seldom for the better; no. 419: All innovation is perilous

FQ, V, ii, 36, 7: All chaunce unsound.

Culman, 6: Humani casus ancipites (Human chances are doubtful).

Seneca, *De Brev.*, xvii, 4: Omne enim quod fortuito obvenit instabile est (For everything that comes to us from chance is unstable). ¶ Tasso, *Jer. Del.*, II, 67, 3: Chance is uncertain. ¶ Hughes, *Misf. of Arthur*, III, i, 142: *Chance* is fraile.

94 **CHANGE** IS SELDOM FOR THE BETTER

Cf. no. 93: All chance is unsound; no 419: All innovation is perilous

Shep. Cal., Sept., 68–69: Ah, fon! now by thy losse art taught That seeldome chaunge the better brought.

Cf. Apperson, 556; W. G. Smith, 572; Tilley, B332.

95 ALL THINGS **CHANGE**

Cf. no. 97: There are many kinds of change; no 770: Time changes all things; no. 772: Time devours (consumes, wears out) all things

Ruines of T., 206: All things doo change that under heaven abide. ¶ *Daphnaïda*, 428–429: All the world . . . changeth ever too and fro. ¶ *FQ*, V, Prol., 4, 5: All things else in time are chaunged quight. ¶ *Ibid.*, VII, vii, 48, 8: Moves them all, and makes them changed be. ¶ *Ibid.*, vii, 58, 2–3: All things stedfastnes doe hate And changed be.

Culman, 3: Omnia mutantur (All things are changed). ¶ *Ibid.*, 14: Omnes res facile mutantur (All things are quickly changed).

Aristotle, *Politics*, v, 10, 1: *τὸ μὴ μένειν μηθὲν ἀλλ' ἔν τινι περιόδῳ μεταβάλλειν* (Nothing is permanent, but everything changes). ¶ Lucretius, *De Rerum Natura*, v, 830–831: Omnia migrant, omnia commutat natura et vertere cogit (All things move, all are changed by nature and compelled to alter). ¶ Ovid, *Metam.*, xv, 165: Omnia mutantur (All things are changing). ¶ Marcus Aurelius, *Meditations*, ix, 19: *Πάντα ἐν μεταβολῇ* (Everything changes). ¶ Erasmus, *Adagia*, 286A: Omnium rerum vicissitudo est (In all things there is change).

Cf. Taverner, 22; Tilley, C233; C. G. Smith, 23.

96 IN ALL THINGS **CHANGE** IS SWEET

Muiopotmos, 178: All change is sweete.

Culman, 7: Jucunda rerum vicissitudo (The interchange of things is pleasant). ¶ *Ibid.*, 13: In omni re varietas delectat (Variety is delightful in everything). ¶ Publilius Syrus (1934), 278: Iucundum nihil est nisi quod reficit varietas (There is nothing pleasant save what variety freshens).

Euripides, *Orestes*, 234: *μεταβολὴ πάντων γλυκύ* (Change is in all things sweet); cf. Aristotle, *E. Ethics*, vii, 1, 9; *N. Ethics*, vii, 14, 8. ¶ Ovid, *Ex Ponto*, iii, 4, 51: Est quoque cunctarum novitas carissima rerum (Novelty in all things is charming). ¶ Erasmus, *Adagia*, 287B: Jucunda vicissitudo rerum (Change in all things is sweet).

Cf. Taverner, 22; Tilley, C229.

97 THERE ARE MANY KINDS OF **CHANGE**

Cf. no. 95: All things change; no. 770: Time changes all things

FQ, VII, vii, 25, 2–3: All the world . . . To thousand sorts of change we subject see.

Culman, 16: Variae sunt rerum vices (The changes of things are divers). ¶ *Ibid.*, 22: Mortalia omnia mutationes multas habent (All mortal things have many changes).

98 AS **CHANGEABLE** AS THE MOON

FQ, VII, vii, 50, 9: *As changefull as the moone* men use to say.

Culman, 27: Stultus, perinde atque luna, immutatur (A fool is changed, just as the moon).

Hawes, *Past. Pleas.*, 83: The minde of men chaungeth as the mone. ¶ *Ibid.*, 156: Chaunge as the mone. ¶ Harvey, *Foure Lett.*, *Works*, I, 227: As changeable as the moone. ¶ Harvey, *Pierces Super.*, *Works*, II, 191: As interchaungeable as the Moone. ¶ Shakespeare, *L. Lab. Lost*, V, ii, 212: Thus change I like the moon.

Cf. Apperson, 91; W. G. Smith, 88; Tilley, M1111.

99 TO **CHECKMATE**

Shep. Cal., Dec., 53: Love . . . gave me checkmate.

Chaucer, *Troilus*, II, 754: Shal noon housbonde seyn to me "chek mat!" ¶ Lydgate, *Fall of P.*, Prol., 181–182: Fortune ful offte . . . seith to hem chekmat. ¶ *Ibid.*, I, 1526: Sey to hem chek-maat. ¶ *Ibid.*, III, 52: I stood chekmaat for feer. ¶ Gascoigne, *Dan Bartholmew*, *Works*, I, 118: Deadly hate, Did play checke mate, With me. ¶ Lyly, *Euph. Anat. of Wit*, *Works*, I, 249: A Milkesoppe, taunted and retaunted, with check and checkemate. ¶ Greene, *Philomela*, *Works*, XI, 119: They wil giue thee . . . a checkmate.

Cf. Tilley, C262.

100 **CHEEK** BY JOWL

FQ, V, ii, 49, 7: Cheeke by cheeke.

Gascoigne, *Epist. to Divines*, *Works*, I, 5: Cheeke by cheek. ¶ Nashe, *Lenten Stuffe*, *Works*, III, 189: March cheeke by iowle with her.

Cf. Apperson, 92; Stevenson, 329:6; Tilley, C263.

101 TO **CHEW** THE CUD

Virgils Gnat, 86: Chaw the tender prickles in her cud. ¶ *Ibid.*, 144: His flock their chawed cuds do eate. ¶ *FQ*, III, x, 18, 1: He chawd the cud of inward griefe. ¶ *Ibid.*, V, v, 27, 2: She chaw'd the cud of lovers carefull plight.

Cf. Apperson, 94; W. G. Smith, 91; Tilley, C896.

102 ONCE A MAN AND TWICE A **CHILD**

Axiochus (Variorum), 167–168: They whose bodies in old age long flourisheth in minde, as the saying is, become twise children.

Culman, 5: Bis pueri senes (Old men are twice children).

Aristophanes, *The Clouds*, 1417: *ἐγὼ δέ γ' ἀντείποιμ' ἂν ὡς δὶς παῖδες οἱ γέροντες* (I would reply that old men are twice boys). ¶ Plautus, *Mercator*, 295–296: Senex quom extemplo est, iam nec sentit nec sapit, aiunt solere eum rusum repuerascere (Once a man gets old and reaches the senseless, witless stage, they do say he's apt to have a second childhood). ¶ Erasmus, *Adagia*, 195B: Bis pueri senes (Twice a boy, once an old man). ¶ Greene, *Mamillia*, *Works*, II, 50: Old folke are twise children.

Cf. Taverner, 16; W. G. Smith, 472; Tilley, M570; C. G. Smith, 25.

103 AS **CLEAR** AS CRYSTAL

Shep. Cal., Julye, 159: More cleare than christall glasse. ¶ *Ibid.*, Aug., 80: As cleare as the christall glasse. ¶ *FQ*, I, vii, 6, 3: As cleare as christall glas. ¶ *Ibid.*, III, i, 15, 4: As cleare as christall stone. ¶ *Visions of B.*, xii, 2: As cleare as christall. ¶ *Amoretti*, xlv, 12: Clearer then christall.

Harvey, *Marginalia*, 103: As cleare, as Christall. ¶ Harvey, *Foure Lett.*, *Works*, I, 211: Clere as a christal. ¶ Greene, *Never Too Late*, *Works*, VIII, 107: As cleare as Christall. ¶ Jonson, *Every Man Out of His Humour*, III, vii, 15–16, *Works*, III, 516: As cleere as christall.

Cf. Apperson, 101; Stevenson, 363:5; Tilley, C875, G135.

104 **CLEMENCY** BREEDS GOODWILL AND FAVOR

Cf. no. 526: Mercy is the mighty's jewel

FQ, V, vii, 22, 8–9: Clemence oft, in things amis, Restraines . . . sterne behests and cruell doomes.

* Publilius Syrus (1934), 90: Bona comparat praesidia misericordia (Pity provides good defenses). ¶ *Ibid.*, 370: Misereri scire sine periclo est vivere (To know how to pity is to live without danger).

Seneca, *De Clem.*, i, 11, 4: Clementia ergo non tantum honestiores sed tutiores praestat ornamentumque imperiorum est simul et certissima salus (Mercy, then, makes rulers not only more honored, but safer, and is at the same time the glory of sovereign power and its surest protection). ¶ Lydgate, *Fall of P.*, III, 4056–4057: The moral Senec doth clerli specifie, The throne of princis be clemence is most stable. ¶ Florio, *First Fruites*, 64: Nothing gendreth loue, mainteyneth concorde, peace, & quietnes among the subjects, then a prince to be clement.

Cf. C. G. Smith, 29.

105 TO HAVE A **CLOAK** FOR YOUR GUILE (CRIME, KNAVERY)

Shep. Cal., Feb., 162: His colowred crime with craft to cloak. ¶ *Mother Hub.*, 344: Abusing manie through their cloaked guile. ¶ *FQ*, II, i, 21, 6–7: Disguysd, To cloke her guile with sorrow and sad teene. ¶ *Ibid.*, vii, 45, 9: She sought for helps to cloke her crime withall. ¶ *Ibid.*, VI, vii, 4, 1–2: False Turpine comming courteously, To cloke the mischiefe which he inly ment.

Publilius Syrus (1835), 640: Odia alia sub vultu, alia sub osculo latent (Some enmities conceal themselves beneath a mask, some under a kiss).

Cf. Apperson, 102; W. G. Smith, 98; Tilley, C419.

106 **CLOTHES** MAKE THE MAN

Colin Clouts, 711: Each mans worth is measured by his weed. ¶ *View*, 639: There is not a litle in the garment to the fashioning of the mynde and conditions.

Erasmus, *Adagia*, 731E: Vestis virum facit (Clothes make the man); cf. 926E. ¶ Jonson, *Every Man Out of His Humour*, II, vi, 45–46, *Works*, III, 490: Rich apparell has strange vertues: it makes him that hath it without meanes, esteemed for an excellent wit. ¶ Shakespeare, *Cymb.*, IV, ii, 82–83: Clothes . . . it seems, make thee.

Cf. Apperson, 13; W. G. Smith, 12; Stevenson, 367:5; Tilley, A283.

107 AFTER **CLOUDS**, CLEAR WEATHER

Cf. no. 728: After a storm comes a calm

Shep. Cal., Sept., 18: When the rayne is faln, the cloudes wexen cleare. ¶ *FQ*, V, iii, 1, 1–2: After long stormes and tempests overblowne, The sunne at length his joyous face doth cleare. ¶ *Hymne in Honour of L.*, 276–277: After stormes, when clouds begin to cleare, The sunne more bright and glorious doth appeare.

Seneca, *Epist.*, cvii, 8: Nubilo serena succedunt (Clear weather follows cloudy).

Cf. Apperson, 103; W. G. Smith, 4; Stevenson, 2244:7; Tilley, C442.

108 A **COCK** IS BOLD ON ITS OWN DUNGHILL

Shep. Cal., Sept., 45–46: So stiffe and so state As cocke on his dunghill crowing cranck. ¶ *View*, 660: Being but of late growen out of the dounghill beginneth nowe to overcrowe soe high mountaynes.

Culman, 20: Gallus in suo sterquilinio plurimum potest (A cock can do very much upon his own dunghill). ¶ Publilius Syrus (1835), 363: In sterculino plurimum gallus potest (A cock has great influence on his own dunghill).

Seneca, *Apoc.*, 7: Gallum in suo sterquilino plurimum posse (The Gallic cock was worth most on his own dunghill). ¶ Erasmus, *Adagia*, 1030A: Gallus in suo sterquilinio plurimum potest (A cock is most powerful on his own dunghill). ¶ Lydgate, *Pilgr.*, 10048: How that every wyht ys bold upon hys owne (erly and late) at the dongel at hys gate. ¶ Sidney, *Defence of P.*, *Works*, III, 22: Cocke of this worldes dunghill.

Cf. Apperson, 105; Tilley, C486.

109 THE **COCKATRICE** KILLS WITH ITS LOOK

Amoretti, xlix, 10: Kill with looks, as cockatrices doo.

Cf. Tilley, C495.

110 MUCH **COIN**, MUCH CARE

Cf. no. 631: Prosperity brings on anxieties; no. 830: Little wealth, little care

FQ, VI, ix, 21, 4: Store of cares doth follow riches store.

Culman, 11: Crescentem sequitur cura pecuniam (As money increases care follows).

Hesiod, *Works and Days*, 380: πλείων μὲν πλεόνων μελέτη (Care increases with possessions). ¶ Horace, *Odes*, iii, 16, 17: Crescentem sequitur cura pecuniam (As money grows, care follows). ¶ *Paradise of D. Dev.*, 33: In getting much, we get but care.

Cf. W. G. Smith, 438; Stevenson, 1834:1; Tilley, C506.

111 FOLLOW **CONCORD**

FQ, II, ii, 31, 1–9: Lovely concord, and most sacred peace, Doth nourish vertue, and fast friendship breeds; . . . Be therefore, . . . pacifide, And this missceming discord meekely lay aside.

Culman, 1: Concordiam sectare (Follow concord).

112 DO NOT **CONDEMN** IGNORANTLY

Cf. no. 66: Do not blame rashly

FQ, IV, Prol., 2, 3–4: They ought not thing unknowne reprove, Ne naturall affection faultlesse blame.

Culman, 19: Damnaveris nullum causa non cognita (Condemn no one before his cause is known). ¶ Publilius Syrus (1835), 815: Quod nescias, damnare summa est temeritas (It is the height of folly to blame without knowledge).

113 **CONFIDENCE** MUST BE HAD IN GOD ALONE

Visions of B., i, 12–14: So I . . . In God alone my confidence do stay.

Culman, 29: Confidentia sola habenda in Deo (Sole confidence must be had in God).

114 OFTEN THE **CONQUERED** CONQUER THE VICTOR

FQ, II, x, 57, 1–4: Fought . . . and him overthrew; Yet in the chace was slaine of them that fled: So made them victors whome he did subdew.

Cato, *Disticha*, ii, 10: Victorem a victo superari saepe videmus (Often we see the victor conquered by the vanquished).

Cf. Stevenson, 403:7.

115 **CONSCIENCE** MAKES BONDSMEN OF US ALL

FQ, I, xii, 30, 5: My conscience cleare with guilty bands would bynd.

Publilius Syrus (1934), 264: Heu, conscientia animi gravis est servitus (Ah, conscience makes bondsmen of us all)!

116 A BAD **CONSCIENCE** IS A SILENT TORTURE OF THE MIND

FQ, I, ix, 49, 3–4: Trembling horror did his conscience daunt, And hellish anguish did his soule assaile.

Publilius Syrus (1934), 490: O tactitum tormentum animi conscientia (O conscience, silent torture of the mind)! ¶ *Ibid.* (1835), 739: Quam conscientia animi gravis est servitus (How oppressive is the weight of an evil conscience)!

Cf. Stevenson, 408:6; C. G. Smith, 36.

117 BEFORE YOU BEGIN, **CONSIDER** YOUR GOAL

Cf. no. 124: Good counsel insures victory

Mother Hub., 122–123: For it behoves, ere that into the race We enter, to resolve first hereupon. ¶ *FQ*, III, x, 40, 7–8: Therefore advise ye well, Before ye enterprise that way to wend.

Publilius Syrus (1934), 561: Quicquid conaris, quo pervenias cogites (In your every endeavor contemplate your goal).

Sallust, *Bellum Catilinae*, i, 6–7: Prius quam incipias, consulto, et ubi consulueris, mature facto opus est (Before you begin, deliberation is necessary; when you have deliberated, prompt action). ¶ Erasmus, *Adagia*, 512F: Antequam incipias, consulto; ubi consulueris, mature facto opus est (Before you begin, consider, and when you have considered, act).

Cf. Taverner, 33.

118 IN THIS LIFE NOTHING IS **CONSTANT**

FQ, VII, vii, 47, 7: Nothing here long standeth in one stay. ¶ *Ibid.*, 56, 1–3: Within this wide great universe Nothing doth firme and permanent appeare, But all things tost and turned by transverse.

Culman, 6: Firmum in vita nihil (Nothing is constant in this life).

Cf. Stevenson, 1233:9.

119 HAPPY IS THE MAN WHO IS **CONTENT** WITH A LITTLE

Cf. no. 120: Happy is the man who is content with his own lot; no. 831: The greatest wealth is contentment with a little

FQ, VI, ix, 20, 2–4: Happie, . . . having small, yet doe I not complaine Of want, ne wish for more it to augment, But doe my selfe, with that I have, content.

Lydgate, *Fall of P.*, I, 904–908: For in this world is no thyng mor parfit, Nor taccomplisshe thyng off mor plesance, Than a man for to haue delit In litil good to hauen suffisance. And be content in his gouernance.

120 HAPPY IS THE MAN WHO IS **CONTENT** WITH HIS OWN LOT

Cf. no. 119: Happy is the man who is content with a little; no. 831: The greatest wealth is contentment with a little

FQ, VI, ix, 29, 8–9: Fittest is, that all contented rest With that they hold.

Publilius Syrus: Qui suis rebus contentus est, huic maximae ac certissimae divitiae (He who is contented with his lot has the greatest and surest riches); cf. Stevenson, 414:7.

Seneca, *De Vita Beata*, vi, 2: Beatus est praesentibus, qualiacumque sunt, contentus amicusque rebus suis (The happy man is content with his present lot, no matter what it is, and is reconciled to his circumstances).

121 TO BE **CORN-FED**

FQ, II, vii, 16, 6: Like corn-fed steed.

Gascoigne, *Steele Glas*, *Works*, II, 170: Cornfed beasts, whose bellie is their God. ¶ Deloney, *Jack Newb.*, *Works*, 56: My folkes are so corne fed, that wee haue much adoo to please them in their dyet.

Cf. Clarke, 99; Stevenson, 422:2; Tilley, C665.

122 **CORRECTION** SHOULD BEGIN AT THE HOUSE OF GOD

View, 646: (As it is sayde) correction should begin at the howse of God.

123 **COUNSEL** IS A SOVEREIGN REMEDY

FQ, I, vii, 40, 7–8: Mishaps are maistred by advice discrete, And counsell mitigates the greatest smart. ¶ *Ibid.*, II, i, 44, 2–3: Goodly counsell, that for wounded hart Is meetest med'cine. ¶ *Ibid.*, III, iii, 5, 4–5: Counsel, that is chiefe And choisest med'cine. ¶ *Ibid.*, VI, iv, 34, 7: In evils counsell is the comfort chiefe. ¶ *Ibid.*, vi, 13, 7–9: If that no salves may us to health restore . . . we need good counsell . . Aread, good sire, some counsell, that may us sustaine.

Culman, 20: In rebus malis opus est bono consilio (In bad matters we need good counsel). ¶ Publilius Syrus (1934), 141: Consilium in dubiis remedium prudentis est (The prudent man's remedy in a crisis is counsel).

Seneca, *Medea*, 155–156: Levis est dolor qui capere consilium potest et clepere sese (Light is the grief which can take counsel and hide itself). ¶ Hawes, *Past. Pleas.*, 67: Councell is medicine. ¶ Pettie, *Petite P.*, 32: The case is light, where counsayle can take place. ¶ Clarke, 22: He that will not be counselled cannot be helped.

Cf. Apperson, 115.

124 GOOD **COUNSEL** INSURES VICTORY

Cf. no. 117: Before you begin, consider your goal

FQ, I, i, 33, 5–6: The way to win Is wisely to advise.

Publilius Syrus (1934), 151: Deliberare utilia mora tutissima est (To think out useful plans is the safest delay).

Euripides, *Phoen. Maidens*, 721: μὴν τὸ νικᾶν ἐστι πᾶν εὐβουλία (Wholly in good counsel victory lies). ¶ Chaucer, *Miller's T.*, 3530: Werk al by conseil, and thou shalt nat rewe.

125 ILL **COUNSEL** MARS ALL

Mother Hub., 128: Things miscounselled must needs miswend.

Cf. W. G. Smith, 315; Tilley, C692.

126 WOMEN'S **COUNSELS** ARE OFTEN FATAL

FQ, III, x, 11, 9: So readie rype to ill, ill wemens counsels bee.

Cf. Stevenson, 2576:4, 6.

127 **COUNTERFEIT** THINGS OFTEN APPEAR TO BE MORE BEAUTIFUL

FQ, IV, v, 15, 9: Forged things do fairest shew.

Pettie, *Petite P.*, 246: Counterfayte coine sheweth more goodly then the good.

128 **COURAGE** MOUNTS WITH OCCASION

Cf. no. 129: In great danger courage is everything

FQ, III, vii, 26, 9: Need her corage taught. ¶ *Ibid.*, IV, iii, 8, 9: Smart daunts not mighty harts, but makes them more to swell.

Publilius Syrus (1934), 447: Non novit virtus calamitati cedere (Bravery knows no yielding to calamity). ¶ *Ibid.*, 450: Nocere casus non solet constantiae (Misfortune seldom hurts steadfastness).

Lucan, *De Bello Civili*, iii, 614: Crevit in adversis virtus (His courage rose with disaster).

Cf. C. G. Smith, 40–41.

129 IN GREAT DANGER **COURAGE** IS EVERYTHING

Cf. no. 74: The semblance of boldness helps one to win; no. 128: Courage mounts with occasion

FQ, I, ii, 17, 6–7: Repining courage yields No foote to foe. ¶ *Ibid.*, IV, ii, 39, 1–3: Bold was the chalenge, as himselfe was bold, And courage full of haughtie hardiment, Approved oft in perils manifold.

Publilius Syrus (1934), 227: Felicitatem in dubiis virtus impetrat (Valor secures success in hazards). ¶ * *Ibid.*, 298: In rebus dubiis plurimi est audacia (Audacity is everything, when the danger is critical). ¶ *Ibid.*, 547: Pericla qui audet ante vincit quam accipit (The bold defeat danger before meeting it).

Ovid, *Metam.*, iii, 54: Iaculum teloque animus praestantior omni (Better than all weapons, a courageous soul). ¶ Ovid, *Ex Ponto*, ii, 7, 75: Animus tamen omnia vincit (Courage conquers all things). ¶ Shakespeare, *3 Hen. VI*, IV, vii, 62: Fearless minds climb soonest unto crowns.

Cf. C. G. Smith, 41.

130 WHERE THERE IS NO **COURAGE** (HONOR) THERE IS NO PITY, NO GRIEF

FQ, VI, vii, 18, 5: For wheres no courage, theres no ruth nor mone.

Herbert, 364: Where there is no honour there is no grief.

131 **COURTESY** BREEDS GOOD WILL AND FAVOR

FQ, VI, ix, 45, 5–6: Courtesie amongst the rudest breeds Good will and favour.

Culman, 5: Comitate vincendi morosi (Froward folks are to be won by fair means). ¶ *Ibid.*, 6: Ferocitas lenitate sedatur (Fierceness is assuaged by mildness).

Erasmus, *Institutio Principis, Christiani*, 591C: Civilitas ubique aut amorem gignit, aut certe lenit odium (Courtesy everywhere engenders love, or at least assuages hatred).

132 ALL **COVET**, ALL LOSE

Shep. Cal., Sept., 58–61: I was so fonde To leave the good that I had in hande, In hope of better, that was uncouth: So lost the dogge the flesh in his mouth.

Culman, 35: Qui plus ambit, minus consequitur (He that covets to get more, gets less).

Lydgate, *Aesop*, 8, 1–3: An old prouerbe hath he sayde and shal . . . who al coveiteth, oft he lesith all. ¶ Foxe, *Acts and Mon.*, IV, 272: The immeasurable desire of that bishop sought more than enough (like to Aesop's dog coveting to have both the flesh and the shadow), not only he missed what he gaped for, but also lost that which he had. ¶ Lodge, *Catharos*, *Works*, II, 31: According to the common prouerbe, Hee that coueteth all, often times looseth much.

Cf. Henderson, 368; W. G. Smith, 7; Stevenson, 443:12; Tilley, A127; C. G. Smith, 43.

133 DO NOT **COVET** OTHER MEN'S THINGS

FQ, IV, i, 11, 3–4: Made repent that he had rashly lusted For thing unlawfull, that was not his owne.

Culman, 5: Aliena concupiscere noli (Do not covet other men's things).

Euripides, *Hecuba*, 996: νυν αὐτὸν μηδ' ἔρα τῶν πλησίον (Covet not thy neighbors' goods). ¶ Cato, *Disticha*, Prol., 54: Alienum noli concupiscere (Do not covet what is another's).

Cf. Stevenson, 443:3.

134 **COVETOUSNESS** CANNOT BE SATISFIED

Cf. no. 135: Nothing is more miserable than covetousness; no. 559: The more a man has, the more he desires

Amoretti, xxxv, 1–3: My hungry eyes, through greedy covetize . . . With no contentment can themselves suffize.

Culman, 5: Cupiditas est inexplebilis (Covetousness is insatiable). ¶ *Ibid.*, 11: Avari non possunt satiari (Covetous men cannot be satisfied).

Horace, *Epist.*, i, ii, 56: Semper avarus eget (The covetous man always wants). ¶ Fuller, 1177: Covetousness is generally incurable.

135 NOTHING IS MORE MISERABLE THAN **COVETOUSNESS**

Cf. no. 134: Covetousness cannot be satisfied

FQ, I, iv, 29, 1–3: Most wretched wight, whom nothing might suffise, . . . Whose need had end, but no end covetise.

Culman, 5: Avaritia nihil miserius (Nothing is more miserable than covetousness).

136 **COWARDS** ARE CRUEL

FQ, VI, vi, 26, 9: For cowardize doth still in villany delight.

Cf. Apperson, 120; W. G. Smith, 116; Stevenson, 449: 7; Tilley, C778.

137 LOSE **CREDIT** AND ONE CAN LOSE NO MORE

FQ, II, i, 3, 8–9: His credit now in doubtfull ballaunce hong; For hardly could bee hurt, who was already stong.

* Publilius Syrus (1835), 267: Fidem qui perdit, perdere ultra nil potest (One who has forfeited his honor can lose nothing more).
Cf. Tilley, C817; C. G. Smith, 44.

138 DO NOT CLOAK **CRIME** WITH CRIME

FQ, I, xii, 30, 7–9: If your selfe . . . ye faulty fynd, . . . With cryme doe not it cover.

Seneca, *Hippolytus*, 721: Scelere velandum est scelus (Crime must be concealed with crime).

139 TO **CROW** OVER

FQ, I, ix, 50, 5: Then gan the villein him to overcraw.

Harvey, *Letter-Book*, 34: Crowing on the on part and more overcrowing on the other. ¶ Harvey, *Pierces Super.*, *Works*, II, 235: To ouer-crow an Asse, is a sory Conquest. ¶ Nashe, *Strange Newes*, *Works*, I, 262: Ouer-crow mee with comparatiue tearmes. ¶ Nashe, *Have with You*, *Works*, III, 114: It will *scare* & *crow* ouer the best.
Cf. Taylor, 190.

140 TO HAVE A **CROW'S-FOOT** GROWING UNDER YOUR EYE

Shep. Cal., Dec., 136: By myne eie the crow his clawe dooth wright.
Chaucer, *Troilus*, II, 403: Til crowes feet be growen under youre yë.
Cf. Tilley, C865.

141 TO DRINK OF THE SAME **CUP**

FQ, V, i, 15, 7: That I mote drinke the cup whereof she dranke.
Cf. Tilley, C908.

142 FULL FLOWING **CUPS** PROVOKE ELOQUENCE

Shep. Cal., Oct., 105–106: Let powre in lavish cups and thriftie bitts of meate; For Bacchus fruite is frend to Phoebus wise.

Horace, *Epist.*, i, 5, 19: Fecundi calices quem non fecere disertum (The flowing bowl—whom has it not made eloquent)? cf. Gascoigne, *Droome of Doomes Day*, *Works*, II, 246. ¶ Nashe, *To the Gent. Students*, *Works*, III, 321: That prouerbiall *foecundi calices*; cf. *Summers Last Will*, *Works*, III, 265. ¶ *Ibid.*, 322: No man writes with conceit, except he take counsell of the cup.

Cf. Mustard, *Mod. Lang. Notes*, XXXIV (1919), 201.

143 TO WISH TO BE CURED IS PART OF THE **CURE**

FQ, VI, vi, 7, 4: Who can him cure, that will be cur'd of none?

Seneca, *Hippolytus*, 249: Pars sanitatis velle sanari fuit (It is part of the cure to wish to be cured).

144 TO **CURRY** FAVOR

FQ, V, v, 35, 5–6: To curry favour With th' Elfin knight. ¶ *View*, 649: The English will currye favour with the Irish.

Foxe, *Acts and Mon.*, VII, 252: Outwardly they curry favour. ¶ Harvey, *Pierces Super.*, *Works*, II, 122: To currie fauour; cf. II, 188. ¶ *Ibid.*, 298: He curred popular fauour. ¶ Nashe, *Lenten Stuffe*, *Works*, III, 219: Curry a little fauour.

Cf. W. G. Smith, 163; Tilley, C724.

145 A **DAINTY** STOMACH BEGGARS THE PURSE

FQ, I, ii, 27, 9: Dainty, they say, maketh derth.

Grange, *Golden Aphr.*, sig. H 4: To die for wante of foode, and yet he feedes on daintie dishes. ¶ Nashe, *Christs Teares*, *Works*, II, 147: Hee that loueth dainty fare shall feele scarcity.

Cf. Apperson, 133; Stevenson, 479:9–10; Tilley, D10.

146 NO **DANGER** INCURRED, NO DANGER REPELLED

Cf. no. 797: Don't turn back when you are just at the goal

FQ, I, i, 12, 7–8: Shame were to revoke The forward footing for an hidden shade. ¶ *Ibid.*, III, xi, 24, 5–9: Shameful thing Yt were t'abandon noble chevisaunce, For shewe of perill, without venturing: Rather let try extremities of chaunce, Then enterprised praise for dread to disavaunce.

* Publilius Syrus (1934), 428: Numquam periclum sine periclo vincitur (A risk is never mastered save by risk).

Cf. C. G. Smith, 51.

147 THE GREATER THE **DANGER**, THE GREATER THE HONOR

FQ, II, ii, 25, 9: So double was his paines, so double be his praise. ¶ *Ibid.*, viii, 26, 5: Honour is least, where oddes appeareth most.

Cicero, *De Offic.*, i, 19, 64: Quo difficilius, hoc praeclarius (The greater the difficulty, the greater the glory). ¶ Seneca, *De Prov.*, iii, 4: Gladiator . . . scit eum sine gloria vinci, qui sine periculo vincitur (A gladiator knows that to win without danger is to win without glory). ¶ *Ibid.*, 9. Quanto plus tormenti tanto plus erit gloriae (The greater his torture is, the greater shall be his glory). ¶ Barclay, *Ship of F.*, I, 32: In greatest honour is greatest ieoperdye. ¶ Greene, *Mamillia*, *Works*, II, 126: The more harde the combat were, the more hauty wer the conquest: the more doubtful the fight, the more worthy the victory. ¶ Greene, *Alcida*, *Works*, IX, 49: The more hard the rebut is, the more hautie is the conquest; the more doubtfull the fight, the more worthy the victorie. ¶ Shakespeare, *3 Hen. VI*, IV, iii, 15: 'Tis the more honour, because more dangerous. ¶ Deloney, *Gentle Craft*, *Works*, 73: The sorer the fight is, the greater is the glory of the victory.

Cf. W. G. Smith, 512; Stevenson, 483:13; 574:9; Tilley, D35.

148 WHEN **DANGER** (DEATH) HAS COME, COUNSEL IS TOO LATE

FQ, IV, xii, 28, 6: It's late, in death, of daunger to advize.

Publilius Syrus (1934), 684: Sero in periclis est consilium quaerere (In perils it is too late to search for advice).

149 DESIRES THAT ENGROSS ONE DURING THE **DAY** PRESENT THEMSELVES IN SLEEP

FQ, IV, v, 43, 9: The things that day most minds, at night doe most appeare.

Menander, *Frag.*, 734K: ἃ γὰρ μεθ' ἡμέραν τις ἐσπούδαζ' ἔχων, ταῦτ' εἶδε νύκτωρ (For what one has dwelt on by day, these things he sees in visions of the night). ¶ Claudian, *Panegyricus De Sexto Consulatu Honorii Augusti*, Pref., 1–2: Omnia, quae sensu volvuntur vota diurno, pectore sopito reddit amica quies (All things that with waking sense desire ponders kindly repose brings back to the slumbering mind); cf. Herodotus, *Hist.*, vii, 16; Cicero, *De Div.*, i, 22, 45. ¶ Nashe, *Terrors of the Night*, *Works*, I, 356: A Dreame is nothing els but the Eccho of our conceipts in the day.

Cf. Stevenson, 623:5; Tilley, S205.

150 THE LONGEST **DAY** HAS AN END

Cf. no. 53: Whatever has a beginning has an end

Epithalamion, 273: Yet never day so long, but late would passe.

Cf. Apperson, 136; W. G. Smith, 382; Stevenson, 495:2; Tilley, D90.

151 FORBEAR TO SLANDER THE **DEAD**

FQ, I, x, 42, 8–9: Even dead we honour should. Ah! dearest God me graunt, I dead be not defould. ¶ *Ibid.*, II, viii, 13, 6–7: Vile is the vengeaunce on the ashes cold, And envy base, to barke at sleeping fame. ¶ *Ibid.*, 29, 6–9: But gentle knight, That doth against the dead his hand upheave, His honour staines with rancour and despight, And great disparagment makes to his former might. ¶ *Ibid.*, VI, ii, 15, 6–7: Full loth I were To rayse a lyving blame against the dead. ¶ *View*, 656: Most untruelye and maliciously doe these evill tonges backbite and slaunder the sacred ashes of that most just and honorable personage.

Sophocles, *Antigone*, 1029–1030: ἀλλ' εἶκε τῷ θανόντι μηδ' ὀλωλότα κέντει τίς ἀλκὴ τὸν θανόντ' ἐπικτανεῖν (O forbear to vex the dead. What glory wilt thou win by slaying twice the slain)? ¶ Euripides, *Phoen. Maidens*, 1663: *μὴ ἐφυβρίζεσθαι νεκρούς* (Outrage not the dead). ¶ Diogenes Laertius, *Chilon*, i, 70: *τὸν τεθνηκότα μὴ κακολογεῖν* (Speak no evil of the dead). ¶ Shakespeare, *L. Lab. Lost*, V, ii, 667: Beat not the bones of the buried. ¶ Shakespeare, *2 Hen. IV*, I, i, 98: He doth sin that doth belie the dead.

Cf. W. G. Smith, 611; Stevenson, 521:9.

152 **DEATH** IS NOT BITTER

Shep. Cal., Nov., 210: *La mort ny mord.* ¶ *Ibid.*, Glosse, 129: *Death biteth not.* ¶ *Daphnaïda*, 447–448: Is it so . . . dolorous to dye?

Vergil, *Aeneid*, xii, 646: Usque adeone mori miserum est (Is it then so very dreadful to die)? ¶ Quintilian, *Inst. Orat.*, viii, 5, 5–6: Mors misera non est (Death is not bitter).

Cf. Stevenson, 504:9.

153 **DEATH** IS THE END OF ALL MISERY

FQ, I, ix, 47, 9: Death is the end of woes. ¶ *Ibid.*, II, i, 56, 4: Ended all her woe in quiet death. ¶ *Ibid.*, III, ii, 39, 9: Till death make one end of my daies and miseree.

Culman, 6: Finis miseriae mors (Death is the end of misery). ¶ * Publilius Syrus (1934), 67: Bona mors est homini vitae quae exstinguit mala (Good for man is death when it ends life's miseries). ¶ *Ibid.*, 672: Spes inopem, res avarum, mors miserum levat (Hope eases the beggar, wealth the miser, death the wretched).

Cato, *Disticha*, iii, 22: Quae [mors] bona si non est, finis tamen illa malorum est (Death, if no boon, is the end of our evils). ¶ Cicero, *Tusc. Disp.*, i, 42, 100: Vitae miserae mors finis esse videtur (Death seems to be the end of a wretched life). ¶ Seneca, *Ad Marciam de Con.* xix, 5: Mors dolorum omnium exsolutio est et finis (Death is a release from, and the end of, all suffering). ¶ Chaucer, *Troilus*, IV, 501: Deth, that endere art of sorwes alle. ¶ Lydgate, *Fall of P.*, II, 1223: Deth maketh an eende off al worldli distresse. ¶ *Ibid.*, VI, 1261–1262: Men seen how deth is fyn of al myscheeff, Eende off aduersite that doth wrechchis tarie. ¶ Painter, *Palace of P.*, III, 119: Death the end of sorrow. ¶ Greene, *Mirrour of Mod.*, *Works*, III, 25: Death cutteth off all miseries. ¶ Greene, *Perymedes*, *Works*, VII, 26: Death . . . is the ende of sorrowe. ¶ Greene, *Never Too Late*, *Works*, VIII, 154: Death cuts off all miseries.

Cf. C. G. Smith, 53.

154 **DEATH** IS THE GRAND LEVELER

FQ, II, i, 59, 1–2: Death is an equall doome To good and bad, the commen in of rest.

Culman, 7: Mors omnia sternit (Death throws down all before it). Publilius Syrus (1835), 1: A morte semper homines tantumdem absumus (As men, we are all equal in the presence of death).

Seneca, *Ad Marciam de Con.*, xx, 1–2: Mors . . . exaequat omnia (Death levels all things). ¶ Seneca, *De Ira*, iii, 43, 2: Mors . . . vos pares faciat (Death will make you equals). ¶ Seneca, *Epist.*, xcix, 9: Exitu aequamur (Death levels us). ¶ Claudian, *De Raptu Proserpinae*, ii, 302: Omnia mors aequat (Death levels all things).

Cf. Tilley, D143; C. G. Smith, 54.

155 **DEATH** KEEPS NO CALENDAR

FQ, I, ix, 42, 9: When houre of death is come, let none ask whence, nor why.

Chaucer, *Clerk's T.*, 125–126: Uncerteyn we alle Been of that day whan deeth shal on us falle. ¶ Greene, *Never Too Late*, *Works*, VIII, 125: Nothing more vncertaine than the houre of death.

Cf. Tilley, D144.

156 A DISHONORABLE **DEATH** IS THE SCORN OF DESTINY

FQ, I, v, 48, 9: Till, scornd of God and man, a shamefull death he dide.

Publilius Syrus (1934), 415: Mala mors necessitatis contumelia est (A dishonorable death is an insult of fate).

157 AN HONORABLE **DEATH** IS BETTER THAN A SHAMEFUL LIFE

Cf. no. 392: Honor is dearer than life

FQ, I, vii, 49, 6: Rather death desire then such despight. ¶ *Ibid.*, III, iv, 38, 8: Sad life worse then glad death. ¶ *Ibid.*, v, 45, 8–9: Fayre death it is, to shonne more shame, to dy: Dye rather, dy, then ever love disloyally. ¶ *Ibid.*, ix, 14, 8–9: Rather had he dy Then, when he was defyde, in coward corner ly. ¶ *Ibid.*, IV, vii, 11, 7–8: Death is to him that wretched life doth lead, Both grace and gaine. ¶ *Ibid.*, V, iv, 32, 8–9: Rather chose to die in lives despight, Then lead that shamefull life, unworthy of a knight. ¶ *Ibid.*, xi, 55, 9: Dye rather, then doe ought that mote dishonor yield.

Culman, 24: Praestat mori, quam foedam vitam vivere (It is better to die than to lead a dishonest life). ¶ Publilius Syrus (1835), 331: Honestam mortem vitae turpi praefero (An honorable death is better than a disgraceful life). ¶ *Ibid.*, 1102: Tolerabilior, qui mori jubet, quam qui male vivere (A sentence of death is more tolerable than a command to live wickedly).

Claudian, *De Bello Gild.*, I, 451: Nonne mori satius, vitae quam ferre pudorem (Is not death preferable to a life disgraced)? ¶ Tacitus, *Agricola*, 33: Honesta mors turpi vita potior (Honorable death is better than dishonorable life). ¶ Juvenal, *Sat.*, viii, 83: Summum crede nefas animam praeferre pudori (Count it the greatest of all sins to prefer life to honor). ¶ Hawes, *Past. Pleas.*, 133: Rather deye in ony maner of wyse, To attayne honour and the lyfe dyspyse, Than for to lyve and remayne in shame. ¶ Wilson, *Arte of Rhet.*, 64: Better to die with honor, then to liue with shame. ¶ Ashley, *Of Honour* (Heltzel), 50: Yt ys much better to die with Honour then to liue with shame.

Cf. Tilley, H576; C. G. Smith, 55.

158 AS CERTAIN AS **DEATH**

Cf. no. 162: There is no remedy for death; no. 179: All men must die

FQ, I, xi, 12, 3: As sure as death.

Culman, 7: Mors est inevitabilis (Death is inevitable).

Plautus, *Captivi*, 732: Non moriri certius (As certain as death).

Cf. Apperson, 611; W. G. Smith, 464; Tilley, D136; C. G. Smith, 56.

159 AT THE DOOR OF **DEATH**

Cf. no. 164: To look death in the face

FQ, I, iv, 28, 1: His life was nigh unto deaths dore yplaste. ¶ *Ibid.*, v, 41, 8: From dore of death. ¶ *Ibid.*, viii, 27, 2: Nigh unto deaths dore. ¶ *Ibid.*, x, 27, 9: Lay at deathes dore. ¶ *Ibid.*, III, v, 46, 2–3: From deathes dore Me brought? ¶ *Virgils Gnat*, 355: Even from the doore of death. ¶ *FQ*, IV, iii, 1, 7: Every houre they knocke at Deathes gate. ¶ *Ibid.*, V, iv, 35, 2: From deathes dore, at which he lately lay. ¶ *Ibid.*, VI, viii, 20, 8: To the dore of death for sorrow drew.

Cf. W. G. Smith, 134; Tilley, D162.

160 THE TIME OF **DEATH** IS CERTAIN

FQ, I, ix, 42, 2–5: Did not He all create, To die againe? All ends, that was begonne. Their times in His eternall booke of fate Are written sure, and have their certein date.

Culman, 33: Mortis certum tempus (The time of death is certain).

161 THE WAGES OF SIN IS **DEATH**

FQ, I, ix, 38, 4: He should dye, who merites not to live. ¶ *Ibid.*, 47, 5: Is not His lawe, Let every sinner die? ¶ *View*, 646: They all shall dye in theyr sinnes for they have all erred and gone out of the way togither.

Culman, 35: Peccatum causa mortis (Sin is the cause of death).

New Testament: *Romans*, vi, 23: τὰ γὰρ ὀψώνια τῆς ἁμαρτίας θάνατος (For the wages of sin is death).

162 THERE IS NO REMEDY FOR **DEATH**

Cf. no 158: As certain as death; no 179: All men must die

FQ, III, xii, 35, 4: Nought may save thee from to dy. ¶ *Ibid.*, V, xii, 21, 4: Nought could him from death protect.

Culman, 30: Contra mortem non est remedium (There is no remedy against death).

Cf. W. G. Smith, 537: Stevenson, 1951:3; Tilley, R69.

163 TO LONG FOR **DEATH** IS TO CONFESS THAT LIFE IS A FAILURE

Cf. no. 165: When to live is torment, death is best

FQ, I, x, 22, 8: Disdeining life, desiring leave to dye. ¶ *Ibid.*, II, i, 36, 6–9: Come . . . sweetest Death, to me, And take away this long lent loathed light: . . . sweete the medicines be, That long captived soules from weary thraldome free. ¶ *Colin Clouts*, 204: Who life doth loath . . . longs death to behold. ¶ *FQ*, IV, viii, 16, 9: And make me loath this life, still longing for to die.

* Publilius Syrus (1934), 120: Crimen relinquit vitae qui mortem appetit (One who longs for death confesses that life is a failure).

164 TO LOOK **DEATH** IN THE FACE

Cf. no. 159: At the door of death

Daphnaïda, 565: As if that Death he in the face had seene.

Cf. Spenser, *Minor Poems* (Variorum), I, 446.

165 WHEN TO LIVE IS TORMENT, **DEATH** IS BEST

Cf. no. 163: To long for death is to confess that life is a failure

FQ, III, iv, 38, 3–4: Farre better I it deeme to die with speed, Then waste in woe and waylfull miserye.

Publilius Syrus (1934), 465: Nemo immature moritur qui moritur miser (No one dies untimely who dies in misery). ¶ *Ibid.*, 701: Ubi omnis vitae metus est, mors est optima (When life is all one terror, death is best).

Cf. Stevenson, 1416:8; C. G. Smith, 58.

166 IT IS EASY (NOT EASY) TO **DECEIVE** ONESELF

FQ, IV, vi, 40, 9: Vaine is the art that seekes it selfe for to deceive.
Cf. Tilley, N295.

167 NOBLE **DEEDS** DIE, IF SUPPRESSED IN SILENCE

FQ, I, ix, 2, 8–9: Least so great good, as he for her had wrought, Should die unknown, and buried be in thankles thought. ¶ *Ibid.*, III, xi, 9, 8–9: What booteth then the good and righteous deed, If goodnesse find no grace, nor righteousnes no meed?

Publilius Syrus (1934), 304: Iacet omnis virtus fama nisi late patet (Every virtue is depressed unless it gains wide recognition).

Pindar, *Eulogy on Alex.*, 121: *θνᾴσκει δὲ σιγαθὲν καλὸν ἔργον* (Every noble deed dies if suppressed in silence).

Cf. Stevenson, 1821:8; C. G. Smith, 59.

168 **DEFEND** ME AND SPEND ME

View, 624: They . . . are very loth to yeld any certayne rent, but onely such spendinges, saying commonly, "Spend me and defend me."

Cf. Apperson, 141; W. G. Smith, 613; Tilley, D192.

169 **DELAY** IS DANGEROUS

View, 683: Delayes . . . are oftentimes . . . most irkesome, the opportunitye there in the meane time passes away, and greate daunger often groweth.

Livy, *Hist.*, xxxviii, 25, 13: In mora periculi (There is danger in delay). ¶ Ovid, *Artis Amat.*, ii, 731: Mora non tuta est (Delay is not safe). ¶ Lucan, *De Bello Civili*, i, 281: Tolle moras; semper nocuit differre paratis (Away with delays; delay is ever fatal to those who are prepared. ¶ Chaucer, *Troilus*, III, 852: Peril is with drecchyng [delay] in ydrawe. ¶ Erasmus, *Colloquia Fam.*, 720C: Dilatio damnum habet, mora periculum (Procrastination brings loss, delay danger).

Cf. Apperson, 141–142; Stevenson, 546:7; 1890:11; Tilley, D195.

170 **DELAY** IS VEXATIOUS

View, 683: Delayes . . . are . . . irkesome.

Culman, 8: Procrastinatio est odiosa (Putting off from day to day is annoying). ¶ * Publilius Syrus (1934), 352: Mora omnis odio est (Delay is always vexatious).

171 WE MUST NOT **DELIGHT** IN EARTHLY THINGS

Ruines of T., 685–686: Unto heaven let your high minde aspire, And loath this drosse of sinfull worlds desire. ¶ *Hymne of Heavenly L.*, 272: In no earthly thing thou shalt delight.

Culman, 28: Ad terrena non respiciendum (We must not think of earthly things).

172 WE **DESIRE** WHAT IS FORBIDDEN

Cf. no. 276: He is a fool who wishes for the impossible

FQ, IV, viii, 30, 8–9: Each unto his lust did make a lawe, From all forbidden things his liking to withdraw. ¶ *Ibid.*, VI, ix, 29, 6: For not that which men covet most is best.

Culman, 10: Vetita magis appetimus (We lust more after things forbidden). ¶ Publilius Syrus (1934), 438: Nihil magis amat cupiditas quam quod non licet (Longing desire likes nothing better than what is not allowed).

Ovid, *Amores*, ii, 19, 3: Quod licet, ingratum est; quod non licet acrius urit (What one may do freely has no charm; what one may not do pricks more keenly on). ¶ *Ibid.*, iii, 4, 25: Quidquid servatur cupimus magis, . . . pauci, quod sinit alter, amant (Whatever is guarded we desire the more; few love what another concedes). ¶ Seneca, *Hercules Oetaeus*, 357: Illicita amantur (What is forbidden we love). ¶ Chaucer, *Wife of Bath's Prol.*, 519: Forbede us thyng, and that desiren we. ¶ Erasmus, *Colloquia Fam.*, 663A: Ita ingenium est hominum, ut perniciosissima quaeque appetant vehementissime (It is the disposition of mankind to be most desirous of those things that are most hurtful): cf. 788A.

Cf. Stevenson, 1893:10; Tilley, F585; C. G. Smith, 64.

173 THE FARTHER OFF, THE MORE **DESIRED**

Colin Clouts, 162: Men use most to covet forreine thing.

Pindar, *Paean.*, iv, 33–35: συγγένει' ἀνδρὶ φίλ' ὤστε καὶ στέρξαι (To foolish men belongs a love for things afar). ¶ Surrey, *The Faithfull Lover Declareth His Paines*, *Tottel's Misc.*, I, 210: The farther of the more desirde. ¶ Jonson, *Catiline*, III, 868–871, *Works*, V, 498: Thought, vnlike the eye . . . thinkes there's nothing great, but what is farre.

Cf. Benham, 623b.

174 HE THAT **DESIRES** BUT LITTLE IS LEAST IN NEED

Cf. no. 175: Who desires most lacks most

Mother Hub., 430: Content with little in condition sicker.

Publilius Syrus (1934), 324: Is minimum eget mortalis qui minimum cupit (That mortal needs least, who wishes least). ¶ *Ibid.* (1835), 216: Eget minus mortalis, quo minus cupit (The less a mortal desires, the less he needs).

Seneca, *Epist.*, cviii, 11: Is minimo eget mortalis, qui minimum cupit (He needs but little who desires but little). ¶ Sidney, *Arcadia*, *Works*, I, 14: A happie people, wanting litle, because they desire not much.

Cf. Apperson, 142; W. G. Smith, 137; Stevenson, 553:4; Tilley, L347a.

175 WHO **DESIRES** MOST LACKS MOST

Cf. no. 174: He that desires but little is least in need

FQ, I, iv, 29, 1–2: Most wretched wight, whom nothing might suffise, Whose greedy lust did lacke in greatest store.

Culman, 5: Avarus semper eget (A covetous person always needs). ¶ *Ibid.*, 10: Avari cupiditas nunquam expletur (The desire of a covetous man is never satisfied). ¶ *Ibid.*, 13: Multa petentibus desunt multa (Many things are wanting to them that desire many things). ¶ *Ibid.*, 16: Semper inops quicunque cupit (Whoever covets is always poor). ¶ *Ibid.*, 25: Pauper est, non qui parum habet, sed qui plus cupit (He is a poor man, not who has little, but who desires much). ¶ Publilius Syrus (1934), 275: Inopiae desunt multa, avaritiae omnia (Beggary lacks much, but greed lacks everything). ¶ *Ibid.*, (1835), 444: Luxuriae desunt multa, avaritiae omnia (The spendthrift lacks many things; the miser lacks everything).

Horace, *Odes*, iii, 16, 42–43: Multa petentibus desunt multa (To those who seek for much, much is ever lacking). ¶ Horace, *Epist.*, i, 2, 56: Semper avarus eget (The covetous man always wants).

176 **DESPAIR** GIVES COURAGE TO A COWARD

Astrophel, 117: Despeyre makes cowards stout.

Sidney, *Arcadia*, *Works*, I, 60: He was driven to make courage of despaire. ¶ *Ibid.*, 267: Despaire made Feare valiant. ¶ Milton, *Par. Lost*, II, 44–45: The strongest and the fiercest Spirit That fought in Heav'n; now fiercer by despair.

Cf. W. G. Smith, 137; Tilley, D216.

177 **DESPERATE** MEN HAVE DESPERATE THOUGHTS

View, 609: Desperat men farr driven . . . wishe the utter ruine of that they cannot redress.

Shakespeare, *Rom. & Jul.*, V, i, 35–36: O mischief, thou art swift To enter the thoughts of desperate men!

178 THE DOOM OF **DESTINY** CANNOT BE AVOIDED

Cf. no. 290: In all human affairs fortune (providence) rules; no. 570: The force of necessity is irresistible; no. 847: What will be, shall be

FQ, I, v, 25, 4: Who can turne the streame of destinee? ¶ *Ibid.*, III, i, 37, 9: Who can shun the chance that dest'ny doth ordaine? ¶ *Ibid.*, iv, 27, 1–2: Who can deceive his destiny, Or weene by warning to avoyd his fate? ¶ *Ibid.*, 36, 9: Ne can thy irrevocable desteny bee wefte. ¶ *Ibid.*, V, iv, 27, 8: Who can scape what his owne fate hath wrought?

Culman, 26: Quod fatis decretum est, nemini licet evitare (What destiny has decreed, no man can avoid).

Homer, *Iliad*, vi, 488: μοῖραν δ' οὔ τινά φημι πεφυγμένον ἔμμεναι ἀνδρῶν (No man has ever escaped his destiny); cf. Plato, *Gorgias*, 512E. ¶ Sophocles, *Antigone*, 1106: ἀνάγκῃ δ' οὐχὶ δυσμαχητέον (To war with destiny is vain). ¶ Euripides, *Rhesus*, 634: οὐκ ἂν δύναιο τοῦ πεπρωμένου πλέον (Thou canst not overpass the doom of fate); cf. *Hercules*, 311; *Hippolytus*, 1256. ¶ Lyly, *Gallathea*, I, i, 69, *Works*, II, 434: Destenie may be deferred, not preuented. ¶ Harvey, *Pierces Super.*, *Works*, II, 273: There is no warring with Destiny.

Cf. Stevenson, 555:7; Tilley, F83; C. G. Smith, 66.

179 ALL MEN MUST **DIE**

Cf. no. 158: As certain as death; no. 162: There is no remedy for death

Teares of the M., 105–106: All that in this world is worthie hight Shall die. ¶ *FQ*, I, ix, 42, 2–3: Did not He all create, To die againe? ¶ *Ibid.*, III, vi, 30, 5–6: All things . . . are borne to live and dye, According to their kynds. ¶ *Ibid.*, V, ii, 41, 1: They live, they die, like as He doth ordaine.

* Publilius Syrus (1934), 360: Mori necesse est, sed non quotiens volueris (You needs must die, but not as often as you have wished). ¶ *Ibid.*, (1835), 522: Morti debetur, quicquid usquam nascitur (Everything which has birth must pay tribute to death).

Pindar, *Olympian Odes*, i, 82: θανεῖν δ' οἷσιν ἀνάγκα (All men must die). ¶ Lucretius, *De Rerum Natura*, iii, 1078–1079: Certa quidem finis vitae mortalibus adstat nec devitari letum pote quin obeamus (There is an end fixed for the life of mortals, and death cannot be avoided, but die we must). ¶ Cicero, *Tusc. Disp.*, i, 5, 9: Moriendum est enim omnibus (For all men have to die). ¶ Cicero, *De Sen.*, xx, 74: Moriendum enim certe est (For it is certain that we must die). ¶ Horace, *Odes*, i, 4, 13–14: Pallida Mors aequo pulsat pede pauperum tabernas regumque turres (Pale death with foot impartial knocks at the poor man's cottage and at princes' palaces). ¶ Seneca, *Epist.*, lxxvii, 11: Nemo tam imperitus est, ut nesciat quandoque moriendum (No one is so ignorant as not to know that we must at some time die). ¶ Erasmus, *Adagia*, 923B: Mors omnibus communis (Death is common to all). ¶ Wilson, *Arte of Rhet.*, 74: We must al die. ¶ Pettie, *Petite P.*, 49: Wee are borne to die, . . . even in our swathe cloutes death may aske his due.

Cf. Tilley, M505; C. G. Smith, 67.

180 TO **DIE** BEFORE ONE'S TIME

Amoretti, xlii, 14: Doe me not before my time to dy.

Erasmus, *Adagia*, 104C: Qui mori nolit ante tempus (He does not desire to die before his time).

Cf. Tilley, T290.

181 TO **DIE** OF HUNGER IS A MISERABLE KIND OF DEATH

FQ, II, vii, 59, 4–7: Most cursed of all creatures under skye . . . I here tormented lye: . . . here I now for want of food doe dye.

Culman, 7: Miserrimum ſame mori (It is a most miserable thing to die of hunger). ¶ *Ibid.*, 21: Miserrimum mortis genus, fame emori (It is a most miserable kind of death to die of hunger).

Erasmus, *Adagia*, 857E: Miserrimum fame mori (It is a very miserable thing to die of hunger).

182 **DILIGENCE** CAN ACCOMPLISH THE HARDEST THINGS

Amoretti, li, 9–10: Ne ought so hard, but he that would attend Mote soften it and to his will allure. ¶ *FQ*, III, xii, 39, 9: And goodly well advaunce, that goodly well was tryde.

Culman, 5: Assiduitas durissima vincit (Continual diligence overcomes the hardest things). ¶ *Ibid.*, 23: Nihil est tam diuturnum, quod non emolliat assiduitas (There is nothing so long-lasting which continual diligence cannot make easy). ¶ *Ibid.*, 26: Res factu ardua, tamen assidua industria evincitur (A thing hard to be done is yet overcome by continual industry).

Seneca, *Epist.*, 1, 6: Nihil est, quod non expugnet pertinax opera et intenta ac diligens cura (There is nothing which persevering effort and unceasing and diligent care cannot overcome). ¶ Florio, *First Fruites*, 63: Diligence is able to make the vneasyest thing, easye: the rawest thing rype, the straungest thyngs, familiar: the hardest thyng, soft.

Cf. Taverner, 30.

183 PRACTICE **DILIGENCE**

FQ, I, x, 23, 6: And streightway sent with carefull diligence. ¶ *Ibid.*, V x, 12, 8: Which long he usd with carefull diligence.

Culman, 1: Diligentiam adhibe (Use diligence).

Cato, *Collectio Dis. Vulg.*, 14: Diligentiam adhibe (Practice diligence).

Cf. C. G. Smith, 68.

184 **DISASTER** EASILY FINDS WHOMEVER IT SEEKS

FQ, II, iv, 17, 2–5: What man can shun the hap, That hidden lyes unwares him to surpryse? Misfortune waites advantage to entrap The man most wary in her whelming lap.

Publilius Syrus (1934), 567: Quemcumque quaerit calamitas facile invenit (Disaster easily finds whomever it seeks).

185 **DISCORD** MAKES CONCORD MORE PLEASANT

Shep. Cal., Ded. Epist., 100–101: Ofentimes a dischorde in musick maketh a comely concordaunce. ¶ *FQ*, III, ii, 15, 9: Dischord ofte in musick makes the sweeter lay.

* Publilius Syrus (1934), 154: Discordia fit carior concordia (Discord gives a relish to concord).

Aristotle, *N. Ethics*, viii, 1, 6: *Ἡράκλειτος τὸ "ἀντίξουν συμφέρον" καὶ "ἐκ τῶν διαφερόντων καλλίστην ἁρμονίαν"* (Heraclitus says, "Opposition unites," and "The fairest harmony springs from discord"). ¶ Erasmus, *Adagia*, 740C: Discordia fit carior concordia (Discord makes concord more pleasant).

186 GREAT THINGS DECAY BY **DISCORD**

Cf. no. 436: Kingdoms decay by discord

FQ, IV, i, 21, 3–8: The sad effects of discord sung: . . . rent robes and broken scepters . . . Altars defyl'd, and holy things defast, Disshivered speares, and shields ytorne in twaine, Great cities ransackt, and strong castles rast, Nations captived, and huge armies slaine.

Culman, 22: Magnae res discordia pereunt, concordia valent (Great things decay by discord, by concord they are made strong).

187 **DISCRETION** IS THE BETTER PART OF VALOR

FQ, III, xi, 23, 1–2: Daunger without discretion to attempt Inglorious and beastlike is.

Euripides, *Suppliants*, 509–510: ἥσυχος καιρῷ σοφός. καὶ τοῦτό τοι τἀνδρεῖον, ἡ προμηθία (The wise in season sitteth still. This too is manful valour, even discretion). ¶ Cicero, *De Offic.*, i, 23, 81: Temere autem in acie versari et manu cum hoste confligere immane quiddam et beluarum simile est (But to mix rashly in the fray and to fight hand-to-hand with the enemy is but a barbarous and brutish kind of business).

Cf. Apperson, 153; W. G. Smith, 147; Tilley, D354.

188 **DISEASES** ARE CAUSED BY SIN

Cf. no. 84: Every calamity is a punishment of sin

Ruines of R., xix, 13: Their great sinnes, the causers of their paine. ¶ *Ibid.*, xxiii, 11–12: In a vicious bodie, grose disease Soone growes.

Culman, 33: Morbi ob peccatum veniunt (Diseases come because of sin).

189 TO **DO** OR DIE

FQ, I, i, 51, 6: He bids me do, or die. ¶ *Ibid.*, III, xii, 35, 7: This doe and live, els dye undoubtedly.

Fletcher, *Isl. Princess*, II, iv: Let us do or die. ¶ Burns, *Scots, Wha Hae*, 4+

24: Let us do, or die. ¶ Campbell, *Gertrude of Wyoming*, III, 37: To-morrow let us do or die!

Cf. Stevenson, 537:5.

190 A **DOG** BITES THE STONE, NOT THE MAN WHO THROWS IT

FQ, IV, viii, 36, 5–6: A curre doth felly bite and teare The stone which passed straunger at him threw.

Cf. Tilley, D542.

191 AS GREEDY AS A **DOG** (HOUND)

FQ, V, viii, 7, 1: Like hound full greedy. ¶ *Ibid.*, VI, xi, 17, 1–4: Like as a sort of hungry dogs . . . stryving each to get The greatest portion of the greedie pray.

Cf. Apperson, 273; Stevenson, 1039:2; Tilley, D434.

192 LIKE A **DOG** IN THE MANGER

Shep. Cal., Ded. Epist., 153–154: Like to the dogge in the maunger.

Lucian, *Timon*. 14: καθάπερ τὴν ἐν τῇ φάτνῃ κύνα (Like the dog in the manger). ¶ Lucian, *Ignorant Book-Collector*, 30: ἀλλὰ τὸ τῆς κυνὸς ποιεῖς τῆς ἐν τῇ φάτνῃ (But you act like the dog in the manger). ¶ Harvey, *Letter-Book*, 114: A dogg in the maunger.

Cf. Apperson, 160; W. G. Smith, 151; Tilley, D513.

193 WHAT'S **DONE** CANNOT BE UNDONE

FQ, I, xii, 19, 5–6: That band ye cannot now release, Nor doen undoe. ¶ *Ibid.*, IV, iv, 27, 1–2: He could not salve, Ne done undoe. ¶ *Ibid.*, V, ii, 42, 1: What ever thing is done, . . . is donne. ¶ *Ibid.*, v, 26, 6: Having chosen, now he might not chaunge. ¶ *Ibid.*, VI, x, 20, 8: Things passed none may now restore. ¶ *View*, 655: All that was formerly done with long labour and great toyle, was (as you say) in a moment undone.

Culman, 26: Quod factum est, infectum fieri non potest (What is done cannot be undone).

Sophocles, *Ajax*, 378: *οὐ γὰρ γένοιτ' ἂν ταῦθ' ὅπως οὐχ ὧδ' ἔχειν* (What's done is done and nothing can alter it); cf. *Trachiniae*, 742–743. ¶ Plautus, *Aulularia*, 741: Factum est illud: fieri infectum non potest (It's done, and it can't be undone). ¶ Cicero, *Pro Rabirio Postumo*, ix, 26: Mutari factum iam nullo modo poterat (But what was done could not be undone). ¶ Erasmus, *Adagia*, 513C: Quod factum est, infectum fieri non potest (What has been done cannot be undone). ¶ Hawes, *Past. Pleas.*, 103: Dede done can not be called agayne. ¶ Harvey, *Foure Lett.*, *Works*, I, 157: That is doone, cannot de facto be vndone. ¶ Harvey, *Pierces Super.*, *Works*, II, 165: That is done on both sides, cannot be vndone.

Cf. Taverner, 33; Bacon, Promus, 951; Tilley, T200; C. G. Smith, 74.

194 TO **DRAW** WATER IN A LEAKY VESSEL

FQ, I, v, 35, 9: And fifty sisters water in leke vessels draw.

Xenophon, *Oeconomicus*, vii, 40: *εἰς τὸν τετρημένον πίθον ἀντλεῖν λεγόμενοι* (To draw water in a leaky jar, as the saying goes). ¶ Plato, *Gorgias*, 493B: *καὶ φοροῖεν εἰς τὸν τετρημένον πίθον ὕδωρ ἑτέρῳ τοιούτῳ τετρημένῳ κοσκίνῳ* (And will carry water into their leaky jar with a sieve which is no less leaky).

Cf. Stevenson, 2462:8.

195 CONSTANT **DROPPING** WILL WEAR AWAY A STONE

Amoretti, xviii, 3–4: Drizling drops . . . The firmest flint doth in continuance weare. ¶ *FQ*, IV, xii, 7, 1–2: Yet loe! the seas I see by often beating, Doe pearce the rockes, and hardest marble weares.

Ovid, *Ex Ponto*, ii, 7, 39–40: Utque caducis percussu crebro saxa cavantur aquis (As the falling drops by their constant force hollow the rock). ¶ *Ibid.*, iv, 10, 5: Gutta cavat lapidem (Drops of water hollow out a stone). ¶ Lucretius, *De Rerum Natura*, i, 313: Stilicidi casus lapidem cavat (The fall of drippings hollows a stone). ¶ Plutarch, *Moralia*: *Ed. of Children*: 2D: ὕδατος πέτρας κοιλαίνουσι (Drops of water make hollows in rocks). ¶ Erasmus, *Adagia*, 782E: Assidua stilla saxum excavat (Constant dripping wears away the rock). ¶ Greene, *Repentance of Robert G.*, *Works*, XII, 161: No flint so harde, but the drops of raine will hollowe.

Cf. Apperson, 112; W. G. Smith, 107; Tilley, D618.

196 THE MORE A MAN WITH **DROPSY** DRINKS THE MORE THIRSTY HE BECOMES

FQ, I, iv, 23, 7: Dry dropsie through his flesh did flow.

Ovid, *Fasti*, i, 215–216: Sic quibus intumuit suffusa venter ab unda, quo plus sunt potae, plus sitiuntur aquae (So he whose belly swells with dropsy, The more he drinks, the thirstier he grows). ¶ Gower, *Conf. Aman.*, V, 253–254: The more ydropesie drinketh, The more him thursteth. ¶ Lydgate, *Fall of P.*, III, 3732–3733: Ther may no tresour ther dropesie weel staunche; The mor thei drynke the mor thei thruste in deede; cf. VII, 996–998. ¶ Pettie, *Petite P.*, 96: As dropsy pacients drink and still be drye . . . the more they drinke the more they desire it. ¶ Lyly, *Euph. Anat. of Wit*, *Works*, I, 289: As with him that hath the dropsie, . . . the more he drincketh the more he thirsteth. ¶ Greene, *Never Too Late*, *Works*, VIII, 140: He that hath the dropsie, drinketh while he bursteth, and yet not satisfied; cf. *Mirrour of Mod.*, *Works*, III, 36. ¶ Sidney, *Poems* (1593), *Works*, II, 219: Like dropsy folke still drinke to be a thyrst.

Cf. Tilley, M211.

197 **DRUNKENNESS** MAKES MEN MAD

FQ, II, i, 52, 2: She makes her lovers dronken mad. ¶ *Ibid.*, V, vii, 11, 3–9: The fruitfull vine, whose liquor blouddy red, Having the mindes of men with fury fraught, . . . Such is the powre of that same fruit, that nought The fell contagion may thereof restraine, Ne within reasons rule her madding mood containe.

Culman, 1: Ebrietas dementat (Drunkenness makes men mad).

Plato, *Laws*, iii, 695B: μαινόμενος ὑπὸ μέθης (Being mad with drink). Cf. C. G. Smith, 76.

198 GIVE EVERYONE HIS **DUE**

FQ, I, ix, 38, 7: To each his dew to give. ¶ *Ibid.*, III, xii, 33, 9: Give him the reward for such vile outrage dew. ¶ *Ibid.*, IV, v, 9, 9: Yeeld the fayrest her due fee. ¶ *Ibid.*, 20, 2: As her dew right, It yielded was. ¶ *Ibid.*, VI, ii, 13, 8–9: Th' unrighteous ire Of her owne knight had given him his owne due hire. ¶ *Ibid.*, ix, 44, 7: Given to Calidore as his due right.

Publilius Syrus (1835), 843: Reddit, non perdit, qui suum quoique tribuit (He who gives to each one his due, does not lose but gives back).

New Testament: Romans, xiii, 7: ἀπόδοτε πᾶσι τὰς ὀφειλάς (Render therefore to all their dues). ¶ Shakespeare, *Timon*, III, i, 37: Give thee thy due.

Cf. Stevenson, 272:6; Tilley, D634.

199 ONLY THE **EAGLE** CAN GAZE AT THE SUN

FQ, I, x, 47, 6: As eagles eie, that can behold the sunne.

Cf. Tilley, E3.

200 TO LEND AN **EAR**

FQ, II, viii, 4, 1: The palmer lent his eare unto the noyce. ¶ *Ibid.*, III, i, 23, 1: To her cry they list not lenden eare. ¶ *Ibid.*, 60, 8: Lent her wary eare to understand. ¶ *Mother Hub.*, 1010–1011: His eare he lent To everie sound that under heaven blew. ¶ *FQ*, IV, vi, 41, 5: To lend an eare. ¶ *Ibid.*, ix, 31, 4: Ne lend an eare. ¶ *Ibid.*, xii, 6, 5: Heaven, that unto all lends equall eare.

Shakespeare, *Rich. III*, III, vii, 101: Lend favourable ear to our requests. ¶ *Ibid.*, IV, ii, 79: Rise, and lend thine ear. ¶ Shakespeare, *T. of Shrew*, IV, i, 62: Lend thine ear. ¶ Shakespeare, *Jul. Caesar*, III, ii, 79:

Lend me your ears. ¶ Shakespeare, *Othello*, I, iii, 245: Lend your prosperous ear. ¶ Jonson, *Every Man in His Humour*, V, iii, 355–356; *Works*, III, 286: Lend me your large eares. ¶ Jonson, *Epigr.*, Dedication to the Earl of Pembroke, 35–36, *Works*, VIII, 26: Lend their long eares. ¶ Jonson, *The Gypsies Metam.*, 255, *Works*, VII, 573: Nowe lend yor eare. ¶ Jonson, *Love Freed from Ignorance*, 156, *Works*, VII, 364: Lend it your best eare.

Cf. Stevenson, 653:14; Tilley, E18.

201 BEWARE OF TURNING **EARNEST** (JEST) INTO JEST (EARNEST)

FQ, II, i, 31, 1: So can he turne his earnest unto game. ¶ *Ibid.*, vi, 23, 9: Therewith she laught, and did her earnest end in jest.

Plautus, *Amphitryon*, 920–921: Si quid dictum est per iocum, non aequom est id te serio praevortier (It is not fair to treat as serious that which is only said in joke). ¶ Chaucer, *Miller's Prol.*, 3186: Men shal nat maken ernest of game. ¶ Chaucer, *Miller's T.*, 3390: Al his ernest turneth til a jape. ¶ Chaucer, *Manciple's* Prol., 100: So kanst turnen ernest into game. ¶ Sidney, *Arcadia*, *Works*, I, 114: Take heede, that this jest do not one day turne to earnest.

Cf. Stevenson, 1266:4; Tilley, J46.

202 THE **EARTH** IS THE MOTHER OF US ALL

FQ, II, i, 10, 6: Earth, great mother of us all. ¶ *Ibid.*, VII, vii, 17, 6: Earth (great mother of us all).

Lucretius, *De Rerum Natura*, v, 795–796: Linquitur ut merito maternum nomen adepta terra sit, e terra quoniam sunt cuncta creata (It remains, therefore, that the earth deserves the name of mother which she possesses, since from the earth all things have been produced). ¶ Ovid, *Metam.*, i, 1, 393: Magna parens terra est (Our great mother is the earth).

Cf. Stevenson, 656:2.

203 TO **EAT** ONE'S HEART OUT

Cf. no. 215: Envy feeds upon itself

Mother Hub., 904: To eate thy heart through comfortlesse dispaires. ¶ *FQ*, I, ii, 6, 3: But did his stout heart eat. ¶ *Ibid.*, IV, vi, 7, 5: Gnaw his gealous hart. ¶ *Ibid.*, ix, 14, 4–5: Bitter corsive . . . did eat Her tender heart. ¶ *Ibid.*, VI, ix, 39, 3–4: For gealousie Was readie oft his owne hart to devoure. ¶ *Hymne in Honour of L.*, 267–268: That monster Gelosie, Which eates the hart, and feedes upon the gall.

Plutarch, *Moralia*: *Ed. of Children*, 12E: "*Μὴ ἐσθίειν καρδίαν*" (Do not eat your heart). ¶ Erasmus, *Adagia*, 17E: Cor ne edito (Do not eat your heart). ¶ Harvey, *Foure Lett.*, *Works*, I, 214: Valiantly eate his owne harte. ¶ Nashe, *Unfor. Trav.*, *Works*, II, 266: Eate out his heart with iealousie.

Cf. Taverner, 68; Apperson, 177; W. G. Smith, 166; Stevenson, 1106:1; Tilley, H330.

204 **END** ALL STRIFE AND ENMITY

FQ, II, ii, 28, 2–3: Her lowd gainsaid, and . . . bad Pursew the end of their strong enmity. ¶ *Ibid.*, III, iv, 8, 7–8: O! doe thy cruell wrath and spightfull wrong At length allay, and stint thy stormy stryfe. ¶ *Ibid.*, V, xi, 54, 3: Stint all strife and troublous enmitie.

Culman, 2: Inimicitias dissolve (Put an end to enmities).

205 IN THE **END** THINGS WILL MEND

Mother Hub., 172: Sildome but some good commeth ere the end.

Cf. Apperson, 182; Tilley, E124.

206 MARK THE **END**

FQ, II, i, 3, 4: He seekes, of all his drifte the aymed end. ¶ *Ibid.*, vii, 32, 7–8: Loe here the end, To which al men doe ayme.

Culman, 6: Finem vitae specta (Look at the end of life). ¶ *Ibid.*, 27:

Spectandus semper est finis & rei exitus (The end and issue of a thing is ever to be looked at).

Erasmus, *Adagia*, 126D: Finem vitae specta (Mark the end of life).

Cf. Taverner, 50; Tilley, E125; C. G. Smith, 78.

207 THE **END** CROWNS (TRIES) ALL

FQ, I, x, 41, 6–7: All is but lost, that living we bestow, If not well ended at our dying day. ¶ *Ibid.*, II, viii, 14, 7: The worth of all men by their end esteeme. ¶ *Ibid.*, IV, iv, 43, 9: So nought may be esteemed happie till the end. ¶ *Ibid.*, v, 8, 8: Last is deemed best.

Publilius Syrus (1934), 190: Extrema semper de ante factis iudicant (The end always passes judgment on what has preceded).

Ovid, *Heroides*, ii, 85: Exitus acta probat (The end judges the act). ¶ Lyly, *Euph. Anat. of Wit*, *Works*, II, 28: Things are not to be iudged by the euent, but by the ende. ¶ Harvey, *A New Lett.*, *Works*, I, 294: All is well that endeth effectually well. ¶ Kyd, *Span. Trag.*, II, iv, 204: The end is crown of every work well done.

Cf. W. G. Smith, 171; Tilley, E116; C. G. Smith, 79.

208 AVOID **ENMITY**

FQ, III, i, 13, 8–9: Let later age . . . Vyle rancor . . . avoid, and cruel surquedry.

Culman, 2: Inimicitias fuge (Avoid enmities).

209 HE THAT HAS **ENOUGH**, LET HIM WISH NO MORE

Cf. no. 210: Who has enough needs no more

FQ, I, iv, 29, 5: Who had enough, yett wished ever more.

Culman, 25: Quod satis est cui contingit, nihil amplius optet (One who has enough, let him wish no more).

Horace, *Epist.*, i, 2, 46: Quod satis est cui contingit, nihil amplius optet (Let him who has enough ask for nothing more).

210 WHO HAS **ENOUGH** NEEDS NO MORE

Cf. no. 209: He that has enough, let him wish no more

FQ, I, x, 38, 8: He had enough; what need him care for more? ¶ *Ibid.*, II, vii, 39, 3–4: All that I need I have; what needeth mee To covet more then I have cause to use?

Publilius Syrus (1934), 603: Quicquid plus quam necesse est possideas premit (Any possession beyond the needful overburdens you).

Cf. Stevenson, 699:6.

211 NO **ENTREATIES** CAN REACH AN UNFRIENDLY MIND

FQ, VI, vii, 40, 1–5: Ne ought it mote availe her to entreat The one or th' other, better her to use: For both so wilfull were and obstinate, That all her piteous plaint they did refuse, And rather did the more her beate and bruse.

Publilius Syrus (1934), 325: Inimici ad animum nullae conveniunt preces (No entreaties are fitted to reach an unfriendly mind).

212 IT IS BETTER TO BE **ENVIED** THAN PITIED

Shep. Cal., Maye, 57–58: I (as I am) had rather be envied, All were it of my foe, then fonly pitied. ¶ *Ibid.*, Glosse, 63–64: *I as I am* seemeth to imitate the commen proverb, *Malim invidere mihi omnes, quam miserescere.*

Culman, 24: Praestat invisum esse, quam miserabilem (It is better to be envied than pitied). ¶ Publilius Syrus (1835), 400: Invidiosum esse praestat quam miserabilem (It is more agreeable to be envied than pitied). ¶ *Ibid.*, 707: Praestare invidiam dico misericordiae (It is better, I say, to be envied than pitied).

Pindar, *Pyth.*, i, 85: *κρέσσων γὰρ οἰκτιρμοῦ φθόνος* (Envy is better than pity). ¶ Herodotus, *Hist.*, iii, 52: *σὺ δὲ μαθὼν ὅσῳ φθονέεσθαι κρέσσον ἐστὶ ἢ οἰκτείρεσθαι* (Nay, bethink you how much better a thing it is to be envied than to be pitied). ¶ Erasmus, *Adagia*, 1044B: Praestat invidiosum esse quam miserabilem (It is better to be envied than pitied).

Cf. Apperson, 42; Stevenson, 703:5; Tilley, E177.

213 AN **ENVIOUS** MAN GROWS LEAN (GRIEVES) WHEN HIS NEIGHBOR WAXES FAT

FQ, I, ix, 39, 6: Most envious man, that grieves at neighbours good.

Culman, 21: Invidus alterius rebus macrescit opimis (An envious man waxes lean at the prosperity of another).

Horace, *Epist.*, i, 2, 57: Invidus alterius macrescit rebus opimis (The envious man grows lean when his neighbor waxes fat).

Cf. Tilley, M96; C. G. Smith, 81.

214 **ENVY** CAN ABIDE NOTHING PRAISEWORTHY

Cf. no. 216: Envy is an enemy of honor

FQ, I, iv, 30, 7: Death it was, when any good he [Envy] saw. ¶ *Ibid.*, 32, 1–9: He hated all good workes and vertuous deeds, And him no lesse, that any like did use . . . Such one vile Envy was. ¶ *Ibid.*, V, xii, 27, 7: Envies cloud still dimmeth vertues ray. ¶ *Ibid.*, 31, 1–3: Her name was Envie, knowen well thereby; Whose nature is to grieve and grudge at all That ever she sees doen prays-worthily.

Culman, 27: Semper malis invisa fuit egregia virtus (Excellent virtue was ever envied by wicked men).

Cf. Stevenson, 703:4; Tilley, E171.

215 **ENVY** FEEDS UPON ITSELF

Cf. no. 203: To eat one's heart out

FQ, I, iv, 30, 1–5: Malicious Envy . . . chawed his owne maw. ¶ *Ibid.*, V, xii, 31, 1–8: Her name was Envie . . . She feedes on her owne maw unnaturall, And of her owne foule entrayles makes her meat.

* Publilius Syrus (1934), 378: Malivolus semper sua natura vescitur (An envious disposition feeds upon itself).

Diogenes Laertius, *Antisthenes*, vi, 5: ἔλεγε τοὺς φθονεροὺς ὑπὸ τοῦ ἰδίου ἤθους κατεσθίεσθαι (The envious are consumed by their own passion).

Cf. Stevenson, 701:7.

216 **ENVY** IS AN ENEMY OF HONOR

Cf. no. 214: Envy can abide nothing praiseworthy

Virgils Gnat, 557–558: For loftie type of honour, through the glaunce Of envies dart, is downe in dust prostrate.

Pindar, *Olympian Odes*, ii, 95: *αἶνον ἔβα κόρος* (Praise is attacked by envy). ¶ Greene, *Euphues His Censure to Phil.*, *Works*, VI, 272: Enuy the secret enemy of honor. ¶ Shakespeare, *Pericles*, IV, Prol., 12–13: That monster, Envy, oft the wrack Of earned praise.

Cf. Benham, 593a.

217 **ENVY** TORMENTS ITS OWNER

FQ, V, xii, 33, 4–5: Envie . . . did . . . murder her owne mynd. ¶ *Ibid.*, 35, 7–8: Envy selfe excelling In mischiefe . . . her selfe she onely vext.

Culman, 13: Invidia suum torquet authorem (Envy torments its owner).

218 THE RANCOR OF **ENVY** IS HOSTILE BUT CONCEALED

FQ, V, xii, 33, 2–5: In bad will and cancred kynd, . . . what so Envie good or bad did fynd She did conceale.

Publilius Syrus (1934), 287: Invidia tacite sed inimice irascitur (Silent but unfriendly is the anger of envy).

219 IT IS GOOD TO PREVENT AN **EVIL** IN THE BEGINNING

FQ, III, ii, 46, 1–2: Represse The growing evill, ere it strength have gott. ¶ *Mother Hub.*, 189–190: Therefore I read that we our counsells call, How to prevent this mischiefe ere it fall. ¶ *FQ*, VI, vi, 8, 2–4: The seede of all this evill . . . at the first, before it had infected, Mote easie be supprest with little thing. ¶ *View*, 683: Greate daunger often groweth, which by such timely prevention might easely be stopped.

Culman, 21: Multo praestat medicari initia, quam finem (It is much better to remedy the beginning than the end). ¶ *Ibid.*, 23: Omne malum nascens facile opprimitur (Every evil at its first coming up is easily suppressed). ¶ *Ibid.*, 27: Satius est initiis mederi, quam fini (It is better to remedy the beginnings than the end). ¶ Publilius Syrus (1835), 881: Satius mederi est initiis quam finibus (Better use medicines at the outset, than at the last moment).

Cicero, *Philip.*, v, 11, 30–31: Omne malum nascens facile opprimitur, inveteratum fit plerumque robustius (Every evil is easily crushed at its birth; become inveterate, it as a rule gathers strength). ¶ Erasmus, *Adagia*, 85F: Satius est initiis mederi, quam fini (It is better to remedy the beginnings than the end). ¶ Pettie, *Petite P.*, 121: Any evill at the first entring in of it may easely bee avoyded.

Cf. Stevenson, 712:2, Tilley, E202.

220 THE **EVIL** THAT MEN DO LIVES AFTER THEM

FQ, II, viii, 28, 9: The trespas still doth live, albee the person dye. ¶ *Ibid.*, 29, 1–2: The evill donne Dyes not, when breath the body first doth leave.

Culman, 13: Mala herba non perit (An evil weed does not die).

Sophocles, *Philoctetes*, 446: *ἐπεὶ οὐδέν πω κακόν γ' ἀπώλετο* (Evil never dies). ¶ Erasmus, *Adagia*, 1007D: Malam herbam non perire (The evil weed never dies).

Cf. Stevenson, 715:4; 2476:6; C. G. Smith, 82.

221 TO DO NO **EVIL**, AVOID THE OCCASION OF EVIL

FQ, VI, vi, 14, 1–2: "The best," sayd he, "that I can you advize, Is to avoide the occasion of the ill."

Northbrooke, *Treatise agst. Dicing*, 173: As the olde saying is, He that will none euill do, Must do nothing belonging therto.

Cf. Apperson, 194; Tilley, I28.

222 EVIL-DOING NEEDS ONLY AN EXCUSE

Cf. no. 225: The wicked always excuse their wickedness

Shep. Cal., Feb., 198: Ay little helpe to harme there needeth.

* Publilius Syrus (1934), 377: Male facere qui vult numquam non causam invenit (The intention to injure can always find a reason).

Aristotle, *Rhetoric*, i, 12, 23–24: *ὥσπερ γὰρ ἡ παροιμία, προφάσεως δεῖται μόνον ἡ πονηρία* (For, as the proverb says, "Evil-doing needs only an excuse").

Cf. Benham, 520b.

223 EVIL-GOTTEN GOODS THRIVE NOT

Mother Hub., 1149: Ill might it prosper, that ill gotten was.

Culman, 7: Male partum dilabitur (A thing evil-gotten is quickly gone). ¶ *Ibid.*, 16: Turpe lucrum adducit infortunium (Dishonest gain brings loss). ¶ *Ibid.*, 21: Lucrum malum damnum semper affert (Evil gain always brings loss). ¶ * Publilius Syrus (1934), 158: Damnum appellandum est cum mala fama lucrum (Ill-famed gain should be called loss).

Hesiod, *Works and Days*, 352: *κακὰ κέρδεα ἶσ' ἀάτῃσιν* (Base gain is as bad as ruin). ¶ Sophocles, *Antigone*, 326: *τὰ δειλὰ κέρδη πημονὰς ἐργάζεται* (The wages of ill-gotten gains is death). ¶ Plautus, *Poenulus*, 844: Male partum male disperit (Ill-gotten, ill-spent). ¶ Cicero, *Philip.*, ii, 27, 65–66: Sed, ut est apud poetam nescio quem, "Male parta male dilabuntur" (But, as some poet says: "Evil gains come to an evil end"). ¶ Ovid, *Amores*, i, 10, 48: Non habet eventus sordida praeda bonos (A sordid gain can bring no good in the end). ¶ Erasmus, *Adagia*, 294F: Male parta, male dilabuntur (Wickedly gained things wickedly go to ruin). ¶ Northbrooke, *Treatise agst. Dicing*, 125: As the poet sayth, *De bonis male quaesitis, vix gaudebit haeres tertius*; euill gotten goods shall neuer prosper.

Cf. Taverner, 23; Apperson, 324; Tilley, G301; C. G. Smith, 86.

224 HE THAT EXALTS HIMSELF SHALL BE ABASED

FQ, V, ii, 21, 5: Made them stoupe, that looked earst so hie. ¶ *Ibid.*, 50, 9: So was the high aspyring with huge ruine humbled.

Culman, 31: Extollens se humiliabitur (He that exalts himself shall be made low).

New Testament: *Matthew*, xxiii, 12: Ὅστις δὲ ὑψώσει ἑαυτὸν ταπεινωθήσεται (And whosoever shall exalt himself shall be abased).

Cf. Stevenson, 1195:12.

225 THE WICKED ALWAYS **EXCUSE** THEIR WICKEDNESS

Cf. no. 222: Evil-doing needs only an excuse

FQ, IV, xii, 30, 8–9: For never wight so evill did or thought, But would some rightfull cause pretend.

Publilius Syrus (1835), 643: Omne vitium semper habet patrocinium suum (Every vicious act has its excuse ever ready).

Seneca, *De Ira*, ii, 13, 1: Cui enim tandem vitio advocatus defuit (For what vice, pray, has ever lacked its defender)? ¶ Jonson, *Catiline*, III, 339, *Works*, V, 480: Bad men excuse their faults.

226 **EXPERIENCE** IS THE MOTHER OF WISDOM

Shep. Cal., Dec., 85: Tryed time yet taught me greater thinges. ¶ *FQ*, II, ix, 54, 4–5: Through continuall practise and usage, He now was growne right wise and wondrous sage.

Publilius Syrus (1835), 448: Magister usus omnium est rerum optimus (In all things, experience is the best instructor).

Quintilian, *Inst. Orat.*, ii, 17, 12–13: Nam id potentissimum discendi genus est (For experience is the best of all schools). ¶ Sidney, *Arcadia*, *Works*, I, 113: All is but lip-wisdome, which wants experience.

Cf. Tilley, E221.

227 **EXPERIENCE** KEEPS A DEAR SCHOOL

Mother Hub., 403–404: Who hath the world not tride From the right way full eath may wander wide.

Ascham, *Scholemaster*, *Eng. Works* (Wright), 214: We know by experience it selfe, that it is a meruelous paine, to finde oute but a short waie, by long wandering.

Cf. W. G. Smith, 182–183.

228 BELIEVE YOUR **EYES** RATHER THAN YOUR EARS

Mother Hub., 1275–1278: He heard each one complaine Of foule abuses both in realme and raine: Which yet to prove more true, he meant to see, And an ey-witnes of each thing to bee.

Culman, 15: Oculi auribus sunt fideliores (The eyes are more faithful than the ears). ¶ *Ibid.*, 18: Certiora quae videntur, quam quae audiuntur (Those things that are seen, are more certain than those that are heard). ¶ *Ibid.*, 21: Libentius oculatis, quam auritis testibus creditur (Men believe eye-witnesses more willingly than ear-witnesses). ¶ *Ibid.*, 23: Oculis magis habenda fides, quam auribus (We are rather to believe our eyes than our ears). ¶ *Ibid.*, 25: Quae cernuntur, certiora sunt, quam quae audiuntur (Those things that are seen are more certain than those that are heard). ¶ Publilius Syrus (1835), 637: Oculis habenda quam auribus est major fides (Put more confidence in your eyes than in your ears).

Herodotus, *Hist.*, i, 8: *ὦτα γὰρ τυγχάνει ἀνθρώποισι ἐόντα ἀπιστότερα ὀφθαλμῶν* (Men trust their ears less than their eyes). ¶ Seneca, *Epist.*, vi, 5: Homines amplius oculis quam auribus credunt (Men put more faith in their eyes than in their ears). ¶ Erasmus, *Adagia*, 67D: Oculis magis habenda fides, quam auribus (Better to trust your eyes than your ears).

Cf. Taverner, 4; Stevenson, 737:9; Tilley, C815; C. G. Smith, 90.

229 RULE YOUR **EYES**

FQ, VI, vi, 7, 8–9: Your eies . . . restraine From that they most affect, and in due termes containe.

Culman, 3: Oculis moderare (Rule your eyes).

230 THE **FACE** IS THE INDEX OF THE MIND

Shep. Cal., Sept., 168: All their craft is in their countenaunce. ¶ *FQ*, I, iii, 9, 9: And ever by her lookes conceived her intent. ¶ *Ibid.*, II, i, 7, 6: By lookes one may the mind aread. ¶ *Astrophel*, 168: His lookes did tell his thought. ¶ *FQ*, VII, vi, 28, 9: So did their ghastly gaze bewray their hidden feares.

Cicero, *Orator*, xviii, 60: Imago est animi voltus (The face is the image of the soul). ¶ Jonson, *Discoveries*, 522, *Works*, VIII, 579: Man is read in his face.

Cf. Apperson, 198; Tilley, F1.

231 TO CARRY TWO **FACES** UNDER ONE HOOD

FQ, V, xi, 56, 7: Under one hood to shadow faces twaine.

Cf. Apperson, 654; W. G. Smith, 679; Stevenson, 741: 8; Tilley, F20.

232 THE MANY **FAIL**, THE FEW SUCCEED

Mother Hub., 894: Few have found, and manie one hath mist. ¶ *FQ*, II, vii, 48, 9: Few gett, but many mis.

Tennyson, *The Day Dream: The Arrival*, 2, 7–8: This proverb flashes thro' his head, "The many fail: the one succeeds."

233 **FAINT** HEART NEVER WON FAIR LADY

FQ, IV, x, 53, 6–7: Doubt and shamefast feare, . . . Ladies love I heard had never wonne.

Greene, *Never Too Late*, *Works*, VIII, 90: A faint heart neuer wonne faire Ladie. ¶ Greene, *Mourning Garment*, *Works*, IX, 174: Faint heart neuer wonne faire Lady. ¶ Lodge, *Rosalynde*, *Works*, I, 64: Faint heart neuer wonne faire Ladie.

Cf. Apperson, 198; W. G. Smith, 185; Stevenson, 1108: 9; Tilley, H302.

234 A **FAIR** (FOUL) MORNING OFTEN TURNS TO A FOUL (FAIR) EVENING

Muiopotmos, 219: Morning faire may bring fowle evening late.

Chaucer, *Troilus*, III, 1060–1061: For I have seyn, of a ful misty morwe Folowen ful ofte a myrie someris day.

Cf. Apperson, 103, 429; W. G. Smith, 98, 222.

235 WHERE **FAIR** MEANS MAY NOT PREVAIL, THERE FOUL MEANS RIGHTLY MAY BE USED

Cf. no. 608: Benevolence tries persuasion first, then severer measures

FQ, III, xii, 28, 1–2: Where force might not availe, there sleights and art She cast to use, both fitt for hard emprize. ¶ *Ibid.*, V, v, 49, 9: Who will not stoupe with good shall be made stoupe with harme. ¶ *View*, 650: Where noe other remedye may be founde, nor noe hope of recoverye had, there must needes this violent meanes be used.

Publilius Syrus (1934), 605: Quem bono tenere non potueris, contineas malo (Him you have failed to control by fair means, you must restrain by foul).

Cf. C. G. Smith, 91.

236 WANT OF **FAITH**, GUILT OF SIN

FQ, I, vii, 45, 8: Want of faith, . . . guilt of sin.

Culman, 35: Peccatum est quod absque fide est (That which is without faith is sin).

New Testament: Romans, 14:23: πᾶν δὲ ὃ οὐκ ἐκ πίστεως ἁμαρτία ἐστίν (Whatsoever is not of faith is sin).

237 THERE IS **FALSEHOOD** (FLATTERY) IN FRIENDSHIP

Prothalamion, 99: Friendships faultie guile.

Culman, 17: Adulatio, maxima in amicitia pestis (Flattery is the greatest plague in friendship).

Seneca, *Epist.*, xlv, 7: Adulatio quam similis est amicitiae (How closely flattery resembles friendship). ¶ Tacitus, *Annals*, ii, 12: Amicis inesse adulationem (Flattery is natural in friendship).

Cf. Apperson, 202; W. G. Smith, 189; Tilley, F41; C. G. Smith, 110.

238 **FAME** (A GOOD NAME) IS BETTER THAN RICHES

Shep. Cal., Oct., 19–20: The prayse is better then the price, The glory eke much greater then the gayne. ¶ *FQ*, V, xi, 63, 6–8: Fie on the pelfe for which good name is sold . . . Dearer is . . . fame then gold.

Culman, 20: Haereditas famae, quam divitiarum honestior (The inheritance of a good name is more honest than that of riches). ¶ * Publilius Syrus (1934), 75: Bona opinio hominum tutior pecunia est (There is more safety in men's good opinion than in money). ¶ *Ibid.*, 96: Bene audire alterum patrimonium est (To have a good name is a second patrimony). ¶ * *Ibid.*, 254: Honestus rumor alterum est patrimonium (An honorable reputation is a second patrimony). ¶ *Ibid.*, 546: Probo bona fame maxima est hereditas (For the upright a good name is the greatest inheritance). ¶ *Ibid.* (1835), 328: Honesta fama est alterum patrimonium (A good reputation is a second patrimony).

Old Testament: Proverbs, xxii, 1: A good name is rather to be chosen than great riches. ¶ Pettie, *Petite P.*, 18: An honest name . . . the cheife ritches I have. ¶ *Ibid.*, 29: Is not the losse of goodes lesse, then of ones good name? ¶ Greene, *Penelopes Web*, *Works*, V, 210: I esteeme more of fame then of gold.

Cf. Apperson, 261; Tilley, N22; C. G. Smith, 94.

239 **FAME** IS A SPUR TO GREAT DEEDS

Teares of the M., 453–454: Deserved meed, Due praise, that is the spur of dooing well.

Culman, 13: Immensum gloria calcar habet (Glory has a very great spur).

Ovid, *Ex Ponto*, iv, 2, 36: Inmensum gloria calcar habet (Renown possesses a mighty spur). ¶ Lodge, *Robert, Sec. Duke of Normandy*,

Works, II, 16: Honours are the spurres of vertue. ¶ Milton, *Lycidas*, 70: Fame is the spur that the clear spirit doth raise.

Cf. C. G. Smith, 93.

240 THE **FARTHER** YOU GO, THE FARTHER BEHIND

FQ, I, ix, 43, 9: The further he doth goe, the further he doth stray.

Lydgate, *Minor Poems* (Percy S.), 74: The more I go, the further I am behynde.

Cf. W. G. Smith, 231; Stevenson, 1999: 10; Tilley, G151.

241 THE **FATES** (PROVIDENCE) CAN FIND A WAY

FQ, I, vi, 7, 1–2: Eternall Providence, exceeding thought, Where none appeares can make her selfe a way. ¶ *Ibid.*, III, iii, 25, 4–5: Fates can make Way for themselves.

Vergil, *Aeneid*, iii, 395: Fata viam invenient (The fates will find a way). ¶ *Ibid.*, x, 113: Fata viam invenient (The fates shall find their way).

Cf. Stevenson, 769: 7.

242 LIKE **FATHER**, LIKE SON

Cf. no. 243: You are your father's own son; no. 684: As the shepherd, so his sheep

FQ, V, vi, 33, 1–2: Three sonnes, all three like fathers sonnes, Like treacherous, like full of fraud and guile.

Erasmus, *Adagia*, 1068D: Qualis pater, talis filius (Like father, like son). ¶ Barclay, *Ship of F.*, I, 236: An olde prouerbe hath longe agone be sayde That oft the sone in maners lyke wyll be Vnto the Father. ¶ Sidney, *Christ. Relig.*, *Works*, III, 325: Whatsoever the Father is, the Sonne is the same.

Cf. Apperson, 366; W. G. Smith, 194; Tilley, F92.

243 YOU ARE YOUR **FATHER'S** OWN SON

Cf. no. 242: Like father, like son; no. 684: As the shepherd, so his sheep

FQ, V, vi, 33, 1: He had three sonnes, all three like fathers sonnes.

Erasmus, *Adagia*, 1013F: Patris est filius (He is his father's son).

Cf. Tilley, F97.

244 WHAT YOU FIND **FAULT** WITH IN OTHERS, YOU SHOULD NOT BE GUILTY OF

FQ, II, ix, 38, 4–5: Him ill beseemes, anothers fault to name, That may unawares bee blotted with the same. ¶ *View*, 676: Take heede, least unawares ye fall into that inconvenience which you formerly found faulte with in others.

Culman, 25: Quod aliis vitio vertas, ipse ne feceris (What you blame others for, you yourself must not do). ¶ Publilius Syrus (1835), 809: Quod aliis vitio vertis, ne ipse admiseris (What you blame in others as a fault, you should not be guilty of yourself).

Aristotle, *Rhetoric*, ii, 23, 7: ἄτοπός ἐστιν, ὅταν τις ἐπιτιμᾷ ἄλλοις ἃ αὐτὸς ποιεῖ ἢ ποιήσειεν ἄν (It is ridiculous for a man to reproach others for what he does or would do himself). ¶ Plautus, *Truculentus*, 160: Qui alterum incusat probri, sumpse enitere oportet (He who damns another's faults had best be a paragon himself). ¶ Cato, *Disticha*, i, 30: Quae culpare soles ea tu ne feceris ipse (Do not yourself what you are wont to blame). ¶ Cicero, *Tusc. Disp.*, iii, 30, 73–74: Est enim proprium stultitiae aliorum vitia cernere, oblivisci suorum (It is a peculiarity of folly to discern the faults of others and be forgetful of its own). ¶ Plutarch, *Moralia*: *Advice about Keeping Well*, 129D: οὕτω τὰ περὶ αὑτὸν ἐν τοῖς πλησίον εὖ τίθεσθαι (A man ought to correct in himself the faults he observes in his neighbors). ¶ Erasmus, *Adagia*, 926C: Quod aliis vitio vertas, ipse ne feceris (What you find fault with in others, you yourself should not do).

Cf. Udall, *Apoph. of Erasm.*, 7:15; Stevenson, 780:4; Tilley, F107; C. G. Smith, 97.

245 WE ARE QUICK-SIGHTED TO OTHER MEN'S **FAULTS**, NOT TO OUR OWN

Colin Clouts, 757–758: For all the rest do most-what far amis, And yet their owne misfaring will not see.

Culman, 20: In aliena vitia natura sumus occulati, non in nostra (We are by nature quick-sighted to other men's faults, not to our own).

Cato, *Collectio Monos.*, 48–49: Cum vitia alterius satis acri lumine cernas nec tua prospicias, fis verso crimine caecus (When with sharp eye another's faults you mind, Not seeing yours, you're blamed in turn as blind). ¶ Seneca, *De Ira*, II, 28, 8: Aliena vitia in oculis habemus, a tergo nostra sunt (The vices of others we keep before our eyes, our own behind our back).

Cf. C. G. Smith, 100.

246 THE MOST **FAULTY** ARE THE MOST SUSPICIOUS

Shep. Cal., Maye, 319: *Πᾶς μὲν ἄπιστος ἀπιστεῖ* (Who doth most mistrust is most false).

Publilius Syrus (1835), 627: Nunquam secura est prava conscientia (A guilty conscience never feels secure). ¶ *Ibid.*, 1103: Tuta saepe, nunquam secura, mala conscientia (An evil conscience is often quiet, but never secure).

Lydgate, *Minor Poems* (Percy S.), 162: No man of kynde is moore suspecious, Than he that is moost vicious and coupable. ¶ Sidney, *Arcadia*, *Works*, I, 341: Who others vertue doubt, themselves are vicious.

Cf. Stevenson, 2382:12; Tilley, F117; C. G. Smith, 101.

247 **FEAR** GIVES WINGS

FQ, II, iv, 32, 1: Feare gave her winges. ¶ *Ibid.*, III, v, 6, 6: Carried away with wings of speedy feare. ¶ *Ibid.*, vi, 54, 9: Fled with wings of idle feare. ¶ *Ibid.*, vii, 26, 9: Fear gave her wings. ¶ *Ibid.*, V, viii, 4, 6–7: Yet fled she fast, . . . Carried with wings of feare.

Vergil, *Aeneid*, viii, 224: Pedibus timor addidit alas (Fear lends wings to his feet). ¶ Sidney, *Arcadia*, *Works*, I, 271: Feare gives him wings.

Cf. Apperson, 206; Stevenson, 787:13; Tilley, F133.

248 **FEAR** RESTRAINS THE WICKED

View, 610: Feare of law . . . restrayneth offences.

Publilius Syrus (1934), 398: Metus improbos compescit non clementia (Fear, not clemency, restrains the wicked).

249 BY CONSTANT **FEAR** A WISE MAN ESCAPES HARM

FQ, I, viii, 44, 5–6: Th' only good, that growes of passed feare, Is to be wise, and ware of like agein.

Publilius Syrus (1934), 666: Semper metuendo sapiens evitat malum (By constant fear the wise man escapes harm).

250 IT IS FOLLY TO **FEAR** WHAT CANNOT BE AVOIDED

Cf. no. 251: There is no advantage in needless fear

FQ, III, ix, 7, 1: In vaine he feares that which he cannot shonne. ¶ *Ibid.*, x, 3, 3: Fond is the feare that findes no remedie.

* Publilius Syrus (1835), 924: Stultum est, timere, quod vitari non potest (It is folly to fear what cannot be avoided).

Seneca, *De Rem. Fortui.* (Palmer), 32–33: Stultum est timere, quod vitare non possis (It is folly to dread what you cannot avoid).

Cf. C. G. Smith, 105.

251 THERE IS NO ADVANTAGE IN NEEDLESS **FEAR**

Cf. no. 250: It is folly to fear what cannot be avoided

FQ, I, i, 54, 4–5: Ne let vaine feares procure your needlesse smart, Where cause is none. ¶ *Ibid.*, iv, 49, 4: Needlesse feare did never vantage none. ¶ *Ibid.*, IV, vi, 37, 6–7: Be nought dismayd With needelesse dread.

Publilius Syrus (1934), 471: Nemo timendo ad summum pervenit locum (Fear never brought one to the top). ¶ *Ibid.*, 728: Virtutis omnis impedimentum est timor (All virtue finds an obstacle in fear).

Sidney, *Arcadia*, *Works*, II, 166: Feare is more paine, then is the paine it feares, Disarming humane mindes, of native might. ¶ Breton, *Crossing of Prov.*, *Works*, II, *e*, 9: Feare it selfe is full of hurt.

252 THERE IS POOR SLEEPING WHEN **FEAR** TORMENTS THE MIND

FQ, IV, v, 43, 6–7: In his soundest sleepe, his dayly feare His ydle braine gan busily molest. ¶ *Hymne in Honour of L.*, 252–256: Feare . . . O how doth it torment His troubled mynd . . . To breake his sleepe and waste his ydle braine.

* Publilius Syrus (1934), 359: Metus cum venit, rarum habet somnus locum (When fear has come, sleep has scanty place).

Cf. C. G. Smith, 272.

253 WHOM WE **FEAR** WE HATE

View, 649: According to the saying "Quem metuunt oderunt."

Cicero, *De Offic.*, ii, 7, 23: Praeclare enim Ennius: Quem metuunt, oderunt (For Ennius says admirably: "Whom they fear they hate"). ¶ Plutarch, *Moralia*: *On Envy and Hate*, 537C: ὅ γὰρ δεδίασι, καὶ μισεῖν πεφύκασιν (What they fear they naturally hate as well). ¶ Erasmus, *Colloquia Fam.*, 675D: Oderint, inquit, dum metuant ("Let them hate me," he says, "so they fear me"). ¶ Shakespeare, *Ant. & Cleop.*, I, iii, 12: In time we hate that which we often fear.

Cf. Stevenson, 1089:4.

254 AFTER **FEASTING**, WEEPING

Cf. no. 426: There is no joy without sorrow

FQ, VI, iii, 4, 8–9: Is this the timely joy, Which I expected long, now turnd to sad annoy?

Culman, 12: Extrema gaudii luctus occupat (Mourning possesses the last of joy).

Beowulf, 128: Aefter wiste wop (After feasting weeping). ¶ Chaucer, *Knight's T.*, 2841: Wo after gladnesse. ¶ Chaucer, *Nun's Priest's T.*, 3205: For evere the latter ende of joye is wo. ¶ Erasmus, *Colloquia Fam.*, 885E: Illud verissime dictum extrema gaudii luctus occupat (The old saying is a true one: "The end of mirth is heaviness").

255 TO HAVE A **FEATHER** IN YOUR CAP

FQ, III, ii, 27, 1: Fether in her lofty crest.

Nashe, *Unfor. Trav.*, *Works*, II, 227: I had my feather in my cap. ¶ Nashe, *Have with You*, *Works*, III, 30: Flourishing with a feather in my cappe. ¶ Nashe, *Lenten Stuffe*, *Works*, III, 174: Feather in his cap for his mistris fauour. ¶ Nashe, *Summers Last Will*, *Works*, III, 262: Like a Caualier that weares a huge feather in his cap.

Cf. Apperson, 207; W. G. Smith, 197; Stevenson, 791:8; Tilley, F157.

256 TO **FEED** (EAT) ONE'S FILL

Virgils Gnat, 78: On the soft greene grasse feeding their fills. ¶ *Mother Hub.*, 337: Whenas they feasted had their fill. ¶ *Muiopotmos*, 205: When he hath both plaid, and fed his fill. ¶ *FQ*, III, ix, 27, 8: On her faire face so did he feede his fill. ¶ *Ibid.*, 32, 1: Of meats and drinks they had their fill. ¶ *Ibid.*, IV, ii, 49, 3: When at last she had beheld her fill. ¶ *Ibid.*, iii, 36, 8: So wearie both of fighting had their fill. ¶ *Ibid.*, VI, vi, 14, 7: Use scanted diet, and forbeare your fill. ¶ *Ibid.*, ix, 7, 6: Fed his fill. ¶ *Amoretti*, lxv, 8: Singes and feeds her fill. ¶ *Ibid.*, lxxiii, 7–8: That wont on your fayre eye To feed his fill.

Lamb. Hom. (1175), 53: To eten hire fulle. ¶ Gascoigne, *Compl. of Philomene*, *Works*, II, 178: They feede their fil. ¶ Greene, *Pinner of Wakefield*, 498–499, *Works*, XIV, 143: They must . . . eate their fill. ¶ *Ibid.*, 527, *Works*, XIV, 145: They now shall feede their fill.

Cf. Tilley, F215.

257 RULE YOUR **FEELINGS** (DESIRES) LEST YOUR FEELINGS (DESIRES) RULE YOU

FQ, II, iv, 34, 1–2: Most wretched man, That to affections does the bridle lend! ¶ *Ibid.*, VI, vi, 14, 6: Subdue desire.

Publilius Syrus (1934), 40: Animo imperabit sapiens, stultus serviet (The sage will rule his feelings, the fool will be their slave). ¶ *Ibid.*, 50: Animo imperato ne tibi animus imperet (Rule your feelings lest your feelings rule you).

258 NO MAN LOVES HIS **FETTERS**, THOUGH THEY ARE MADE OF GOLD

FQ, III, ix, 8, 4–5: A foole I doe him firmely hold, That loves his fetters, though they were of gold. ¶ *Amoretti*, xxxvii, 13–14: Fondnesse it were for any, being free, To covet fetters, though they golden bee.

Cf. Apperson, 387; W. G. Smith, 393; Stevenson, 795:6; Tilley, M338.

259 TO **FILE** YOUR TONGUE

FQ, I, i, 35, 7: And well could file his tongue. ¶ *Ibid.*, II, i, 3, 6: His fayre fyled tonge. ¶ *Ibid.*, III, ii, 12, 4–5: Ye fyle Your courteous tongue. ¶ *Colin Clouts*, 701: A filed toung.

Chaucer, *Cant. T.*, Gen. Prol., 712: And wel affile his tonge. ¶ Chaucer, *Troilus*, II, 1681: Pandarus gan newe his tong affile. ¶ Gower, *Conf. Aman.*, I, 678: For whanne he hath his tunge affiled. ¶ *Ibid.*, III, 516–517: Ne so wel can noman affile His tunge. ¶ Skelton, *Colyn Cloute*, 852, *Works*, I, 344: But they theyr tonges fyle. ¶ Wilson, *Arte of Rhet.*, 3: Euery Orator should earnestly labour to file his tongue. ¶ Shakespeare, *L. Lab. Lost*, V, i, 10–12: His humour is lofty, his discourse peremptory, his tongue filed.

260 **FIRE** THAT IS CLOSEST KEPT BURNS MOST FURIOUSLY

FQ, II, xi, 32, 1–5: A fire, the which in hollow cave Hath long bene underkept and down supprest, . . . At last breakes forth with furious unrest. ¶ *Ibid.*, V, v, 53, 7–9: Her private fire . . . in her entrayles fryde, The more that she it sought to cover and to hyde. ¶ *Brief Note of Ireland* (Variorum), 112–113: A fire the longer it is kept vnder the more violentlie it burneth when it breaketh out.

Ovid, *Metam.*, iv, 64: Quoque magis tegitur, tectus magis aestuat ignis (The more they covered up the fire, the more it burned). ¶ Chaucer, *Troilus*, II, 538–539: And wel the hotter ben the gledes rede, That men hem wrien with asshen pale and dede. ¶ Chaucer, *Leg. Good Women*, 735: Wry the glede, and hotter is the fyr. ¶ Greene, *Carde of F.*, *Works*, IV, 100: To represse the fire, is to make it flame more furiouslie. ¶ Lodge, *Rosalynde*, *Works*, I, 114: Fire supprest growes to the greater flame.

Cf. Apperson, 214; W. G. Smith, 203; Stevenson, 810:2; Tilley, F265.

261 **FIRE** THAT IS DIVIDED BURNS WITH LESS FORCE

FQ, VII, vii, 24, 1–4: The fire: . . . every day, Wee see his parts, so soone as they do sever, To lose their heat, and shortly to decay.

Publilius Syrus (1835), 204: Divisus ignis extinguetur celerius (Fire that is divided is more easily extinguished).

Cf. Tilley, F257.

262 DO NOT PUT **FIRE** TO FLAX

FQ, III, i, 47, 6–7: Her fickle hart conceived hasty fyre, Like sparkes of fire which fall in sclender flex.

Cf. Apperson, 213; Stevenson, 807:6; Tilley, F278.

263 THERE IS NO **FIRE** WITHOUT SMOKE

FQ, I, i, 12, 4: Oft fire is without smoke.

Publilius Syrus (1934), 434: Numquam ubi diu fuit ignis defecit vapor (Where there has been fire for long, there's never a lack of smoke).

Cicero, *De Partit. Orat.*, x, 34: Declarat, ut fumus ignem (As smoke is a certain indication of fire). ¶ Plautus, *Curculio*, 53: Flamma fumo est proxima (Flame is nearest to smoke). ¶ Seneca, *Epist.*, ciii, 2: Praenuntiat fumus incendium (Smoke is the forerunner of fire). ¶ Erasmus, *Adagia*, 189A: Flamma fumo est proxima (Fire is very near to smoke). ¶ Erasmus, *Colloquia Fam.*, 859A: Non est fortassis ignis absque fumo (Perhaps there is no fire, but there is some smoke).

Cf. Taverner, 53; Tilley, F282, S569.

264 TO FLEE FROM THE **FIRE** AND TO FALL INTO THE WATER

Cf. no. 314: Out of the frying-pan into the fire

View, 652: Flying from the fire shall fall into the water, and out of one daunger into another.

Shakespeare, *Two Gent.*, I, iii, 78–79: Thus have I shunn'd the fire for fear of burning And drench'd me in the sea, where I am drown'd.

265 TO KINDLE **FIRE** WITH ICE (SNOW)

Amoretti, xxx, 9–12: Miraculous thing . . . That . . . yse . . . Should kindle fyre.

Shakespeare, *Two Gent.*, II, vii, 19: As soon go kindle fire with snow.

Cf. Tilley, F284.

266 IT IS A SILLY **FISH** THAT IS CAUGHT TWICE WITH THE SAME BAIT

FQ, II, i, 4, 9: The fish that once was caught, new bait wil hardly byte.

Ovid, *Ex Ponto*, ii, 7, 9–10: Qui semel est laesus fallaci piscis ab hamo, omnibus unca cibis aera subesse putat (The fish which has once felt the hook suspects the crooked metal in every food which offers).

Cf. Tilley, F316.

267 ALL **FLESH** IS FRAIL

FQ, II, i, 52, 6: All flesh doth frayltie breed. ¶ *Ibid.*, VI, i, 41, 7: All flesh is frayle. ¶ *Amoretti*, lviii, 5: All flesh is frayle.

Gower, *Conf. Aman.*, V, 6416–6417: The frele fleissh, whos nature is Ai redy forto sporne and falle. ¶ *Chester Plays* (E.E.T.S.), II, 351: Flesh is frayle. ¶ Barnfield, *Aff. Shep.*, 28: Remember flesh is fraile.

Cf. Tilley, F363.

268 MEN ARE **FLESH** AND BLOOD

Shep. Cal., Sept., 238: We bene of fleshe, men as other bee.

Jonson, *Every Man Out of His Humour*, II, iv, 11–12, *Works*, 480: I am a man, and I have limmes, flesh, bloud, Bones, sinews, and a soule. ¶ Jonson, *Magnetic Lady*, V, vii, 48, *Works*, VI, 587: I am a man of flesh, and blood.

Cf. Tilley, F367.

269 EVERY **FLOW** HAS ITS EBB

FQ, VII, vii, 20, 4: Every river still doth ebbe and flowe.

Hawes, *Past. Pleas.*, 174: After an ebbe there cometh a flowynge tyde. ¶ Harvey, *Lett. between Spenser and Harvey*, *Works*, I, 148: The sea ebbith and flowith. ¶ Greene, *Tullies Love*, *Works*, VII, 124: The lowest ebbe may haue his flow.

Cf. Apperson, 220; W. G. Smith, 211; Tilley, F378.

270 THE **FLOWER** OF CHIVALRY

Ded. Sonnets, x, 2: The flowre of chevalry, now bloosming faire. ¶ *FQ*, I, iv, 45, 8: The flowre of grace and chevalrye. ¶ *Ibid.*, viii, 26, 7: Fayre braunch of noblesse, flowre of chevalrie. ¶ *Prothalamion*, 150: Faire branch of honor, flower of chevalrie.

Cf. Stevenson, 347:1; 835:9.

271 TO FADE LIKE A **FLOWER**

Visions of P., vi, 9: She languisht as the gathered floure. ¶ *Amoretti*, lxxix, 14: All other fayre, like flowres, untymely fade.

Cf. Apperson, 201; Stevenson, 835:4; Tilley, F386.

272 THERE IS NO **FLYING** WITHOUT WINGS

FQ, III, vi, 24, 9: He clip his wanton wings, that he no more shall flye.

Culman, 26: Sine pennis volare haud facile est (It is not easy to fly without wings).

Plautus, *Poenulus*, 871: Sine pennis volare hau facilest (It is not easy to fly without wings). ¶ Erasmus, *Adagia*, 847C: Sine pennis volare haud facile est (It is difficult to fly without wings).

Cf. W. G. Smith, 212; Stevenson, 838:5; Tilley, F407; C. G. Smith, 111.

273 THE **FOE** THAT LURKS IN THE HEART IS ONE TO BE FEARED

FQ, II, ix, 42, 3–5: Other ill to feare . . . in the secret of your hart close lyes, From whence it doth, as cloud from sea, aryse.

* Publilius Syrus (1835), 303: Gravior est inimicus qui latet in pectore (The most formidable enemy lies hidden in one's own heart).

274 **FOLLY** AND WISDOM OFTEN DWELL TOGETHER

FQ, IV, ii, 9, 9: And prov'd himselfe most foole in what he seem'd most wise.

Publilius Syrus (1835), 873: Sapientiae plerumque stultitia est comes (Folly is very often the companion of wisdom).

Shakespeare, *Meas. for Meas.*, II, ii, 119: Most ignorant of what he's most assur'd.

275 HE IS A **FOOL** WHO PLANS FOR A FORTUNE BY VOWS

FQ, VI, ix, 30, 7–8: Fooles therefore They are, which fortunes doe by vowes devize.

Publilius Syrus (1934), 169: Deos ridere credo cum felix vovet (I am sure the gods must laugh when the lucky man makes his vow [for more]).

276 HE IS A **FOOL** WHO WISHES FOR THE IMPOSSIBLE

Cf. no. 172: We desire what is forbidden

Shep. Cal., Aprill, 158–159: I hold him for a greater fon, That loves the thing he cannot purchase.

Culman, 21: Impossibilia optare sibi, delirantis est (He is a fool who wishes for things impossible to himself).

Ovid, *Tristia*, iii, 8, 11–12: Stulte, quid haec frustra votis puerilibus optas, quae non ulla tibi fertque feretque dies (Fool! why pray in vain like a child for such things as these—things which no day brings you or will bring)?

Cf. Stevenson, 849:12.

277 THERE IS NOTHING SO INTOLERABLE AS A FORTUNATE **FOOL**

Shep. Cal., Maye, 140–141: Of all burdens that a man can beare, Moste is, a fooles talke to beare and to heare.

Culman, 13: Insipiente fortunato nihil intolerabilius (Nothing is more intolerable than a fortunate fool).

Cicero, *De Amicitia*, xv, 55: Nec quicquam insipiente fortunato intolerabilius fieri potest (Nor can anything in the world be more insufferable than one of fortune's fools). ¶ Fuller, 4867: There cannot be a more intolerable thing than a fortunate fool.

278 **FOOLHARDINESS** IS DANGEROUS

Cf. no. 639: Rashness provokes mischief

FQ, II, iv, 42, 9: Least thy foolhardize worke thy sad confusion.

Culman, 1: Aud aciapericulosa (Foolhardiness is dangerous).

279 **FORBEARANCE** IS NO ACQUITTANCE

FQ, IV, iii, 11, 5: To forbeare doth not forgive the det.

Seneca, *De Prov.*, iv, 7–8: Quisquis videtur dimissus esse, dilatus est (Whoever seems to have been released has only been reprieved). ¶ Greene, *Repentance of Robert G.*, *Works*, XII, 179: *Quod defertur non aufertur*, that which is deferde is not quittanst.

Cf. Henderson, 381; Apperson, 229; W. G. Smith, 219, 474; Stevenson, 864:1; Tilley, F584.

280 **FORGET** (FORGET NOT) WHAT YOU ARE

Visions of the Worlds V., xii, 12: Forget not what you be.

* Publilius Syrus (1934), 179: Etiam oblivisci quid sis interdum expedit (Sometimes it is fitting even to forget what you are).

Gower, *Conf. Aman.*, II, 21: I myself foryete, That I wot nevere what I am. ¶ Shakespeare, *Rich. II*, III, ii, 83: I had forgot myself. Am I not King?

Cf. Stevenson, 867:4.

281 THERE IS NO **FORT** SO STRONG THAT IT CANNOT BE TAKEN

FQ, I, ix, 11, 1–3: No fort can be so strong, Ne fleshly brest can armed be so sownd, But will at last be wonne with battrie long. ¶ *Ibid.*, III, x, 10, 1–2: No fort so fensible, no wals so strong, But that continuall battery will rive.

Chaucer, *Wife of Bath's Prol.*, 263–264: Thou seyst men may nat kepe a castel wal, It may so longe assailled been over al. ¶ Lydgate, *Reson & Sen.* (E.E.T.S.), 6919–6921: And castel ys ther non so stronge, The sege ther-at may be so longe That at the last yt wil be wonne. ¶ Hawes, *Past. Pleas.*, 76: No castell can be of so great a strength, Yf that there be a sure syege to it layde, It muste yelde vp or elles me be wonne at lengt. ¶ *Par. of D. Dev.*, 29: A seeged fort with forraine force, for want of ayde, must yeelde at last; cf. 59, 84, 207. ¶ Greene, *Menaphon, Works*, VI, 55: No fort so wel defenced, but strong batterie will enter.

282 **FORTUNE** DOES NOT ALWAYS LEND A READY EAR

FQ, VI, viii, 10, 1: Fortune aunswerd not unto his call.

Culman, 14: Non semper arridet fortuna (Fortune does not always smile). ¶ Publilius Syrus (1934), 457: Non semper aurem facilem habet felicitas (Good fortune does not always lend a ready ear).

Cf. C. G. Smith, 115.

283 **FORTUNE** FAVORS THE BOLD

Virgils Gnat, 301–304: God or fortune would assist his might . . . made him bold . . . To overcome. ¶ *FQ*, IV, ii, 7, 6: Fortune friends the bold.

Culman, 5: Audentes fortuna juvat (Fortune helps adventurous men). ¶ *Ibid.*, 6: Fortes fortuna adjuvat (Fortune helps resolute men).

Terence, *Phormio*, 203: Fortis fortuna adiuvat (Fortune favors the brave). ¶ Vergil, *Aeneid*, x, 284: Audentis Fortuna iuvat (Fortune aids the daring). ¶ Ovid, *Metam.*, x, 586: Audentes deus ipse iuvat (God himself helps those who dare). ¶ Erasmus, *Adagia*, 88C. ¶ Fortes fortuna adjuvat (Fortune aids the bold). ¶ Greene, *Carde of F., Works*, IV, 44: Fortune euer fauoureth them that are valiant. ¶ Greene, *Alcida, Works*, IX, 33–34: *Audaces fortuna adiuuat:* Loue and fortune fauoreth them that are resolute.

Cf. Taverner, 10; Apperson, 231; W. G. Smith, 221; Tilley, F601.

284 **FORTUNE** GIVES SECRET FAVOR

Mother Hub., 594: Fortune doth you secret favour give.

* Publilius Syrus (1934), 221: Facit gradum Fortuna quem nemo videt (Fortune takes the step that no one sees).

285 **FORTUNE** IS BLIND

FQ, III, iv, 9, 6–9: Love . . . And Fortune . . . both are bold and blinde. ¶ *Ibid.*, VI, x, 38, 7: Fortune, fraught with malice, blinde and brute.

Cf. Stevenson, 870:6; Tilley, F604.

286 **FORTUNE** IS FICKLE (CHANGEABLE)

FQ, I, iv, 50, 1–2: I feare the fickle freakes . . . Of Fortune. ¶ *Ibid.*, ix, 44, 8: Fickle Fortune. ¶ *Ibid.*, IV, iii, 17, 6–7: Long delay Of doubtfull fortune wavering to and fro. ¶ *Ibid.*, VI, i, 41, 7–8: Full of ficklenesse, Subject to fortunes chance, still chaunging new. ¶ *Virgils Gnat*, 247: Inconstant Fortune.

* Publilius Syrus (1934), 335: Levis est Fortuna: cito reposcit quod dedit (Fickle is fortune: she soon demands back what she gave).

Cato, *Disticha*, iv, 26: Tranquillis rebus semper diversa timeto (When all is calm, dread ever fortune's change). ¶ Ovid, *Tristia*, v, 8, 15–18: Passibus ambiguis Fortuna volubilis errat . . . et tantum constans in levitate sua est (Changeable fortune wanders abroad with aimless steps, steadfast only in its own fickleness). ¶ Seneca, *Medea*, 219: Rapida fortuna ac levis (Swift and fickle is fortune). ¶ Seneca, *Epist.*, xiii, 11: Habet etiam mala fortuna levitatem (Even bad fortune is fickle). ¶ Chaucer, *Knight's T.*, 1242: By some cas, syn Fortune is chaungeable. ¶ Greene, *Farewell to F.*, *Works*, IX, 321: Fortune . . . is euer fickle.

Cf. Apperson, 231; Stevenson, 876:8–9; Tilley, F606; C. G. Smith, 116.

287 **FORTUNE** IS NOT SATISFIED WITH HURTING ANYONE ONCE

FQ, VI, xi, 2, 5–7: Fortune, not with all this wrong Contented, greater mischiefe on her threw, And sorrowes heapt on her in greater throng.

Publilius Syrus (1934), 213: Fortuna obesse nulli contenta est semel (Fortune is not content with hurting anyone once).

288 **FORTUNE** MAKES MEN INSOLENT

Mother Hub., 1134–1136: But crueltie, the signe of currish kinde, And sdeignfull pride, and wilfull arrogaunce; Such followes those whom fortune doth advaunce.

Culman, 5: Fortuna reddit insolentes (Fortune makes men insolent).

Erasmus, *Adagia*, 934A: Fortuna reddit insolentes (Success leads to insolence).

289 **FORTUNE** TOSSES OFF HER WHEEL THE DESTINIES OF KINGS

FQ, VI, ix, 27, 7–9: Fortunes wrackfull yre . . . tosseth states, and under foot doth tread The mightie ones.

Publilius Syrus (1835), 847: Regum fortuna casus praecipites rotat (Fortune tosses off her wheel the destinies of kings).

Seneca, *Agamemnon*, 71–72: Praecipites regum casus Fortuna rotat (Fortune turns on her wheel the headlong fates of kings).

290 IN ALL HUMAN AFFAIRS **FORTUNE** (PROVIDENCE) RULES

Cf. no. 178: The doom of destiny cannot be avoided; no. 506: More by luck than by wit

Shep. Cal., Sept., 251: Froward fortune doth ever availe. ¶ *FQ*, I, ix, 6, 8–9: The secret meaning of th' Eternall Might, That rules mens waies, and rules the thoughts of living wight. ¶ *Ibid.*, III, iii, 31, 5–6: But at the last to th' importunity Of froward fortune shall be forst to yield.

¶ *Ibid.*, v, 27, 1: Providence hevenly passeth living thought. ¶ *Ibid.*, vii, 4, 4: Fortune all in equall launce doth sway. ¶ *Ibid.*, x, 3, 1–2: He must abie What fortune and his fate on him will lay. ¶ *Ibid.*, xii, 46, 9: Fate n'ould let her. ¶ *Ibid.*, V, iv, 27, 9: The worke of heavens will surpasseth humaine thought.

Culman, 31: Eveniunt non quae nos instituimus, sed quae Deus decrevit (Those things befall not, which we determine, but which God has decreed). ¶ Publilius Syrus (1934), 222: Fortuna plus homini quam consilium valet (Luck avails a man more than policy). ¶ *Ibid.* (1835), 999: Vitam regit fortuna, non sapientia (Fortune is mistress of life, and not wisdom).

Sophocles, *Philoctetes*, 1316–1317: *ἀνθρώποισι τὰς μὲν ἐκ θεῶν τύχας δοθείσας ἔστ' ἀναγκαῖον φέρειν* (What fates the gods allot to men they needs must bear). ¶ Euripides, *Hecuba*, 491: *τύχην δὲ πάντα τἀν βροτοῖς ἐπισκοπεῖν* (Chance controls all things among men). ¶ Demosthenes, *Olynthiac*, ii, 22: *μεγάλη γὰρ ῥοπή, μᾶλλον δ' ὅλον ἡ τύχη παρὰ πάντ' ἐστὶ τὰ τῶν ἀνθρώπων πράγματα* (For fortune is indeed a great weight in the scales; I might almost say it is everything in human affairs); cf. Plutarch, *Moralia*: *On the Fortune of the Romans*, 329–330. ¶ Plautus, *Captivi*, 304: Fortuna humana fingit artatque ut lubet (Fortune molds us, pinches us, to suit her whims). ¶ Cicero, *Tusc. Disp.*, v, 9, 25: Vitam regit fortuna, non sapientia (Fortune, not wisdom, rules the life of men). ¶ Ovid, *Ex Ponto*, iv, 3, 49: Ludit in humanis divina potentia rebus (Divine power plays with human affairs); cf. *Metam.*, viii, 619. ¶ Seneca, *Hippolytus*, 978–979: Res humanas ordine nullo Fortuna regit (Fortune without order rules the affairs of men). ¶ Seneca, *Octavia*, 924: Regitur fatis mortale genus (Our mortal race is ruled by fate). ¶ Statius, *Thebaidos*, vii, 197–198: Immoto deducimur orbe fatorum (It is fate's unchanging wheel that ordains our destiny).

Cf. C. G. Smith, 120.

291 MAN'S PLANS AND THE PLANS OF **FORTUNE** ARE EVER AT VARIANCE

FQ, VI, viii, 15, 5: But Fortune did not with his will conspire.

Publilius Syrus (1934), 253: Homo semper aliud, Fortuna aliud cogitat (Man's plans and the plans of fortune are ever at variance).

292 USE THY **FORTUNE**

FQ, II, viii, 52, 2: Use thy fortune.

Vergil, *Aeneid*, xii, 932: Utere sorte tua (Use thou thy fortune). ¶ Sidney, *Arcadia*, *Works*, I, 418: The young Knight . . . bad him use his fortune. ¶ Tasso, *Jer. Del.*, xix, 22: Usa la sorte tua (Use thy fortune).

Cf. *FQ* (Variorum), II, 277; Stevenson, 312:15.

293 WHAT **FORTUNE** HAS MADE YOURS IS NOT YOURS

Daphnaïda, 498–503: And ye, fond men, on Fortunes wheele that ride, Or in ought under heaven repose assurance, Be it riches, beautie, or honors pride, Be sure that they shall have no long endurance, But ere ye be aware will flit away; For nought of them is yours. ¶ *FQ*, V, iv, 14, 1–5: Whether it indeede be so or no, This doe I say, that what so good or ill Or God or Fortune unto me did throw, Not wronging any other by my will, I hold mine owne, and so will hold it still.

Publilius Syrus (1835), 600: Non est tuum, fortuna quod fecit tuum (That is not yours which fortune has made yours).

Seneca, *Epist.*, viii, 10: Non est tuum, fortuna quod fecit tuum (What chance has made yours is not really yours).

294 WHEN **FORTUNE** FAVORS, YOU CAN DO ALMOST ANYTHING

FQ, I, iii, 37, 8–9: And whilest him fortune favourd, fayre did thrive In bloudy field.

Publilius Syrus (1835), 192: Deo favente, naviges vel vimine (When Providence favors, you can make a safe voyage on a twig).

Plutarch, *Moralia*: *Oracles of Delphi*, 405B: θεοῦ θέλοντος, κἂν ἐπὶ ῥιπὸς πλέοις (God willing, you may voyage on a mat).

295 **FORTUNE'S** WHEEL IS EVER TURNING

FQ, V, x, 20, 7–8: Fortunes headlong wheele Begins to turne.

Shakespeare, *K. Lear*, II, ii, 180: Fortune, good night; smile once more, turn thy wheel.

Cf. Stevenson, 877:4; Tilley, F617.

296 DO NOT TRUST THE GUILE OF **FORTUNE'S** BLANDISHMENT

Colin Clouts, 668–671: I, silly man . . . Durst not . . . trust the guile of Fortunes blandishment.

Culman, 20: Fortuna prospera, dum blanditur, perdit (Prosperity undoes you while it fawns upon you). ¶ * Publilius Syrus (1934), 197: Fortuna cum blanditur captatum venit (When fortune flatters, it comes to ensnare).

297 AS WILY AS A **FOX**

Muiopotmos, 401: Like as a wily foxe.

Cf. Tilley, F629.

298 BEWARE OF **FRAUD**

Shep. Cal., Maye, 224: Sperre the yate fast, for feare of fraude. ¶ *FQ*, I, iv, 1, 3: Beware of fraud. ¶ *Ibid.*, IV, x, 43, 5: Some fearing fraud.

Culman, 1: Dolum time (Fear cozenage).

299 AS **FRESH** AS A DAY IN SUMMER

FQ, I, xii, 7, 7: As fayre Diana, in fresh sommers day. ¶ *Ibid.*, VI, iii, 13, 8: Calidore, rising up as fresh as day. ¶ *Prothalamion*, 70: So fresh they seem'd as day.

Chaucer, *Merchant's T.*, 1896: As fressh as is the brighte someres day.

Cf. Stevenson, 889:5.

300 AS **FRESH** AS A FLOWER IN MAY

FQ, I, xii, 22, 1: So faire and fresh, as freshest flowre in May. ¶ *Ibid.*, IV, x, 37, 9: Flowres, as fresh as May. ¶ *Colin Clouts*, 106: Fresh as floure of May.

Chaucer, *Rom. Rose*, 2277: Floures as fresh as May. ¶ Warner, *Alb.*

Eng., XXXI, 4: As fresh as flowers in May. ¶ Deloney, *Gentle Craft, Works*, 187: As fresh as flowers in May.

Cf. Apperson, 235; Stevenson, 889:4; Tilley, F389.

301 AS **FRESH** AS A ROSE

FQ, II, ix, 36, 7: Faire and fresh as morning rose. ¶ *Ibid.*, IV, iii, 51, 7: As fresh as morning rose.

Chaucer, *Wife of Bath's Prol.*, 448: As fresh as is a rose. ¶ Lydgate, *Troy Book*, V, 2897: With swetenes freshe as any rose. ¶ *Cov. Myst.* (Sh. S.), 154: Fayr and fresche, as rose on thorn. ¶ *Roxb. Ballads* (B.S.), VI, 166: Cheeks as fresh as rose in June.

Cf. Apperson, 235; W. G. Smith, 225; Stevenson, 889: 6; Tilley, R176.

302 A **FRIEND** SHOULD BEAR A FRIEND'S INFIRMITIES

FQ, II, i, 28, 9: Your court'sie takes on you anothers dew offence.

Publilius Syrus (1934), 522; Peccatum amici veluti tuum recte putes (You would do right to consider your friend's fault as if it were your own).

Plautus, *Captivi*, 151: Laudo, malum cum amici tuom ducis malum (I appreciate this, that you consider your friend's disaster your own).

Cf. C. G. Smith, 123.

303 A FALSE **FRIEND** IS A DANGEROUS ENEMY

FQ, IV, ii, 18, 8–9: So mortall was their malice and so sore Become of fayned friendship which they vow'd afore. ¶ *Ibid.*, iv, 1, 3: Friends profest are chaungd to foemen fell. ¶ *Ibid.*, ix, 27, 8–9: But sooth is said, and tride in each degree, Faint friends when they fall out most cruell fomen bee.

Publilius Syrus (1835), 907: Simulans amicum inimicus inimicissimus (A false friend is the most dangerous of enemies).

Kendall, *Flowres of Epigr.* (Sp. S.), XV, 139: Moste sure a wretched foe is he, whiche frendship firme doeth faine: And sekes by all the shifts he can, his frende to put to paine.

304 BETTER A NEW **FRIEND** THAN AN OLD FOE

FQ, I, ii, 27, 4: Better new friend then an old foe is said.

Bodenham, *Belvedere* (Sp. S.), 94: Better a new friend than an old foe. Cf. Apperson, 41; Tilley, F686.

305 THE LOSS OF A **FRIEND** IS THE GREATEST OF LOSSES

FQ, III, i, 25, 5–6: All losse is lesse, and lesse the infamy, Then losse of love to him that loves but one.

Publilius Syrus (1835), 37: Amicum perdere, est damnorum maximum (The loss of a friend is the greatest of losses).

306 **FRIENDS** HAVE BUT ONE SOUL

FQ, II, iv, 19, 8: Love, that two harts makes one, makes eke one will. ¶ *Ibid.*, IV, ii, 28, 5–6: Each to other did his faith engage, Like faithfull friends thenceforth to joyne in one. ¶ *Ibid.*, 43, 1–3: These three did love each other dearely well, And with so firme affection were allyde, As if but one soule in them all did dwell.

Erasmus, *Adagia*, 14F: Amicus alter ipse (A friend is a second self). ¶ Edwards, *Damon and P.*, 637: Ah my Damon, another myself. ¶ Sidney, *To Hubert Languet*, *Works*, III, 92: *Cum amico id est se ipso.* ¶ Pettie, *Petite P.*, 117–118: Of al greifes it is most gripyng when freindes are forced to parte eche from other, . . . when ownes selfe is separated from him selfe, or at least his seconde selfe. ¶ Greene, *Mamillia*, *Works*, II, 15: They were two bodyes and one soule. ¶ Lodge, *Rosalynde*, *Works*, I, 31: Custome had wrought an vnion of our nature, and the sympathie of our affections such a secrete loue, that we haue two bodies, and one soule. ¶ Shakespeare, *Sonnets*, xlii, 13: But here's the joy—my friend and I are one.

Cf. Tilley, F696; Charles G. Smith, *Spenser's Theory of Friendship*, 37–46; W. G. Smith, 227.

307 AMONG **FRIENDS** ALL THINGS ARE COMMON

FQ, IV, ii, 13, 3–5: Well know'st thou, when we friendship first did sweare, The covenant was, that every spoyle or pray Should equally be shard betwixt us tway.

Publilius Syrus (1835), 1051: Minime amicus sum, fortunae particeps nisi tuae (I am not your friend unless I share in your fortunes).

Plato, *Republic*, iv, 424A: παροιμίαν πάντα ὅ τι μάλιστα κοινὰ τὰ φίλων ποιεῖσθαι (The proverbial goods of friends that are common); cf. *Phaedrus*, 279C; Euripides, *Andromache*, 376–377; *Orestes*, 725. ¶ Aristotle, *Politics*, ii, 2, 4: κατὰ τὴν παροιμίαν κοινὰ τὰ φίλων (Friends' goods common goods, as the proverb says); cf. *N. Ethics*, viii, 9, 1. ¶ Terence, *Adelphoe*, 803–804: Vetus verbum hoc quidemst, communia esse amicorum inter se omnia (It's an old saying that friends have all things in common). ¶ Cicero, *De Offic.*, i, 16, 51: In Graecorum proverbio est, amicorum esse communia omnia (In the light indicated by the Greek proverb: "Amongst friends all things in common"). ¶ Seneca, *De Benef.*, vii, 12, 5: Quidquid habet amicus, commune est nobis (Whatever our friend possesses is common to us). ¶ Erasmus, *Adagia*, 13F: Amicorum communia omnia (Among friends all things are common). ¶ Painter, *Palace of P.*, II, 104: For frendship sake . . . Their goodes were common betwene them.

Cf. Taverner, 65; Bacon, *Promus*, 984; Stevenson, 903:1–4; Tilley, F729; C. G. Smith, 125.

308 HELP YOUR **FRIENDS**

FQ, I, i, 38, 5: To aide his friendes. ¶ *Ibid.*, viii, 21, 2: To ayde his frend.

Culman, 1: Amicis opitulare (Help thy friends).

Lucilius, *Sat.*, Frag., 1187: Prodes Amicis (Help your friends).

309 FALSE **FRIENDSHIP** (LOVE) CANNOT LAST

FQ, I, x, 62, 9: Loose loves, they'are vaine, and vanish into nought. ¶ *Ibid.*, IV, i, 35, 4: For light . . . love, . . . soone is lost. ¶ *Ibid.*, ii, 29, 6–8: Ne certes can that friendship long endure, How ever gay and goodly be the style, That doth ill cause or evill end enure. ¶ *Ibid.*, iv, 1,

8–9: Friendship, which a faint affection breeds Without regard of good, dyes like ill grounded seeds.

Edwards, *Damon and P.*, 326–327: But such as for profit in friendship do link, When storms come they slide away sooner than a man will think. ¶ Greene, *Royal Exch.*, *Works*, VII, 243: The difference betweene true and fained freendship, the one beeing momentarie, depending on the fauour of Fortune, the other perpetual.

Cf. Charles G. Smith, *Spenser's Theory of Friendship*, 46–49.

310 TRUE **FRIENDSHIP** (LOVE) IS BASED ON SIMILARITY

Cf. no. 466: Like will to like

FQ, III, xi, 33, 6–7: Faire Alcmena better match did make, Joying his love in likenes more entire. ¶ *Ibid.*, IV, i, 32, 7: Two companions of like qualitie. ¶ *Ibid.*, viii, 55, 9: For never two [friends] so like did living creature see. ¶ *Hymne in Honour of B.*, 197–198: Love is a celestiall harmonie Of likely harts.

Elyot, *Governour*, II, xi, Everyman ed., 162: Amitie . . . requireth . . . semblable or muche like maners. ¶ Taverner, 8: Likenes of maners, egaltie of age, similitude in all thinges wonderfullie knitteth persons together and gendreth frenship. ¶ Edwards, *Damon and P.*, 102: They say Morum similitudo consuit amicitias. ¶ Lyly, *Euph. Anat. of Wit*, *Works*, I, 235: Friendshippe betweene man and man . . . proceedeth of the similitude of maners. ¶ Sidney, *Arcadia*, *Works*, I, 524: Likeness is a great cause of liking.

Cf. Aristotle, *N. Ethics*, viii, 3, 6; Plutarch, *Moralia: How to Tell a Flatterer*, 51D; Erasmus, *Apophthegmata*, 198F; Charles G. Smith, *Spenser's Theory of Friendship*, 33–37.

311 TRUE **FRIENDSHIP** (LOVE) IS BASED ON VIRTUE

FQ, IV, ii, 29, 9: Vertue is the band that bindeth harts most sure. ¶ *Ibid.*, vi, 46, 8–9: For vertues onely sake, which doth beget True love and faithfull friendship, she by her did set.

Aristotle, *N. Ethics*, viii, 3, 6: *Τελεία δ' ἐστὶν ἡ τῶν ἀγαθῶν φιλία καὶ κατ' ἀρετὴν ὁμοίων* (The perfect form of friendship is that between the good, and those who resemble each other in virtue. ¶ Cicero, *De Amicitia*, v, 18: Nisi in bonis amicitiam esse non posse (Friendship cannot exist except among good men). ¶ *Ibid.*, vi, 20–21: Virtus amicitiam et gignit et continet, nec sine virtute amicitia esse ullo pacto potest (Virtue is the parent and preserver of friendship and without virtue friendship cannot exist at all). ¶ *Ibid.*, xiv, 50: Bonis inter bonos quasi necessariam benevolentiam, qui est amicitiae fons a natura constitutus (The good have for the good, as if from necessity, a kindly feeling which nature has made the fountain of friendship). ¶ Elyot, *Governour*, II, xi, Everyman ed., 162: Frendshippe can nat be but in good men, ne may nat be without vertue. ¶ Edwards, *Damon and P.*, 127–128: But true friendship, indeed, Of nought but of virtue doth truly proceed. ¶ Pettie, *Petite P.*, 235: True freindship . . . is grounded only on that which is good and honest. ¶ Greene, *Morando*, *Works*, III, 60: Perfect loue euer springeth from vertue and honestie. ¶ *Ibid.*, 152: The opinion of vertue is the fountaine of Friendship. ¶ Sidney, *Arcadia*, *Works*, II, 197: That sweete and heavenly uniting of the mindes, which properly is called love, hath no other knot but vertue; cf. *ibid.*, II, 193; IV, 374. ¶ Jonson, *The Underwood*, XLV, 12, *Works*, VIII, 216: 'Tis vertue alone, or nothing, that knits friends.

Cf. Charles G. Smith, *Spenser's Theory of Friendship*, 27–30; Tilley, V84.

312 TRUE **FRIENDSHIP** (LOVE) IS ETERNAL

Astrophel, 179–180: Death their hearts cannot divide, Which living were in love so firmly tide. ¶ *Daphnaïda*, 291: So shall our love for ever last. ¶ *Amoretti*, vi, 9–10: So hard it is to kindle new desire [love] In gentle brest, that shall endure for ever. ¶ *FQ*, IV, vi, 31, 6–9: Love . . . is the crowne of knighthood, and the band Of noble minds derived from above, Which being knit with vertue, never will remove. ¶ *Ibid.*, x, 27, 7–9: All that ever had bene tyde In bands of friendship, there did live for ever; Whose . . . loves decayed never.

Publilius Syrus (1835), 734: Quae desiit amicitia, ne coepit quidem (The friendship that can come to an end, never really began).

Aristotle, *N. Ethics*, ix, i, 3: *ἡ* [friendship] *δὲ τῶν ἠθῶν καθ' αὑτὴν οὖσα μένει* (Friendship based on character is disinterested, and therefore lasting). ¶ Cicero, *De Amicitia*, ix, 32: Verae amicitiae sempiternae sunt (Real friendships are eternal). ¶ Edwards, *Damon and P.*, 1638: Other precious things do fade; friendship will never decay. ¶ Sidney, *Arcadia*, *Works*, I, 50: Love; which no likenes can make one, no commaundement dissolve, no foulnes defile, nor no death finish. ¶ Greene, *Royal Exch.*, *Works*, VII, 243: The difference betweene true and fained freendship, the one beeing momentarie, depending on the fauour of Fortune, the other perpetual, which stretcheth *vsque ad Aras*. ¶ Harvey, *Trimming of Thomas Nashe*, *Works*, III, 46: True Frends . . . death it selfe could neuer seperate.

Cf. Tilley, L539; C. G. Smith, 131.

313 TO **FROWN** LIKE GOOD FRIDAY

Shep. Cal., Feb., 30: So semest thou like Good Fryday to frowne.

Greene, *Groatsworth of Wit*, *Works*, XII, 120: The Foxe made a Friday face, counterfeiting sorrow. ¶ Day, *Blind Beggar of Bednal Green* (1659), III: Friday-faced, as a term of reproach. ¶ Robertson, *Phraseol. Gen.* (1693), 1092: What makes you look so sad, and moodily? with such a Friday face.

Cf. Spenser, *Minor Poems* (Variorum), I, 256.

314 OUT OF THE **FRYING-PAN** INTO THE FIRE

Cf. no. 264: To flee from the fire and to fall into the water

View, 659: This then were but to leape out of the pann into the fire.

Cf. Apperson, 240; W. G. Smith, 230; Stevenson, 814:1; Tilley, F784.

315 TO ADD **FUEL** TO THE FIRE

FQ, II, v, 8, 4: Added flame unto his former fire. ¶ *Ibid.*, IV, vi, 11, 2: New matter added to his former fire.

Plato, *Laws*, ii, 666: *οὐ χρὴ πῦρ ἐπὶ πῦρ ὀχετεύειν* (It is wrong to pour fire upon fire). ¶ Livy, *Hist.*, xxi, 10, 4: Velut materiam igni praebentes (As though adding fuel to the fire). ¶ Horace, *Sat.*, ii, 3, 321: Oleum adde camino (Throw oil on the fire). ¶ Warner, *Alb. Eng.*, LIX, 27: All adding fewel to the fire. ¶ Sidney, *Arcadia*, *Works*, I, 442: Her eyes give to my flames their fuell. ¶ Milton, *Samson*, 1351: By adding fuel to the flame.

Cf. Stevenson, 807: 1.

316 ONE MAN'S **GAIN** IS ANOTHER MAN'S LOSS

FQ, I, v, 25, 9: To make one great by others losse is bad excheat. ¶ *Ibid.*, V, xii, 32, 8–9: In anothers losse . . . she had got thereby, and gayned a great stake.

Culman, 17: Alterius salus, alterius est exitium (One man's welfare is another man's ruin). ¶ * Publilius Syrus (1934), 337: Lucrum sine damno alterius fieri non potest (Gain cannot be made without another's loss).

Cicero, *De Fin.*, iii, 21, 70: Fatentur alienum esse a iustitia . . . detrahere quid de aliquo quod sibi assumat (To enrich oneself by another's loss is an action repugnant to justice). ¶ Seneca, *De Ira*, ii, 8, 2: Nulli nisi ex alterius iniuria quaestus est (No one makes gain save by another's loss). ¶ More, *Utopia*, tr. Robinson (Arber), 69: The healpe of one causeth anothers harme: forasmuche as nothinge can be geuen to annye one, onles it be taken from an other. ¶ Pettie, *Petite P.*, 163: Can one be exalted without anothers wracke? Can I be preferred to pleasure without some others paine?

Cf. Tilley, M337; C. G. Smith, 132.

317 EVERY **GARDEN** HAS ITS WEEDS

FQ, III, i, 49, 6: Emongst the roses grow some wicked weeds.

Chaucer, *Troilus*, I, 946–949: For thilke grownd that bereth the wedes wikke Bereth ek thise holsom herbes, as ful ofte Next the foule netle, rough and thikke, The rose waxeth swoote. ¶ Barclay, *Ship of F.*, II, 41: Amonge swete herbys oft growyth stynkynge wedes. ¶ Gascoigne, *Glasse of Govt.*, III, vi, *Works*, II, 59: Even as weedes, which fast by flowres do growe. ¶ Harvey, *Pierces Super.*, *Works*, II, 288: What garden of flowers without weedes? ¶ Shakespeare, *Lucrece*, 870: Unwholesome weeds take root with precious flow'rs. ¶ Cawdray, *Treasurie or Store-House of Similies* (1600), 660: No Garden without weedes.

Cf. Stevenson, 936:3; Tilley, G37.

318 **GENTLE** IS THAT GENTLE DOES

FQ, VI, iii, 1, 2: The gentle minde by gentle deeds is knowne. ¶ *Ibid.*, vii, 1, 1–2: Like as the gentle hart it selfe bewrayes In doing gentle deedes with franke delight.

Chaucer, *Wife of Bath's T.*, 1170: He is gentil that dooth gentil dedis.

Cf. Apperson, 244; W. G. Smith, 235.

319 AS **GENTLE** AS A FALCON

FQ, V, v, 15, 2: A gentle faulcon.

Cf. Apperson, 243; Tilley, F35.

320 **GENTLENESS** WINS FRIENDS

Astrophel, 20–22: With gentle usage and demeanure myld, . . . all mens hearts . . . He stole away. ¶ *FQ*, VI, i, 2, 3–6: In whom it seemes that gentlenesse of spright And manners mylde were planted naturall; To which he adding comely guize withall, And gracious speach, did steale mens hearts away.

Culman, 5: Comitas amicos parit (Gentleness gets friends). ¶ *Ibid.*, 8: Obsequium amicos parit (Smooth carriage gets friends).

Terence, *Andria*, 67–68: Obsequium amicos . . . parit (Complaisance makes friends).

321 **GIFTS** CAN PERSUADE EVEN THE GODS

FQ, V, v, 49, 3–4: Gifts of great availe, With which the gods themselves are mylder made.

Hesiod, *Frag.*, 6: δῶρα θεοὺς πείθει (Gifts move the gods); cf. Plato, *Republic*, iii, 390E: Euripides, *Medea*, 964. ¶ Ovid, *Artis Amat.*, iii, 653–654: Munera . . . capiunt hominesque deosque: Placatur donis Iuppiter ipse datis (Bribes, believe me, buy both gods and men; Jupiter himself is appeased by the offering of gifts). ¶ Erasmus, *Adagia*, 120A: Muneribus vel Dii capiuntur (By gifts even the gods are taken captive). ¶ Pettie, *Petite P.*, 150–151: The Goddes them selves are pleased with gifts.

Cf. Stevenson, 951:9.

322 **GIFTS** OFTEN CATCH MEN

FQ, V, xi, 50, 4–6: With golden giftes . . . Entyced her, to him for to accord. O who may not with gifts . . . be tempted?

Culman, 7: Munera capiunt homines (Gifts do catch men).

Ovid, *Artis Amat.*, iii, 653: Munera . . . capiunt hominesque deosque (Bribes buy both gods and men).

Cf. C. G. Smith, 135.

323 A COVETOUS KING IS PACIFIED WITH **GIFTS** (GOLD)

FQ, III, iii, 39, 9: But shall with guifts his lord Cadwallin pacify.

Culman, 10: Auro placatur rex avarus (A covetous king is pacified with gold).

Plato, *Republic*, iii, 390E: δῶρα θεοὺς πείθει, δῶρ' αἰδοίους βασιλῆας (Gifts move the gods and gifts persuade dread kings).

Cf. Stevenson, 951:9.

324 IT IS BETTER TO **GIVE** THAN TO TAKE (RECEIVE)

Shep. Cal., Aprill, Glosse, 161–163: Men first ought to be gracious and bountiful to other freely, then to receive benefits at other mens hands. ¶ *FQ*, VI, x, 24, 9: Good should from us goe, then come, in greater store.

Publilius Syrus (1835), 706: Praestare cuncta pulchrum est, exigere nihil (To give everything and not demand anything in return, that is beautiful).

New Testament: *Acts*, xx, 35: Μακάριόν ἐστιν μᾶλλον διδόναι ἢ λαμβάνειν (It is more blessed to give than to receive). ¶ Gower, *Conf. Aman.*, V, 7725: Betre is to yive than to take.

Cf. W. G. Smith, 40; Tilley, G119; C. G. Smith, 136.

325 ONE WHO **GIVES** ALL POSSESSES ALL

FQ, IV, i, 6, 5: All is his justly, that all freely dealth.

Publilius Syrus (1934), 541: Probo beneficium qui dat ex parte accipit (The giver of a benefit to the good is in part the receiver). ¶ *Ibid.*, 582: Quicquid bono concedas, des partem tibi (Give to the good and a share returns to yourself).

Seneca, *De Benef.*, vi, 3, 1: Hoc habeo, quodcumque dedi (Whatever I have given, that I still possess). ¶ Chaucer, *Rom. Rose*, 1159–1160: The more she yaf awey The more, ywys, she hadde alwey.

Cf. Tilley, G128; C. G. Smith, 134.

326 **GOD** FEEDS HIS OWN

Mother Hub., 433–437: To feede mens soules . . . is not in man: . . . But God it is that feedes them with his grace.

Culman, 31: Deus pascit ac servat nos ultra nostram curam (God feeds and preserves us beyond our care). ¶ *Ibid.*, 35: Pascit Deus suos certissime (God is most sure to feed his own).

327 **GOD** HAS A CARE FOR US

Mother Hub., 1195–1196: Let God . . . care for the manie, I for my selfe must care before els anie.

Culman, 30: Cura omnis Deo committenda (All care is to be committed to God). ¶ *Ibid.*: Deus curam nostri habet (God has a care for us).

328 **GOD** (HEAVEN) IS THE SOURCE OF ALL GOOD THINGS

Visions of B., i, 8: Heaven, whence all good gifts do come. ¶ *Hymne of Heavenly L.*, 99–100: That Eternall Fount of love and grace, Still flowing forth his goodnesse unto all.

Culman, 30: Deus fons omnium bonorum (God is the fountain of all good things).

New Testament: *James*, i, 17: πᾶσα δόσις αγαθὴ καὶ πᾶν δώρημα τέλειον ἄνωθέν (Every good gift and every perfect gift is from above).

Cf. Stevenson, 951:11.

329 **GOD** SEES AND HEARS EVERYTHING

Astrophel, 181: Gods . . . all things see. ¶ *Hymne of Heavenly B.*, 172–173: To God all mortall actions here, And even the thoughts of men, do plaine appeare.

Culman, 31: Deus videt et audit omnia (God sees and hears all things).

Pindar, *Olympian Odes*, i, 64: εἰ δὲ θεὸν ἀνήρ τις ἔλπεταί τι λαθέμεν, ἔρδων, ἁμαρτάνει (But, if any man hopes, in whatever he does, to escape the eye of God, he is grievously wrong). ¶ Plautus, *Captivi*, 313: Est profecto deus, qui quae nos gerimus auditque et videt (There is indeed a God who hears and sees what we do).

Cf. Stevenson, 975:2.

330 NOTHING IS HIDDEN FROM **GOD**

FQ, V, vii, 21, 6: Can from th' immortall gods ought hidden bee?

Culman, 30: Deò nihil est occultum (Nothing is hidden from God). ¶ *Ibid.*, 31: Deum humana astutia nihil celare potest (Man's cunning can hide nothing from God).

331 OBEY **GOD** RATHER THAN MEN

FQ, V, ii, 40, 9: All creatures must obey the voice of the Most Hie.

Culman, 30: Deo omnia parent (All things obey God). ¶ *Ibid.*, 31:

Deo plus obediendum, quam hominibus (We must obey God rather than men).

New Testament: *Acts*, v, 29: Πειθαρχεῖν δεῖ θεῷ μᾶλλον ἢ ἀνθρώποις (We ought to obey God rather than men).

Cf. Stevenson, 1708:3.

332 THE WORKS AND COUNSELS OF **GOD** ARE INSCRUTABLE

Cf. no. 333: What God gives to all it is granted to few to comprehend

FQ, V, ii, 42, 5–7: In vaine . . . doest thou now take in hand, To call to count, or weigh His [God's] workes anew, Whose counsels depth thou canst not understand.

Culman, 31: Dei consilia nobis abscondita (God's counsels are hidden from us). ¶ *Ibid.*: Dei opera & consilia inscrutabilia (The works and counsels of God are inscrutable).

Pindar, *Dithyrambs*: *Frag.*, 61: οὐ γὰρ ἔσθ' ὅπως τὰ θεῶν βουλεύματ' ἐρευνάσει βροτέᾳ φρενί (For man is not able with his human mind to search out the counsels of the gods). ¶ Chaucer, *Miller's T.*, 3453–3454: I thoghte ay wel how that it sholde be! Men sholde nat knowe of Goddes pryvetee.

Cf. Stevenson, 975:1.

333 WHAT **GOD** GIVES TO ALL IT IS GRANTED TO FEW TO COMPREHEND

Cf. no. 332: The works and counsels of God are inscrutable

FQ, I, ix, 6, 6–9: "Full hard it is," quoth he, "to read aright The course of heavenly cause, or understand The secret meaning of th' Eternall Might, That rules mens waies, and rules the thoughts of living wight."

Publilius Syrus (1934), 528: Paucorum est intellegere quid donet deus (It is granted to few to comprehend what God gives to all).

334 WITH **GOD** THERE IS NO RESPECT OF PERSONS

FQ, V, Prol., 10, 2–4: God in his imperiall might . . . both to good and bad . . . dealeth right.

Culman, 31: Deus non respicit personas (God does not respect persons). ¶ *Ibid.*, 35: Personarum acceptio non est apud Deum (There is no respect of persons with God).

New Testament: *Romans*, ii, 11: οὐ γάρ ἐστιν προσωποληµψία παρὰ τῷ θεῷ (For there is no respect of persons with God). ¶ *Ibid.*, *Acts.*, x, 34: οὐκ ἔστιν προσωπολήµπτης ὁ θεός (God is no respecter of persons).

Cf. Stevenson, 970:6.

335 WE CAN DO NOTHING WITHOUT **GOD'S** HELP

Cf. no. 582: Trusting in ourselves alone, we can do nothing

FQ, I, x, 1, 6–9: Ne let the man ascribe it to his skill, That thorough grace hath gained victory. If any strength we have, it is to ill, But all the good is Gods, both power and eke will.

Culman, 27: Sine ope divina nihil valemus (We can do nothing without God's help). ¶ *Ibid.*, 28: Absque Deo nihil possumus (We can do nothing without God).

336 ALL IS NOT **GOLD** THAT GLITTERS

FQ, II, viii, 14, 5: Yet gold al is not, that doth golden seeme.

Lydgate, *Fall of P.*, IV, 2944: Al is nat gold that shyneth briht. ¶ Wager, *Enough is as Good as a Feast*, sig. D ii: It is an olde prouerbe and of an ancient time: Which saith, it is not all Golde, that like Golde dooth shine. ¶ Gascoigne, *Grief of Joye*, *Works*, II, 524: All is not golde, which glistereth faire and bright. ¶ Harvey, *Lett. between Spenser and Harvey*, *Works*, I, 47: All is not gould that glistereth. ¶ Greene, *Mamillia*, *Works*, II, 26: Al is not gold that glysters. ¶ Nashe, *Unfor. Trav.*, *Works*, II, 234: All is not gold that glisters.

Cf. Henderson, 278; Apperson, 6; Taylor, 138; W. G. Smith, 249; Stevenson, 990:13; Tilley, A146.

337 AS YELLOW (SHINING) AS **GOLD**

Ruines of T., 10: Her yeolow locks, like wyrie golde. ¶ *Virgils Gnat*, 260–261: His creste . . . did shine like scalie golde. ¶ *Visions of the Worlds*

V., vi, 3: Shields of brasse, that shone like burnisht golde. ¶ *Visions of B.*, xii, 3: Yeallow, like the golden grayle. ¶ *FQ*, II, iii, 30, 1: Her yellow lockes, crisped like golden wyre. ¶ *Ibid.*, IV, vi, 20, 7: It did glister like the golden sand. ¶ *Ibid.*, V, ix, 28, 6–7: Bright sunny beams, Glistring like gold. ¶ *Epithalamion*, 154: Her long loose yellow locks lyke golden wyre.

Chaucer, *Knight's T.*, 2141: Yelewe and brighte as any gold.

Cf. Apperson, 717; Tilley, G280.

338 **GOOD** FOR NOTHING

FQ, II, ix, 32, 2: Not good . . . for ought. ¶ *Ibid.*, IV, ii, 3, 5: Not good for ought.

Cf. Tilley, N258.

339 A **GOOD** MAN NEVER COQUETS WITH INIQUITY

Mother Hub., 232: Gay without good is good hearts greatest loathing. ¶ *Amoretti*, liii, 12: Good shames to be to ill an instrument.

* Publilius Syrus (1934), 70: Bonus animus numquam erranti obsequium commodat (Good judgment never humors one who is going wrong).

340 DO NOT CEASE FROM DOING **GOOD** TO MORTALS

FQ, III, v, 10, 9: Do one or other good, I you most humbly pray.

Culman, 33: Laborandum est ut proximo prosimus (We must labor to do good to our neighbor).

Plutarch, *Moralia*: *Old Men in Public Affairs*, 791D: μή τι πανσώμεσθα δρῶντες εὖ βροτούς (Let us ne'er cease from doing good to mortals).

Cf. Stevenson, 996:5.

341 OUT OF ALL EVIL SOME **GOOD** COMES

FQ, I, viii, 43, 6: Good growes of evils priefe.

Publilius Syrus (1835), 619: Nullum sine auctoramento est magnum malum (There is no great evil which does not bring with it some advantage).

Cf. Stevenson, 1005:6; Tilley, N328; C. G. Smith, 84.

342 THE **GOOD** MAN IS THE HAPPY MAN

FQ, I, i, 35, 4: The noblest mind the best contentment has.

Publilius Syrus (1835), 503: Miser dici bonus vir, esse non potest (The good man can be called miserable, but he is not so).

Cicero, *In Pisonem*, 42: Non posset esse umquam vir bonus non beatus (The good man can never be otherwise than happy); cf. *De Fin.*, iii, 22, 76. ¶ Seneca, *De Prov.*, iii, 1: Persuadebo deinde tibi, ne umquam boni viri miserearis; potest enim miser dici, non potest esse (I shall induce you, in fine, never to commiserate a good man. For he can be called miserable, but he cannot be so).

343 TO KNOW ONE'S OWN **GOOD**

FQ, I, x, 7, 5: And knew his good to all of each degree. ¶ *Ibid.*, VI, ii, 1, 6–7: Ought they well to know Their good.

Cf. Tilley, G321.

344 WHAT IS **GOOD** IS DIFFICULT

Cf. no. 363: Things hard to come by are much set by

Amoretti, li, 7–8: Sith never ought was excellent assayde, Which was not hard t' atchive and bring to end.

Culman, 23: Optima quaeque difficiles habent exitus (All the best things have difficult ends).

Plato, *Republic*, iv, 435C: τὸ λεγόμενον ἀληθές, ὅτι χαλεπὰ τὰ καλά (Th saying is true that fine things are difficult); cf. *Republic*, vi, 497D; *Hippias Major*, 304E. ¶ Cicero, *Tusc. Disp.*, iii. 34, 84: Quid autem praeclarum non idem arduum (But what noble undertaking is not also hard?). ¶ Ovid, *Artis Amat.*, ii, 537: Nulla, nisi ardua, virtus (What is meritorious must needs be difficult). ¶ Plutarch, *Moralia*: *Ed. of Children*, 6C: κατὰ τὴν παροιμίαν "χαλεπὰ τὰ καλά" (According to the proverb, "Good things are hard"). ¶ Erasmus, *Adagia*, 410C: Difficilia quae pulchra (Things that are excellent are difficult); cf. *Enchiridion*, 16B; *Institutio Principis Christiani*, 580C; *Colloquia Fam.*, 696F. ¶ Shakespeare, *Lucrece*, 334: Pain pays the income of each precious thing.

Cf. Taverner, 28; W. G. Smith, 256; Stevenson, 172:7; Tilley, T181.

345 **GOODS** ARE THEIRS THAT ENJOY THEM

Shep. Cal., Maye, 71: Good is no good, but if it be spend.

Cf. Apperson, 265; W. G. Smith, 259; Tilley, G302.

346 THE **GRACE** OF GOD IS GEAR ENOUGH

FQ, I, x, 38, 6–8: The grace of God he layd up still in store . . . He had enough.

Cf. Tilley, G393.

347 THE **GREAT** ONES EAT UP THE LITTLE ONES

Cf. no. 517: The many overpower the few

FQ, V, ix, 1, 6: The stronger doth the weake devoure.

Barclay, *Cast. of Labour*, sig. E 2: Euery daye well mayst thou se That the grete doth ete the small. ¶ Stubbes, *Anatomie of Abuses* (N. S. S.), I, 117: Rich men eat vp poore men, as beasts doo eat grasse. ¶ Shakespeare, *Pericles*, II, i, 31–32: The great ones eat up the little ones.

Cf. Henderson, 328; Stevenson, 1034:5; Tilley, R102.

348 AS **GREEN** AS A GOURD (GRASS, LEEK)

Virgils Gnat, 164: As greene as any goord.

Cf. Apperson, 273; Stevenson, 1039:10; Tilley, G412, L176.

349 PENT UP **GRIEF** WILL BURST THE HEART

Cf. no. 549: Misery without a voice is a hell; no. 761: By telling our woes we often lessen them

Shep. Cal., Sept., 15–16: Sorrow close shrouded in hart, I know, to kepe is a burdenous smart. ¶ *FQ*, I, ii, 34, 5: Double griefs afflict concealing harts.

Publilius Syrus (1835), 671: Pejora querulo cogitat mutus dolor (Mute grief feels a keener pang than that which cries aloud).

Ovid, *Tristia*. v, 1, 63: Strangulat inclusus dolor atque exaestuat intus (A suppressed sorrow chokes and seethes within). ¶ Greene, *Never Too Late*, *Works*, VIII, 103: In the Aphorismes of Philosophers . . . passions concealed, procure the deeper sorrowes. ¶ Greene, *Vision*, *Works*, XII, 211: Greefes smoothered, if they burst not out will make the heart to breake.

Cf. Tilley, G449; C. G. Smith, 144, 227.

350 WORDS FITLY SPOKEN EASE **GRIEF** (SORROW)

FQ, I, x, 24, 1–9: Comming to that sowle-diseased knight . . . his grief . . . knowne . . . he gan apply relief . . . And there to added wordes of wondrous might: By which to ease he him recured brief, And much aswag'd the passion of his plight, That he his paine endur'd, as seeming now more light.

Culman, 9: Sermo medetur tristitiae (Talking with anyone cures sorrow). ¶ *Ibid.*, 24: Placidis dictis dolor recte curabitur (Grief will be well eased with sweet words).

Shakespeare, *Lucrece*, 1330: Sorrow ebbs, being blown with wind of words. ¶ Shakespeare, *L. Lab.*, *Lost*, V, ii, 762: Honest plain words best pierce the ear of grief.

351 GREAT **GRIEFS** ARE SILENT

FQ, I, vii, 41, 1–2: Great griefe will not be tould, And can more easily be thought then said. ¶ *Ibid.*, 51, 9: This is my cause of griefe, more great then may be told.

Seneca, *Hippolytus*, 607: Curae leves locuntur, ingentes stupent (Light troubles speak; the weighty are struck dumb).

Cf. W. G. Smith, 598; Stevenson, 1041:9; Tilley, S664.

352 THE **GUILER** HIMSELF SHALL BE BEGUILED

Cf. no. 88: Caught in one's own trap

FQ, II, v, 34, 8: He them deceives, deceivd in his deceipt. ¶ *Ibid.*, vii, 64, 9: So goodly did beguile the guyler of his pray. ¶ *Ibid.*, IV, i, 36, 5–6; Him selfe he did of his new love deceave, And made him selfe thensample of his follie. ¶ *Ibid.*, V, ix, 19, 7: So did deceipt the selfe deceiver fayle.

Chaucer, *Reeve's T.*, 4321: A gylour shal hymself bigyled be. ¶ Gower, *Conf. Aman.*, VI, 1379–1381: Often he that wol beguile Is guiled with the same guile, And thus the guilour is beguiled. ¶ Painter, *Palace of P.*, I, 229: The deceiuour shalbe begiled. ¶ Greene, *Conny-Catching*, *Works*, X, 101: *Fallere fallentem non est fraus*, euery deceipt hath his due.

Cf. Tilley, D179.

353 HE IS A RASCAL WHO THROWS HIS OWN **GUILT** UPON ANOTHER

FQ, V, i, 15, 8–9: I . . . die guiltie of the blame, The which another did, who now is fled with shame.

Publilius Syrus (1934), 595: Quam malus est culpam qui suam alterius facit (What a rascal he is who throws his own guilt upon another)!

354 TO MAKE ONE'S **HAIR** STAND ON END

FQ, I, ix, 22, 2–3: Curld uncombed heares Upstaring stiffe. ¶ *Ibid.*, II, iii, 20, 5: Their haire on end does reare. ¶ *Ibid.*, ix, 13, 9: Staring with hollow eies, and stiffe upstanding heares. ¶ *Ibid.*, III, x, 54, 7–8: Bestadd, With upstart haire. ¶ *Ibid.*, xii, 36, 6: Her faire locks up stared stiffe on end. ¶ *Ibid.*, V, vii, 20, 7: With long locks up-standing, stifly stared. ¶ *Ibid.*, VI, xi, 27, 4–5: Lockes upstaring hye, As if he did from some late daunger fly.

Shakespeare, *Rich. III*, I, iii, 304: My hair doth stand an end. ¶ Shakespeare, *Hamlet*, I, v, 19: Each particular hair to stand an end. ¶ *Ibid.*, III, iv, 121–122: Your bedded hairs, . . . Start up and stand an end.

Cf. Stevenson, 788:13.

355 THE LEFT **HAND** RUBS THE RIGHT

Axiochus (Variorum), 127–128: Saying of *Epicharmus*, One hand rubbeth another: giue somewhat, and somewhat take. ¶ *FQ*, IV, i, 40, 8–9: Your selfe for this; my selfe will for you fight, As ye have done for me: the left hand rubs the right.

Seneca, *Apoc.*, 9: Manus manum lavat (One hand washes the other). ¶ Erasmus, *Adagia*, 40C: Manus manum fricat (Hand rubs hand). ¶ Harvey, *A New Lett.*, *Works*, I, 269: One hand washeth an other, and it apperteineth vnto him, that taketh something, to giue something.

Cf. Apperson, 471; Stevenson, 1059:9; Tilley, H87.

356 WITH CONSTANT **HANDLING** THE HARDEST SUBSTANCE IS WORN TO NOTHING

Amoretti, xviii, 2: The hardest steele in tract of time doth teare.

Ovid, *Artis Amat.*, i, 473: Ferreus adsiduo consumitur anulus usu (An iron ring is worn by constant use). ¶ Erasmus, *Similia*, 573A: Ut stilla cavat assiduitate saxum, ut ferrum contractatione atteritur: Ita assiduitas etiam durissima vincit (As a drop by repetition hollows a stone, as iron is worn away by handling: so repetition conquers even the hardest things). ¶ Lyly, *Euph. Anat. of Wit*, *Works*, I, 263: Yron wyth often handlinge is worne to nothinge. ¶ Sidney, *Arcadia*, *Works*, II, 11: There is no flint but may be mollifyed.

357 TO WASH YOUR **HANDS** OF A THING

FQ, I, x, 60, 8: Wash thy hands from guilt of bloody field. ¶ *Ibid.*, II, ii, 3, 4–5: His guiltie handes from bloody gore to cleene, He washt them oft and oft.

Cf. Stevenson, 2456:7–8; Tilley, H122.

358 **HAP** GOOD, HAP ILL

Shep. Cal., Julye, 229–230: Ah, good Algrin! his hap was ill, But shall be bett in time.

Shakespeare, *3 Hen. VI*, II, iii, 8: What hap? What hope of good?

Cf. Apperson, 283; Stevenson, 1069:6; Tilley, H137.

359 WHAT CAN **HAPPEN** TO ANY CAN HAPPEN TO ALL

Cf. no. 360: What has happened before may happen again

FQ, I, ii, 31, 5: Least to you hap that happened to me. ¶ *Ibid.*, III, vi, 21, 9: The like that mine, may be your paine another tide. ¶ *Daphnaïda*, 516–517: And thinke that such mishap as chaunst to me May happen unto the most happiest wight. ¶ *FQ*, VI, i, 41, 9: What haps to day to me to morrow may to you.

Publilius Syrus (1934), 133: Cunctis potest accidere quod cuivis potest (What can happen to any can happen to all).

Seneca, *Ad Marciam de Con.*, ix, 5: Cuivis potest accidere quod cuiquam potest (Whatever can one man befall can happen just as well to all)! ¶ Seneca, *De Tran.*, xi, 10: Quicquid in ullum incurrit posse in te quoque incurrere (Whatever befalls any man can you also). ¶ *Ibid.*, xi, 12: Quicquid fieri potest pro futuro habes (Whatever can happen is likely to happen to you).

Cf. Apperson, 637; W. G. Smith, 312; Tilley, M406, T371.

360 WHAT HAS **HAPPENED** BEFORE MAY HAPPEN AGAIN

Cf. no. 359: What can happen to any can happen to all

Shep. Cal., Maye, 104: Ought may happen, that hath bene beforne.

Seneca, *Epist.*, lxiii, 15–16: Hodie fieri potest, quicquid umquam potest (Whatever can happen at any time can happen today). ¶ Quintilian, *Inst. Orat.*, v, 10, 90: Quod semel, et saepius (What can happen once may happen often). ¶ Harvey, *Pierces Super.*, *Works*, II, 185: Accidents, that haue happened, may happen agayne.

361 DO NOT FIND YOUR **HAPPINESS** IN ANOTHER'S MISFORTUNE (SORROW)

FQ, I, iv, 30, 9: But when he heard of harme, he wexed wondrous glad.

Publilius Syrus (1934), 421: Malum ne alienum feceris tuum gaudium (Make not another's misfortune your joy). ¶ *Ibid.* (1835), 22: Alterius damnum, gaudium haud facias tuum (Do not find your happiness in another's sorrow).

362 ONE MAN'S **HAPPY** HOUR IS BUT ANOTHER'S BITTER TIME OF TRIAL

FQ, II, ix, 35, 1–8: Diverse delights they fownd them selves to please; Some song in sweet consort, some laught for joy, Some plaid with strawes, some ydly satt at ease; But other some could not abide to toy, All pleasaunce was to them griefe and annoy: This fround, that faund, the third for shame did blush, Another seemed envious, or coy, Another in her teeth did gnaw a rush.

* Publilius Syrus (1934), 62: Bona nemini hora est ut non alicui sit mala (Nobody has a good time without its being bad for someone).

Erasmus, *Adagia*, 1055C: Bona nemini hora est, quin alicui sit mala (One man's happy hour is but another's bitter time of trial).

Cf. Stevenson, 1810:7; Tilley, R136; C. G. Smith, 256.

363 THINGS **HARD** TO COME BY ARE MUCH SET BY

Cf. no. 344: What is good is difficult

FQ, IV, x, 28, 9: Much dearer be the things which come through hard distresse. ¶ *Amoretti*, xxvi, 11–12: Easie things, that may be got at will,

Most sorts of men doe set but little store. ¶ *Hymne in Honour of L.*, 168: Things hard gotten men more dearely deeme.

Publilius Syrus (1934), 573: Quod vix contingit ut voluptatem parit (What pleasure is produced by what is won with difficulty)! ¶*Ibid.*, 700: Voluptas e difficili data dulcissima est (Out of difficulty comes the sweetest pleasure).

Aristotle, *Rhetoric*, i, 7, 15: τὸ χαλεπώτερον τοῦ ῥάονος (That which is more difficult is preferable to that which is easier of attainment). ¶ Juvenal, *Sat.*, xi, 16: Magis illa iuvant quae pluris emuntur (The greater the price, the greater the pleasure). ¶ Chaucer, *Rom. Rose*, 2738–2739: A man loveth more tendirly The thyng that he hath bought most dere. ¶ Deloney, *Gentle Craft*, *Works*, 73: The harder a woman is to be won, the sweeter is her loue when it is obtained.

Cf. W. G. Smith, 278; Tilley, T201; C. G. Smith, 240.

364 EVEN **HARES** (PUPPIES) CAN TAUNT DEAD LIONS

Ruines of R., xiv, 5–8: The coward beasts use to despise The noble lion after his lives end, Whetting their teeth, and with vaine foolhardise Daring the foe, that cannot him defend.

Publilius Syrus (1835), 428: Leo a leporibus insultatur mortuus (Hares can gambol over the body of a dead lion). ¶ *Ibid.*, 429: Leonem mortuum etiam catuli morsicant (When the lion is dead, even puppies can bite him).

Greek Anthology: *Epigr.*, xvi, 4: νεκροῦ σῶμα λέοντος ἐφυβρίζουσι λαγωοί (The very hares insult the body of a dead lion). ¶ Erasmus, *Adagia*, 1118A: Mortuo leoni et lepores insultant (Hares taunt the dead lion). ¶ Guazzo, *Civ. Conv.*, *Works*, I, 73: This saying rose, That the Lion being dead, the verie Hares triumph over him.

Cf. Apperson, 285; W. G. Smith, 279; Stevenson, 1435:1; Tilley, H165; C. G. Smith, 146.

365 TO BE ABLE TO DO **HARM** AND NOT DO IT IS NOBLE

Cf. no. 591: It is better to overlook an injury than to avenge it; no. 712: It is noble to spare the vanquished

FQ, V, x, 2, 8–9: It is greater prayse to save then spill, And better to reforme then to cut off the ill. ¶ *Amoretti*, xxxviii, 12: To spill were pitty, but to save were prayse. ¶ *Ibid.*, xlix, 4: Greater glory thinke to save then spill.

Publilius Syrus (1934), 442: Nocere posse et nolle laus amplissima est (Power to harm without the will is the most ample fame).

Ovid, *Heroides*, xii, 75–76: Perdere posse sat est, siquem iuvet ipsa potestas; sed tibi servatus gloria maior ero (To have power to ruin is enough, if anyone delight in power for itself; but to save me will be greater glory).

Cf. Tilley, H170; C. G. Smith, 147.

366 **HASTE** BREEDS ERROR

Cf. no. 647: Repentance follows on a hasty plan

Shep. Cal., Julye, 15–16: Though one fall through heedlesse hast, Yet is his misse not mickle. ¶ *FQ*, I, iv, 34, 9: How many mischieves should ensue his heedlesse hast.

Culman, 23: Omnis res properando parit errorem (By making haste everything breeds error).

Cf. Stevenson, 1082:8; C. G. Smith, 148.

367 MAKE **HAY** WHILE THE SUN SHINES

Cf. no. 369: He that will not when he may, when he will he shall have nay; no. 777: Take time by the forelock

Shep. Cal., Maye, 65–67: Reapen the fruite thereof, that is pleasure, The while they here liven, at ease and leasure? For when they bene dead, their good is ygoe. ¶ *Ibid.*, 154–155: While times enduren of tranquillitie, Usen we freely our felicitie. ¶ *FQ*, II, xii, 75, 6: Gather therefore the rose, whilest yet is prime. ¶ *Ibid.*, 8: Gather the rose of love, whilest yet is time.

Ovid, *Fasti*, v, 353: Et monet aetatis specie, dum floreat, uti (And she warns to use life's flower, while it still blooms). ¶ Ovid, *Artis Amat.*, iii, 79–80: Carpite florem, Qui nisi carptus erit, turpiter ipse cadet (Pluck the flower, which save it be plucked will basely wither). ¶ Greene, *Menaphon*, *Works*, VI, 105: Make hay while the Sunne shined. ¶ Lodge, *Robert*, *Sec. Duke of Normandy*, *Works*, II, 42: Whil'st occasion giues you seasure, Feede your fancies and your sight: After death when you are gone, Joy and pleasure is there none. ¶ Greene, *Conny-Catching*, *Works*, X, 105: Take time while time serues, and make hay while the Sunne shines.

Cf. Apperson, 291; W. G. Smith, 398; Stevenson, 1092:5; Tilley, H235.

368 IT IS **HAZARDOUS** TO PLUCK A BONE FROM THE GREEDY JAW OF CERBERUS

FQ, I, xi, 41, 4–5: Harder was from Cerberus greedy jaw To plucke a bone, then from his cruell claw.

Erasmus, *Adagia*, 990C: Clavam extorquere Herculi (To tear away the club from Hercules).

Cf. *FQ* (Variorum), I, 303; Bland, II, 127.

369 **HE** THAT WILL NOT WHEN HE MAY, WHEN HE WILL HE SHALL HAVE NAY

Cf. no. 367: Make hay while the sun shines

FQ, V, v, 39, 5–7: "Unworthy sure," quoth he, "of better day, That will not take the offer of good hope, And eke pursew, if he attaine it may."

Cato, *Disticha*, iv, 45: Quam primum rapienda tibi est occasio prona, ne rursus quaeras iam quae neglexeris ante (The lucky chance you must secure with speed, Lest you go seeking what you failed to heed). ¶ Gascoigne, *Droome of Doomes Day*, *Works*, II, 263: It is but meete and right that they which would not when they might, should be barred to have power when they would. ¶ Greene, *Alphonsus*, 1913–1914, *Works*, XIII, 406: He that will not when he may, When he desires, shall surely purchase nay. ¶ Sidney, *Arcadia*, *Works*, I, 405: Let not some . . . perswade you to lose the hold of occasion, while it may not only be taken, but offers, nay sues to be taken: which if it be not now taken, will never hereafter be overtaken.

Cf. Apperson, 292; Stevenson, 1724:2; Tilley, N54.

370 AS MANY **HEADS** AS HYDRA

Visions of B., x, 10–12: This Hydra new . . . With seven heads. ¶ *FQ*, VI, xii, 32, 1–5: The hell-borne Hydra . . . labourd long in vaine To crop his thousand heads, the which still new Forth budded, and in greater number grew.

Cf. W. G. Smith, 285; Stevenson, 1097:3; Tilley, H278.

371 SO MANY **HEADS** (MEN), SO MANY WITS (MINDS)

FQ, IV, v, 11, 5: Diverse wits affected divers beene.

Culman, 15: Quot capita, tot sensus (So many men so many minds). ¶ *Ibid.*, Quot homines, tot sententiae (So many men, so many opinions).

Terence, *Phormio*, 454: Quot omines tot sententiae (So many men so many minds). ¶ Erasmus, *Adagia*, 114A: Quot homines, tot sententiae (There are as many opinions as there are men); cf. *Colloquia Fam.*, 842E. ¶ Foxe, *Acts and Mon.*, III, 659: There were as many minds as there were men. ¶ Sidney, *Arcadia*, *Works*, I, 311: So many as they were, so many almost were their mindes.

Cf. Apperson, 586; W. G. Smith, 406, 418; Tilley, M583

372 **HEALTH** IS GREAT RICHES

Shep. Cal., July, 211–212: When folke bene fat, and riches rancke, It is a signe of helth.

Cf. Stevenson, 1100:5; Tilley, H288.

373 A **HEART** AS HARD AS A STONE (FLINT, MARBLE)

FQ, I, ii, 26, 8: Hart of flint. ¶ *Ibid.*, iii, 44, 3: Stony hart. ¶ *Ibid.*, viii, 41, 5: A stony hart. ¶ *Ibid.*, II, i, 42, 2: His hart gan wexe as starke as marble stone. ¶ *Ibid.*, vii, 23, 8: Hart of flint. ¶ *Ibid.*, III, viii, 1, 7: The hardest hart of stone. ¶ *Ibid.*, ix, 39, 6: Stony hart. ¶ *Teares of the M.*, 110: A stonie heart. ¶ *Daphnaïda*, 246: Hart so stony hard. ¶ *FQ*, IV, xii, 7, 3: Hard rocky hart. ¶ *Ibid.*, 13, 1: Stony hart. ¶ *Hymne of Heavenly L.*, 246: Flinty hart. ¶ *View*, 654: Stonye harte.

Cf. Stevenson, 1075:9; 1115:13; Tilley, H311.

374 TAKE GOOD **HEART**

Mother Hub., 1003: Mine owne deare brother, take good hart. ¶ *FQ*, III, x, 26, 1–2: Take good hart, And tell thy griefe.

Terence, *Adelphoe*, 96: Bono animo est (Be of good heart). ¶ Palsgrave, *Acolastus* (E.E.T.S.), 175: I take good harte. ¶ Shakespeare, *As You Like It*, IV, iii, 174–175: Take a good heart and counterfeit to be a man.

Cf. Stevenson, 1107:4.

375 WHAT THE **HEART** THINKS THE TONGUE SPEAKS

Cf. no. 878: Words are (speech is) the image of the mind

View, 638: Out of the aboundaunce of the harte, the tonge speaketh.

New Testament: *Matthew*, xii, 34: ἐκ γὰρ τοῦ περισσεύματος τῆς καρδίας τὸ στόμα λαλεῖ. (For out of the abundance of the heart the mouth speaketh). ¶ Erasmus, *Similia*, 571A: Si quid delectat, ibi linguam habemus, id est, libentur ejus rei facimus mentionem (If anything delights us, there we have a tongue, that is, we freely make mention of that thing). ¶ Sidney, *Arcadia*, *Works*, II, 28: The tongue is but a servant of the thoughtes; cf. IV, 191. ¶ Greene, *Royal Exch.*, *Works*, VII, 255: Olde English prouerbe, what the hart thinketh, the tongue clacketh.

Cf. Apperson, 295; W. G. Smith, 288; Stevenson, 1112:16; Tilley, H334.

376 TO HANG BY THE **HEELS**

FQ, VI, vii, 27, 1–2: For greater infamie, He by the heeles him hung upon a tree.

Shakespeare, *1 Hen. IV*, II, iv, 480: Hang me up by the heels. ¶ Shakespeare, *2 Hen. IV*, I, ii, 141: To punish you by the heels. ¶ Jonson, *News from the New World*, 224–226, *Works*, VII, 520: Hung up by the heeles . . . to give the wiser sort warning.

Cf. Tilley, H388.

377 TO TAKE TO ONE'S **HEELS**

FQ, VI, vi, 29, 2: Unto his heeles himselfe he did betake.

Plautus, *Cistellaria*, 161: Pedibus perfugium peperit (He found himself a haven in his heels). ¶ Terence, *Eunuchus*, 844: Ego me in pedes quantum queo (I took to my heels and ran full speed).

Cf. Udall, *Apoph. of Erasm.*, 142:138; Stevenson, 1122:9; Tilley, H394.

378 **HELL** IS PAVED WITH GOOD INTENTIONS

Shep. Cal., Maye, 101–102: Often times, when as good is meant, Evil ensueth of wrong entent.

Taverner, 60: Many ther be which while they studie to do a man good do him muche harme.

Cf. Apperson, 297; W. G. Smith, 290; Stevenson, 1128:8; Tilley, H404.

379 **HELP** NEVER COMES TOO LATE

FQ, II, i, 44, 9: Help never comes too late.

Cf. Tilley, H411.

380 THE WISH TO **HELP** WITHOUT THE POWER MEANS SHARING MISERY

FQ, IV, xii, 12, 6–9: For griefe of minde he oft did grone, And inly wish that in his powre it weare Her to redresse: but since he meanes found none, He could no more but her great misery bemone.

Publilius Syrus (1934), 499: Prodesse qui vult nec potest, aeque est miser (The wish to help without the power means sharing misery).

Cf. C. G. Smith, 309.

381 FROM **HENCE** TO [SOME DISTANT PLACE]

Teares of the M., 505: From hence wee mount aloft unto the skie. ¶ *Ruines of R.*, i, 6: From hence to depth of darkest hell. ¶ *FQ*, V, v, 4, 5–6: From hence Their sound did reach unto the heavens hight.

Cf. Tilley, H429.

382 A **HESITANT** MIND IS THE HANDMAID OF WISDOM

FQ, IV, iii, 41, 9: And some, that would seeme wise, their wonder turnd to dout.

Publilius Syrus (1934), 320: Incertus animus dimidium est sapientiae (The hesitant mind is the half of wisdom).

Sidney, *Arcadia*, *Works*, I, 178: The handmaid of wisdome is slow belief.

Cf. C. G. Smith, 151.

383 **HIDDEN** DANGERS ARE THE WORST

FQ, II, xii, 35, 5: Worse is the daunger hidden then descride. ¶ *Ibid.*, III, ii, 26, 6: Of hurt unwist most daunger doth redound.

* Publilius Syrus (1934), 233: Gravius malum omne est quod sub adspectu latet (It is always a more serious evil that lurks out of sight). ¶ *Ibid.*, 494: O pessimum periclum quod opertum latet (The worst danger is that which is concealed)!

384 THINGS TOO **HIGH** SHOULD BE AVOIDED

Colin Clouts, 616–619: Thou hast forgot Thy selfe, me seemes, too much, to mount so hie: Such loftie flight base shepheard seemeth not,

From flocks and fields to angels and to skie. ¶ *Ibid.*, 935–936: Not then to her, . . . But to my selfe the blame, that lookt so hie.

Culman, 6: Fuge nimis alta (Shun things that are too lofty). ¶ *Ibid.*, 12: Fugienda sunt nimis alta (Too high things are to be avoided).

385 THE **HIGHER** THE CLIMB, THE GREATER THE FALL

Cf. no. 386: The higher the standing, the lower the fall

Shep. Cal., Julye, 11–12: This reede is ryfe, that oftentime Great clymbers fall unsoft. ¶ *Ruines of R.*, xxxi, 12–14: When thou wast in greatest hight To greatnes growne, through long prosperitie, Thou then adowne might'st fall more horriblie.

* Publilius Syrus (1934), 189: Excelsis multo facilius casus nocet (The exalted are much more readily hurt by a fall).

Greene, *Carde of F.*, *Works*, IV, 103: In climing to high, thou catch the sorer fall.

Cf. W. G. Smith, 282; Tilley, C414; C. G. Smith, 152.

386 THE **HIGHER** THE STANDING, THE LOWER THE FALL

Cf. no. 385: The higher the climb, the greater the fall

Amoretti, lviii, 11–12: He that standeth on the hyghest stayre Fals lowest.

Lydgate, *Fall of P.*, IX, 3491: Moost grevous fal, of them that sitte aloffte. ¶ Pettie, *Petite P.*, 77: The higher the place is the sooner and sorer is the fall.

Cf. Tilley, S823.

387 FROM THE **HIGHEST** (GREATEST) TO THE LOWEST (SMALLEST)

Ruines of T., 25: From highest staire to lowest step. ¶ *FQ*, V, ii, 37, 9: From the most . . . to the least. ¶ *Ibid.*, VI, x, 3, 2: From so high step to . . . so low. ¶ *Ibid.*, xii, 24, 8: From most to least.

New Testament: Matthew (Wycliff), xxvii, 51: Fro the hiest to the lowest. ¶ Chaucer, *Boece*, II, pr. 2, 58–60: The loweste to the heyeste, and the heyeste to the loweste. ¶ *Ibid.*, m. 7, 19: The heygheste to the loweste. ¶ Foxe, *Acts and Mon.*, I, 372: From the highest estate to the lowest; cf. IV, 480; V, 466. ¶ Painter, *Palace of P.*, II, 279: From highest title to meanest degree. ¶ Sidney, *Arcadia*, *Works*, I, 305: From the hiest to the lowest. ¶ Deloney, *Jack Newb.*, *Works*, 30: From the highest to the lowest.

388 IT IS LOST LABOR TO STOP ONE **HOLE** AND MAKE MANY

View, 649: Lost labour, by patching up one hole to make manye.

Cf. Tilley, T347.

389 THERE IS NO **HONEY** WITHOUT GALL

Cf. no. 426: There is no joy without sorrow; no. 745: Every sweet has its sour

Astrophel, 26: Honny without gall.

Chaucer, *Monk's T.*, B 3537: Fortune hath in hire hony galle.

Cf. Tilley, H556.

390 **HONOR** BELONGS ONLY TO GOD

FQ, V, x, 27, 8–9: And forced it the honour that is dew To God to doe unto his idole most untrew.

Culman, 32: Honor solius Dei est (Honor belongs only to God).

391 **HONOR** FOLLOWS WHEN TOIL HAS MADE THE WAY

FQ, II, iii, 40, 9: Who seekes with painfull toile, shal Honor soonest fynd. ¶ *Ibid.*, IV, ii, 27, 8–9: And save her honour with your ventrous paines; That shall you win more glory. ¶ *Ibid.*, xi, 22, 8–9: For sparing litle cost or paines, Loose . . . immortall glory, and . . . endlesse gaines.

¶ *Ibid.*, VI, ii, 2, 9: Yet praise likewise deserve good thewes, enforst with paine. ¶ *Ibid.*, ix, 2, 1–9: Calidore . . . toyle endured, . . . Reaping eternall glorie of his restlesse paines.

Culman, 6: Gloriae fundamentum labor (Labor is the foundation of glory). ¶ *Ibid.*, 7: Labores gloriae fundamentum (Labors are the foundation of glory). ¶ *Ibid.*, 13: Innumeris laboribus honos constat (Honor costs innumerable pains). ¶ Publilius Syrus (1934), 676: Solet sequi laus, cum viam fecit labor (Praise ever follows when toil has made the way).

392 **HONOR** IS DEARER THAN LIFE

Cf. no. 157: An honorable death is better than a shameful life

FQ, IV, i, 6, 6–7: Her honor, dearer then her life, She sought to save.

Painter, *Palace of P.*, III, 153: Honor . . . is to be preferred before life, bicause without honor life is of no regard. ¶ Greene, *Pandosto*, *Works*, IV, 311: Rather choose death then dishonour. ¶ Greene, *Spanish Masquerado*, *Works*, V, 270: Sweete it were to die rather than to liue with dishonour.

Cf. Tilley, H565.

393 **HONOR** IS STAINED WHEN IT IS BESTOWED ON THE UNWORTHY

FQ, VI, vi, 36, 4–5: For shame is to adorne With so brave badges one so basely borne.

* Publilius Syrus (1934), 332: Loco ignominiae est apud indignum dignitas (Honor is stained when it is bestowed on the unworthy). ¶ *Ibid.* (1835), 332: Honestatem laedes, quum pro indigno petes (You stain honor when you seek it for the unworthy).

Cf. C. G. Smith, 153.

394 **HONOR** IS THE REWARD OF VICTORY

FQ, III, i, 13, 6: Honour was the meed of victory.

Erasmus, *Colloquia Fam.*, 648D: Victori abunde magnum praemium est gloria (Glory is a reward sufficient for victory).

395 HONOR IS THE REWARD OF VIRTUE

Cf. no. 625: Praise is the reward of virtue

FQ, II, iii, 10, 8: Honour, vertues meed. ¶ *Ibid.*, III, x, 31, 7: Fame is my meed, and glory vertues pay.

* Publilius Syrus (1934), 263: Honos honestum decorat, inhonestum notat (Honor adorns the honorable; the dishonorable it brands). ¶ *Ibid.*, 590: Quicquid fit cum virtute fit cum gloria (A deed of valor is a deed of fame).

Cicero, *Brutus*, lxxxi, 281: Honos sit praemium virtutis (Honor is a reward of virtue). ¶ Erasmus, *Similia*, 594C: Gloria virtutem sequitur (Renown follows virtue). ¶ Erasmus, *Enchiridion*, 60D: Verus honor non opum, sed virtutis est praemium (True honor is not the reward of riches but of virtue). ¶ Ashley, *Of Honour* (Heltzel), 23: Honor . . . ys the reward of vertue. ¶ *Ibid.*, 28: Honor . . . (as great Philosophers affirme) ys the reward of vertue.

Cf. Stevenson, 1162:11; Tilley, H571; C. G. Smith, 312.

396 HONOR NOURISHES ART

Colin Clouts, 320: There learned arts do florish in great honor.

Culman, 6: Honos alit artes (Honor nourishes art).

Cicero, *Tusc. Disp.*, i, 2, 4: Honos alit artes omnesque incenduntur ad studia gloria (Public esteem is the nurse of the arts, and all men are fired to application by fame). ¶ Erasmus, *Adagia*, 330F: Honos alit artes (Honor nourishes the arts). ¶ Greene, *A Quippe for an Upstart C.*, *Works*, XI, 229: Honor norisheth Art.

Cf. Apperson, 308; Tilley, H574.

397 BY HOOK OR CROOK

FQ, III, i, 17, 6: By hooke or crooke. ¶ *Ibid.*, V, ii, 27, 8: By hooke and crooke.

Tusser, *Husb.* (E.D.S.), 98: By hooke or by crooke. ¶ Harvey, *Pierces Super.*, *Works*, II, 59: By hooke or crooke; cf. II, 304. ¶ Greene, *Scot. Hist. of James the Fourth*, 2018, *Works*, XIII, 292: By hooke or crooke.

Cf. Apperson, 308; W. G. Smith, 303; Stevenson, 1165:1; Tilley, H588.

398 **HOPE** BEARS UP THE MINDS OF MEN

FQ, I, i, 2, 6: Soveraine hope . . . in his helpe he had. ¶ *Ibid.*, III, xii, 44, 6–7: Faire Amoret, whose gentle spright Now gan to feede on hope. ¶ *Muiopotmos*, 25–26: With fruitfull hope his aged breast he fed Of future good.

Culman, 16: Spes mentes hominum fovet (Hope bears up the minds of men).

Pindar, *Frag.*, 214: γλυκεῖά οἱ καρδίαν ἀτάλλοισα γηροτρόφος συναορεῖ (With him lives sweet hope, the nurse of age, the fosterer of his heart).

Cf. Stevenson, 1167:18.

399 **HOPE** FOR THE BEST, BUT FEAR THE WORST

FQ, IV, vi, 37, 9: Its best to hope the best, though of the worst affrayd.

Cicero, *Epist. ad Fam.*, ix, 17, 3: Tu tamen pro tua sapientia debebis optare optima, cogitare difficillima, ferre quaecumque erunt (Be that as it may, it will be your duty, with characteristic wisdom, to hope for the best, to contemplate the worst, and bear whatever happens). ¶ Plutarch, *Moralia*: *Tranq. of the Mind*, 474C: εὔχεται μὲν ὁ νοῦν ἔχων τα βελτίονα προσδοκᾶ δὲ καὶ θάτερα (He that is master of himself wishes for the better, but expects the worse). ¶ Greene, *Mamillia*, *Works*, II, 192: Although it is good to doubt the worst, yet suppose the best. ¶ Sidney, *Arcadia*, *Works*, I, 278: Learned, so to hope for good, and feare of harm.

Cf. Apperson, 310; W. G. Smith, 303; Stevenson, 1166:8; Tilley, B328.

400 **HOPE** IS THE BEST MEDICINE FOR THE MISERABLE

FQ, III, ii, 15, 3–4: Hart that is inly hurt is greatly eased With hope of thing that may allegge his smart. ¶ *Ibid.*, V, x, 22, 9: Good hart in evils doth the evils much amend.

Culman, 9: Spes servat afflictos (Hope preserves the afflicted).

Erasmus, *Adagia*, 1039C: Spes servat afflictos (Hope supports the afflicted). ¶ Hill, *Com.-Book* (E.E.T.S.), 129: Ner hope harte wold breste. ¶ Shakespeare, *Meas. for Meas.*, III, i, 2–3: The miserable have no other medicine But only hope.

Cf. Tilley, H602; C. G. Smith, 155.

401 TO WIN THE **HORSE** (SADDLE) AND LOSE THE SADDLE (HORSE)

FQ, IV, v, 22, 5: To winne the saddle, lost the steed.

Breton, *Packet of Mad Lett.*, *Works*, II, *h*, 9: I will either winne the Horse, or lose the Saddle. ¶ Davies, *Sco. of Folly*, *Works*, II, *k*, 17: Ile recouer the horse or lose the saddle.

Cf. W. G. Smith, 711; Stevenson, 2529:4; Tilley, H639, S15.

402 AS **HOT** AS FIRE

Shep. Cal., March, 41: As whott as fyre. ¶ *FQ*, VII, vii, 36, 1: Hot July boyling like to fire.

Barclay, *Ship of F.*, II, 316: Hote as fyre. ¶ Foxe, *Acts and Mon.*, V, 147: As hot as fire.

Cf. Apperson, 315; Tilley, F247.

403 SOON **HOT**, SOON COLD

FQ, II, ix, 39, 5: Now seeming flaming whott, now stony cold. ¶ *Ibid.*, VII, vii, 23, 3: Now, boyling hot: streight, friezing deadly cold.

Udall, *Ralph Roister D.*, IV, viii, 38: So soone hotte, so soone colde. ¶ Greene, *Menaphon*, *Works*, VI, 136: Soone hote soone colde. ¶ Greene, *Never Too Late*, *Works* VIII, 135: Soone hot and soone colde.

Cf. W. G. Smith, 604; Stevenson, 1186:4; Tilley, H732.

404 TO BE A **HOTSPUR**

FQ, IV, i, 35, 5: The hot-spurre youth.

Harvey, *Foure Lett.*, *Works*, I, 204: Dunces, and hypocriticall hoat spurres. ¶ *Ibid.*, 232: Quarreling Hoatspurres. ¶ Nashe, *Pierce P.*, *Works*, I, 161: Hypocriticall hot-spurres. ¶ Shakespeare, *1 Hen. IV*, V, ii, 19: A hare-brain'd Hotspur, govern'd by a spleen. ¶ Davies, *Sco. of Folly*, *Works*, II, *k*, 29: Thou art as hot-spurre.

Cf. *FQ* (Variorum), IV, 171; Apperson, 315; Stevenson, 1186:8.

405 ONE **HOUR** CAN RESTORE WHAT MANY YEARS HAVE TAKEN AWAY

FQ, I, iii, 30, 2–3: One loving howre For many yeares of sorrow can dispence.

Publilius Syrus (1934), 668: Solet hora quod multi anni abstulerunt reddere (An hour often restores what many years have taken away). ¶ *Ibid.* (1835), 1040: Hora saepe reddidit una, quod decennium abstulit (A single hour may often compensate for the losses of ten years).

406 **HOURS** OF PLEASURE ARE SHORT

Amoretti, lxxxvi, 14: But joyous houres doo fly away too fast.

Cf. Apperson, 501; Tilley, H747.

407 **HOUSE** OF AGONIES (CARE, NIGHT, PAIN, WOE)

FQ, I, v, 33, 7: The house of endlesse paine. ¶ *Ibid.*, II, ix, 52, 9: The house of agonyes. ¶ *Teares of the M.*, 123: The house of heavinesse. ¶ *FQ*, III, v, 22, 3: The balefull house of endlesse night. ¶ *Ibid.*, IV, vi, 2, 1: That restlesse House of Care. ¶ *Ibid.*, V, x, 10, 8: The house of Night. ¶ *Ibid.*, xi, 14, 9: The house of dole.

Milton, *Par. Lost*, II, 823: Dismal house of pain. ¶ *Ibid.*, X, 465: The house of woe.

408 IN **HUGGER-MUGGER**

Mother Hub., 139: In hugger mugger.

Skelton, *Colyn Cloute*, 69–70, *Works*, I, 313–314: For in hoder moder The Churche is put in faute. ¶ Udall, *Apoph. of Erasm.*, 240: To be doen secretely in hugger mugger. ¶ Foxe, *Acts and Mon.*, III, 432: In hugger-mugger; cf. IV, 452. ¶ Harvey, *Pierces Super.*, *Works* II, 214: Deale in hugger-mugger. ¶ Nashe, *Unfor. Trav.*, *Works*, II, 213: So iniuriously abused in hugger mugger.

Cf. Spenser, *Minor Poems* (Variorum), II, 353; F. O. Matthiessen, *Translation: An Eliz. Art* (1931), 83; W. G. Smith, 309; Stevenson, 1195:4; Tilley, H805.

409 HE MUST **HUNGER** IN FROST WHO WILL NOT WORK IN HEAT

View, 653: Bread he hathe none, he ploughed not in sommer.

Barclay, *Ship of F.*, II, 43: Who that maketh for hymselfe no purueaunce. Of fruyt and corne in somer season clere. Whan of the same is store and habundaunce Shal after lyue in hunger all the yere. ¶ *Ibid.*, 46: In wynter he abydeth a lyfe myserable Whiche in the Somer prouydyd hath no thynge. ¶ *Ibid.*, 47: For he that wyll nat his mynde therto aply In youth and Somer to labour without fere In age and wynter shall lyue in penury.

Cf. W. G. Smith, 310; Tilley, F772.

410 HE THAT **HURTS** ANOTHER HURTS HIMSELF

Cf. no. 88: Caught in one's own trap

FQ, III, ix, 4, 3: He others wrongs and wreckes himselfe.

Hesiod, *Works and Days*, 265–266: Οἷ γ' αὐτῷ κακὰ τεύχει ἀνὴρ ἄλλῳ κακὰ τεύχων, ἡ δὲ κακὴ βουλὴ τῷ βουλεύσαντι κακίστη (He does mischief to himself who does mischief to another, and evil planned harms the plotter most). ¶ Aristotle, *Rhetoric*, iii, 9, 6: οἷ τ' αὐτῷ κακὰ τεύχει ἀνὴρ ἄλλῳ κακὰ τεύχων (A man does harm to himself in doing harm to another). ¶ Erasmus, *Adagia*, 1135C: Sibi parat malum, qui alteri parat (One who prepares evil for another, prepares evil for himself).

Cf. Stevenson, 1244:9, 1967:4; Tilley, H830.

411 BE NOT **IDLE**

Mother Hub., 735: Lothefull idleness he doth detest. ¶ *FQ*, IV, vii, 23, 9: Banish sloth.

Culman, 3: Otiosus ne sis (Be not idle). ¶ *Ibid.*: Otium fuge (Avoid idleness).

Cato, *Disticha*, iii, 4: Segnitiem fugito, quae vitae ignauia fertur (Shun slackness, which means idling all your days). ¶ Chaucer, *Man of Law's T.*, Int., 32: Lat us nat mowlen thus in ydelnesse. ¶ Lyly, *Euph. Anat. of Wit*, *Works*, I, 281: Not to lye in idleness, that is, that sloth shoulde be abhorred. ¶ Shakespeare, *1 Hen. VI*, I, i, 79: Let not sloth dim your honours new begot.

Cf. Tilley, I6.

412 **IDLENESS** IS THE CANKER OF THE MIND

Mother Hub., 735–736: Lothefull idlenes, . . . The canker worme of everie gentle brest. ¶ *FQ*, IV, vii, 23, 9: Sloth . . . oft doth noble mindes annoy.

Culman, 8: Otium ingenii rubigo (Idleness is the rust of the wit).

Ovid, *Tristia*, v, 12, 21–22: Adde quod ingenium longa rubigine laesum torpet et est multo, quam fuit ante, minus (And besides my talent, injured by long neglect, is dull, much inferior to what it was before). ¶ Ovid, *Ex Ponto*, i, 5, 7–8: Et mihi siquis erat ducendi carminis, usus, deficit estque minor factus inerte situ (For me, too, whatever skill I had in shaping song is failing, diminished by inactive sloth).

Cf. Apperson, 322; W. G. Smith, 312; Tilley, I14.

413 IDLENESS IS THE NURSE OF EVIL

Cf. no. 699: Sloth is the mother of poverty

FQ, I, iv, 18, 6: Sluggish Idlenesse, the nourse of sin. ¶ *Ibid.*, II, iii, 40, 5: Where ease abownds, yt's eath to doe amis. ¶ *Ibid.*, III, vii, 12, 9: Such laesinesse both lewd and poore attonce him made.

Culman, 12: Ex otio vitia proveniunt (Vices come from idleness). ¶ *Ibid.*, 14: Otium multa docet vitia (Idleness teaches many vices). ¶ *Ibid.*, 22: Multa mala affert hominibus otium (Idleness is the occasion of many mischiefs to men). ¶ *Ibid.*, 25: Quam multa mala hominibus affert otium (How many mischiefs does idleness bring upon men)? ¶ Publilius Syrus (1835), 321: Homines nihil agendo agere consuescunt male (By doing nothing, men learn to do ill).

Erasmus, *Colloquia Fam.*, 652D: Nam nihil malorum non docet ocium (For idleness is the root of all evil). ¶ Golding, *Ovid*, Epist., 113–114: Idlenesse Is cheefest nurce and cherisher of all volupteousnesse. ¶ Greene, *Mourning Garment*, *Works*, IX, 178: Idle life is the mother of all mischiefe.

Cf. Udall, *Apoph. of Erasm.*, 10:21; W. G. Smith, 313; Tilley, D547; C. G. Smith, 157.

414 IGNORANCE IS THE CURSE OF MANKIND

Teares of the M., 188–189: Brutish Ignorance, ycrept of late Out of dredd darknes of the deep abysme. ¶ *Ibid.*, 259–260: Hellish horrour, Ignorance, Borne in the bosome of the black abysse. ¶ *Ibid.*, 496–497: Hell and darkenesse and the grislie grave Is ignorance, the enemie of grace.

Plato, *Epist.*, vii, 336B: τόλμαις ἀμαθίας ἐξ ἧς πάντα κακὰ πᾶσιν ἐρρίζωται (Acts of ignorance—that ignorance which is the root whence all evils for all men spring). ¶ Guazzo, *Civ. Conv.*, *Works*, I, 213: It is an ordinary saying, that ignorance is a kinde of folly. ¶ Northbrooke, *Treatise agst. Dicing*, 29: Ignorance . . . called the mother . . . of all mischiefe and vice. ¶ Shakespeare, *2 Hen. VI*, IV, vii, 78: Ignorance is the curse of God. ¶ Shakespeare, *Twelfth N.*, IV, ii, 46–47: There is no darkness but ignorance. ¶ Shakespeare, *Troilus*, II, iii, 30–31: The common curse of mankind, folly and ignorance.

Cf. Spenser, *Minor Poems* (Variorum), II, 323.

415 THE **IGNORANT** FALL EASILY INTO HIDDEN TRAPS

FQ, III, i, 54, 8–9: The bird, that knowes not the false fowlers call, Into his hidden nett full easely doth fall. ¶ *Ibid.*, IV, x, 49, 9: Luring baytes oftimes doe heedlesse harts entyse.

Publilius Syrus (1934), 459: Ni qui scit facere insidias nescit metuere (He can best guard against a snare who knows how to set one).

416 HE THAT DOES **ILL** (EVIL) HATES THE LIGHT

FQ, III, iv, 58, 9: All that lewdnesse love doe hate the light to see.

Cf. W. G. Smith, 150, 315; Tilley, I26.

417 THERE IS NO GREATER SHAME TO MAN THAN **INHUMANITY**

FQ, VI, i, 26, 9: No greater shame to man then inhumanitie.

Cf. Stevenson, 1519:1.

418 THE **INNOCENT** ARE FREE FROM FEAR (BLAME)

FQ, III, i, 19, 9: Ne evil thing she feard, ne evill thing she ment.

Publilius Syrus (1835), 176: Culpa vacare maximum est solatium (The greatest of comforts is to be free from blame).

Shakespeare, *Meas. for Meas.*, III, i, 215–216: Virtue is bold, and goodness never fearful. ¶ Dryden, *The Hind and the Panther*, 4: She fear'd no danger, for she knew no sin.

Cf. Stevenson, 1249:2.

419 ALL **INNOVATION** IS PERILOUS

Cf. no. 93: All chance is unsound; no. 94: Change is seldom for the better

FQ, V, ii, 36, 7: All change is perillous. ¶ *View*, 649: All Innovation is perilous.

Lydgate, *Fall of P.*, I, 3528: For sodeyn chaungis been hatful to nature. ¶ Sidney, *Disc. to the Q. Majesty*, *Works*, III, 52: Any soudain change is not without perill.

Cf. Erasmus, *Institutio Principis Christiani*, 593A.

420 AS **IRISH** AS O'HANLAN'S BREECHES

View, 637: As Irish as Ohanlans breeche, as the proverbe there is.

421 THE WILD **IRISH**

View, 621: The wild Irish. ¶ *Ibid.*, 636: The very wild Irish. ¶ *Ibid.*: Degenerate . . . as the wild Irish. ¶ *Ibid.*, 674: The verye wilde Irish. ¶ *Ibid.*, 675: Growen to be wilde and meere Irish. ¶ *Ibid.*: Woorse then the wilde Irish.

Libell of Eng. Policy, *Wright's Political Songs and Poems* (Rolls S.), II, 187: God forbid that a wylde Irish wyrlynge Shulde be chosen. ¶ Boorde, *Introd. Knowl.* (1870), III, 132: The wilde Irysh. ¶ Harvey, *Letter-Book*, 100: Wylde Irish. ¶ Melbancke, *Phil.*, sig. Y2: The nature of a wild Irishman. ¶ Webster, *White Devil*, IV, i, 141: Like the wild Irish. ¶ Milton, *Hist. of Britain*, *Works* (Columbia, 1931), X, 49: Worse then wild Irish.

422 THE MORE YOU BEAT **IRON** THE HARDER IT GROWS

Amoretti, xxxii, 11: And harder growes, the harder she is smit.

Cf. Tilley, I96.

423 **IRREVERENT** MEN SCORN GOD'S GIFTS

Colin Clouts, 326–327: For God his gifts there plenteously bestowes, But gracelesse men them greatly do abuse. ¶ *FQ*, IV, viii, 15, 5–9: If . . . wilful scorne Of life it be, then better doe advise; For he whose daies in wilfull woe are worne, The grace of his Creator doth despise, That will not use his gifts for thanklesse nigardise.

Culman, 33: Impii dona Dei contemnunt (Irreverent men scorn God's gifts).

424 LIKE **JANUS**, TWO-FACED

FQ, IV, x, 12, 3–5: His name was Doubt, that had a double face, Th' one forward looking, th' other backeward bent, Therein resembling Janus.

Cato, *Disticha*, ii, 27: Illum imitare Deum, qui partem spectat utraque (Like Janus, facing both ways equally). ¶ Vergil, *Aeneid*, vii, 180: Ianique bifrontis imago (The likeness of two-faced Janus). ¶ Erasmus, *Adagia*, 1007A: Jano bifronte (Like Janus, two-faced).

Cf. Stevenson, 866:3; Tilley, J37.

425 SECRET **JOY** IS A SWEET TORTURE

FQ, VI, Prol., 2, 1–6: Secret comfort and . . . heavenly pleasures, Ye sacred imps . . . Into the mindes of mortall men doe well, And goodly fury into them infuse. ¶ *Muiopotmos*, 393–394: Secrete joy therefore Did tickle inwardly in everie vaine.

Publilius Syrus (1934), 487: O dulce tormentum ubi reprimitur gaudium (It is a sweet torture when joy is held in).

426 THERE IS NO **JOY** WITHOUT SORROW

Cf. no. 254: After feasting, weeping; no. 389: There is no honey without gall; no. 745: Every sweet has its sour; no. 829: There is no weal without woe

Ruines of T., 322: Sad joy, made of mourning and anoy!

Culman, 6: Gaudium dolori junctum (Joy is joined to grief).

Erasmus, *Adagia*, 943A: Gaudium dolori junctum (Joy is joined to grief). ¶ Greene, *Mamillia*, *Works*, II, 115: For euery ynch of ioy, I catch an ell of annoy.

Cf. Apperson, 448; Tilley, P420; C. G. Smith, 160.

427 ON EARTH **JOYS** DO NOT LAST

Ruines of T., 568–569: What can long abide above this ground In state of blis, or stedfast happinesse? ¶ *FQ*, I, viii, 44, 9: Blisse may not abide in state of mortall men. ¶ *Ibid.*, III, i, 10, 7: Nothing on earth mote alwaies happy beene. ¶ *Ibid.*, V, iii, 9, 1: What on earth can alwayes happie stand? ¶ *Ibid.*, VI, xi, 1, 7: Here on earth is no sure happinesse.

* Publilius Syrus (1934), 485: O vita misero longa, felici brevis (O life, long for woe but brief for joy)!

Martial, *Epigr.*, i, 15, 8: Gaudia non remanent, sed fugitiva volant (Joys abide not, but fugitive they fly). ¶ Chaucer, *Man of Law's T.*, 1133–1134: Joye of this world, for tyme wol nat abyde; Fro day to nyght it changeth as the tyde. ¶ Chaucer, *Merch. T.*, 2055: Worldly joye may not alwey dure. ¶ Florio, *First Fruites*, 32: The ioyes of this worlde dure but litle.

Cf. Stevenson, 1072:9.

428 **JUDGE** JUSTLY

FQ, V, iv, 1, 2: True justice unto people to divide. ¶ *Ibid.*, vii, 42, 7: Did true justice deale. ¶ *Ibid.*, ix, 36, 4: Dealing of justice with indifferent grace.

Culman, 2: Aequum judica (Judge indifferently). ¶ *Ibid.*: Juste judicato (Judge justly).

Cato, *Collectio Dis. Vulg.*, 43: Aequum iudica (Judge fairly).

429 DO NOT **JUDGE** BY APPEARANCES

Mother Hub., 649–650: Not by that which is, the world now deemeth, (As it was wont) but by that same that seemeth.

Martial, *Epigr.*, i, 24, 4: Nolito fronti credere (Do not credit his appearances). ¶ Juvenal, *Sat.*, ii, 8: Frontis nulla fides (In appearances place no trust). ¶ Shakespeare, *Merch. of V.*, III, ii, 73–74: So may the outward shows be least themselves; The world is still deceiv'd with ornament.

Cf. Christy, I, 13, 572; W. G. Smith, 328; Stevenson, 82:3, 4.

430 IN **JUSTICE** ALL VIRTUE IS FOUND IN SUM

FQ, I, ix, 53, 6: Where justice growes, there grows eke greter grace.

Aristotle, *N. Ethics*, v, 1, 15: *παροιμιαζόμενοί φαμεν ἐν δὲ δικαιοσύνῃ συλλήβδην πᾶσ' ἀρετὴ 'νί* (We have the proverb: In justice all virtue is found in sum). ¶ Marcus Aurelius, *Meditations*, xi, 10: *γένεσις δικαιοσύνης, ἀπὸ δὲ ταύτης αἱ λοιπαὶ ἀρεταὶ ὑφίστανται* (The origin of justice, and in justice all other virtues have their root). ¶ Erasmus, *Adagia*, 513F: Justitia in se virtutem complectitur omnem (Justice comprises in itself all virtue).

Cf. Taverner, 33; Stevenson, 1285:3; Tilley, J105.

431 THE PRINCIPLE OF **JUSTICE** IS THE PRINCIPLE OF EQUALITY

FQ, V, iv, 19, 1: Equall right in equall things doth stand.

Aristotle, *Politics*, iii, 7, 1: *δοκεῖ δὴ πᾶσιν ἴσον τι τὸ δίκαιον εἶναι* (It is therefore thought by all men that justice is some sort of equality). ¶ Painter, *Palace of P.*, III, 149: The balance of iustice is equall, and wayeth downe no more of one side than of other. ¶ Harvey, *Pierces Super.*, *Works*, II, 160: Equality in things equall, is a just Law.

Cf. Aristotle, *E. Ethics*, vii, 9, 1.

432 **KEEP** WHAT YOU GET

FQ, II, i, 47, 9: Take not away now got, which none would give to me.

Culman, 8: Parta sunt conservanda (Things gotten are to be kept).

Plautus, *Mostellaria*, 801: Lucri quidquid est, id domum trahere oportet (Get what you can, and keep what you get).

Cf. Stevenson, 948:2.

433 NEITHER IN **KENT** NOR IN CHRISTENDOM

Shep. Cal., Sept., 153: Nor in all Kent, nor in Christendome.

Cf. Apperson, 338; W. G. Smith, 332; Tilley, K16.

434 WE OUGHT TO DEAL **KINDLY** WITH OUR ENEMIES

FQ, V, viii, 17, 9: And even to her foes her mercies multiply.

Culman, 30: Cum hostibus benefice agendum (We must deal kindly with our enemies). ¶ Publilius Syrus (1835), 123: Bonum est etiam bona verba inimicis reddere (It is fitting to speak kind words even to one's enemies).

Cf. Stevenson, 686:13.

435 **KINDNESS** CAN WIN WHAT FORCE CANNOT

FQ, V, v, 17, 9: No fayrer conquest then that with goodwill is gayned.

Publilius Syrus (1934), 718: Virtute quod non possis blanditia auferas (You can accomplish by kindness what you cannot by force).

Cf. Tilley, L487; C. G. Smith, 165.

436 **KINGDOMS** DECAY BY DISCORD

Cf. no. 186: Great things decay by discord

FQ, II, x, 36, 4–5: The noble braunch from th' antique stocke was torne Through discord, and the roiall throne forlorne. ¶ *Ibid.*, 54, 2–4: Great trouble in the kingdome grew, That did her selfe in sondry parts divide, And with her powre her owne selfe overthrew. ¶ *Ibid.*, IV, i, 19, 2–4: Dissention, which doth dayly grow Amongst fraile men . . . many a publike state And many a private oft doth overthrow.

Culman, 5: Discordia dilabuntur regna (Kingdoms decay by discord).

Sallust, *Jugurtha*, x, 6: Concordia parvae res crescunt, discordia maxumae dilabuntur (Harmony makes small states great, while discord undermines the mightiest empires).

Cf. Stevenson, 583:12.

437 GREEDY DESIRE FOR **KINGSHIP** IS RUTHLESS

FQ, II, x, 35, 1–2: The greedy thirst of royall crowne . . . knowes no kinred, nor regardes no right. ¶ *Ibid.*, V, xii, 1, 2–7: Impotent desire of men to raine, Whom neither dread of God, that devils bindes, Nor lawes of men, that common weales containe, Nor bands of nature, that wilde beastes restraine, Can keepe from outrage and from doing wrong, Where they may hope a kingdome to obtaine.

Cicero, *De Offic.*, i, 8, 26: Nulla sancta societas Nec fides regni est (There is no fellowship inviolate, No faith is kept, when kingship is concerned).

Cf. Stevenson, 1301:6.

438 TO **KISS** THE GROUND

Cf. no. 59: To bite the dust

FQ, I, ii, 19, 6: With bloudy mouth his mother earth did kis. ¶ *Ibid.*, xii, 25, 7: Kist the ground. ¶ *Ibid.*, IV, vii, 46, 8: The ground he kist. ¶ *Ibid.*, viii, 13, 2: Kist the ground on which her sole did tread.

Sidney, *Arcadia*, *Works*, I, 253: There would she kisse the ground. ¶ Milton, *Par. Lost*, IX, 526: Fawning, and licked the ground whereon she trod.

Cf. W. G. Smith, 340; Tilley, D651.

439 **KNOW** THYSELF

Teares of the M., 503: By knowledge wee do learne our selves to knowe.

Culman, 1: Cognosce teipsum (Know thy selfe).

Plato, *Alcibiades I*, 124B: *Δελφοῖς γράμματι, γνῶθι σαυτόν* (The Delphic motto: *Know thyself*). ¶ Aristotle, *Rhet.*, ii, 21, 13: *Γνῶθι σαυτόν* (Know thyself). ¶ Cicero, *Tusc. Disp.*, 1, 22, 52: Cum igitur: *Nosce te*, dicit, hoc dicit: *Nosce animum tuum* (When, therefore, he [Apollo] says, "Know thyself," he says, "Know thy soul"). ¶ Seneca, *Epist.*, xciv, 28: Te nosce (Know thyself). ¶ Plutarch, *Moralia*: *Tranq. of the Mind*, 472C: *δεῖ τῷ Πυθικῷ γράμματι πειθόμενον αὐτόν καταμαθεῖν* (One must, obeying the Pythian inscription, "know one's self"). ¶ Juvenal, *Sat.*, xi, 27: E caelo descendit *γνῶθι σεαυτόν* ("Know thyself" descended from heaven). ¶ Erasmus, *Adagia*, 258D: Nosce teipsum (Know thyself). ¶ Ascham, *Toxoph.*, *Eng. Works* (Wright), 111: That wise prouerbe of Apollo, Knowe thy selfe. ¶ Sidney, *Christ. Relig.*, *Works*, III, 324: The chiefest wisedome is to knowe ones selfe.

Cf. Taverner, 19; Stevenson, 2066:4; Tilley, K175; C. G. Smith, 167.

440 HARD **LABOR** OVERCOMES ALL THINGS

FQ, I, viii, 40, 4–6: With constant zele, and corage bold, After long paines and labors manifold, He found the meanes that prisoner up to reare. ¶ *Amoretti*, lxix, 13–14: Happy purchase of . . . glorious spoile, Gotten at last with labour and long toyle.

Culman, 7: Labore omnia florent (All things flourish by labor). ¶ *Ibid.*, 13: Labor improbus omnia vincit (Hard labor overcomes all things).

Menander, *The Peevish Man*, *Frag.*, 132K: ἁλωτὰ γίνετ' ἐπιμελείᾳ καὶ πόνῳ ἅπαντα (All things are attained by diligence and toil). ¶ Vergil, *Georgics*, i, 145–146: Labor omnia vicit improbus (Unrelenting labor conquered all things). ¶ Seneca, *Epist.*, 1, 6: Nihil est, quod non expugnet pertinax opera (There is nothing which persistent labor will not conquer).

Cf. Stevenson, 1334:3; Tilley, L5.

441 TO LOSE YOUR **LABOR**

Cf. no. 811: To labor in vain

Mother Hub., 636: Loose thy labour. ¶ *Ruines of T.*, 89–90: To tell my forces . . . were but lost labour. ¶ *FQ*, I, iii, 24, 2: Shee backe retourned with some labour lost. ¶ *Ibid.*, II, xi, 25, 9: Labour lost it was. ¶ *Ibid.*, 44, 2: Thought his labor lost. ¶ *Ibid.*, III, i, 32, 1–2: To tell the sumptuous aray . . . should be labour lost. ¶ *Ibid.*, vii, 34, 8: To see his whole yeares labor lost. ¶ *Ibid.*, viii, 47, 2: Thy labour all is lost. ¶ *Ibid.*, IV, ii, 34, 2: That I thy labours lost may thus revive.

Plautus, *Casina*, 424: Meam operam luserim (I would lose my labor). ¶ Plautus, *Persa*, 233: Operam perdo (I lose my labor). ¶ Plautus, *Poenulus*, 332: Oleum et operam perdidi (I've lost my oil and my labor). ¶ *Ibid.*, 880: Omnem operam perdis (That's all labor lost). ¶ Terence, *Heauton*, 693: Frustra operam opinor sumo (It seems to me mine is lost labor). ¶ Shakespeare, *Merry Wives*, II, i, 247: I lose not my labour.

¶ Shakespeare, *Com. of Errors*, V, i, 97: Lose my labour in assaying it. ¶ Shakespeare, *Merch. of V.*, II, vii, 73–74: "Your suit is cold" . . . and labour lost. ¶Shakespeare, *Macb.*, V, viii, 8: Thou losest labour.

Cf. Stevenson, 1334:6, 1334:9; Tilley, L9.

442 AS CHASTE AS A **LAMB**

FQ, I, i, 5, 1–2: So pure and innocent, as that same lambe, She was in life and every vertuous lore.

Cf. Tilley, L33.

443 TO SEE (DISCOVER, BE IN VIEW OF) **LAND**

Muiopotmos, 286: The land she saw. ¶ *Colin Clouts*, 265: At length we land far off descryde. ¶ *FQ*, II, vi, 22, 5: Guyon of that land had sight. ¶ *Ibid.*, xii, 2, 2: Ne ever land beheld. ¶ *Ibid.*, 10, 8: Lo! I the land descry. ¶ *Ibid.*, IV, x, 24, 5: The lands about to vew.

Erasmus, *Adagia*, 1126E: Terram video (I see the land). ¶ Shakespeare, *2 Hen. VI*, III, ii, 105: My earnest-gaping sight of thy land's view. ¶ Shakespeare, *3 Hen. VI*, III, i, 14: To greet mine own land with my wishful sight.

Cf. Stevenson, 1344:3; Tilley, L56.

444 TO SING LIKE A **LARK**

FQ, II, vi, 3, 3: She song, as lowd as larke in ayre.

Cf. W. G. Smith, 591; Tilley, L70.

445 **LAST** BUT NOT LEAST

Colin Clouts, 444: Though last not least, is Aetion.

Sidney, *Arcadia*, *Works*, I, 27: The last . . . would not seeme the least unto me. ¶ Nashe, *To the Gent. Students*, *Works*, III, 323: The last, though not the least of them all.

Cf. Apperson, 350; W. G. Smith, 350; Stevenson, 1348:1; Tilley, L82.

446 FOR MAN, NEITHER LIFE NOR LUCK IS **LASTING**

Cf. no. 447: On earth nothing is long lasting

Daphnaïda, 498–502: And ye, fond men, on Fortunes wheele that ride, Or in ought under heaven repose assurance, Be it riches, beautie, or honors pride, Be sure that they shall have no long endurance, But ere ye be aware will flit away.

Publilius Syrus (1934), 456: Nec vita nec fortuna hominibus perpes est (Neither life nor luck is lasting for man).

447 ON EARTH NOTHING IS LONG **LASTING**

Cf. no. 446: For man, neither life nor luck is lasting; no. 12: All things come to an end

Mother Hub., 1176: For what thing can ever last? ¶ *Muiopotmos*, 217: What on earth can long abide in state? ¶ *Visions of the Worlds V.*, xi, 14: Nought on earth can chalenge long endurance. ¶ *Visions of P.*, vi, 11: On earth so nothing doth endure. ¶ *FQ*, II, x, 40, 1: For what may live for ay? ¶ *Amoretti*, lviii, 12: On earth nought hath enduraunce.

Culman, 2: Nihil diuturnum (Nothing is long lasting).

Cicero, *Philip.*, xi, 14, 39: Nihil enim semper floret, aetas succedit aetati (For nothing is for ever flourishing; age succeeds to age). ¶ Seneca, *Ad Polybium de Con.*, i, 1: Nihil perpetuum (Nothing is everlasting). ¶ Harvey, *Foure Lett.*, *Works*, I, 231: What can last allwayes, quoth the neat Tayler, when his fine seames began to cracke their credit at the first drawing-on. ¶ Greene, *Groatsworth of Wit*, *Works*, XII, 104: All mortall things are momentarie.

Cf. Tilley, G58; C. G. Smith, 168.

448 **LAW** CANNOT PERSUADE WHERE IT CANNOT PUNISH

View, 638: What doe statutes avayle without penaltyes, or lawes without charge of execution?

Fuller, 3148: Law cannot persuade, where it cannot punish.

Cf. Tilley, L101.

449 IT IS A UNIVERSAL **LAW** WHICH ORDAINS BIRTH AND DEATH

FQ, I, ix, 41, 2–3: The terme of life is limited, Ne may a man prolong, nor shorten it. ¶ *Ibid.*, 42, 8: Death ordaynd by destinie. ¶ *Ibid.*, IV, ii, 50, 4–5: The measure of their utmost date, To them ordained by eternall Fate. ¶ *Ibid.*, 52, 1–2: Since, . . . the terme of each mans life For nought may lessened nor enlarged bee.

* Publilius Syrus (1934), 336: Lex universa est quae iubet nasci et mori (It is a universal law which ordains birth and death).

450 AMONG WEAPONS **LAWS** ARE SILENT

View, 614: It is then a very unseasonable time to pleade lawe, when a swoord is drawen in the hand of the vulgar. ¶ *Ibid.*, 646: It is an ill time to preache amongest swoordes.

Culman, 5: Arma nesciunt leges (Weapons regard not laws). ¶ *Ibid.*, 13: Inter arma silent leges (Laws are silent among weapons).

Cicero, *Pro Milone*, iv, 11: Silent enim leges inter arma (When arms speak, the laws are silent).

Cf. Tilley, D624.

451 AS **LEAN** AS A RAKE

FQ, II, xi, 22, 2: Leane and meagre as a rake.

Chaucer, *Cant. T.*, Gen. Prol., 287: As leene was his hors as is a rake.

Cf. Apperson, 356; W. G. Smith, 357; Tilley, R22.

452 **LEARN** FROM THE LEARNED

Shep. Cal., Nov., 29: Learne of hem that learned bee.

Culman, 26: Sapientia est a viro sapiente discere (It is wisdom to learn of a wise man).

Cato, *Disticha*, iv, 23: Disce sed a doctis (Learn from the learned). ¶ Erasmus, *Colloquia Fam.*, 838A: Disce, inquit cato, sed a doctis (Cato bids us learn of those that are learned).

Cf. C. G. Smith, 171.

453 **LEARNING** (ART, KNOWLEDGE) HAS NO ENEMY BUT IGNORANCE

Teares of the M., 67–72: They that dwell in lowly dust, The sonnes of darknes and of ignoraunce . . . Despise the brood of blessed Sapience.

Publilius Syrus (1835), 581: Nisi ignorantes, ars osorem non habet (It is only the ignorant who despise education).

Cunningham, *Cosmogr. Glasse* (1559), 46: Knowledge hath no enemy but ignorance. ¶ Harvey, *Letter-Book*, 163: Scientia non habet inimicum nisi ignorantem (Learning has no enemy except ignorance). ¶ Lyly, *Euph. Anat. of Wit*, *Works*, I, 285: The ignoraunt . . . are alwayes enemyes to learning.

Cf. Apperson, 347; Stevenson, 1220:12; Tilley, A331, S142.

454 **LEARNING** MAKES MANNERS GENTLE

FQ, II, x, 25, 9: And with sweet science mollifide their stubborne harts. ¶ *View*, 613: Temper theyr warlick couradge with sweete delight of learning and sciences. ¶ *Ibid.*, 626: Learning (as the Poet sayth) "Emollit mores, nec sinit esse feros." ¶ *Ibid.*, 678: Learning hath that wonderfull power in it selfe, that it can soften and temper the most sterne and savage nature.

Culman, 9: Studium humanos reddit (Study makes men courteous).

Ovid, *Ex Ponto*, ii, 9, 47–48: Ingenuas didicisse fideliter artes emollit mores nec sinit esse feros (A faithful study of the liberal arts humanizes character and permits it not to be cruel). ¶ Guazzo, *Civ. Conv.*, *Works*, I, 184: This saying is most true, that gentry is the daughter of knowledge: and that knowledge doeth gentellise him that possesseth it.

455 A WISE MAN **LEARNS** FROM ANOTHER MAN'S CALAMITY

Cf. no. 456: A wise man learns from another man's follies (faults)

FQ, II, ii, 45, 5: Ill by ensample good doth often gayne. ¶ *Ibid.*, IV, x, 3, 6–7: Then hearke, ye gentle knights and ladies free, My hard mishaps, that ye may learne to shonne.

* Publilius Syrus (1934), 60: Bonum est fugienda adspicere in alieno malo (In another's misfortune it is good to observe what to avoid). ¶ *Ibid.* (1835), 841: Recte sapit, periclo qui alieno sapit (He is truly wise who gains wisdom from another's mishap).

Erasmus, *Adagia*, 496E: Felix, quem faciunt aliena pericula cautum (Happy is he that can beware by another man's jeopardy); cf. *Enchiridion*, 57F. ¶ Greene, *Mamillia*, *Works*, II, 63: Good to beware by another mans harme. ¶ Greene, *Arbasto*, *Works*, III, 183: It is good . . . by other mens harmes to learne to beware. ¶ Lodge, *Rosalynde*, *Works*, I, 111: If they haue that wit by others harmes to beware.

Cf. Taverner, 4; Tilley, M612.

456 A WISE MAN **LEARNS** FROM ANOTHER MAN'S FOLLIES (FAULTS)

Cf. no. 455: A wise man learns from another man's calamity

Mother Hub., 725–726: Heares and sees the follies of the rest, And thereof gathers for himselfe the best.

Culman, 14: Optimum aliena insania frui (It is the best to make use of another man's folly). ¶ *Ibid.*, 19: Ex vitio alterius sapiens emendat suum (From another man's faults a wise man amends his own). ¶ * Publilius Syrus (1934), 177: Ex vitio alterius sapiens emendat suum (From a neighbor's fault a wise man corrects his own).

Erasmus, *Adagia*, 496D: Optimum aliena insania frui (It is best to learn wisdom from the follies of others).

457 ALL MEN ARE **LIARS**

View, 626: All men be lyars.

Old Testament: Psalms, cxvi, 11: All men are liars. ¶ Foxe, *Acts and Mon.*, IV, 495: All men by nature are liars. ¶ Nashe, *Pierce P.*, *Works*, I, 232: All bee giuen to lie by nature.

458 ALL MEN LOVE **LIBERTY**

View, 675: It is the nature of all men to love libertye.

Dionysius of Halicarnassus, *Roman Antiq.*, iv, 83, 2: ἔμφυτος ἅπασιν ἀνθρώποις ὁ τῆς ἐλευθερίας πόθος (The desire of liberty is implanted by nature in the minds of all men). ¶ Painter, *Palace of P.*, II, 290: Euery man desireth to haue hys liberty. ¶ Dryden, *Palamon and A.*, II, 291: The love of liberty with life is given.

Cf. Christy, I, 622–623.

459 TO **LICK** THE FAT FROM ONE'S BEARD

Shep. Cal., Sept., 122–123: But they that shooten neerest the pricke, Sayne, other the fat from their beards doen lick. ¶ *Mother Hub.*, 78: From my beard the fat away have swept.

Cf. W. G. Smith, 363; Tilley, F80.

460 **LIFE** IS A PILGRIMAGE

FQ, I, x, 61, 3–4: Peaceably thy painefull pilgrimage To yonder same Hierusalem doe bend. ¶ *Daphnaïda*, 372–373: I will walke this wandring pilgrimage, Throughout the world. ¶ *Axiochus* (Variorum), 61–62: Common saying, which is worne in all mens mouths; That this our life is a Pilgrimage.

Seneca, *De Rem. Fortui.* (Palmer), 30: Peregrenatio est vita (This life is but a pilgrimage). ¶ Erasmus, *Adagia*, 1177A: Vita hominis peregrinatio (The life of man is a pilgrimage). ¶ Pettie, *Petite P.*, 249: Desirous to passe the pilgrimage of this short life in pleasure.

Cf. W. G. Smith, 365; Stevenson, 1400:6; Tilley, L249; Roland M. Smith, "Three Obscure English Proverbs," *Mod. Lang. Notes*, LXV (1950), 443–447.

461 **LIFE** SEEMS LONGER BECAUSE OF ITS ILLS

Amoretti, lx, 10–12: Fourty yeares . . . I have wasted in long languishment, That seemd the longer for my greater paines.

Publilius Syrus (1934), 92: Brevis ipsa vita est sed malis fit longior (Life is short, but its ills make it seem longer).

Lucian, *Greek Anthology*: *Epigr.*, x, 28: Τοῖσι μὲν εὖ πράττουσιν πᾶς ὁ βίος βραχύς ἐστιν, τοῖς δὲ κακῶς μία νὺξ ἄπλετός ἐστι χρόνος (For men who are fortunate all life is short, but for those who fall into misfortune one night is infinite time).

Cf. C. G. Smith, 177.

462 AN ILL **LIFE**, AN ILL END

FQ, II, viii, 12, 9: To proove he lived il, that did thus fowly dye.

Publilius Syrus (1835), 465: Male vivet quisquis nesciet mori bene (He must have lived ill, who knows not how to die well).

Seneca, *De Tran.*, xi, 4: Male vivet quisquis nesciet bene mori (That man will live ill who does not know how to die well). ¶ Erasmus, *Moriae Encomium*, 446A: Non male peribis, si bene vixeris (You will not die badly, if you live well).

Cf. W. G. Smith, 316; Stevenson, 519:11; Tilley, L247; C. G. Smith, 178.

463 MAN'S **LIFE** IS A LOAN, NOT A GIFT

FQ, II, i, 36, 7: This long lent loathed light [life]. ¶ *Ibid.*, x, 2, 2: All that lives does borrow life and light. ¶ *Ruines of T.*, 387: And interchanged life unto them lent.

* Publilius Syrus (1934), 257: Homo vitae commodatus non donatus est (Man is only lent to life, not given).

Lucretius, *De Rerum Natura*, iii, 971: Vitaque mancipio nulli datur, omnibus usu (To no man is life given in free hold; all are tenants). ¶ Cicero, *Tusc. Disp.*, i, 39, 93: Natura . . . dedit usuram vitae tamquam pecuniae (Nature has granted the use of life like a loan).

464 IT IS FOOLISH TO SEEK FOR A DEFENSE AGAINST **LIGHTNING**

FQ, VI, viii, 8, 5–6: Nought the course thereof could stay, No more then lightening from the lofty sky.

Publilius Syrus (1934), 640: Remedium frustra est contra fulmen quaerere (It is vain to look for a defense against lightning).

465 **LIKE** REJOICES IN ITS LIKE

Cf. no. 466: Like will to like

Hymne of Heavenly L., 118–119: Love doth love the thing belov'd to see, That like it selfe in lovely shape may bee.

Culman, 9: Simile simili gaudet (Like rejoices in its like).

Plutarch, *Moralia: How to Study Poetry*, 30F: εἴγε δὴ τὰ ὅμοια χαίρειν τοῖς ὁμοίοις πέφυκεν (It is the nature of like to delight in like). ¶ Erasmus, *Adagia*, 79E: Simile gaudet simili (Like enjoys like).

Cf. Stevenson, 1431:2.

466 **LIKE** WILL TO LIKE

Cf. no. 310: True friendship (love) is based on similarity; no. 465: Like rejoices in its like

Mother Hub., 48: Lyeke with his lyeke. ¶ *Colin Clouts*, 863: Thenceforth they gan each one his like to love.

Culman, 24: Pares cum paribus facile congregantur (Like are easily gathered together with like). ¶ *Ibid.*, 27: Semper similem ducit Deus ad similem (God always brings like to like). ¶ Publilius Syrus (1835), 690: Plerumque similem ducit ad similem Deus (God generally finds a way for like to meet like).

Homer, *Odyssey*, xvii, 218: ὡς αἰεὶ τὸν ὁμοῖον ἄγει θεὸς ὡς τὸν ὁμοῖον (As ever, the god is bringing like and like together). ¶ Plato, *Lysis*, 214D: τὸ ὅμοιον τῷ ὁμοίῳ φίλον (Like is friend to like). ¶ Aristotle, *N. Ethics*, viii, 1, 6: ὅμοιον τοῦ ὁμοίου ἐφίεσθαι (Like seeks after like); cf. *Rhet.*, i, 11, 25. ¶ Cicero, *De Sen.*, iii, 7: Pares autem vetere proverbio cum paribus facillime congregantur (And according to the old adage, like with like most readily foregathers); cf. Quintilian, *Inst. Orat.*, v, 11, 41. ¶ Plutarch, *Moralia*: *Obsolescence of Oracles*, 430D: προσχωρεῖν ἀεὶ τὰ ὅμοια τοῖς ὁμοίοις (Like always draws near to like).

Cf. Udall, *Apoph. of Erasm.*, 215:22; Taverner, 8; Stevenson, 1431:2; Tilley, L286; C. G. Smith, 180.

467 AS FIERCE (VALIANT) AS A **LION**

Muiopotmos, 434: Like a grimme lyon rushing with fierce might. ¶ *FQ*, I, i, 17, 1–2: The valiant Elfe . . . lept As lyon fierce upon the flying pray. ¶ *Ibid.*, VI, vi, 22, 4: Like a fell lion at him fiercely flew.

Chaucer, *Second Nun's T.*, 198: Lyk a fiers leoun. ¶ Shakespeare, *Troilus & Cres.*, I, ii, 20–21: He is as valiant as the lion.

Cf. Stevenson, 1436:1, 9; Tilley, L308.

468 ONCE THE **LION** (WOLF) BY THE LAMB DID LIE

FQ, IV, viii, 31, 1: The lyon there did with the lambe consort.

Publilius Syrus (1835), 709: Prius ovem, credo, ducet uxorem lupus (First, I think the wolf will consort with the sheep).

Tasso, *Jer. Del.*, X, 51, 5: The lambs and wolves shall in one fold abide. ¶ Sidney, *Arcadia*, *Works*, I, 134: Once the Lion by the Lambe did lie; cf. II, 75; IV, 239. ¶ Nashe, *Unfor. Trav.*, *Works*, II, 214: It is not for the lambe to liue with the wolfe.

Cf. *Old Testament: Isaiah*, xi, 6.

469 THE **LION** SPARES THE SUPPLIANT

Amoretti, xx, 5–8: The lyon, that is lord of power, And reigneth over every beast in field, In his most pride disdeigneth to devoure The silly lambe that to his might doth yield.

Ovid, *Artis Amat.*, ii, 183: Obsequium tigresque domat Numidasque leones (Compliance tames tigers and Numidian lions). ¶ Pliny, *Nat. Hist.*, viii, 19, 48: Leoni tantum ex feris clementia in supplices (The lion alone of wild animals shows mercy to suppliants). ¶ Erasmus, *Similia*, 611B: Leo . . . simplicibus ac prostratis parcit (The lion spares the innocent and the prostrate).

Cf. Tilley, L316.

470 AS **LITHE** AS LASS OF KENT

Shep. Cal., Feb., 74: His dewelap as lythe as lasse of Kent.

Cf. Apperson, 370; W. G. Smith, 372; Tilley, L73.

471 SAY **LITTLE**, THINK MORE

FQ, V, xii, 29, 9: Yet spake she seldom, but thought more, the lesse she sed.

Cf. Tilley, L367.

472 THE **LONGER** THE LIFE, THE GREATER THE MISERY

FQ, I, ix, 43, 1–2: The lenger life, I wote, the greater sin, The greater sin, the greater punishment. ¶ *Daphnaïda*, 361: By living long . . . multiplie their paine. ¶ *FQ*, IV, iii, 2, 2–3: In seeking for her children three Long life, thereby did more prolong their paine.

Culman, 13: Longior vita, diuturna calamitas (A longer life is a long-lasting calamity). ¶ *Ibid.*, 21: Longior vita solet plurima incommoda afferre (A longer life usually brings more troubles). ¶ *Ibid.*, 33: Longior vita, diuturna calamitas (The longer life is a long-lasting misery). ¶ Publilius Syrus (1835), 441: Longaeva vita mille fert molestias (A long life makes acquaintance with a thousand ills).

Tottel's Misc., I, 127: The lenger lyfe, the more offence: The more offence, the greater payn. ¶ Cotgrave, *Dict.* (s. v. Plus): The longer life the more affliction.

Cf. Tilley, L260; C. G. Smith, 183.

473 **LOSE** A FOE AND FIND A FRIEND

FQ, I, ii, 27, 2–3: Found a new friend you to aid, And lost an old foe.

474 BETTER **LOSE** A PART THAN LOSE ALL

Shep. Cal., Sept., 134–135: Better leave of with a little losse, Then by much wrestling to leese the grosse. ¶ *FQ*, III, v, 43, 3: Madnesse to save a part, and lose the whole! ¶ *Ibid.*, V, x, 2, 3–4: To preserve inviolated right, Oft spilles the principall, to save the part.

Chaucer, *Troilus*, IV, 1375–1376: Men ful ofte, iwys, Mote spenden part the remenant for to save.

475 THE **LOT** OF KINGS IS HARDER THAN THE LOT OF THEIR SUBJECTS

FQ, VI, iii, 5, 5–9: Bale and bitter sorrowings . . . is the state of keasars and of kings. Let none therefore, that is in meaner place, Too greatly grieve at any his unlucky case.

Publilius Syrus (1835), 1085: Regibus pejus est multo, quam ipsis servientibus (Much harder is the lot of kings than that of their subjects).

Shakespeare, *Hen. V*, IV, i, 249–254: The King . . . must bear all. O hard condition, Twin-born with greatness . . . What infinite heart's-ease Must Kings neglect that private men enjoy!

Cf. Stevenson, 1301:8.

476 TO **LOUT** LOW

FQ, I, i, 30, 1: He faire the knight saluted, louting low. ¶ *Ibid.*, x, 44, 6: He humbly louted in meeke lowlinesse. ¶ *Ibid.*, II, iii, 13, 4: Tho to him louting lowly did begin. ¶ *Ibid.*, III, x, 23, 9: And comming him before, low louted on the lay. ¶ *Ibid.*, 37, 9: To him louted low. ¶ *Ruines of T.*, 202: The courting masker louteth lowe. ¶ *FQ*, IV, ii, 23, 3: And lowly to her lowting. ¶ *Ibid.*, iii, 5, 8: Thrise lowted lowly to the noble mayd. ¶ *Ibid.*, vi, 28, 7: To see you lout so low on ground. ¶ *Ibid.*, vii, 44, 7: He louted lowly, as did him becum. ¶ *Ibid.*, xi, 30, 5: Ne none disdained low to him to lout. ¶ *Ibid.*, V, iii, 34, 9: Louted low on knee. ¶ *Ibid.*, VI, x, 16, 7: Low to lout.

Chaucer, *Troilus*, III, 683: Took his leve, and gan ful lowe loute. ¶ *World & Child* (Roxb. Cl.), B j: To me men lewte full lowe. ¶ Drayton, *Poly-Olbion*, V, 131: All lowting lowe to him, him humbly they observe.

477 **LOVE** ABOUNDS WITH BOTH HONEY AND GALL

Cf. no. 482: Love is a sweet torment

Shep. Cal., March, 122–123: *Of hony and of gaule in love there is store: The honye is much, but the gaule is more.* ¶ *FQ*, IV, x, 1, 2: Love with gall and hony doth abound.

Plautus, *Cistellaria*, 69: Amor et melle et felle est fecundissimus (Love is fairly overflowing with honey and gall both). ¶ Pettie, *Petite P.*, 237: For every pinte of hony hee [the lover] shall taste a gallon of gall. ¶ Sidney, *Wooing-Stuffe*, *Works*, II, 340: Faint Amorist: What, do'st thou think To tast Loves Honey, and not drink One dram of Gall?

Cf. Stevenson, 1476:2; Tilley, H557.

478 LOVE AND FEAR CANNOT MIX

FQ, II, vi, 46, 2: So love the dread of daunger doth despise. ¶ *Ibid.*, III, xi, 2, 3–5: Sweete Love . . . Untroubled of vile feare or bitter fell. ¶ *Ibid.*, V, i, 27, 9: True love despiseth shame, when life is cald in dread.

Publilius Syrus (1835), 40: Amor misceri cum timore non potest (Love and fear cannot mix).

Seneca, *Epist.*, xlvii, 18: Non potest amor cum timore misceri (Love and fear cannot be mingled).

Cf. C. G. Smith, 189

479 LOVE AND LORDSHIP LIKE NO FELLOWSHIP

Shep. Cal., Oct., 98–99: Lordly Love is such a tyranne fell, That, where he rules, all power he doth expell. ¶ *Mother Hub.*, 1026: Love and lordship bide no paragone. ¶ *Hymne in Honour of L.*, 251: Love can not endure a paragone.

Ovid, *Metam.*, ii, 846–847: Non bene conveniunt nec in una sede morantur maiestas et amor (Majesty and love do not go well together, nor tarry long in the same dwelling-place). ¶ Ovid, *Artis Amat.*, iii, 564: Non bene cum sociis regna Venusque manent (In partnership neither thrones nor love stand sure). ¶ Greene, *Conny-Catching*, *Works*, X, 254: Loue and Lordshippe brookes no fellowship. ¶ Deloney, *Gentle Craft*, *Works*, 190: An old saying, loue and Lordship brookes no fellowship.

Cf. Taverner, 61; Apperson, 384; W. G. Smith, 388; Stevenson, 1465:5; Tilley, L495.

480 **LOVE** CANNOT BE COMPELLED

Cf. no. 494: Coaxing, not compulsion, makes love sweet

FQ, III, i, 25, 7: Ne may love be compeld by maistery. ¶ *Colin Clouts*, 129: Love will not be drawne, but must be ledde. ¶ *Ibid.*, 914: Who can love compell? ¶ *FQ*, IV, i, 46, 8–9: Love is free, and led with selfe delight, Ne will enforced be with maisterdome or might.

Chaucer, *Franklin's T.*, 764: Love wol nat been constreyned by maistrye.

Cf. Stevenson, 1466:4; Tilley, L499.

481 **LOVE** CONQUERS ALL THINGS

FQ, III, i, 29, 8–9: Trew love most of might, That for his trusty servaunts doth so strongly fight. ¶ *Colin Clouts*, 883–884: Love is lord of all the world by right, And rules the creatures by his powrfull saw. ¶ *FQ*, VI, ix, 37, 9: Love so much could.

Culman, 5: Amor vincit omnia (Love overcomes all things).

Vergil, *Eclog.*, x, 69: Omnia vincit Amor (Love conquers all). ¶ Gower, *Conf. Aman.*, I, 35: Love is maister wher he wile. ¶ *Ibid.*, V, 4556: Love is lord in every place. ¶ Greene, *Mamillia*, *Works*, II, 122: Loue is aboue king or keisar, Lorde or lawes.

Cf. Stevenson, 1472:12; Tilley, L527.

482 **LOVE** IS A SWEET TORMENT

Cf. no. 477: Love abounds with both honey and gall

Shep. Cal., Jan., 54: Ah God! that love should breede both joy and payne! ¶ *FQ*, IV, vi, 32, 7: Lovers heaven must passe by sorrowes hell. ¶ *Ibid.*, x, 3, 8–9: Though sweet love to conquer glorious bee, Yet is the paine thereof much greater then the fee.

Publilius Syrus (1934), 306: In venere semper certat dolor et gaudium (In love, pain is ever at war with joy).

Watson, *Eng. Parnassus* (Crawford), 141: For euery pleasure that in loue is found, A thousand woes and more therein abound.

Cf. Tilley, L505a; C. G. Smith, 185.

483 **LOVE** IS A YOUNG MAN'S PLEASURE, AN OLD MAN'S REPROACH

Shep. Cal., Maye, 2–18: When love lads masken in fresh aray . . . such follies fitte, But we tway bene men of elder witt. ¶ *Ibid.*, June, 33–36: And I, whylst youth and course of carelesse yeeres Did let me walke withouten lincks of love, In such delights did joy amongst my peeres: But ryper age such pleasures doth reprove.

* Publilius Syrus (1934), 29: Amare iuveni fructus est, crimen seni (Love is the young man's enjoyment, the old man's reproach).

Cf. Tilley, P421.

484 **LOVE** IS BLIND

Cf. no. 496: It is impossible to love and be wise

FQ, II, iv, 24, 9: Blind abused love. ¶ *Ibid.*, III, iv, 6, 8: Her blinded guest [Love]. ¶ *Ibid.*, 9, 6–9: Love . . . And Fortune . . . both are bold and blinde. ¶ *Ibid.*, x, 4, 3–4: False Love, why do men say thou canst not see, And . . . feigne thee blinde? *Ibid.*, IV, v, 29, 5: Making blind Love her guide.

Plato, *Laws*, v, 731E: τυφλοῦται γὰρ περὶ τὸ φιλούμενον ὁ φιλῶν (For the lover is blind in his view of the object loved); cf. Plutarch, *Moralia*: *How to Profit by One's Enemies*, 90A. ¶ Sidney, *Arcadia*, *Works*, I, 176: O Love, how farre thou seest with blind eyes? ¶ Jonson, *Case Is Altered*, IV, ii, 49–50, *Works*, III, 151: Blind excuse, Blinder then Loue himselfe.

Cf. Apperson, 384; W. G. Smith, 389; Tilley, L506.

485 **LOVE** IS BRED BY LOOKING

Shep. Cal., Aug., 79–84: With glauncing eye . . . love into thy hart did streame. ¶ *Amoretti*, xxi, 6–14: She to her love doth lookers eyes allure . . . With such strange termes her eyes she doth inure, That with one looke she doth my life dismay, And with another doth it streight recure: . . . Thus doth she traine and teach me with her lookes: Such art of eyes I never read in bookes.

Culman, 11: Amorem oculi potissimum conciliant (The eyes

especially win love). ¶ *Ibid.*, 12: Ex aspectu nascitur amor (Love is bred by looking at one). ¶ Publilius Syrus (1934), 497: Oculi (occulte) amorem incipiunt consuetudo perficit (The eyes start love secretly; intimacy perfects it).

Ovid, *Artis Amat.*, iii, 510: Comibus est oculis alliciendus amor (By gentle eyes must love be enticed). ¶ Erasmus, *Adagia*, 100E: Ex adspectu nascitur amor (From looking love is born).

Cf. Taverner, 11; Tilley, L501; C. G. Smith, 186.

486 **LOVE** IS FULL OF ANXIETY (FEAR)

FQ, III, vii, 20, 9: And love to frenzy turnd, sith love is franticke hight. ¶ *Ibid.*, V, vi, 3, 9: A thousand feares . . . love-sicke fancies faine to fynde.

Publilius Syrus (1934), 34: Amor otiosae causa est sollicitudinis (Love causes worry in the leisure hour).

Ovid, *Heroides*, i, 12: Res est solliciti plena timoris amor (Love is a thing ever filled with anxious fear). ¶ Chaucer, *Troilus*, IV, 1645: Love is thyng ay ful of bisy drede. ¶ Gower, *Conf. Aman.*, V, 6059: Men sein that every love hath drede. ¶ Sidney, *Arcadia*, *Works*, II, 116; (According to the nature of love) fearing the worst. ¶ Sidney, *To Hubert Languet*, *Works*, III, 79: *Plena timoris amor.* ¶ Shakespeare, *Venus & A.*, 1021: Fie, fie, fond love, thou art so full of fear.

Cf. Apperson, 384-385; Tilley, L507.

487 **LOVE** IS INCURABLE

Shep. Cal., Aug., 104: Love is a curelesse sorrowe.

Culman, 10: Amor non est sanabilis (Love is not curable).

Ovid, *Metam.*, i, 523: Ei mihi, quod nullis amor est sanabilis herbis (Alas, that love is curable by no herbs!) ¶ Ovid, *Heroides*, v, 149: Me miseram, quod amor non est medicabilis herbis! (Alas, wretched me, that love may not be healed by herbs!) ¶ Lyly, *Euph. Anat. of Wit*, *Works*, I, 208: O ye gods haue ye ordayned for euerye maladye a medicine, . . . leuing only loue remedilesse?

Cf. Stevenson, 1471: 3, 6.

488 LOVE IS LAWLESS

FQ, VI, viii, 23, 3: No law in love.

Boethius, *De Con. Phil.*, iii, meter 12, 47–48: Quis legem det amantibus? Maior lex amor est sibi (Who can give law to lovers? Love is a greater law to itself). ¶ Gower, *Conf. Aman.*, VIII, 263: Lust of love excedeth lawe. ¶ Lydgate, *Minor Poems* (E. E. T. S.), 108: Poetys seyen howe loue hath no law. ¶ Painter, *Palace of P.*, I, 108: Who is able to prescribe lawes to loue? ¶ Greene, *Arbasto*, *Works*, III, 197: Loue is without lawe. ¶ Greene, *Euphues His Censure to Phil.*, *Works*, VI, 178: Loue is . . . without law, and therefore aboue all lawe. ¶ Greene, *Never Too Late*, *Works*, VIII, 52: She breathed out this saw, Oh, that loue hath no law. ¶ *Ibid.*: Fie on loue that hath no law.

Cf. W. G. Smith, 390; Tilley, L508.

489 LOVE IS THE REWARD OF LOVE

FQ, II, viii, 2, 8: All for love, and nothing for reward.

Cf. Stevenson, 1477:2; Tilley, L515.

490 LOVE IS THE SOURCE OF ALL GOOD DEEDS

FQ, III, i, 49, 8–9: For love does alwaies bring forth bounteous deeds, And in each gentle hart desire of honor breeds. ¶ *Ibid.*, iii, 1, 4–9: Love . . . Whence spring all noble deedes and never dying fame. ¶ *Ibid.*, IV, Prol., 2, 6–7: For it [love] of honor and all vertue is The roote, and brings forth glorious flowres of fame.

Painter, *Palace of P.*, III, 11: Loue pricketh and prouoketh the spirite to do well. ¶ Herbert, 370: He that hath love in his breast hath spurs in his sides; cf. Fuller, 2160.

491 LOVE NOT AT FIRST SIGHT

Hymne in Honour of B., 209–210: Streight do not love: for love is not so light, As streight to burne at first beholders sight.

Marlowe, *Hero and Leander*, 175: Who ever lov'd, that lov'd not at first sight? cf. Shakespeare, *As You Like It*, III, v, 82.

Cf. W. G. Smith, 391; Tilley L426.

492 **LOVE** STARTS BUT IS NOT DROPPED AT WILL

Shep. Cal., March, 99–102: But soone it [love] sore encreased. And now it ranckleth more and more, And inwardly it festreth sore, Ne wote I how to cease it.

* Publilius Syrus (1934), 5: Amor animi arbitrio sumitur, non ponitur (Love starts but is not dropped at will).

Cf. Tilley, M234.

493 **LOVE** YOUR FRIEND, BUT LOOK TO YOURSELF

FQ, I, v, 18, 7–9: Foolish man, . . . Forgetfull of his owne, that mindes an others cares. ¶ *Ibid.*, vi, 47, 5–6: Most sencelesse man he, that himselfe doth hate, To love another. ¶ *Astrophel*, 111–112: Ill mynd, so much to mynd anothers ill, As to become unmyndfull of his owne. ¶ *FQ*, IV, vii, 10, 9: Selfe to forget to mind another, is oversight. *Ibid.*, VI, iii, 12, 1–3: She perceiving, did with plenteous teares His care more then her owne compassionate, Forgetfull of her owne, to minde his feares.

Publilius Syrus (1934), 54: Amicis ita prodesto ne noceas tibi (Benefit friends without hurt to yourself).

Cato, *Disticha*, i, 11: Dilige sic alios, ut sis tibi charus amicus; sic bonus esto bonis, ne te mala damna sequatur (Love other men; yet be your own true friend; Do good to good men so no loss attend).

Cf. C. G. Smith, 187.

494 COAXING, NOT COMPULSION, MAKES **LOVE** SWEET

Cf. no. 480: Love cannot be compelled

FQ, I, vi, 3, 8–9: For greater conquest of hard love he gaynes, That workes it to his will, then he that it constraines. ¶ *Amoretti*, lxv, 5–6:

Sweet be the bands the which true love doth tye, without constraynt or dread of any ill. ¶ *FQ*, IV, v, 25, 9: Sweete is the love that comes alone with willingnesse.

* Publilius Syrus (1934), 69: Blanditia non imperio fit dulcis venus (Coaxing, not ordering, makes love sweet).

Cf. C. G. Smith, 188.

495 IF YOU **LOVE** YOURSELF ALONE, MANY WILL HATE YOU

FQ, IV, xii, 9, 9: And let him live unlov'd, or love him selfe alone.

Publilius Syrus (1835), 902: Si tutemet te amaris, erunt, qui te oderint (There will always be some to hate you, if you love yourself).

Erasmus, *Adagia*, 690B: Multi te oderint, si teipsum amas (Many will hate you, if you love yourself).

Cf. Taverner, 45.

496 IT IS IMPOSSIBLE TO **LOVE** AND BE WISE

Cf. no. 484: Love is blind

Shep. Cal., March, 119–120: *To be wise and eke to love, Is graunted scarce to god above.*

* Publilius Syrus (1934), 22: Amare et sapere vix deo conceditur (Wisdom with love is scarcely granted to a god). ¶ *Ibid.*, 131: Cum ames non sapias aut cum sapias non ames (Love means you can't be wise: wisdom means you can't be in love).

Erasmus, *Adagia*, 476E: Amare et sapere, vix Deo conceditur (To love and to be wise is scarcely granted to God). ¶ Cotgrave, *Dict.* (*s. v.* Aimer): Love and knowledge live not together. ¶ Bacon, *Essays: Of Love:* It is well said, "That it is impossible to love and to be wise."

Cf. W. G. Smith, 388; Tilley, L558; C. G. Smith, 190.

497 NEW **LOVE** DRIVES OUT OLD LOVE

FQ, VI, ix, 40, 9: Old love is litle worth when new is more prefard.

Cicero, *Tusc. Disp.*, iv, 35, 75: Etiam novo quidam amore veterem amorem tamquam clavo clavum eiiciendum putant (Some think, too, that old love can be driven out by new, as one nail can be driven out by another). ¶ Ovid, *Rem. Amoris*, 462: Successore novo vincitur omnis amor (All love is vanquished by a succeeding love). ¶ Chaucer, *Troilus*, IV, 415: The newe love out chaceth ofte the olde. ¶ Erasmus, *Similia*, 606B: Amor pellat amorem (Love expels love).

Cf. W. G. Smith, 441; Tilley, L538.

498 NO ONE CAN ESCAPE **LOVE** OR DEATH

FQ, III, ii, 46, 7: Love or death must bee thy lott.

Publilius Syrus (1934), 478: Nec mortem effugere quisquam nec amorem potest (There is no one who can escape either death or love).

Painter, *Palace of P.*, III, 279: Death and Loue, choose whether thou lyst.

499 THE GREATER THE **LOVE**, THE GREATER THE LOSS

FQ, I, vii, 27, 6: For greater love, the greater is the losse.

500 THE LESS THE HOPE, THE HOTTER THE **LOVE**

FQ, IV, ii, 37, 1–2: So much the more as she refusd to love, So much the more she loved was and sought. ¶ *Ibid.*, VI, vii, 30, 3–4: The more she did all love despize, The more would wretched lovers her adore.

Terence, *Eunuchus*, 1053: Quanto minus spei est tanto magis amo (The less my hope, the hotter my love). ¶ Lodge, *Glaucus and Scilla*, *Works*, I, 24: And more she loues the more the Sea-god hated. ¶ Shakespeare, *Two Gent.*, IV, ii, 14–15: The more she spurns my love, The more it grows. ¶ Shakespeare, *Mids. Night's D.*, I, i, 198: The more I hate, the more he follows me. ¶ *Ibid.*, II, i, 201–202: I do not nor I cannot love you? And even for that do I love you the more.

Cf. Stevenson, 1470:10.

501 THE MADNESS OF **LOVE** IS ALWAYS SWEET

Amoretti, xxxix, 6–10: When on me thou shinedst late in sadnesse, A melting pleasance ran through every part, And me revived with hart robbing gladnesse: Whylst rapt with joy resembling heavenly madnes, My soule was ravisht quite, as in a traunce.

Publilius Syrus (1934), 314: In venere semper dulcis est dementia (To lose your wits in love is always sweet).

502 THE ONE WHO CAUSES ALSO CURES THE WOUND OF **LOVE**

FQ, II, xii, 73, 2–3: With her false eyes fast fixed in his sight, As seeking medicine whence she was stong. ¶ *Ibid.*, VI, x, 31, 4–8: The rigour of his smart . . . to recure, no skill of leaches art Mote him availe, but to returne againe To his wounds worker, that with lovely dart Dinting his brest, had bred his restlesse paine.

* Publilius Syrus (1934), 31: Amoris vulnus idem sanat qui facit (The one who causes also cures the wound of love).

Cf. Taylor, 44; Tilley, H90.

503 THEY THAT **LOVE** MOST SPEAK LEAST

FQ, II, x, 31, 2: Love is not, where most it is profest.

Cf. Stevenson, 1478:3; Tilley, L165.

504 TRUE **LOVE** KNOWS NO MEAN OR MEASURE

FQ, IV, ix, 21, 3–4: Claribell . . . With fervent flames . . . loved out of measure. ¶ *Ibid.*, VII, vi, 44, 3–6: Where-as shee had out of measure Long lov'd the Fanchin, . . . he would undertake for this to get her To be his love.

Culman, 17: Amor verus nullum novit habere modum (True love does not know how to keep any measure).

Phineas Fletcher, *Piscatorie Eclog.*, iii, 17, 7: Love knows no mean nor measure.

Cf. Stevenson, 1473:5.

505 A **LOW** KIND OF LIFE IS THE SAFEST

Shep. Cal., Julye, Glosse, 173–177: He taketh occasion to prayse the meane and lowly state, as that wherein is safetie without feare, and quiet without danger. ¶ *Mother Hub.*, 909–910: Sweete home, where meane estate In safe assurance, without strife or hate.

Culman, 12: Humile vitae genus tutissimum (A mean kind of life is the safest). ¶ *Ibid.*, 20: Humilis fortuna tutior est quam excelsa (A mean fortune is safer than a lofty fortune).

Tacitus, *Annals*, xiv, 60: Ex mediocritate fortunae, pauciora pericula sunt (In modesty of fortune there are fewer dangers).

Cf. Stevenson, 1604:4; C. G. Smith, 118.

506 MORE BY **LUCK** THAN BY WIT

Cf. no. 290: In all human affairs fortune (providence) rules

FQ, IV, x, 4, 9: My lucky lot; sith all by lot we hold. ¶ *Ibid.*, VI, iii, 51, 8: Chaunces oft exceed all humaine thought.

Publilius Syrus (1835), 60: Ars non ea est, quae casu ad effectum venit (Skill avails nothing, when chance determines the issue).

Stubbes, *Anat. of Abuses* (N. Sh. S.), II, 53: It is by meere chance, and not by any knowledge of theirs. ¶ Draxe, 779 (*s. v.* Fortune): More by chance then by any good cunning. ¶ Jonson, *Underwoods*, XXV, 52, *Works*, VIII, 179: More through luck, then wit.

Cf. Tilley, C225.

507 THERE IS **LUCK** IN ODD NUMBERS

FQ, III, ii, 50, 8–9: Spitt thrise upon me, thrise upon me spitt; Th' uneven nomber for this busines is most fitt.

Vergil, *Ciris*, 372–373: "Ter in gremium mecum," inquit, "despue, virgo, despue ter, virgo: numero deus impare gaudet" (She cries: "Spit thrice into my bosom, as I do, maiden; spit thrice, maiden: in an uneven number heaven delights").

Cf. Apperson, 388; W. G. Smith, 394; Tilley, L582.

508 THERE IS NO **LUCK** SO GOOD BUT YOU COULD MAKE SOME COMPLAINT ABOUT IT

FQ, VI, viii, 32, 2–9: She thought Her selfe now past the perill of her feares . . . And sitting downe, . . . often did of love, and oft of lucke complaine.

* Publilius Syrus (1934), 429: Nulla tam bona est fortuna de qua nihil possis queri (There is no luck so good but you could make some complaint about it).

509 THE **LUST** OF THE EYE DECEIVES

FQ, II, v, 34, 5–8: Whiles through their lids his wanton eies do peepe, To steale a snatch of amorous conceipt, . . . he them deceives.

Culman, 34: Oculorum concupiscentia decipit (The lust of the eye deceives us).

510 TO HAVE THE EYES OF **LYNCEUS** (A LYNX)

FQ, II, xi, 8, 6: And every one of them had lynces eyes.

Aristophanes, *Plutus*, 210: ὀξύτερον τοῦ Λυγκέως (Keener-sighted than Lynceus). ¶ Horace, *Sat.*, i, 2, 90–91: Lyncei contemplere oculis (To survey with the eyes of Lynceus). ¶ Erasmus, *Adagia*, 427E: Lyncei perspicacitas in proverbium abiit (The sharp-sightedness of Lynceus has developed into a proverb). ¶ Sidney, *Arcadia*, *Works*, II, 201: Had *Lynces* eyes. ¶ Nashe, *Pierce P.*, *Works*, I, 226: *Linceus* eyes, that see through stone walles.

Cf. Stevenson, 2106:1.

511 IF YOU CANNOT **MAKE** IT BETTER, DO NOT MAKE IT WORSE

FQ, I, ii, 26, 4: Doe none ill, if please ye not doe well. ¶ *Mother Hub.*, 384: Ne make one title worse, ne make one better.

Erasmus, *Colloquia Fam.*, 740F: Si non datur prodesse, damus operam ne quem laedamus (If we find no opportunity of doing good, we take care to do nobody any harm).

Cf. Tilley, M47.

512 TO **MAKE** OR MAR

FQ, III, ii, 3, 8: And, striving fit to make, I feare doe marre. ¶ *Ibid.*, IV, i, 29, 3: One did make, the other mard againe.

Sidney, *Arcadia*, *Works*, I, 131: He is mard that is for others made. ¶ Harvey, *Pierces Super.*, *Works*, II, 58: Whome they will not make, shall not marre. ¶ Shakespeare, *Mids. Night's D.*, I, ii, 39: Make and mar. ¶ Shakespeare, *Macb.*, II, iii, 36: It makes him, and it mars him.

Cf. W. G. Smith, 399; Tilley, M48.

513 **MAN** IS SUBJECT TO CALAMITY

FQ, I, viii, 1, 1–2: How many perils doe enfold . . . man, to make him daily fall. ¶ *Ibid.*, III, v, 36, 6–7: Wee mortall wights . . . lives and fortunes bee To commun accidents stil open layd. ¶ *Muiopotmos*, 221–222: Thousand perills lie in close awaite About us daylie, to worke our decay.

Culman, 32: Homo calamitosum animal (Man is a living creature subject to calamity).

Cato, *Disticha*, i, 33: Cum dubia incertis versetur vita periclis (Since our frail life through dangers sure must run). ¶ Lucretius, *De Rerum Natura*, ii, 15–16: Qualibus in tenebris vitae quantisque periclis degitur hoc aevi quodcumquest (In what gloom of life, in how great perils is passed all your poor span of time)! ¶ *Ibid.*, vi, 29–31: Quidve mali foret in rebus mortalibus passim, quod fieret naturali varieque volaret seu casu seu vi (He showed what evil there was everywhere in human affairs, which comes about and flies to us in different ways, by natural chance or violence).

514 LET EVERY **MAN** HAVE HIS OWN

FQ, V, Prol., 3, 7: All men sought their owne, and none no more. ¶ *Ibid.*, iv, 20, 6: So was their discord by this doome appeased, And each one had his right.

Cf. Tilley, M209.

515 NOTHING IS MORE MISERABLE THAN **MAN**

Teares of the M., 127–128: Most miserable creature under sky Man without understanding doth appeare.

Culman, 14: Nihil est homine calamitosius (Nothing is more miserable than man).

Homer, *Iliad*, xvii, 446–447: *οὐ μὲν γάρ τί πού ἐστιν ὀϊζυρώτερον ἀνδρὸς πάντων ὅσσα τε γαῖαν ἔπι πνείει τε καὶ ἕρπει* (For in sooth there is naught, I ween, more miserable than man among all things that breathe and move upon earth).

Cf. Stevenson, 1591:13.

516 YOU MAY KNOW A **MAN** BY HIS MANNERS

FQ, VI, iii, 1, 3–4: A man by nothing is so well bewrayed As by his manners.

Cf. Tilley, M440.

517 THE **MANY** OVERPOWER THE FEW

Cf. no. 347: The great ones eat up the little ones

View, 675: The greater number will carrye away the less.

Vergil, *Aeneid*, ii, 424: Ilicet obruimur numero (Straight way we are overwhelmed with odds). ¶ O'Rahilly, 291: Many overpower few.

518 TO MISS THE **MARK**

Cf. no. 519: To shoot wide of the mark

Shep. Cal., Nov., 155: Doe misse the marked scope. ¶ *FQ*, I, viii, 8, 3: Missing the marke of his misaymed sight. ¶ *Ibid.*, IV, iii, 18, 8: Who, missing of the marke which he had eyde. ¶ *Ibid.*, VI, vii, 7, 6: Th' one did misse his marke.

Cf. Stevenson, 1598:3; Tilley, M669.

519 TO SHOOT WIDE OF THE **MARK**

Cf. no. 518: To miss the mark

Shep. Cal., Nov., 155: Shooting wide, doe misse the marked scope. ¶ *View*, 632: He shootes wyde on the bowe hand, and very farr from the marke.

Cf. Tilley, M668.

520 HE CANNOT **MASTER** OTHERS WHO MASTERS NOT HIMSELF

FQ, II, v, 15, 9: Vaine others overthrowes who selfe doth overthrow. ¶ *Ibid.*, VI, i, 41, 5–6: In vaine he seeketh others to suppresse, Who hath not learnd him selfe first to subdew.

Publilius Syrus (1835), 928: Stultum, imperare reliquis, qui nescit sibi (It is folly for him to rule over others who cannot govern himself).

Cicero, *Pro Lege Manilia*, xiii, 38: Neque enim potest exercitum is continere imperator, qui se ipse non continet (No commander can control an army who does not control himself). ¶ Claudian, *Penegyricus De Quarto Consulatu Honorii Augusti*, 261–262: Tunc omnia iure tenebis, cum poteris rex esse tui (When thou canst be king over thyself then shalt thou hold rightful rule over the world).

Cf. W. G. Smith, 105; Tilley, C552.

521 ONE WHO CANNOT **MASTER** LITTLE THINGS CANNOT MASTER BIG THINGS

FQ, V, ii. 43, 9: Ill can he rule the great, that cannot reach the small.

522 **MASTERY** MOWS THE MEADOW DOWN

FQ, IV, ix, 2, 4: And them with maystring discipline doth tame. ¶ *Ibid.*, VI, xii, 38, 1–2: The maystring might Of doughty Calidore, supprest and tamed.

Wyntoun, *Chron.* (1425), LXXX, 1499: It is said in commone sawis that mastry mawis the medow doune. ¶ Ray, *Prov.* (1678), 384: Maisterie mawes the meadows down.

Cf. W. G. Smith, 413; Stevenson, 1545:5.

523 KEEP THE GOLDEN **MEAN** IN ALL THINGS

Cf. no. 817: Virtue is a mean

FQ, II, i, 58, 1–2: Temperaunce . . . can measure out a meane. ¶ *Ibid.*, ii, 38, 1–4: The faire Medina . . . With equall measure . . . did moderate The strong extremities of their outrage. ¶ *Ibid.*, xii, 33, 4: A solemne meane unto them measured. ¶ *Teares of the M.*, 379–380: I that rule in measure moderate The tempest of that stormie passion.

Culman, 5: Temperantiam exerce (Use temperance). ¶ *Ibid.*, 8: Ne quid nimis (Do nothing too much). ¶ *Ibid.*, 10: Adest unicuique rei modus (Every thing has a mean). ¶ *Ibid.*, 21: Modus omnibus in rebus optimus habendus (A mean is to be accounted the best in all things). ¶ Publilius Syrus (1835), 1091: Temperamentum tene (Keep the golden mean).

Plato, *Gorgias*, 507D: τὸν βουλόμενον, ὡς ἔοικεν, εὐδαίμονα εἶναι σωφροσύνην μὲν διωκτέον καὶ ἀσκητέον (Anyone, as it seems, who desires to be happy must pursue and practice temperance). ¶ Aristotle, *N. Ethics*, ii, 7, 3: μεσότης μὲν σωφροσύνη (The observance of the mean is temperance). ¶ Aristotle, *Rhetoric*, ii, 21, 13: Μηδὲν ἄγαν (Nothing in excess). ¶ Plautus, *Poenulus*, 237: Modus omnibus rebus (Moderation in all things). ¶ Terence, *Andria*, 61: Ne quid nimis (Moderation in all things). ¶ Cicero, *De Fin.*, iii, 22, 73: Nihil nimis (Moderation in all things). ¶ Seneca, *Epist.*, xciv, 43: Nil nimis (Nothing in excess). ¶ Erasmus, *Adagia*, 259E: Ne quid nimis (Nothing too much). ¶ Chaucer, *Parson's T.*, 833: Attemperaunce, that holdeth the meene in alle thynges. ¶ Barclay, *Ship of F.*, I, 97: In eche thynge ought to be had measure.

Cf. Taverner, 19; Stevenson, 1602:1–4; C. G. Smith, 208.

524 TO ENJOY IN **MEMORY** ONE'S PAST LIFE IS TO LIVE TWICE OVER

Colin Clouts, 38–39: Of good passed newly to discus, By dubble usurie doth twise renew it.

Martial, *Epigr.*, x, 23, 7–8: Hoc est vivere bis, vita posse priore frui (To be able to enjoy the recollection of one's past life, this is to live twice over).

525 THINGS PAST CANNOT BE **MENDED**

FQ, VI, xi, 34, 7: He could not mend thing past.

Culman, 24: Praeterita reprehendi possunt, corrigi non possunt (Things may be blamed, but they cannot be amended).

526 **MERCY** IS THE MIGHTY'S JEWEL

Cf. no. 104: Clemency breeds goodwill and favor

FQ, II, vi, 36, 5–6: Such is the might Of courteous clemency in gentle hart. ¶ *Amoretti*, xlix, 3: Mercy is the Mighties jewell.

Seneca, *Octavia*, 442: Magnum . . . remedium clementia est (Clemency is a sovereign cure). ¶ Shakespeare, *Merch. of V.*, IV, i, 184–188: Mercy . . . 'Tis mightiest in the mightiest.

527 HE SHALL FIND **MERCY** THAT MERCIFUL IS

FQ, VI, i, 42, 1–2: Who will not mercie unto others shew, How can he mercy ever hope to have?

New Testament: *Matthew*, v, 7: μακάριοι οἱ ἐλεήμονες, ὅτι αὐτοὶ ἐλεηθήσονται (Blessed are the merciful: for they shall obtain mercy). ¶ Seneca,

De Clem., i, 1, 9: Ex clementia omnes idem sperant (From mercy men all hope to have the same). ¶ Shakespeare, *Merch. of V.*, IV, i, 88: How shalt thou hope for mercy, rend'ring none?

Cf. Stevenson, 1565:9; Tilley, M895.

528 **MERRY** ENGLAND (LONDON)

FQ, I, x, 61, 9: *Saint George* of mery *England*, the signe of victoree. ¶ *Prothalamion*, 127–128: They all to mery London came, To mery London.

Cf. W. G. Smith, 420.

529 AS **MERRY** AS POPE JOHN

FQ (Globe), II, vi, 3, 4: As merry as Pope Jone.

Foxe, *Acts and Mon.* (1563), 178: As merry as pope John, a proverb. ¶ Pilkington, *Lett. to Archbishop of Cant.*, *Works* (Parker S.), VII: As merry as Pope Joan. ¶ Edwards, *Damon and P.*, 1230: As merry as Pope John. ¶ Harvey, *Pierces Super.*, *Works*, II, 185: If Flesh prooue not a Pope Ioane. ¶ Harington, *Nugae Antiq.* (1779), II, 195: As the phrase is, as mery as Pope Joane. ¶ Deloney, *Gentle Craft*, *Works*, 149: As merry as pope John.

Cf. *FQ* (Variorum), II, 242.

530 IT IS GOOD TO BE **MERRY** AND WISE

Shep. Cal., Aug., 144: With mery thing its good to medle sadde.

Horace, *Odes*, iv, 12, 27: Misce stultitiam consiliis brevem (Mingle, while thou mayst, brief folly with thy wisdom). ¶ Martial, *Epigr.*, ii, 41, 1: Ride si sapis (Laugh, if you are wise). ¶ Udall, *Ralph Roister D.*, I, 1, 5–6: An-other sayd sawe doth men aduise That they be together both mery and wise. ¶ Edwards, *Damon and P.*, 657: It is very good to be merry and wise. ¶ Harvey, *Pierces Super.*, *Works*, II, 247: It is good, they say, to be merry, and wise.

Cf. Apperson, 413; W. G. Smith, 420; Stevenson, 1567:5; Tilley, G324.

531 THE **MERRY** MONTH OF MAY

Shep. Cal., Maye, 1: The mery moneth of May.

Cf. Apperson, 414; W. G. Smith, 413; Stevenson, 1549:6; Tilley, M1106.

532 **MIGHT** MAKES RIGHT

FQ, V, iv, 1, 9: Powre is the right hand of Justice truely hight.

Plato, *Republic*, i, 338C: *φημὶ γὰρ ἐγὼ εἶναι τὸ δίκαιον οὐκ ἄλλο τι ἢ τὸ τοῦ κρείττονος ξυμφέρον* (I affirm that might is right, justice the interest of the stronger). ¶ Seneca, *Hercules Furens*, 253: Ius est in armis (Might is right). ¶ Greene, *A Quippe for an Upstart C.*, *Works*, XI, 252: Howsoeuer right bee, might carries awaie the verdict. ¶ Shakespeare, *Troilus & Cres.*, I, iii, 116: Force should be right.

Cf. Stevenson, 1572:1.

533 WITH **MIGHT** AND MAIN

Shep. Cal., March, 86: With might and maine. ¶ *FQ*, I, xi, 43, 4: With all his might and maine. ¶ *Ruines of T.*, 62: Of their might and maine. ¶ *Virgils Gnat*, 524: With his might and maine. ¶ *FQ*, IV, iv, 44, 8: With all his might and maine. ¶ *Ibid.*, viii, 45, 3: With all his might and maine. ¶ *Ibid.*, V, iii, 12, 3: Joyned might and maine. ¶ *Ibid.*, ix, 19, 3: With so huge might and maine. ¶ *Ibid.*, x, 32, 3: With so huge might and maine. ¶ *Ibid.*, xii, 23, 6: With all his might and maine. ¶ *Ibid.*, VI, iv, 7, 4: With all his might and maine. *Ibid.*, vi, 23, 3: With might and maine.

Cursor M., 17028: Mikel might and main. ¶ *Melayne* (1400), 282: Hase loste both Mayne & myght. ¶ *World & Child* (Manly), 195: With mayne and all my myght. ¶ Gascoigne, *Grief of Joye*, *Works*, II, 529: Withe verie maine & might.

Cf. Clarke, 60; Tilley, M923.

534 **MILESIAN** LIES

View, 627: All which are in very trueth fables, and very Mylesian lyes (as the Latine proverbe is).

Camden, *Britannia* (1586), 491: *Nugae Milesiae* (Milesian jokes).
Cf. Spenser, *Prose Works* (Variorum), 319; Tilley, L242.

535 A MAN'S **MIND** OFTEN WARNS HIM OF IMPENDING EVIL

FQ, I, i, 13, 2–8: I better wot then you . . . wisedome warnes, whilest foot is in the gate, To stay the steppe, ere forced to retrate . . . I read beware.

Culman, 7: Mens praesaga futuri (The mind foreknows of a thing to come). ¶ *Ibid.*, 13: Mens est praesaga futuri (The mind is a foreteller of that which is to come).

Cf. Tilley, M475; C. G. Smith, 197.

536 GOOD AND EVIL ARE CHIEFLY IN THE **MIND**

FQ, VI, Prol., 5, 8–9: But Vertues seat is deepe within the mynd, And not in outward shows, but inward thoughts defynd. ¶ *Ibid.*, ix, 30, 1: It is the mynd that maketh good or ill.

Seneca, *Hippolytus*, 735: Mens impudicam facere, non casus solet ('Tis thinking makes impure, not circumstance). ¶ Marcus Aurelius, *Mediations*, ix, 42: τὸ δὲ κακόν σου καὶ τὸ βλαβερὸν ἐνταῦθα πᾶσαν τὴν ὑπόστασιν ἔχει (But it is in thy mind that the evil for thee and the harmful have their existence); cf. xii, 8. ¶ Shakespeare, *Hamlet*, II, ii, 255–257: There is nothing either good or bad but thinking makes it so. ¶ Donne, *Progresse of the Soule*, 518–520, *Poetical Works* (Grierson), I, 316: Ther's nothing simply good, nor ill alone, . . . The onely measure is, and judge, opinion.

Cf. Tilley, M254.

537 MAN'S **MIND** IS IMMORTAL

Axiochus (Variorum), 381: Euery mans minde is immortall. ¶ *Hymne in Honour of L.*, 103–104: Man . . . breathes a more immortall mynd . . . for eternitie. ¶ *FQ*, VII, vii, 19, 8: Their [men's] minds (which they immortall call).

Lucretius, *De Rerum Natura*, iii, 624–626: Immortalis natura animaist et sentire potest secreta a corpore nostro (The nature of the mind is immortal and can feel when separated from our body). ¶ *Ibid.*, 670–671: Immortalis natura animai constat (The nature of the mind is immortal). ¶ Cicero, *De Sen.*, xxiii, 85: Si in hoc erro, qui animos hominum immortalis esse credam libenter erro (If I err in my belief that the souls of men are immortal, I gladly err).

538 PAIN OF THE **MIND** IS MORE SEVERE THAN PAIN OF BODY

FQ, VI, v, 28, 3–4: Both in minde, the which most grieveth me, And body have receiv'd a mortall wound. ¶ *Ibid.*, vii, 49, 6–8: With bitter mockes and mowes He would him scorne, that to his gentle mynd Was much more grievous then the others [physical] blowes.

Publilius Syrus (1934), 166: Dolor animi (nimio) gravior est quam corporis (Pain of the mind is far more severe than bodily pain).

539 THE **MIND** ALWAYS FEARS THE UNKNOWN EVIL MORE

FQ, I, i, 12, 3–4: The danger hid, the place unknowne and wilde, Breedes dreadful doubts.

Publilius Syrus (1934), 655: Semper plus metuit animus ignotum malum (The mind always fears the unknown evil more).

Gismond of Salerne (1567–1568), V, i, 35–36: For drede of things unknowen doeth allway cause Man drede the worst, till he the better know.

Cf. Tilley, H166; C. G. Smith, 198.

540 THE DISPOSITION OF THE **MIND** FOLLOWS THE TEMPERATURE (COMPOSITION, CONSTITUTION, COMPLEXION) OF THE BODY

View, 638: The mynd followeth much the temperature of the bodye.

Guazzo, *Civ. Conv.*, *Works*, II, 47: The disposition of the mynd, followeth the complexion of the body. ¶ Harvey, *Letter-Book*, 88: The temperature and disposition [and] inclination of the mindes followythe the temperature and composition of the bodye. ¶ Greene, *Penelopes Web*, *Works*, V, 152: The disposition of the senses followes truely the temperature and constitution of their bodies.

Cf. Tilley, D381.

541 THE STEADFAST **MIND** ADMITS NO VARIABLE OPINION

FQ, IV, vii, 16, 5: Nothing could my fixed mind remove. ¶ *Ibid.*, xi, 2, 7–8: Neither gifts nor graces kind Her constant mind could move at all. ¶ *Ibid.*, VI, xi, 5, 1–2: But all that ever he could doe or say Her constant mynd could not a whit remove.

* Publilius Syrus (1934), 232: Gravis animus dubiam non habet sententiam (The steadfast mind admits no halting opinion).

542 THE **MINDS** OF MEN ARE CHANGEABLE

Lett. to Harvey, 45: Minds of nobles varie, as their estates. ¶ *FQ*, VII, vii, 19, 8–9: Their [men's] minds . . . Still change and vary thoughts, as new occasions fall.

Culman, 6: Hominum mentes variae (The minds of men are changeable). ¶ *Ibid.*: Ingenia hominum varia (The inclinations of men are changeable).

Hawes, *Past. Pleas.*, 83: The mynde of men chaungeth.

543 THE MARRIAGE OF TRUE **MINDS** IS THE STRONGEST OF TIES

FQ, IV, ix, 1, 8–9: The band of vertuous mind, Me seemes, the gentle hart should most assured bind.

Publilius Syrus (1934), 529: Perenne coniugium animus, non corpus, facit (Mind, not body, makes lasting wedlock). ¶ * *Ibid.* (1835), 149:

Conjunctio animi maxima est cognatio (The marriage of true minds is the strongest of ties).

Erasmus, *Colloquia Fam.*, 696A: Magis erit animorum quam corporum conjugium (The wedlock of minds will be greater than that of bodies).

Cf. C. G. Smith, 199.

544 THEY PASS PEACEFUL LIVES WHO IGNORE "**MINE**" AND "THINE"

Mother Hub., 148–150: That there might be no difference nor strife, Nor ought cald mine or thine: thrice happie then Was the condition of mortall men.

Publilius Syrus (1835), 804: Quieta vita his qui tollunt *meum*, *tuum* (They pass peaceful lives who ignore *mine* and *thine*).

Plato, *Republic*, v, 462C: *'Εν ᾗτινι δὴ πόλει πλεῖστοι ἐπὶ τὸ αὐτὸ κατὰ ταὐτὰ τοῦτο λέγουσι τὸ ἐμὸν καὶ τὸ οὐκ ἐμόν. αὕτη ἄριστα διοικεῖται* (That city, then, is best ordered in which the greatest number use the expression "mine" and "not mine" of the same things in the same way).

545 BETTER A **MISCHIEF** THAN AN INCONVENIENCE

View, 618: For better is a mischeif, then an inconvenience. ¶ *Ibid.*, 624: But (as you earst sayd) better a mischeif then an inconvenience.

Shakespeare, *Merry Wives*, IV, ii, 75–76: Any extremity rather than a mischief.

Cf. Apperson, 41; W. G. Smith, 37; Tilley, M995.

546 NO ONE IS **MISERABLE** EXCEPT BY HIS OWN FAULT

FQ, II, v, 1, 8–9: His owne woes author, who so bound it findes, As did Pyrochles.

Culman, 33: Homo sibi ipsi calamitatum author (Man is the author of calamities to himself).

Seneca, *Epist.*, lxx, 15: Nemo nisi vitio suo miser est (No one is miserable except by his own fault).

Cf. Stevenson, 2169:14.

547 **MISERY** NEVER QUITS HIM WHOSE THOUGHTS ALWAYS RUN WITH HIS FEARS

FQ, II, iv, 44, 6–7: Woe never wants, where every cause is caught, And rash Occasion makes unquiet life.

Publilius Syrus (1934), 458: Numquam non miser est qui quod timeat cogitat (Misery never quits him whose thoughts run on something to dread).

Cf. C. G. Smith, 202.

548 **MISERY** WILL HUMBLE THE HAUGHTIEST HEART

Mother Hub., 256: Miserie doth bravest mindes abate.

Nashe, *Strange Newes*, *Works*, I, 294: Misery will humble the haughtiest heart in the world. ¶ Deloney, *Gentle Craft*, *Works*, 185: Want makes men lowly, and commonly gentle.

549 **MISERY** WITHOUT A VOICE IS HELL

Cf. no. 349: Pent up grief will burst the heart; no. 761: By telling our woes we often lessen them

Colin Clouts, 659: Most wretched he, that is and cannot tell.

* Publilius Syrus (1934), 248: Heu dolor quam miser est qui in tormento vocem non habet (How pitiful the pain that has no voice amid tortures)!

Cf. Stevenson, 1041:2.

550 IN **MISERY** EVEN LIFE IS AN INSULT

Daphnaïda, 91: For harts deep sorrow hates both life and light.

Publilius Syrus (1934), 283: In miseria vita etiam contumelia est (In misery even life is an insult).

551 IN **MISERY** (TROUBLE) IT IS GOOD TO HAVE COMPANY

Daphnaïda, 67: Griefe findes some ease by him that like does beare. ¶ *FQ*, IV, v, 30, 4–5: Whereto great comfort in her sad misfare Was Amoret, companion of her care.

Culman, 26: Solatium in miseriis amicus compatiens (A friend that suffers with us is a comfort in miseries). ¶ Publilius Syrus (1835), 1012: Calamitatum habere socios miseris est solatio (It is consolation to the wretched to have companions in misery).

Cato, *Collectio Monos.*, 63: Quisque miser casu alterius solatia sumit (Another's woe consoles all wretched folk). ¶ Seneca, *Ad Marciam de Con.*, xii, 5: Solacii genus est turba miserorum (A crowd of fellow sufferers is a kind of comfort in misery). ¶ Erasmus, *Epist.*, 427E: Societas miseriam levat (Fellowship lightens misery). ¶ Chaucer, *Troilus*, I, 708–709: Men seyn, "to wrecche is consolacioun To have another felawe in hys peyne." ¶ Greene, *Mamillia*, *Works*, II, 213: There is no greater comfort than to haue companions in sorrow; cf. *Tullies Love*, *Works*, VII, 144. ¶ Sidney, *Arcadia*, *Works*, II, 10: Sorrow especially glad to find fellowes; cf. II, 137; IV, 306. ¶ Lodge, *Rosalynde*, *Works*, I, 35: Solamen miseris socios habuisse doloris. ¶ Jonson, *Cynthia's R.*, V, iv, 595–596, *Works*, IV, 156: When men disgraces share, The lesser is the care.

Cf. Stevenson, 1042:6–9; Tilley, C571; C. G. Smith, 30.

552 MAN IS BORN TO **MISERY**

Cf. no. 560: There is no mortal whom distress cannot reach; no. 870: We begin life in woe, we end it in misery

Mother Hub., 907: Unhappie wight, borne to desastrous end.

Culman, 32: Homo ad calamitatem nascitur (Man is born to misery).

553 THE EYES AND EARS OF THE **MOB** ARE OFTEN FALSE WITNESSES

FQ, V, iii, 17, 9: So feeble skill of perfect things the vulgar has. ¶ *View*, 609: A vayne conceit of simple men, which judge thinges by theyre effectes, and not by theyre causes.

Culman, 10: Vulgi judicium stultum (The judgment of the common people is fond). ¶ Publilius Syrus (1835), 867: Saepe oculi et aures vulgi sunt testes mali (The eyes and ears of the mob are often false witnesses).

Cicero, *Pro Roscio Comoedo*, x, 29–30: Sic est vulgus; ex veritate pauca, ex opinione multa aestimat (This is the way of the crowd; its judgments are seldom founded on truth, mostly on opinion).

Cf. C. G. Smith, 206.

554 WITH **MOCKS** AND MOWS

FQ, VI, vii, 49, 6–7: With bitter mockes and mowes He would him scorne.

Gascoigne, *Arte of Venerie*, *Works*, II, 360: Of antikes, mocks, & mowes. ¶ Guazzo, *Civ. Conv.*, I, 77: Mops and mowes. ¶ Fulbecke, *First Pt. Parall.* (1602), 71: Taunts with mockes, and mowes. ¶ Rich, *Faults and Nothing but Faults* (1606), 7: See how hee mops and how he mowes.

Cf. Tilley, M1030.

555 PRACTICE **MODESTY**

FQ, VI, x, 23, 8–9: We should our selves demeane, to low, to hie, To friends, to foes; which skill men call civility.

Culman, 3: Pudorem serva (Keep modesty). ¶ *Ibid.*: Verecundiam serva (Practice modesty).

Cato, *Collectio Dis. Vulg.*, 12: Verecundiam serva (Preserve your modesty).

556 **MONEY** CAN DO ANYTHING

FQ, II, vii, 11, 2–4: Money can thy wantes at will supply . . . all things for thee meet It can purvay. ¶ *Mother Hub.*, 153: Without golde now nothing wilbe got.

Culman, 5: Auro nihil inexpugnabile (Nothing is unconquerable with gold). ¶ *Ibid.*, 8: Pecuniae obediunt omnia (All things obey money). ¶ *Ibid.*, 27: Sola pecunia possunt expugnari alioqui invicta

(Things otherwise invincible may be overcome only with money). ¶ Publilius Syrus (1934), 506: Pecunia (una) regimen est rerum omnium (Money alone is the ruling principle of the world).

Chaucer, *Mel.*, VII, 1550: Salomon seith that "alle thynges obeyen to moneye". ¶ Erasmus, *Adagia*, 144D: Pecuniae obediunt omnia (All things obey money). ¶ Florio, *First Fruites*, 18: Money ruleth al things.

Cf. Apperson, 421; Stevenson, 1618:2; Tilley, T163; M1084; C. G. Smith, 209.

557 **MONEY** IS (RICHES ARE) THE ROOT OF ALL EVIL

FQ, II, vii, 12, 1–2: All otherwise, . . . I riches read, And deeme them roote of all disquietnesse. ¶ *Ibid.*, III, x, 31, 8–9: Minds of mortal men are muchell mard And mov'd amisse with massy mucks unmeet regard. ¶ *Ibid.*, VI, ix, 33, 5: That mucky masse [gold], the cause of mens decay.

Culman, 5: Divitiae vitiorum ministrae (Riches are the occasions of vices). ¶ *Ibid.*, 30: Cupiditas habendi radix omnium malorum (The desire of having is the root of all evil).

New Testament: *I Timothy*, vi, 10: *ῥίζα γὰρ πάντων τῶν κακῶν ἐστὶν ἡ φιλαργυρία* (For the love of money is the root of all evil). ¶ Rutilius Namatianus, *De Ruditu Suo*, i, 358: Auri caecus amor ducit in omne nefas (Blind lust of gold leads into every crime).

Cf. Stevenson, 1608:1; Tilley, C746.

558 WHY HAVE **MONEY**, IF YOU CANNOT USE IT?

FQ, II, vi, 17, 6: What bootes it al to have, and nothing use?

Publilius Syrus (1934), 618: Quid tibi pecunia opus est, si uti non potes (What good is money to you, if you cannot use it)?

559 THE **MORE** A MAN HAS, THE MORE HE DESIRES

Cf. no. 134: Covetousness cannot be satisfied

FQ, I, iv, 29, 4: Whose welth was want. ¶ *Ibid.*, VI, ix, 30, 3–4: Some, that hath abundance at his will, Hath not enough, but wants in greatest store.

Publilius Syrus (1934), 55: Avarus animus nullo satiatur lucro (No gain satisfies a greedy mind). ¶ *Ibid.* (1835), 71: Avarum irritat, non satiat pecunia (Money does not sate avarice, but stimulates it).

Lucretius, *De Rerum Natura*, iv, 1089–1090: Plurima habemus, tam magis ardescit dira cuppedine pectus (The more we have the more fierce burns the heart with fell craving). ¶ Horace, *Odes*, iii, 16, 42–43: Multa petentibus desunt multa (To those who seek for much, much is ever lacking). ¶ Horace, *Epist.*, ii, 2, 147–148: Quanto plura parasti, tanto plura cupis (The more you get, the more you want). ¶ Ovid, *Fasti*, i, 212: Cum possideant plurima, plura petunt (They who have the most possessions still crave for more). ¶ Seneca, *De Benef.*, ii, 27, 3: Maiora cupimos, quo maiora venerunt (The more we get, the more we covet). ¶ Seneca, *Epist.*, cxix, 6: Qui multum habet, plus cupit (He who has much desires more). ¶ Sidney, *Arcadia*, *Works*, I, 253: I waile for want, and yet am chokte with store. ¶ Sidney, *Astro. and S.*, xxiv, 4, *Works*, II, 252: Welth breeding want, more rich, more wretched grow.

Cf. Tilley, M1144; M1287; C. G. Smith, 210.

560 THERE IS NO **MORTAL** WHOM DISTRESS CANNOT REACH

Cf. no. 552: Man is born to misery; no. 870: We begin life in woe, we end it in misery

FQ, III, xi, 14, 8–9: For who nill bide the burden of distresse Must not here thinke to live: for life is wretchednesse.

Publilius Syrus (1835), 519: Mortalis nemo est, quem non attingat dolor (There is no mortal whom distress cannot reach).

561 TO MAKE **MUCH** OUT OF NOUGHT

FQ, II, v, 19, 6: So matter did she make of nought.

Harvey, *Foure-Lett.*, *Works*, I, 181: To make something of nothing.

Cf. Tilley, M1280.

562 **MUCK** OF THE WORLD

FQ, II, vii, 10, 5: Regard of wordly mucke doth fowly blend.
Cf. Tilley, M1298.

563 TO ANSWER **MUM**

FQ, IV, vii, 44, 5: And unto every thing did aunswere mum.

Harvey, *Letter-Book*, 136: Not halfe a word more but mumme. ¶ Harvey, *Lett. between Spenser and Harvey*, *Works*, I, 134: Lett it be mum to all the world; cf. *Pierces Super.*, *Works*, II, 210. ¶ Harvey, *Pierces Super.*, Works, II, 302: His Aunswere should haue bene Mum.

Cf. Tilley, M1310; N279, W767.

564 **MUSIC** EASES THE TROUBLED MIND

FQ, I, v, 3, 4–5: Minstrales maken melody, To drive away the dull melancholy. ¶ *Ibid.*, 17, 6–8: Most heavenly melody About the bed sweet musicke did divide, Him to beguile of griefe and agony. ¶ *Ibid.* (Globe), viii, 44, 4: Musicke breeds delight in loathing eare. ¶ *Ibid.*, xii, 38, 6–8: Sweete musicke did apply . . . the warbling notes to play, To drive away the dull melancholy. ¶ *Ibid.*, IV, ii, 3, 1–2: Such [music] us'd Glauce to that wrathfull knight, To calme the tempest of his troubled thought.

Painter, *Palace of P.*, II, 149: Musike, easeth the troubled mynde.

Cf. Henderson, 235; Stevenson, 1643:5.

565 **NATURE** DOES NOT ALLOW A WOMAN TO RULE

FQ, V, v, 25, 1–9: Women kynd . . . wise Nature did . . . strongly bynd, T' obay the heasts of mans well ruling hand, . . . Unlesse the heavens them lift to lawfull soveraintie.

Culman, 22: Natu a non dedit imperare foeminis (Nature has not granted to women to rule). ¶ *Ibid.:* Natura non sinit praeesse foeminam (Nature does not suffer a woman to bear rule).

566 **NATURE** IS CONTENT WITH A LITTLE

FQ, II, vii, 15, 3–4: With how small allowaunce Untroubled nature doth her selfe suffise. ¶ *Ibid.*, VI, ix, 17, 8–9: Nature satisfyde . . . doth little crave, contented to abyde. ¶ *Ibid.*, 20, 6–7: So taught of nature, which doth litle need Of forreine helpes to lifes due nourishment.

Culman, 7: Natura paucis contenta (Nature is content with a few things). ¶ *Ibid.*, 14: Naturae necessitas exiguo placatur (Nature's necessity is satisfied with a little).

Seneca, *Epist.*, xvi, 8: Exiguum natura desiderat (Nature's wants are slight).

Cf. Tilley, N45.

567 **NATURE**, NOT RANK, MAKES THE GENTLEMAN

FQ, VI, iii, 2, 2: Gentle bloud will gentle manners breed.

Publilius Syrus (1934), 501: Pudor doceri non potest, nasci potest (Modesty is born, not taught). ¶ *Ibid.*, 713: Virum bonum natura non ordo facit (Nature, not rank, makes the gentleman).

Cf. Tilley, V85; C. G. Smith, 317.

568 THE **NEARER** THE CHURCH, THE FARTHER FROM GOD

Shep. Cal., Julye, 97–98: To kerke the narre, from God more farre, Has bene an old sayd sawe.

Cf. Apperson, 438; W. G. Smith, 445; Stevenson, 351:4; Tilley, C380.

569 **NECESSITY** IS A LAW THAT JUSTIFIES ITSELF

View, 618: By application, or rather necessitye, it is made just; and this only respect maketh all lawes just.

Publilius Syrus (1835), 329: Honesta lex est temporis necessitas (Necessity is a law that justifies itself).

570 THE FORCE OF **NECESSITY** IS IRRESISTIBLE

Cf. no. 178: The doom of destiny cannot be avoided; no. 847: What will be, shall be

FQ, I, v, 25, 4–5: Who can . . . breake the chayne of strong necessitee? ¶ *Ibid.*, ix, 42, 6: Who then can strive with strong necessitie?

Culman, 8: Necessitati nihil repugnat (Nothing resists necessity). ¶ Publilius Syrus (1934), 448: Necessitas ab homine quae vult impetrat (Necessity wins what she wants from man). ¶ *Ibid.*, 454: Necessitas quod poscit nisi des eripti (Necessity snatches what she asks, unless you give it). ¶ *Ibid.*, 464: Necessitas quam pertinax regnum tenet (How firm the hold of necessity upon her throne)! ¶ *Ibid.*, 470: Nihil aliud scit necessitas quam vincere (Necessity knows nought else but victory).

Aeschylus, *Prometh.*, 104: τὸ τῆς ἀνάγκης ἔστ' ἀδήριτον σθένος (The might of necessity brooks no resistance). ¶ Euripides, *Helen*, 513–514: λόγος γάρ ἐστιν οὐκ ἐμός, σοφῶν δ' ἔπος, δεινῆς ἀνάγκης οὐδὲν ἰσχύειν πλέον (Not mine the saying is, but wisdom's saw—"Stronger is nought than dread necessity"). ¶ Euripides, *Suppliants*, 63–64: ὑπ' ἀνάγκας δὲ προπίπτουσα προσαιτοῦσ' (But as overmastering might of necessity constrains). ¶ Greene, *Mamillia*, *Works*, II, 55: The law of necessitie, saith Plato, is so hard, that the Gods them selues are not able to resist it; cf. Plato, *Laws*, vii, 818B. ¶ Greene, *Euphues His Censure to Phil.*, *Works*, VI, 213: Fate and necessitie may not be auoided.

571 **NEED** MAKES SCHOLARS

FQ, III, iii, 53, 3: Need new strength shall teach. ¶ *FQ* (Globe), III, iii, 53, 3: Need makes good schollers. ¶ *FQ*, III, vii, 4, 3: Need teacheth her this lesson hard and rare.

Horman, *Vulgaria*, 52: Nede taught hym wytte.

Cf. Jones, 180.

572 **NEGLECT** A DANGER, AND IT WILL TAKE YOU BY SURPRISE

Cf. no. 90: One can never be too cautious; no. 826: Good watch prevents misfortune

Muiopotmos, 389–392: The foolish flie, without foresight, As he that did all danger quite despise, Toward those parts came flying careleslie, Where hidden was his hatefull enemie. ¶ *Virgils Gnat*, 364: Shun'd destruction doth destruction render.

* Publilius Syrus (1934), 107: Citius venit periclum cum contemnitur (Danger comes more quickly when underestimated). ¶ *Ibid.*, 617: Quod est timendum decipit si neglegas (The object of your fear tricks you, if you overlook it).

Cf. C. G. Smith, 216.

573 HE BLAMES **NEPTUNE** UNJUSTLY WHO SUFFERS SHIPWRECK MORE THAN ONCE

Shep. Cal., Feb., 33–34: The soveraigne of seas he blames in vaine, That, once seabeate, will to sea againe. ¶ *Ibid.*, Glosse, 13–15: The saying is borrowed of Mimus Publianus, which used this proverb in a verse, "Improbè Neptunum accusat, qui iterum naufragium facit."

* Publilius Syrus (1934), 331: Improbe Neptunum accusat qui iterum naufragium facit (It is an outrage in a man twice shipwrecked to blame Neptune).

Cf. Tilley, S172.

574 **NIGHT** IS THE MOTHER OF COUNSEL

FQ, I, i, 33, 3: Untroubled night, they say, gives counsell best.

Menander, *Arbitrants*, 733K: ἐν νυκτὶ βουλὴν δ', ὅπερ ἅπασι γίγνεται (But over night comes counsel, as it does to all). ¶ Erasmus, *Adagia*, 462B: In nocte consilium (In the night comes counsel). ¶ Herbert, 379: Night is the mother of counsel.

Cf. Apperson, 445; W. G. Smith, 452; Stevenson, 1685:17; Tilley, N174.

575 **NIGHT** IS THE MOTHER OF TROUBLESOME THOUGHTS (CARES, FEARS)

FQ, III, iv, 55, 1–2: Night, thou foule mother of annoyaunce sad, Sister of heavie Death, and nourse of Woe. ¶ *Ibid.*, 57, 2–5: Thou [night] art the roote and nourse of bitter cares, Breeder of new, renewer of old smarts: In stead of rest thou lendest rayling teares, In stead of sleepe thou sendest troublous feares.

Guazzo, *Civ. Conv.*, *Works*, II, 207: Troublesome thoughts (of the which they say, that the night is the nourse and mother). ¶ Shakespeare, *Lucrece*, 117: Sable Night, mother of dread and fear.

576 WHAT IS DONE BY **NIGHT** APPEARS BY DAY

FQ, III, iv, 59, 1: Day discovers all dishonest wayes. ¶ *Ibid.*, VI, viii, 51, 7: Day . . . doth discover bad and good.

Cf. W. G. Smith, 154; Stevenson, 537:9; Tilley, N179.

577 UNDER ONE'S **NOSE**

View, 659: Lyeth under theyr nose.

Hall, *Chron.*, (1548), 38: Before a realme under your nose. ¶ Harrison, *England* (1577), II, i: Kings and princes dwelled not under his nose. ¶ Norden, *Surv. Dial.* (1607), I, 7: Things passing dayly under your nose. ¶ Cotton, *Espernon* (1670), I, iv, 153: They . . . suffer'd the Duke . . . to continue his work under their noses.

578 **NOTHING** IS PLEASANT TO A TROUBLED HEART

Shep. Cal., Aug., 5–6: When the hart is ill assayde, How can bagpipe or joynts be well apayd? ¶ *FQ*, I, vii, 39, 1–3: What worlds delight, or joy . . . Can hart, so plungd in sea of sorrowes deep . . . reach?

Culman, 15: Perturbato cordi nihil jucundum (Nothing is pleasant to a troubled heart). ¶ *Ibid.*, 24: Perturbato cordi nihil est jucundum (Nothing is pleasant to a troubled heart).

Cf. Stevenson, 1268:11.

579 **NOTHING** IS WELL SAID OR DONE IN ANGER

Shep. Cal., Feb., 199: Anger nould let him speake to the tree.

Culman, 5: Consilio inimica iracundia (Anger is an enemy to counsel). ¶ *Ibid.*, 13: Irati nihil recte faciunt (Angry folks do nothing well). ¶ *Ibid.*, 24: Pessimi sunt consultores ira & cupido (Anger and lust are the worst advisers). ¶ Publilius Syrus (1835), 178: Cupido atque ira consultores pessimi (Anger and inordinate desire are the worst of counsellors).

Cicero, *De Offic.*, i, 38, 136: Cum qua nihil recte fieri, nihil considerate potest (For in anger nothing right or judicious can be done).

Cf. Tilley, N307; C. G. Smith, 219.

580 OUT OF NOTHING **NOTHING** COMES

FQ, II, iv, 39, 9: For not to grow of nought he it conjectured.

Plutarch, *Moralia*: *On Borrowing*, 829C: μηδὲν ἐκ τοῦ μὴ ὄν τος γενέσθαι (Nothing arises out of nothing). ¶ Boethius, *De Consolatione*, v, 1, 24–25: Nihil ex nihilo existere uera sententia est (It is a true sentence that of nothing comes nothing).

Cf. Apperson, 454; W. G. Smith, 462: Stevenson, 1699:2; Tilley, N285.

581 THERE IS **NOTHING** TOO HARD FOR A DETECTIVE'S INDUSTRY

FQ, V, ii, 39, 9: There is nothing lost, that may be found, if sought. ¶ *View*, 609: Nothing soe hard but that, through wysedome, it may be mastred and subdued.

Publilius Syrus, (1835), 1064: Nil tam difficile est quin quaerendo investigari possiet (There is nothing so difficult that it cannot be solved by investigation).

Terence, *Heauton*, 675: Nil tam difficilest quin quaerendo investigari possiet (Nothing is too hard for a detective's industry). ¶ Seneca, *De Ira*, ii, 12, 3: Nihil est tam difficile et arduum quod non humana mens vincat et in familiaritatem perducat adsidua meditatio (Nothing is so hard and difficult that it cannot be conquered by the human intellect and be brought through persistent study to intimate acquaintance).

Cf. Taverner, 30.

582 TRUSTING IN OURSELVES ALONE, WE CAN DO **NOTHING**

Cf. no. 335: We can do nothing without God's help

Amoretti, lviii, 9–10: None is so rich or wise, so strong or fayre, But fayleth, trusting in his own assurance.

Culman, 34: Nihil possumus ex nobis (We can do nothing of our selves).

583 THE **NUT** IS SWEET, THE SHELL IS BITTER

Amoretti, xxvi, 6: Sweet is the nut, but bitter is his pill.

Cf. Tilley, N360.

584 THROUGH **OBEDIENCE** LEARN TO COMMAND

View, 661: Any one, before he come to be a captayne, should have bene a soldiour; for, "Parere qui nescit, nescit imperare."

Aristotle, *Politics*, vii, 13, 4: *τόν τε γὰρ μέλλοντα καλῶς ἄρχειν ἀρχθῆναί φασι δεῖν πρῶτον* (For he who is to be a good ruler must have first been ruled, as the saying is). ¶ Cicero, *De Legibus*, iii, 2, 5: Qui bene imperat, paruerit aliquando necesse est (One who commands efficiently must have obeyed others in the past). ¶ Seneca, *De Ira*, ii, 15, 4–5: Nemo autem regere potest nisi qui et regi (No man is able to rule unless he can also submit to be ruled. ¶ Plutarch, *Moralia*: *Precepts of Stagecraft*, 806F: *οὐδ' ἄρξαι καλῶς τοὺς μὴ πρότερον ὀρθῶς δουλεύσαντας, ᾗ φησιν ὁ Πλάτων, δυναμένους* (No one can ever command well who has not first learned rightly to obey, as Plato says); cf. Plato, *Laws*, vi, 762E. ¶ Erasmus, *Adagia*, 25F: Non bene imperat, nisi qui paruerit imperio (No one commands ably unless he himself obeyed discipline). ¶ Guazzo, *Civ. Conv.*, *Works*, II, 98: Those onlye knowe well how to commaund, which know well howe to obaye. ¶ Gascoigne, *Glasse of Govt.*, II, ii, *Works*, II, 28: Neyther shall they ever become able to beare rule them selves, whiche cannot bee content to obay the aucthoritie of others. ¶ Milton, *Par. Reg.*, III, 195–196: Best reign who first Well hath obeyed.

Cf. W. G. Smith, 467; Stevenson, 382:3; Tilley, S246.

585 **OBEY** THE LAW

FQ, III, xi, 30, 9: T' obay her servaunts law! ¶ *Ibid.*, IV, x, 42, 9: And to his law compels all creatures to obay. ¶ *Ibid.*, V, iv, 49, 2–3: He shall obay My law. ¶ *Ibid.*, v, 22, 3: Bound t' obay that Amazons proud law. ¶ *View*, 610: Learne obedience unto lawe.

Culman, 2: Legibus pare (Obey the laws).

586 **OFFENDERS** SHOULD BE PUNISHED

Cf. no. 887: It is not wrong to harm one who has harmed you

Virgils Gnat, 366: Punishment is due to the offender.

Culman, 7: Delinquentes sunt corrigendi (Offenders are to be punished).

587 NEVER REFUSE A GOOD **OFFER**

FQ, II, vii, 18, 9: Thing refused doe not afterward accuse.

Cato, *Disticha*, Appendix, 2: Oblatum auxilium stultum est dimittere cuiquam (He is a fool who fails to heed proffered aid).

Cf. Henderson, 263; Tilley, O17.

588 WHEN THE **OIL** IS CONSUMED, THE LIGHT GOES OUT

FQ, II, x, 30, 1–2: When the oyle is spent, The light goes out.

Greene, *Mamillia*, *Works*, II, 165: The oyle consumed the lampe goeth out. ¶ Shakespeare, *1 Hen. VI*, II, v, 8–9: Lamps whose wasting oil is spent, Wax dim. ¶ Shakespeare, *Ant. & Cleop.*, IV, xv, 85: Our lamp is spent; it's out!

589 **OLD** MEN HAVE NO FEAR OF GOD

Shep. Cal., Feb., 251–252: *Niuno vecchio Spaventa Iddio.* ¶ *Ibid.*, Glosse, 129–156: A byting and bitter proverbe . . . Although it please Erasmus

. . . to construe it, in his Adages, for his own behoofe, that by the proverbe, "Nemo senex metuit Jovem," is not meant, that old men have no feare of God at al.

590 BE OFF WITH THE **OLD** BEFORE YOU ARE ON WITH THE NEW

View, 646: Ere the newe be brought in, the old must be removed. ¶ *Ibid.*, 650: Evills must first be cutt away with a strong hand, before any good can be planted. ¶ *Brief Note of Ireland* (Variorum), 185–186: Before newe building were erected the olde should haue bene plucked downe.

591 IT IS BETTER TO **OVERLOOK** AN INJURY THAN TO AVENGE IT

Cf. no. 365: To be able to do harm and not do it is noble

FQ, II, iv, 44, 4–5: Happy who can abstaine, when Rancour rife Kindles revenge.

Publilius Syrus (1835), 1088: Saepe dissimulare, quam vel ulcisci, satius est (It is often better to overlook an injury than to avenge it).

Seneca, *De Ira*, ii, 33, 1: Saepe autem satius fuit dissimulare quam ulcisci (It is often, however, better to feign ignorance of an act than to take vengeance for it).

Cf. C. G. Smith, 225.

592 THE SCREECH **OWL** AND THE NIGHT RAVEN ARE MESSENGERS OF DEATH

Shep. Cal., June, 23–24: Here no night ravens lodge . . . nor gastly owles doe flee. ¶ *FQ*, I, v, 30, 6–7: The messenger of death, the ghastly owle, With drery shriekes did also her bewray. ¶ *Ibid.*, II, vii, 23, 3–5: After him owles and night-ravens flew, The hatefull messengers of heavy things, Of death. ¶ *Ibid.*, xii, 36, 4–5: The ill-faste owle, deaths dreadfull messengere, The hoars night-raven, trump of dolefull drere.

¶ *Epithalamion*, 345–346: Let not the shriech oule, nor the storke be heard, Nor the night raven that still deadly yels.

Ovid, *Metam.*, v, 550: Ignavus bubo, dirum mortalibus omen (The slothful screech owl, a bird of evil omen to men). ¶ *Ibid.*, x, 452–453: Ter omen funereus bubo letali carmine fecit (Thrice did the funereal screech owl warn her by his uncanny cry). ¶ Seneca, *Hercules Furens*, 687–688: Illic luctifer bubo gemit omenque triste resonat infaustae strigis (There the dole-bringing owl utters its cry, and the sad omen of the gruesome screech owl sounds); cf. *Medea*, 733–734. ¶ Statius, *Thebaidos*, iii, 510–512: Dirae stridunt in nube volucres nocturnaeque gemunt striges et feralia bubo damna canens (Direful birds clamour in the clouds, nocturnal screech owls cry, and the horned owl with its dismal funeral chant). ¶ Chaucer, *Parl. of Fowls*, 343: The oule ek, that of deth the bode bryngeth. ¶ Chaucer, *Troilus*, V, 318–320: I mot nedes dye. The owle ek . . . Hath after me shright all thise nyghtes two; cf. V, 381–382. ¶ Shakespeare, *3 Hen. VI*, II, vi, 56–57: That fatal screech owl . . . nothing sung but death to us and ours. ¶ Shakespeare, *Rich. III*, IV, iv, 507: Out on ye, owls! Nothing but songs of death? ¶ Shakespeare, *Lucrece*, 165: No noise but owls' and wolves' death-boding cries. ¶ Deloney, *Thomas of Reading*, *Works*, 258: The scritch owle cried piteously, and anone after the night rauen sate croking hard by his window . . . an ill fauoured cry. ¶ Shakespeare, *Mids. Night's D.*, V, i, 383–385: The screech owl, screeching loud, Puts the wretch that lies in woe In remembrance of a shroud. ¶ Shakespeare, *Macb.*, II, ii, 3: It was the owl that shriek'd the fatal bellman.

Cf. Tilley, R33.

593 NO **PAINS**, NO PROFIT

FQ, II, x, 14, 9: Each his paynes to others profit still employd. ¶ *Ibid.*, III, x, 28, 9: Your worthy paine shall wel reward with guerdon rich. ¶ *Mother Hub.*, 236: Yeeld them timely profite for their paine.

Culman, 15: Parsimonia & labore crescunt res (Goods increase by sparing and pains).

Erasmus, *Colloquia Fam.*, 746B: Nihil homini citra laborem contingit in hac vita (There is nothing to be attained in this life without pains).

Cf. Tilley, P24; C. G. Smith, 228.

594 IN MUSIC **PAN** IS SUPERIOR TO APOLLO

Shep. Cal., June, 68: I heard that Pan with Phoebus strove.

Ovid, *Metam.*, xi, 153–155: Pan ibi dum teneris iactat sua carmina nymphis et leve cerata modulatur harundine carmen ausus Apollineos prae se contemnere cantus (There, while Pan was singing his songs to the soft nymphs and playing airy interludes upon his reeds close joined with wax, he dared speak slightingly of Apollo's music in comparison with his own). ¶ Wyatt, *Of the Courtiers Life*, *Tottel's Misc.*, I, 86: Pan Passeth Appollo in musicke manifold.

595 A **PARAGON** OF PEERLESS PRICE

Colin Clouts, 548–549: Sweet Charillis is the paragone Of peerlesse price. ¶ *FQ*, IV, ii, 8, 1–2: Proud man himselfe the other deemed, Having so peerelesse paragon ygot.

Cf. Tilley, P49.

596 **PASSION** BLINDS THE EYE OF REASON

FQ, I, ii, 5, 7: The eie of reason was with rage yblent. ¶ *Ibid.*, II, i, 57, 4–5: Raging passion with fierce tyranny Robs reason of her dew regalitie. ¶ *Ibid.*, iv, 7, 7: Reason, blent through passion, nought descryde. ¶ *Ibid.*, III, vii, 21, 5: So strong is passion that no reason heares. ¶ *Virgils Gnat*, 310–311: For feare and yre Had blent so much his sense, that lesse he feard. ¶ *FQ*, IV, ii, 5, 5: With sting of lust, that reasons eye did blind. ¶ *Ibid.*, 11, 5: So blind is lust, false colours to descry.

Culman, 32: Furor depravat judicia (Rage depraves the judgment). ¶ Publilius Syrus (1835), 1063: Nil rationis est, ubi res semel in affectum venit (Reason avails nothing when passion has the mastery).

Euripides, *Medea*, 1079: *θυμὸς δὲ κρείσσων τῶν ἐμῶν βουλευμάτων* (Passion overmasters sober thought). ¶ Cato, *Disticha*, ii, 4: Impedit ira animum, ne possis cernere verum (Temper bars minds from seeing what is true). ¶ Cicero, *Tusc. Disp.*, iii, 5, 11: Furorem autem esse rati sunt mentis ad omnia caecitatem (Frenzy, however, they regarded as a blindness of the mind in all relations). ¶ Quintilian, *Inst. Orat.*, vi, 2, 6:

Sensum oculorm praecipit animus (Passion forestalls the sense of sight). ¶ Sidney, *Arcadia*, *Works*, I, 339: Is not Reason dimde with Passions might?

Cf. C. G. Smith, 230.

597 **PATIENCE** IS THE BEST MEDICINE (REMEDY)

FQ, I, x, 23, 7–9: A leach, the which had great insight In that disease . . . well could cure the same: his name was Patience. ¶ *Ibid.*, 28, 8–9: Yet all with patience wisely she did beare; For well she wist, his cryme could els be never cleare. ¶ *Ibid.*, xi, 38, 9: Ne might his rancling paine with patience be appeased.

* Publilius Syrus (1934), 111: Cuivis dolori remedium est patientia (Patience is a cure for any pain). ¶ *Ibid.* (1835), 229: Et miseriarum portus est patientia (Patience is affliction's haven).

Cato, *Disticha*, iii, 23: Uxoris linguam, si frugi est, ferre memento; namque malum est non velle pati nec posse tacere (A thrifty wife may talk and talk: endure: lost patience and loud brawling are no cure). ¶ Florio, *First Fruites*, 12: There is no remedie, but patience. ¶ *Ibid.*, 44: Pacience is the best medicine that is, for a sicke man, the most precious plaister that is, for any wounde. ¶ Breton, *Crossing of Prov.*, *Works*, II, *m*, 4: Patience is a plaister for all paine.

Cf. Apperson, 486; W. G. Smith, 489; Stevenson, 1754:2.

598 **PATIENCE** PERFORCE

FQ, II, iii, 3, 3–4: Patience perforce: helplesse what may it boot To frett for anger, or for griefe to mone? ¶ *Ibid.*, III, x, 3, 1–2: But patience perforce, he must abie What fortune and his fate on him will lay.

Gascoigne, *Patience Perforce*, *Works*, I, 461: Content thy selfe with patience perforce. ¶ Gascoigne, *Fruite of Fetters*, *Works*, I, 378: Patience is founde in prison (though perforce). ¶ Florio, *First Fruites*, 36: What remedie is there, but pacience perforce? ¶ Greene, *Euphues His Censure to Phil.*, *Works*, VI, 190: To vse patience perforce.

Cf. Apperson, 486; Tilley, P111.

599 OFTEN IT IS EASIER TO CONQUER WITH **PATIENCE** THAN WITH FORCE

FQ, II, viii, 47, 6–8; 48, 9: Well knew The Prince, with pacience and sufferaunce sly So hasty heat soone cooled to subdew . . . And suffred rash Pyrochles waste his ydle might.

Culman, 27: Saepe vincas patientia, quem non viceris impetu (Often you may conquer him with patience, whom you cannot conquer with force).

Cato, *Disticha*, i, 38: Quem superare potes interdum vince ferendo; maxima enim est hominum semper patientia virtus (Sometimes put up with him you might beat down; of human virtues patience is the crown). ¶ Chaucer, *Franklin's T.*, 773–775: Pacience is an heigh vertu, certeyn, For it venquysseth, as thise clerkes seyn, Thinges that rigour sholde nevere atteyne.

Cf. Stevenson, 1754:1; 1756:5.

600 WHEN **PATIENCE** IS PROVOKED, IT TURNS TO FURY

FQ, V, xii, 42, 1–5: Most bitter wordes they spake, Most shamefull, most unrighteous, most untrew, That they the mildest man alive would make Forget his patience, and yeeld vengeaunce dew To her, that so false sclaunders at him threw.

* Publilius Syrus (1934), 208: Furor fit laesa saepius patientia (Patience too often wounded turns to frenzy).

Cf. Tilley, P113.

601 TO **PAY** EACH IN HIS OWN COIN

FQ, VI, i, 42, 3: To pay each with his owne is right and dew.

Pliny the Younger, *Lett.*, iii, 9: Dedi malum, et accepi (We are paid in our own coin). ¶ Erasmus, *Colloquia Fam.*, 693E: Par pari, quod ajunt, referens (Pay her in her own coin, according to the old proverb). ¶ Greene, *Mamillia*, *Works*, II, 155: Pay *Pharicles* his debt in the same coine. ¶ Sidney, *Arcadia*, *Works*, I, 98: To paie him in his owne monie.

¶ Harvey, *Pierces Super.*, *Works*, II, 126: Pay you with the vsury of your owne coyne.

Cf. Apperson, 487; W. G. Smith, 491; Tilley, C507.

602 **PEACE** IS THE END OF ALL WARS

Shep. Cal., Aprill, 124–125: Olives bene for peace, When wars doe surcease. ¶ *Amoretti*, xi, 13: Every war hath peace.

Cf. Stevenson, 2453:7; Tilley, W55.

603 AS PROUD AS A **PEACOCK**

Shep. Cal., Feb., 8: Perke as peacock, ¶ *FQ*, I, iv, 17, 8: Fayre pecocks, that excell in pride.

Chaucer, *Troilus*, I, 210: As proud a pekok. ¶ Sidney, *Arcadia*, *Works*, I, 238: It made me set up my peacocks tayle with the hiest. ¶ Sidney, *Poems* (1593), *Works*, II, 233: The peacockes pride.

Cf. Apperson, 514; W. G. Smith, 521; Tilley, P157.

604 PLAY WITH YOUR **PEERS**

FQ, III, ix, 4, 8: She does joy to play emongst her peares. ¶ *Ibid.*, V, i, 6, 3: Amongst his peres playing his childish sport.

Cf. Benham, 873B; W. G. Smith, 506; Stevenson, 1807:2; Tilley, P180.

605 WHAT **PENELOPE** WOVE DURING THE DAY, SHE ALL UNWOVE AT NIGHT

Amoretti, xxiii, 1–4: Penelope, for her Ulisses sake, Deviz'd a web her wooers to deceave, In which the worke that she all day did make, The same at night she did againe unreave.

Cicero, *Academ.*, ii, 29, 95: Quid, quod eadem illa ars quasi Penelope telam retexens tollit ad extremum superiora (What of the fact that this same science destroys at the end the steps that came before, like Penelope unweaving her web?). ¶ Claudian, *Carminum Minorum Corpusculum*, xxx, 31–32: Penelope trahat arte procos fallatque furentes stamina nocturnae relegens Laertia telae (Let Penelope by artful delays deceive the madness of the suitors and, ever faithful to Ulysses, delude their solicitations, ever winding up again by night the warp of her day-spun web). ¶ Erasmus, *Adagia*, 168B: Penelopes telam retexere (To unweave Penelope's web). ¶ Erasmus, *Colloquia Fam.*, 817D: Penelopes telas texunt ac retexunt (They weave and unweave Penelope's web). ¶ Lyly, *Euph. Anat. of Wit*, *Works*, I, 211: Penelope no less constaunt then shee, yet more wyse, woulde bee wearie to unweaue that in the nyght, she spunne in the daye. ¶ Harvey, *A New Lett.*, *Works*, I, 284: Unwouen like Penelopes web. ¶ Nashe, *Lenten Stuffe*, *Works*, III, 168: Raueling out signifies *Penelopes telam retexere*, the vnweauing of a webbe before wouen contexted.

Cf. W. G. Smith, 494; Tilley, P186.

606 A BETTER **PENNY**

Mother Hub., 523: Thou maist compound a better penie.

Cf. Tilley, P189.

607 **PERSEVERE** TO THE END

FQ, III, x, 40, 9: One may his journey bring too soone to evill end.

Culman, 34: Non satis bene coepisti, nisi perseveres (You have not begun well enough, unless you go to the end).

608 BENEVOLENCE TRIES **PERSUASION** FIRST, THEN SEVERER MEASURES

Cf. no. 235: Where fair means may not prevail, there foul means rightly may be used

FQ, III, ix, 9, 1–5: Let us first . . . entreat The man by gentle meanes, to let us in; . . . Then if all fayle, we will by force it win.

Publilius Syrus (1835), 932: Suadere primum, dein corrigere, est benevoli (Benevolence tries persuasion first, then severer means).

Foxe, *Acts and Mon.*, II, 146: He who would not be ruled by reason, must with force be constrained. ¶ Greene, *Penelopes Web*, *Works*, V, 211: That which intreatie could not commaund, force would constrayne. ¶ Greene, *Euphues His Censure to Phil.*, *Works*, VI, 216: What hee cannot perswade with woordes, hee seeketh to constrayne with weapons.

609 NOT TO CARE A **PIN** (POINT, WHIT)

FQ, I, ii, 12, 9: Cared not for God or man a point. ¶ *Ibid.*, v, 4, 3–4: Who not a pin Does care. ¶ *Astrophel*, 49: He for none of them did care a whit. ¶ *FQ*, VI, ix, 10, 7–8: Neither she for him nor other none Did care a whit.

Cf. Apperson, 496; W. G. Smith, 78; Tilley, P333.

610 HE THAT TOUCHES **PITCH** SHALL BE DEFILED

Shep. Cal., Maye, 74: Who touches pitch mought needes be defilde.

Wilson, *Arte of Rhet.*, Prol., sig. A v: Who that toucheth Pitch shall be filed with it. ¶ Guazzo, *Civ. Conv.*, *Works*, I, 44: Hee which toucheth pitch shalbe defiled therwith. ¶ Northbrooke, *Treatise agst. Dicing*, 157: He that toucheth pitche shall be defiled with it. ¶ Greene, *Mirrour of Mod.*, *Works*, III, 35: Whoso handleth pitch must needs be defiled therwith; cf. VIII, 139.

Cf. Apperson, 498; W. G. Smith, 667; Tilley, P358.

611 **PITY** MELTS THE MIND TO LOVE

FQ, IV, xii, 13, 9: And learne to love, by learning lovers paines to rew.

Chaucer, *Leg. of Good Women*, 1078–1079: Anon hire herte hath pite of his wo, And with that pite love com in also. ¶ Shakespeare, *Twelfth N.*, III, i, 134–135: I pity you.—That's a degree to love. ¶ Daniel, *Queen's Arcadia*, III, i: Pity is sworn servant unto love. ¶ Beaumont and Fletcher, *Knight of Malta*, I, i, 73: Of all the paths that lead to a woman's love Pity's the straightest. ¶ Dryden, *Alexander's Feast*, 96: Pity melts the mind to love.

Cf. Apperson, 499; Stevenson, 1801:9; Tilley, P370.

612 THE MORE IS THE **PITY**

View, 655: The more the pittye.

Wilson, *Arte of Rhet.*, 131: The more is the pitie. ¶ Foxe, *Acts and Mon.*, II, 463: The more was the pity. ¶ Northbrooke, *Treatise agst. Dicing*, 94: The more is the pittie. ¶ Greene, *Arbasto*, *Works*, III, 240: The more is the pitie; cf. XI, 78; XIV, 272. ¶ Nashe, *Pierce P.*, *Works*, I, 161: The more is the pittie. ¶ Sidney, *Arcadia*, *Works*, II, 161: The more pittie it is.

613 TO **PITY** THE AFFLICTED IS TO REMEMBER ONE'S OWN LOT

Ruines of T., 466–469: Let him behold the horror of my fall, And his owne end unto remembrance call; That of like ruine he may warned bee, And in himselfe be moov'd to pittie mee.

* Publilius Syrus (1934), 243: Homo qui in homine calamitoso est misericors meminit sui (Pity for a stricken fellow-man is to remember one's own lot).

614 TO APPEAL TO ONE WHO CANNOT **PITY** IS IN VAIN

FQ, III, xi, 16, 1–2: What boots it . . . sow vaine sorrow in a fruitlesse eare? ¶ *Virgils Gnat*, 358: The praise of pitie vanisht is in vaine. ¶ *FQ*, V, viii, 41, 9: Crying to them in vaine, that nould his crying heare. ¶ *Ibid.*, VI, ii, 10, 9: Weeping to him in vaine, and making piteous woe.

* Publilius Syrus (1934), 200: Frustra rogatur qui misereri non potest (Vain is the appeal to him who cannot pity).

615 WHEREVER WE MEET MISERY WE OWE **PITY**

Shep. Cal., Maye, 61: For pittied is mishappe that nas remedie. ¶ *FQ*, IV, xii, 21, 9: To see an helpelesse evill double griefe doth lend.

Publilius Syrus (1934), 143: Contubernia sunt lacrimarum ubi misericors miserum adspicit (When pity sees misery, there comes the comradeship of tears).

Cawdray, *Treasurie or Store-House of Similies* (1600), 464: We be iustly moued to pitie, by beholding . . . any miseries of men. ¶ Fuller, 5642: Where-ever we meet misery, we owe pity.

616 EVERYONE TRIES TO **PLEASE** HIMSELF

Shep. Cal., June, 72: I play to please my selfe.

Culman, 9: Sibi quisque placet (Every man pleases himself).

617 SEEK TO **PLEASE**

FQ, VI, xii, 41, 9: Seeke to please, that now is counted wisemens threasure.

Culman, 2: Multitudini place (Please the multitude). ¶ *Ibid.*: Omnibus placeto (Please everybody).

Ovid, *Artis Amat.*, i, 596: Quacumque potes dote placere, place (Please by whatever gifts you can). ¶ Shakespeare, *Twelfth N.*, III, iv, 25: Please one, and please all. ¶ *Ibid.*, V, i, 417: We'll strive to please you every day.

618 SURFEITED **PLEASURES** BECOME DISGUSTING

FQ, II, vii, 15, 5–6: Superfluities they would despise, Which with sad cares empeach our native joyes.

Publilius Syrus (1835), 614: Nulla est voluptas, quin assiduae taedeat (There is no pleasure which continued enjoyment cannot render disgusting). ¶ *Ibid.*, 656: Parvo fames constat, magno fastidium (Hunger goes with stinted supplies, disgust attends on abundance).

Seneca, *Epist.*, xxiii, 6: In praecipiti voluptas ad dolorem vergit, nisi modum tenuit (Pleasure, unless it has been kept within bounds, tends to rush headlong into the abyss of sorrow).

Cf. Tilley, S1011; C. G. Smith, 260, 281.

619 **PLENTY** MAKES POOR

Shep. Cal., Sept., 261: *Inopem me copia fecit.* ¶ *Ibid.*, Glosse, 127: Plentye made him poore. ¶ *FQ*, I, iv, 29, 4: Plenty made him pore. ¶ *Amoretti*, xxxv, 8: So plenty makes me poore.

Ovid, *Metam.*, iii, 466: Inopem me copia fecit (Plenty has made me poor); cf. Nashe, *Unfor. Trav.*, *Works*, II, 276.

Cf. Apperson, 503; W. G. Smith, 507; Stevenson, 1815:7; Tilley, P427.

620 **POETRY** COMES FINESPUN FROM CAREFREE MINDS

Shep. Cal., Oct., 100–101: The vaunted verse a vacant head demaundes, Ne wont with crabbed Care the Muses dwell.

Ovid, *Heroides*, xv, 14: Vacuae carmina mentis opus (Songs are the labor of carefree minds). ¶ Ovid, *Tristia*, i, 1, 39–41: Carmina proveniunt animo deducta sereno; . . . carmina secessum scribentis et otia quaerunt (Poetry comes finespun from a mind at peace; . . . poetry requires the writer to be in privacy and at ease). ¶ Sidney, *Arcadia*, *Works*, I, 28: Ease, the Nurse of Poetrie.

Cf. Spenser, *Minor Poems* (Variorum), I, 389.

621 TO **POLL** AND PILL THE POOR

FQ, V, ii, 6, 8: Which pols and pils the poore in piteous wize. ¶ *View*, 674: They poll and utterly undoe the poore.

Sandys, *Serm.* (Parker S.), 287: To poll and pill. ¶ Foxe, *Acts and Mon.*, IV, 269: So excessively did pill and poll the simple people. ¶ *Ibid.*, 540: Pilling, and polling of the poor people. ¶ Nashe, *Christs Teares*, *Works*, II, 152: Being pilled and pould vnconsionably.

622 ANY **PORT** IN A STORM

FQ, II, vi, 23, 8: Better safe port, then be in seas distrest.

Cf. Apperson, 12; W. G. Smith, 11; Stevenson, 1831:8.

623 RATHER THAN DIE OF HUNGER AND MISERY, **POVERTY** COMPELS MEN TO MANY UNTRIED EXPEDIENTS

View, 662: Who will not accept allmost of any condicions, rather then dye of hunger and miserye?

* Publilius Syrus (1934), 247: Hominem experiri multa paupertas iubet (Poverty compels men to many untried expedients).

624 **PRACTICE** MAKES MASTERY

FQ, III, iii, 53, 8–9: Skil, which practize small Wil bring, and shortly make you a mayd martiall.

Culman, 5: Exercitatio potest omnia (Exercise can do all things). ¶ *Ibid.*, 10: Assidua exercitatio omnia potest (Daily exercise can do all things).

Erasmus, *Adagia*, 466A: Exercitatio potest omnia (All things are possible with practice).

Cf. Taverner, 30; W. G. Smith, 684; Tilley, U24; C. G. Smith, 235.

625 **PRAISE** IS THE REWARD OF VIRTUE

Cf. no. 395: Honor is the reward of virtue

FQ, II, iii, 37, 9: All vertue merits praise. ¶ *Teares of the M.*, 451–454: Who would ever care to doo brave deed, Or strive in vertue others to excell, If none should yeeld him his deserved meed, Due praise?

Culman, 7: Laus merces virtutis (Praise is the reward of virtue).

Shakespeare, *Titus Andr.*, I, i, 390: He lives in fame that died in virtue's cause.

Cf. C. G. Smith, 237.

626 TO SHOOT NIGH THE **PRICK**

Shep. Cal., Sept., 122: They . . . shooten neerest the pricke.

Cf. Tilley, P571.

627 **PRIDE** GOES BEFORE AND SHAME COMES AFTER

Cf. no. 628: Pride will have a fall

FQ, VI, i, 40, 8–9: Put away proud looke, and usage sterne, The which shal nought to you but foule dishonor yearne.

* Publilius Syrus (1934), 109: Cito ignominia fit superbi gloria (The boast of arrogance soon turns to shame).

Old Testament: Proverbs, xi, 2: When pride cometh, then cometh shame. ¶ Barclay, *Ship of Fools*, II, 164: Pryde goth before, but shame do it ensue.

Cf. Stevenson, 1882:6; Tilley, P576.

628 **PRIDE** WILL HAVE A FALL

Cf. no. 627: Pride goes before and shame comes after

FQ, I, v, 51, 3–4: After their wofull falles Through wicked pride. *Virgils Gnat*, 559–560: All that vaunts in worldly vanitie Shall fall through fortunes mutabilitie.

Foxe, *Acts and Mon.*, II, 806: Commonly said . . . that pride will have a fall; cf. IV, 272. ¶ Greene, *Looking-Glasse*, 1805, *Works*, XIV, 80: Pride will haue a fall.

Cf. Apperson, 512; W. G. Smith, 518; Tilley, P581.

629 PUFFED UP WITH **PRIDE**

Shep. Cal., Feb., 223: Puffed up with pryde. ¶ *Ruines of* R., xi, 3: Puft up with pride. ¶ *Colin Clouts*, 759: Puffed up with pride. ¶ *Hymne of Heavenly L.*, 78–79: Pride . . . Did puffe them up.

Skelton, *Colyn Cloute*, 595, *Works*, I, 333: Ye are so puffed with pryde. ¶ Guazzo, *Civ. Conv.*, *Works*, I, 80: Puffed up with pride; cf. I, 100, 210. ¶ Gascoigne, *Glasse of Govt.*, IV, vii, *Works*, II, 71: Some puffe us up with pride. ¶ Gascoigne, *Droome of Doomes Day*, *Works*, II, 251: He is puffed up with pryde. ¶ *Ibid.*, 256: The daughters of Syon are puffed up with pryde. ¶ Gascoigne, *Grief of Joye*, *Works*, II, 534: Pufte vp with pride. ¶ Greene, *Pandosto*, *Works*, IV, 270: Puffed vp with pride. ¶ Sidney, *Arcadia*, *Works*, I, 138: Pride so puffes up the hart.

630 KEEP YOUR **PROMISE**

Cf. no. 822: A vow (promise) is a bond

FQ, I, xii, 19, 6: For vowes may not be vayne. ¶ *Ibid.*, II, i, 60, 9: Bynempt a sacred vow, which none should ay releace. ¶ *Ibid.*, iii, 1, 5–7: Mindfull of his vow yplight, Uprose . . . and him addrest Unto the journey which he had behight. ¶ *Ibid.*, III, vii, 51, 5–7: That thousand deathes me lever were to dye, Then breake the vow . . . I plighted have, and yet keepe stedfastly. ¶ *Ibid.*, VI, vii, 15, 7: Therefore now yeeld, as ye did promise make. ¶ *Amoretti*, xlii, 8: Yield for pledge.

Old Testament: Deut., xxiii, 21: When thou shalt vow a vow unto the Lord thy God, thou shalt not slack to pay it. ¶ Plautus, *Mostellaria*, 1023: Fides servanda est (A promise must be kept). ¶ Foxe, *Acts and Mon.*, VI, 698: Promise must be kept. ¶ Shakespeare, *Mids. Night's D.*, I, i, 179: Keep promise. ¶ Shakespeare, *As You Like It*, IV, i, 200: Keep your promise. ¶ Shakespeare, *Hen. V*, IV, vii, 146–147: It is necessary . . . that he keep his vow and his oath. ¶ *Ibid.*, 151: Then keep thy vow.

Cf. Stevenson, 1895:14.

631 **PROSPERITY** BRINGS ON ANXIETIES

Cf. no. 110: Much coin, much care; no. 830: Little wealth, little care

FQ, VI, ix, 21, 3: They that have much, feare much to loose thereby.

Publilius Syrus (1835), 854: Res inquieta est in se ipsam felicitas (Prosperity is ever providing itself with anxieties).

Cf. Tilley, R109; C. G. Smith, 253.

632 **PROSPERITY** IS THE NURSE OF HAUGHTINESS

Shep. Cal., Maye, 117–118: Long prosperitie, . . . nource . . . of insolencie.

Culman, 5: Divitiae fastum pariunt (Riches bring forth haughtiness). ¶ Publilius Syrus (1835), 1004: Vitium sollemne fortunae est superbia (Haughtiness is the common vice of prosperity).

Erasmus, *Adagia*, 943A: Fortuna reddit insolentes (Success leads to insolence).

Cf. C. G. Smith, 241.

633 TO FEEL A PERSON'S **PULSE**

FQ, II, i, 43, 3–4: Then gan softly feel Her feeble pulse. ¶ *Ibid.*, viii, 9, 6: With trembling hand his troubled pulse gan try. ¶ *Ibid.*, III, iv, 41, 7: Did feele his pulse. ¶ *Ibid.*, v, 31, 3: Feeling by his pulses beating rife.

Shakespeare, *Com. of Errors*, IV, iv, 55: Give me your hand, and let me feel your pulse. ¶ *Ibid.*, V, i, 243: Gazing in mine eyes, feeling my pulse.

Cf. Stevenson, 1915:11; Tilley, P240.

634 LET THE **PUNISHMENT** FIT THE OFFENCE

FQ, III, ix, 9, 6–7: We will . . . reward the wretch for his mesprise, As may be worthy of his haynous sin.

Culman, 35: Reddetur unicuique juxta facta sua (It shall be rendered to everyone according to his deeds).

New Testament: Romans, ii, 5–6: *δικαιοκρισίας τοῦ θεοῦ, ὃς 'ΑΠΟ-ΔΏΣΕΙ 'ΕΚΆΣ ΤΩ ΚΑΤΑ ΤᾺ "ΕΡΓΑ ΑΎΤΟΫ* (Judgment of God; Who will render to every man according to his deeds). ¶ Cicero, *De Legibus*, iii, 20, 46: Noxiae poena par esto (Let the punishment fit the offence).

635 THE **PUNISHMENT** OF WICKED MEN IS ETERNAL

FQ, I, v, 33, 7–9: The house of endlesse paine . . . In which . . . cursed creatures doe eternally torment. ¶ *Ibid.*, II, viii, 45, 7–9: His ghost . . . to th' infernall shade Fast flying, there eternall torment found For all the sinnes wherewith his lewd life did abound.

Culman, 35: Poena impiorum aeterna (The punishment of wicked men is eternal).

636 TO TOUCH TO THE **QUICK**

FQ, III, xi, 15, 7: Those feeling words so neare the quicke did goe.

Cf. Stevenson, 1927:1; Tilley, Q13.

637 **RARE** THINGS ARE PRECIOUS THINGS

Cf. no. 638: It is rarity that gives zest to pleasure

FQ, I, vii, 29, 9: Stones most pretious rare. ¶ *Ibid.*, viii, 50, 9: Dainty was and rare. ¶ *Ibid.*, IV, x, 39, 6: Rare and pretious to esteeme.

Culman, 11: Charum est quod rarum est (That is precious which is rare).

Shakespeare, *Mids. Night's D.*, III, ii, 226–227: To call me . . . rare, Precious. ¶ Shakespeare, *King Lear*, I, i, 57–58: Dearer than eyesight . . . Beyond what can be valued, rich or rare. ¶ Shakespeare, *Winter's T.*, I, ii, 452: A precious creature. And she's rare.

Cf. Stevenson, 1935:2; Tilley, T145.

638 IT IS **RARITY** THAT GIVES ZEST TO PLEASURE

Cf. no. 637: Rare things are precious things

Teares of the M., 549–552: Pleasures, Now being let to runne at libertie By those which have no skill to rule them right, Have now quite lost their naturall delight.

Culman, 16: Voluptates commendat rarior usus (The more seldom use commends pleasures). ¶ Publilius Syrus (1934), 630: Rarum esse oportet quod diu carum velis (Rare must be that which you would long hold dear).

Martial, *Epigr.*, iv, 29, 3: Rara iuvant (Rare things please one). ¶ Juvenal, *Sat.*, xi, 208: Voluptates commendat rarior usus (It is rarity that gives zest to pleasure). ¶ Erasmus, *Colloquia Fam.*, 888B: Voluptates commendat rarior usus (Rare use commends pleasure).

Cf. Stevenson, 1812:17, 1935:3–4; C. G. Smith, 246.

639 **RASHNESS** PROVOKES MISCHIEF

Cf. no. 278: Foolhardiness is dangerous

FQ, I, i, 12, 1–2: Be well aware . . . Least suddaine mischiefe ye too rash provoke.

Culman, 3: Periculosa temeritas (Rashness is dangerous). ¶ *Ibid.*, 14: Nocet temeritas multum mortalibus (Rashness does much hurt to men).

640 LET **REASON** RULE YOUR ACTIONS

FQ, II, ii, 11, 1: He harkned to his reason. ¶ *Ibid.*, IV, v, 24, 9: Ne judges powre, ne reasons rule, mote them restraine.

Culman, 3: Rationi obtempera (Obey reason). ¶ Publilius Syrus (1835), 692: Plus conscientiae quam famae attenderis (Harken rather to your conscience than to opinion).

Diogenes Laertius, *Solon*, i, 60: *νοῦν ἡγεμόνα ποιοῦ* (Be led by reason). ¶ Seneca, *De Benef.*, iv, 10, 2: Nihil enim sine ratione faciendum est (Nothing is to be done without reason). ¶ Seneca, *Epist.*, xxxvii, 4: Si vis omnia tibi subicere, te subice rationi (If you wish to subject all things to yourself, subject yourself to reason).

Cf. Stevenson, 1941:12, 1942:3; Tilley, R43; C. G. Smith, 247.

641 AS **RED** AS A ROSE

FQ, II, i, 41, 4–5: His ruddy lips did smyle, and rosy red Did paint his chearefull cheekes. ¶ *Ibid.*, viii, 39, 2: Red as the rose. ¶ *Amoretti*, lxiv, 6: Ruddy cheekes lyke unto roses red.

Chaucer, *Leg. Good Women*, 112: The sonne, that roos as red as rose. ¶ Chaucer, *Sir Thopas*, 1916: His lippes rede as rose. ¶ Hawes, *Past. Pleas.*, 146: Ruddy as a rose.

Cf. Apperson, 526; W. G. Smith, 535; Tilley, R177.

642 SCOTS AND **REDSHANKS**

View, 616: Scottes and Redd-shankes. ¶ *Ibid.*, 658: Scottes and Redd-shankes.

Elder, *Lett. to Hen. VIII*, *Bannatyne Misc.* (1827), I, 10: The Yrische lordes of Scotland, commonly callit the Redshanckes. ¶ Boorde, *Introd. Knowl.* (1870), III, 132: The other parte of Irland is called the wilde Irysh; and the Redshankes be among them. ¶ Nashe, *Lenten Stuffe*, *Works*, III, 188: The Scotish Iockies of Redshanks (so surnamed of their immoderate raunching vp the red shanks or red herrings).

Cf. Spenser, *Prose Works* (Variorum), 293.

643 **RELIGION** IS POTENT IN MAKING FOR GOODNESS

Colin Clouts, 322–323: Religion hath lay powre to rest upon her, Advancing vertue and suppressing vice. ¶ *FQ*, VI, viii, 43, 9: Religion held even theeves in measure.

Cf. *FQ* (Variorum), VI, 235.

644 THERE IS NO **REMEDY** FOR FEAR

FQ, VI, xi, 38, 2: Nought may feare disswade.

Cf. W. G. Smith, 417; Stevenson, 784:1.

645 PLEASANT IS THE **REMEMBRANCE** OF PERILS (LOSSES, WOES) THAT ARE PAST

FQ, IV, ix, 40, 9: Past perils well apay.

Publilius Syrus (1835), 212: Dulcis malorum praeteritorum memoria (Pleasant is the remembrance of the ills that are past).

Cicero, *De Fin.*, ii, 32, 105: Iucunda memoria est praeteritorum malorum (The memory of past evils is pleasant). ¶ Seneca, *Hercules Furens*, 656–657: Quae fuit durum pati, meminisse dulce est (What was hard to bear, it is pleasant to recall). ¶ Statius, *Thebaidos*, v, 48: Dulce loqui miseris veteresque reducere questus (It is pleasant to the unhappy to speak and recall the sorrows of old time). ¶ Erasmus, *Adagia*, 1149F: Jucunda malorum praeteritorum memoria (The memory of past evils is pleasant); cf. *Colloquia Fam.*, 712B.

Cf. Apperson, 481; W. G. Smith, 538; Tilley, R73; C. G. Smith, 249.

646 **REMORSE** IS A SEVERE MENTAL PUNISHMENT

FQ, I, x, 21, 9: So much the dart of sinfull guilt the soule dismayes. ¶ *Ibid.*, III, x, 18, 3–4: When he mused on his late mischiefe, Then still the smart thereof increased more.

Publilius Syrus (1934), 231: Gravis animi poena est quem post facti paenitet (Heavy the penalty on the mind which afterwards regrets a deed).

Seneca, *De Ira*, iii, 26, 2–3: Nec quisquam gravius adficitur quam qui ad supplicium paenitentiae traditur (No man is more heavily punished than he who is consigned to the torture of remorse).

647 **REPENTANCE** FOLLOWS ON A HASTY PLAN

Cf. no. 366: Haste breeds error; no. 648: When harm has been done, repentance is too late

FQ, II, v, 13, 8–9: Hasty wroth, and heedlesse hazardry, Doe breede repentaunce late, and lasting infamy.

Culman, 19: Festinationis comites sunt error & poenitentia (Error and repentance are the companions of haste). ¶ * Publilius Syrus (1934), 32: Ad paenitendum properat, cito qui iudicat (Hasty judgment means speedy repentance). ¶ *Ibid.*, 734: Velox consilium sequitur paenitentia (Repentance follows on a hasty plan). ¶ *Ibid.*, (1835), 1029: Festinationis error comes et poenitentia (Error and repentance are the attendants on hasty decisions).

Pettie, *Petite P.*, 192: Bargains made in speede, are commonly repented at leasure. ¶ Tasso, *Jer. Del.*, II, 65, 6: Things done in haste at leisure be repented.

Cf. Tilley, H191.

648 WHEN HARM HAS BEEN DONE, **REPENTANCE** IS TOO LATE

Cf. no. 647: Repentance follows on a hasty plan

Shep. Cal., Feb., 228–229: Nowe no succoure was seene him nere. Now gan he repent his pryde to late. ¶ *FQ*, I, vi, 47, 1–4: What fury mad

Hath thee incenst to hast thy dolefull fate? Were it not better I that lady had Then that thou hadst repented it too late? ¶ *Colin Clouts*, 668–675: I, silly man, . . . Durst not adventure such unknowen wayes . . . But rather chose back to my sheep to tourne . . . Then, having learnd repentance late, to mourne Emongst those wretches which I there descryde. ¶ *FQ*, IV, ix, 34, 9: And being brought in daunger, to relent [repent] too late. ¶ *Hymne of Heavenly B.*, 290–293: With false Beauties flattring bait misled, . . . now have left thee nought But late repentance, through thy follies prief.

Lydgate, *Fall of P.*, III, 915: Harm doon, to late folweth repentaunce. ¶ Ray, 22: When all is consum'd, repentance comes too late. ¶ Fuller, 5545: When all is gone, repentance comes too late.

Cf. Apperson, 528; W. G. Smith, 539.

649 IN SORROW (CALAMITY, MISERY) **REPROACH** IS CRUEL

FQ, III, vi, 21, 7–8: Ill beseemes it to upbrayd A dolefull heart with so disdainfull pride. ¶ *Ibid.*, 22, 9: Spare, gentle sister, with reproch my paine to eeke. ¶ *Ibid.*, viii, 1, 9: For misery craves rather mercy then repriefe.

Culman, 5: Calamitas nemini exprobranda (His misery is to be upbraided to no man). ¶ *Ibid.*, 7: Infelicitas nemini objicienda (Misfortune is to be objected to nobody). ¶ *Ibid.*, 12: Exprobratio calamitatis nemini objicienda (No man must be upbraided with his calamity). ¶ * Publilius Syrus (1934), 101: Crudelis est in re adversa obiurgatio (Rebuke is cruel in adversity). ¶ * *Ibid.*, 147: Damnare est obiurgare cum auxilio est opus (When there's need of help, reproach is to make things worse). ¶ *Ibid.*, 486: Obiurgari in calamitate gravius est quam calamitas (To be scolded in misfortune is harder than misfortune itself).

Cf. C. G. Smith, 250.

650 PROTECT YOUR **REPUTATION**

Ruines of R., viii, 14: Her name and endles honour keep. ¶ *FQ*, IV, iv, 27, 2: To salve his name, And purchase honour.

Culman, 1: Existimationem retine (Keep your good name).

Cato, *Collectio Dis. Vulg.*, 42: Existimationem retine (Hold fast to your reputation). ¶ Shakespeare, *Merry Wives*, I, iii, 86–87: Keep the haviour of reputation. ¶ *Ibid.*, II, ii, 257–258: Drive her then from the ward of her purity, her reputation. ¶ *Ibid.*, III, iii, 126: Defend your reputation.

651 THE WOUNDS OF BASE **REPUTE** CANNOT BE CURED

FQ, VI, vi, 1, 3–6: The poysnous sting, which infamy Infixeth in the name of noble wight . . . by no art, nor any leaches might, It ever can recured be againe.

Publilius Syrus (1934), 572: Quem fama semel oppressit vix restituitur (To restore one whom ill report has once crushed is hard).

Cato, *Collectio Monos.*, 5: Numquam sanantur deformis vulnera famae (The wounds of base repute are never cured).

Cf. C. G. Smith, 61.

652 WITHOUT **REST**, NOTHING CAN LONG EXIST

Shep. Cal., Sept., 240–241: What ever thing lacketh chaungeable rest, Mought needes decay, when it is at best. ¶ *FQ*, III, vii, 3, 5: Nought that wanteth rest can long aby.

Ovid, *Heroides*, iv, 89: Quod caret alterna requie, durabile non est (That which lacks its alternations of repose will not endure); cf. Northbrooke, *Treatise agst. Dicing*, 51. ¶ Chaucer, *Merch. T.*, 1862–1863: For every labour somtyme moot han reste, Or elles longe may nat endure.

653 THE **REVEALING** (REMEMBRANCE) OF GRIEF IS A RENEWING OF SORROW

FQ, I, iv, 51, 6–7: That is double death . . . my sorrow to renew. ¶ *Ibid.*, vii, 41, 5: "But griefe," quoth she, "does greater grow displaid." ¶ *Ibid.*, viii, 44, 2–3: The things, that grievous were to doe, or beare, Them to renew, I wote, breeds no delight. ¶ *Ruines of T.*,

478–482: My thought returned . . . Renewing her complaint with passion . . . Whose wordes recording in my troubled braine, I felt such anguish wound my feeble heart.

Publilius Syrus (1934), 545: Post calamitatem memoria alia est calamitas (After misfortune, remembrance is misfortune renewed).

Cf. Tilley, R89; C. G. Smith, 248.

654 **REVENGE** ON AN ENEMY IS TO GET A NEW LEASE ON LIFE

FQ, IV, iv, 35, 1–5: With that he drives at them with dreadfull might, Both in remembrance of his friends late harme, And in revengement of his owne despight; So both together give a new allarme, As if but now the battell wexed warme.

* Publilius Syrus (1934), 270: Inimicum ulcisci vitam accipere est alteram (Revenge on an enemy is to get a new lease on life).

655 THE **REWARD** OF VALOR MAKES TOIL A DELIGHT

Amoretti, lxix, 13–14: The happy purchase of my glorious spoile, Gotten at last with labour and long toyle.

Publilius Syrus (1934), 716: Virtutis spolia cum videt, gaudet labor (To see the spoils of valor makes toil a delight).

Cato, *Collectio Monos.*, 53: Dulcis enim labor est, cum fructu ferre laborem (To bear fruitful labor is sweet labor).

656 TO PLAY **REX**

View, 659: To suffer such a caytiff to playe such *Rex*.

Cf. W. G. Smith, 505; Tilley, R96.

657 THE **RICH** HAVE MANY FRIENDS

Shep. Cal., Julye, 193–194: They han great stores and thriftye stockes, Great freendes and feeble foes.

Culman, 5: Amicos pecuniae faciunt (Money makes friends). ¶ *Ibid.*, 14: Opes amicos conciliant (Wealth wins friends).

Erasmus, *Adagia*, 829D: Felicitas multos habet amicos (Good fortune has many friends).

Cf. W. G. Smith, 541; Tilley, R103; C. G. Smith, 252.

658 **RICHES** ARE GOTTEN WITH PAIN, KEPT WITH CARE, AND LOST WITH GRIEF

FQ, I, iv, 28, 7–9: [Avarice] thorough daily care To get, and nightly feare to lose his owne, He led a wretched life.

Guazzo, *Civ. Conv.*, *Works*, III, 52: Riches are gotten with travayle, kept with feare, and lost with greife.

Cf. Apperson, 530; Stevenson, 1978: 12; Tilley, R108.

659 **RICHES** ARE THE CAUSE OF MUCH WRANGLING

FQ, II, vii, 12, 1–7: I riches read, And deeme them roote of . . . Infinite mischiefes . . . Strife and debate, bloodshed and bitternesse.

Culman, 12: Divitiae sunt causa jurgiorum (Riches are the cause of brawlings).

660 **RICHES** FLY AWAY

Daphnaïda, 500–502: Riches . . . have no long endurance, But ere ye be aware will flit away.

Culman, 8: Opes celeriter dilabuntur (Riches pass away swiftly).

Cf. W. G. Smith, 541; Stevenson, 1977:3; Tilley, R111.

661 PUT YOUR TRUST IN **RIGHT**, NOT IN MIGHT

FQ, II, ii, 29, 8–9: Vaine is the vaunt, and victory unjust, That more to mighty hands then rightful cause doth trust. ¶ *Ibid.*, V, viii, 30, 9: More in his causes truth he trusted then in might. ¶ *Ibid.*, xi, 17, 3–5: Deedes ought not be scand By . . . the doers might, But by their trueth and by the causes right.

662 SEEK WHAT IS **RIGHT**

FQ, I, x, 10, 4: Seeke the right.

Culman, 3: Rectum quaere (Seek what is right).

Cf. Stevenson, 1989:4.

663 TO **RIP** UP OLD SORES

Shep. Cal., Sept., 12–13: Gall not my old griefe: Sike question ripeth up cause of newe woe. ¶ *FQ*, I, vii, 39, 8: Rip up griefe, where it may not availe. ¶ *Ibid.*, IV, ix, 37, 3: To rip up wrong that battell once hath tried.

Erasmus, *Adagia*, 253A: Refricare cicatricem (To open a wound afresh). ¶ Nashe, *Summers Last Will*, *Works*, III, 246: Old sores . . . may not be ript vp.

Cf. Milton, *Complete Prose Works* (Yale, 1953), I, 882, 903; Henderson, 215; Stevenson, 2167:10; Tilley, S649.

664 ALL **RIVERS** RUN INTO THE SEA

FQ, IV, xi, 43, 7–8: All [rivers] . . . doe at last accord To joyne in one, ere to the sea they come. ¶ *Ibid.*, VI, prol., vii, 4–5: So from the ocean all rivers spring, And tribute backe repay as to their king.

Cf. W. G. Smith, 544; Stevenson, 1998:2; Tilley, R140.

665 AS FIXED (FIRM) AS A **ROCK**

FQ, I, ii, 16, 7: So stood these twaine, unmoved as a rocke. ¶ *Ibid.*, vi, 4, 5: As rock of diamond stedfast evermore.

Homer, *Odyssey*, xvii, 463–464: ὁ δ' ἐστάθη ἠΰτε πέτρη ἔμπεδον (But he stood firm as a rock). ¶ Vergil, *Aeneid*, vii, 586: Velut pelagi rupes immota (Immovable like a steep rock of the sea).

Cf. Stevenson, 1075:9, 2001:7; Tilley, R151.

666 ALL **ROOTLESS** THINGS SOON DIE

FQ, IV, i, 51, 5: All things not rooted well will soone be rotten.

New Testament: *Mark*, iv, 6: διὰ τὸ μὴ ἔχειν ῥίζαν ἐξηράνθη (Because it had no root, it withered away). ¶ Chaucer, *Troilus*, IV, 769–770: For which ful ofte a by-word here I seye, That "rootles moot grene soone deye." ¶ Shakespeare, *Rich. III*, II, ii, 41: Why grow the branches when the root is gone?

667 RULE YOUR TONGUE

FQ, VI, vi, 7, 8–9: Your tongue, your talke restraine From that they most affect, and in due termes containe.

Culman, 2: Linguam tempera (Rule your tongue). ¶ *Ibid.*, 26: Summa cura lingua regi debet (The tongue must be ruled with a great deal of care).

Plautus, *Rudens*, 1254: Linguae tempera (Control your tongue)! ¶ Cato, *Disticha*, i, 3: Virtutem primam esse puto, compescere linguam (To rule the tongue is the height of virtue, I think). ¶ Chaucer, *Troilus*, III, 292–294: Thise wise clerkes that ben dede Han evere thus proverbed to us yonge, That "firste vertu is to kepe tonge." ¶ Chaucer, *Manciple's Tale*, 242–243: The firste vertu, sone, if thou wolt leere, Is to restreyne and kepe wel thy tonge.

Cf. C. G. Smith, 258.

668 BY BAD RULING THE MOST EXALTED RULE IS LOST

Mother Hub., 1039–1040: For government of state Will without wisedome soone be ruinate.

* Publilius Syrus (1934), 380: Male imperando summum imperium amittitur (By bad ruling the most exalted rule is lost).

669 IT IS BEST TO RUN (DRIFT, SWIM) WITH THE STREAM

Cf. no. 734: Strive (swim, struggle, row) not against the stream

View, 675: Runne with the streame.

Euripides, *Daughters of Troy*, 103: πλεῖ κατὰ πορθμόν, πλεῖ κατὰ δαίμονα (You must drift with the stream, you must drift with the tides of fortune). ¶ Vergil, *Georgics*, iii, 447: Secundo defluit amni (He drifts with the stream). ¶ Nashe, *Unfor. Trav.*, *Works*, II, 245: To swim with the stream. ¶ Shakespeare, *Com. of Errors*, I, i, 86: Floating straight, obedient to the stream.

Cf. Stevenson, 2227:4; Tilley, S930.

670 TO SIT ON HORSEBACK LIKE **SAINT** GEORGE

FQ, I, ii, 11, 8–9: When he sate uppon his courser free, Saint George himselfe ye would have deemed him to be.

Cf. Apperson, 9; W. G. Smith, 556; Stevenson, 946:7; Tilley, S42.

671 ONE **SALVE** FOR ALL SORES

Amoretti, l, 14: With one salve both hart and body heale.

Cf. Tilley, S82.

672 THERE IS A **SALVE** FOR EVERY SORE

Shep. Cal., Aug., 103: Ne can I find salve for my sore. ¶ *FQ*, III, ii, 35, 7: For never sore, but might a salve obtaine. ¶ *Ibid.*, VI, vi, 5, 9: Give salves to every sore.

Cf. Apperson, 549; W. G. Smith, 560; Tilley, S84.

673 TO BUILD ON **SAND**

Visions of B., xiv, 2–4: A citie . . . that on sand was built.

Cf. Stevenson, 253:2; Tilley, S88.

674 TO SOW IN THE **SAND**

Ruines of R., x, 4: Dragons teeth, sowne in the sacred sand.

Cf. W. G. Smith, 608; Stevenson, 2177:5; Tilley, S87.

675 IT IS EASIER TO NUMBER THE **SANDS** IN THE SEA

Cf. no. 720: It is easier to count the stars

FQ, IV, xi, 53, 1–2: More eath [easy] it were for mortall wight To tell the sands.

Cf. Tilley, S91.

676 WITH A **SARDONIC** SMILE

FQ, V, ix, 12, 6: With Sardonian smyle.

Homer, *Odyssey*, xx, 301: *μείδησε δὲ θυμῷ σαρδάνιον μάλα τοῖον* (In his heart he smiled a sardonic smile). ¶ Cicero, *Epist. ad Fam.*, vii, 25, 1: Rideamus *γέλωτα σαρδόνιον* (We may laugh a sardonic laugh). ¶ Lucian, *Zeus Rants*, 16: *ὁ Δᾶμις δὲ τὸ σαρδάνιον ἐπιγελῶν* (Damis with his sardonic laughter). ¶ Erasmus, *Adagia*, 825A: Risus Sardonius (A sardonic laugh); cf. 1173F.

Cf. *FQ* (Variorum), V, 235; Stevenson, 1353:7; 2145:10.

677 **SCORN** BASE THINGS

Amoretti, v, 6: Scorn of base things. ¶ *Ibid.*, lxi, 11–12: Scorne Base things.

Culman, 2: Fuge turpia (Avoid base things).

678 THOSE WHO PLOW THE **SEA** DO NOT CARRY THE WINDS IN THEIR HANDS

FQ, II, vi, 23, 2–3: Who fares on sea may not commaund his way, Ne wind and weather at his pleasure call.

Publilius Syrus (1835), 774: Qui maria sulcant, ventum in manibus non habent (They who plow the sea do not carry the winds in their hands).

679 HE THAT IS TOO **SECURE** IS NOT SAFE

Muiopotmos, 381–382: Litle wist he his fatall future woe, But was secure; the liker he to fall. He likest is to fall into mischaunce, That is regardles of his governaunce. ¶ *Visions of the Worlds V.*, xii, 13–14: For he that of himselfe is most secure Shall finde his state most fickle and unsure. ¶ *FQ*, III, iv, 27, 3–4: When he sleepes in most security And safest seemes, him soonest doth amate. ¶ *Amoretti*, lviii, 3–4: Soonest fals, when as she most supposeth Her selfe assurd, and is of nought affrayd.

Culman, 13: Innumera mala parit securitas (Security breeds many mischiefs). ¶ Publilius Syrus (1934), 280: Irritare est calamitatem cum te felicem voces (To call yourself fortunate is to provoke disaster).

Greene, *Mamillia*, *Works*, II, 238: Be not secure least want of care procure thy calamitie. ¶ Harvey, *A New Lett.*, *Works*, I, 287: Security cannot be too precise or scrupulous.

Cf. Apperson, 641; W. G. Smith, 569; Tilley, W152; C. G. Smith, 263.

680 **SEEING** IS BELIEVING

FQ, II, i, 11, 3: None but that saw . . . would weene for troth [truth]. ¶ *Ibid.*, viii, 22, 3: Soone shalt thou see, and then beleeve for troth [truth].

Aristophanes, *The Ecclesiazusae*, 772: ἀλλ' ἰδὼν ἐπειθόμην (I saw it and believed). ¶ Plautus, *Asinaria*, 202: Credunt quod vident (They believe what they see). ¶ Cicero, *Epist. ad Att.*, xvi, 1: Tum crederes, cum ipse cognosses (Believe it only when you see it).

Cf. Apperson, 556; W. G. Smith, 571; Stevenson, 2105:12; Tilley, S212.

681 **SHAME** TAKE HIM THAT SHAME THINKS

FQ, IV, vi, 6, 1: Shame be his meede . . . that meaneth shame. ¶ *Ibid.*, VI, i, 25, 9: Shame shal thee with shame requight.

Cf. Apperson, 560; W. G. Smith, 314; Tilley, S277.

682 PAST **SHAME**, PAST AMENDMENT (GRACE)

FQ, II, i, 20, 5: No amendes of shame.

Culman, 25: Pudore amisso omnis virtus ruit (When shame is lost, all virtue quickly decays). ¶ * Publilius Syrus (1934), 196: Fidem qui perdit quo rem servat relicuam (With credit lost, what means are there of saving what remains)?

Plautus, *Bacchides*, 487: Nam ego illum periise dico quoi quidem periit pudor (For perished I say he has, when his sense of shame has perished).

Cf. Tilley, S271; C. G. Smith, 264.

683 AS MANY **SHAPES** AS PROTEUS

FQ, I, ii, 10, 3–4: As many formes and shapes . . . As ever Proteus to himselfe could make.

Ovid, *Metam.*, viii, 730–731: Quibus in plures ius est transire figuras, ut tibi, . . . Proteu (To others the power is given to assume many forms, as to thee Proteus). ¶ Erasmus, *Adagia*, 473B: Proteo mutabilior (More changeable than Proteus). ¶ Sidney, *Arcadia*, *Works*, I, 247: He could have turned himself to as many formes as *Proteus*. ¶ Nashe, *Pierce P.*, *Works*, I, 186: More shapes than *Proteus*.

Cf. W. G. Smith, 579; Tilley, S285.

684 AS THE **SHEPHERD**, SO HIS SHEEP

Cf. no. 242: Like father, like son; no. 243: You are your father's own son

Shep. Cal., Sept., 141: Sike as the shepheards, sike bene her sheepe.

Cf. W. G. Smith, 588; Tilley, S328.

685 LIKE A **SHIP** WITHOUT A HELM (STERN, STEERSMAN, BALLAST)

Teares of the M., 141–142: Like a ship in midst of tempest left Withouten helme or pilot her to sway. ¶ *FQ*, II, vi, 5, 1–3: Her shallow ship . . . Withouten care of pilot it to guide.

Cf. Stevenson, 1795:9; Tilley, S347.

686 TO BE OVER **SHOES**

FQ, I, viii, 16, 9: Over shoes in blood he waded on the grownd.

Shakespeare, *Two Gent.*, I, i, 24: He was more than over shoes in love.

Cf. Stevenson, 2096:6; Tilley, S380.

687 **SHORT** PLEASURE (PAIN), LONG LAMENT (EASE)

FQ, I, ix, 40, 6: Short payne well borne . . . bringes long ease. ¶ *Ruines of T.*, 526: O short pleasure bought with lasting paine!

Cf. Apperson, 567; W. G. Smith, 585; Tilley, P419.

688 COMPULSORY **SILENCE** IS INTOLERABLE

Amoretti, xliii, 2–6: If I speake, her wrath renew I shall: And if I silent be, my hart will breake, Or choked be with overflowing gall. What tyranny is this, both my hart to thrall, And eke my toung with proud restraint to tie!

* Publilius Syrus (1934), 355: Miserum est tacere cogi quod cupias loqui (It's wretched to be forced to conceal what you'd like to reveal).

689 IN **SILENCE** THERE IS SAFETY

FQ, I, i, 41, 8–9: But carelesse Quiet lyes, Wrapt in eternall silence farre from enimyes. ¶ *Ibid.*, VI, ix, 32, 8: And in this quiet make you safer live.

Culman, 9: Silentium ubicunque tutum (Silence is safe everywhere).

Horace, *Odes*, iii, 2, 25–26: Est et fideli tutu silentio merces (There is also a sure reward for trusty silence). ¶ Erasmus, *Adagia*, 829B: Silentii tutum praemium (Safety is the reward of silence).

Cf. Stevenson, 2111:1.

690 AS BRIGHT AS **SILVER**

Muiopotmos, 89: His shinie wings, as silver bright.
Cf. Tilley, S453.

691 NOTHING IS MORE WRETCHED THAN THE SERVITUDE OF **SIN**

FQ, II, xi, 1, 9: No wretchednesse is like to sinfull vellenage.

Publilius Syrus (1835), 565: Nil est miserius, quam mali animus conscius (There is nothing more wretched than a mind conscious of its own wickedness).

Erasmus, *Colloquia Fam.*, 882E: Nihil est miserius quam animus sibi male conscius (Nothing can be more wretched than a mind conscious of its own evil).

692 OUR **SIN** IS DERIVED FROM ADAM

FQ, I, xi, 47, 9: That tree through one mans fault hath doen us all to dy. ¶ *Ibid.*, II, x, 50, 3–4: From wretched Adams line . . . purge away the guilt of sinfull crime.

Culman, 28: Ab Adamo peccatum in nos derivatum est (Sin is derived to us from Adam).

693 THE THREE FATAL **SISTERS**

Daphnaïda, 14: Those three Fatall Sisters. ¶ *FQ*, IV, ii, 47, 4: To the three Fatall Sisters house she went.

Cf. W. G. Smith, 654; Tilley, S490.

694 **SLANDER** IS MORE INJURIOUS THAN OPEN VIOLENCE

FQ, IV, iv, 4, 9: Evill deedes may better then bad words be bore.

Publilius Syrus (1835), 386: Injuriae plus in maledicto est quam in manu (Slander is more injurious than open violence). ¶ *Ibid.*, 695: Plus in maledicto quam in manu est injuriae (Slander is a greater outrage than personal violence).

Cf. C. G. Smith, 270.

695 **SLEEP** IS THE BROTHER (IMAGE) OF DEATH

FQ, II, vii, 25, 7: Next to Death is Sleepe to be compard.

Culman, 9: Somnus mortis imago (Sleep is the image of death).

Homer, *Iliad*, xiv, 231: ἔνθ' Ὕπνῳ ξύμβλητο, κασιγνήτῳ Θανάτοιο (There she met Sleep, the brother of Death). ¶ Cato, *Collectio Monos.*, 19: Mortis imago iuvat somnus (Death's copy, sleep, delights). ¶ Vergil, *Aeneid*, vi, 278: Consanguineus Leti Sopor (Death's own brother Sleep). ¶ *Ibid.*, 522: Dulcis et alta quies placidaeque simillima morti (Sleep sweet and deep, very image of death's peace). ¶ Ovid, *Amores*, ii, 41: Quid est somnus, gelidae nisi mortis imago (What else is sleep but the image of chill death)? ¶ Erasmus, *Colloquia Fam.*, 846C: Somnus enim mors quaedam est . . . & ab Homero mortis germanus dictus est (Sleep is a kind of death, and it is called by Homer the cousin-german of death).

Cf. W. G. Smith, 596; Stevenson, 2137:9; Tilley, S526–S527; C. G. Smith, 271.

696 **SLEEP** TAKES AWAY ALL CARES AND WOES

FQ, II, v, 30, 8–9: Slomber made him to forget His . . . payne. ¶ *Virgils Gnat*, 243–245: Careles sleep . . . In quiet rest his molten heart did steep, Devoid of care, and feare of all falshedd. ¶ *Visions of B.*, i, 3–4: Sleepe doth drowne The carefull thoughts of mortall miseries. ¶ *FQ*, VI, viii, 36, 9: Now drowned in the depth of sleepe all fearelesse lay.

Homer, *Odyssey*, xx, 56: ὕπνος ἔμαρπτε, λύων μελεδήματα θυμοῦ, λυσιμελής (Limb-relaxing sleep, that loosens the cares of the heart). ¶ Euripides, *Bacchae*, 282: ὕπνον τε λήθην τῶν καθ' ἡμέραν κακῶν (Sleep, the oblivion of our daily ills). ¶ Ovid, *Metam.*, xi, 623–625: Somne, quies rerum, placidissime, Somne, deorum, pax animi, quem cura fugit, qui corpora duris fessa ministeriis mulces reparasque labori (O Sleep, rest of all things, Sleep, mildest of the gods, balm of the soul, who puts care to flight, soothes our bodies worn with hard ministries, and prepares them for toil again). ¶ Shakespeare, *Mids. Night's D.*, III, ii, 435: Sleep, that sometimes shuts up sorrow's eye. ¶ Shakespeare, *Macb.*, II, ii, 37–40: Sleep that knits up the ravell'd sleave of care, The death of each day's life, sore labour's bath, Balm of hurt minds, great nature's second course, Chief nourisher in life's feast. ¶ Sidney, *Astrophel and Stella*, xxxix, 1–2, *Works*, II, 258: Sleepe, the certaine knot of peace . . . the balme of woe.

Cf. Stevenson, 2134:6.

697 TO **SLIP** ONE'S NECK OUT OF THE COLLAR

Mother Hub., 269: He would have slipt the coller handsomly.

Guazzo, *Civ. Conv.*, *Works*, II, 95: He hadde shrunke his heade oute of the coller. ¶ *Ibid.*, 165: Drawe not your head out of the coller. ¶ Nashe, *Christ's Teares*, *Works*, II, 94: Hee slyps his necke out of the Coller. ¶ Nashe, *Unfor. Trav.*, *Works*, II, 214: Askt his Lordship what hee meant to slip his necke out of the collar so sodainly.

Cf. Spenser, *Minor Poems* (Variorum), II, 356; Apperson, 579; W. G. Smith, 446; Tilley, N69.

698 TO GIVE THE **SLIP**

View, 658: Giveth them the slip.

Golding, *Ovid*, i, 861–862: Often had she given the slippe both to the *Satyrs* quicke And other Gods that dwell in Woods; cf. xiii, 873. ¶ Harvey, *Letter-Book*, 58: Giving them or me the slipp. ¶ *Ibid.*, 115: At thy pleasure give her the slipp. ¶ Pettie, *Petite P.*, 171: To give them the slip. ¶ Harvey, *Pierces Super.*, *Works*, II, 56: Giue him the slipp. ¶ *Ibid.*, 112: Deuise to giue him the cleanly slipp. ¶ Nashe, *Unfor. Trav.*, *Works*, II, 321: For feare hee should giue me the slip; cf. I, 128–129; II, 258. ¶ Shakespeare, *Rom. & Jul.*, II, iv, 50–51: What counterfeit did I give you? — The slip, sir, the slip. ¶ Jonson, *Every Man in His Humour*, II, v, 145–146, *Works*, III, 338: Let the world thinke me a bad counterfeit, if I cannot giue him the slip, at an instant.

Cf. Stevenson, 2139:2.

699 **SLOTH** IS THE MOTHER OF POVERTY

Cf. no. 413: Idleness is the nurse of evil

FQ, III, vii, 12, 9: Such laesinesse . . . poore . . . him made. ¶ *Mother Hub.*, 99–100: To wexe olde at home in idlenesse Is disadventrous, and quite fortunelesse.

Herbert, 388: An idle youth, a needy age. ¶ Ray (1670), 14: Idleness is the key of beggery.

Cf. Apperson, 321; Henderson, 403; W. G. Smith, 597.

700 **SMALL** THINGS ARE NOT TO BE DESPISED

Vision of Worlds V., v, 13–14: I learned have, not to despise What ever thing seemes small in common eyes.

Culman, 15: Parva non sunt contemnenda (Small things are not to be slighted).

Cf. Stevenson, 1445:6.

701 FROM THE **SMALLEST** COMES THE GREATEST

Shep. Cal., Nov., Glosse, 49: *A minore ad majus.* ¶ *FQ*, IV, ii, 54, 7: Great matter growing of beginning small.

Culman, 12: Ex minimis initiis maxima (The greatest things arise from small beginnings). ¶ *Ibid.*: Ex parvis fiunt magna (Great things are made of little things). ¶ *Ibid.*, 19: Ex parvo initio res magna oritur (A great thing arises from a small beginning). ¶ *Ibid.*, 26: Res initio pusilla crescit in majus (A small matter in the beginning increases to a greater). ¶ Publilius Syrus (1934), 435: Necesse est minima maximorum esse initia (Very big things must have very small beginnings).

Erasmus, *Institutio Principis Christiani*, 607C: E minimo maximum (From the smallest comes the greatest).

Cf. Tilley, L362.

702 HE WAS WRAPPED IN HIS MOTHER'S **SMOCK**

Epigrams (Globe), iv, 41–42: She tooke him streight full pitiously lamenting, And wrapt him in her smock.

Cf. Stevenson, 186:3; Tilley, M1203.

703 AS **SMOOTH** AS GLASS

FQ I, i, 35, 7: As smooth as glas.

Jonson, *Devil Is an Ass*, IV, iv, 50–51: Smooth, As any looking-glasse.

Cf. Apperson, 582; Stevenson, 2147:12; Tilley, G136.

704 **SNAKE** IN THE GRASS

FQ, I, ix, 28, 8: Creeping close, as snake in hidden weedes. ¶ *Ibid.*, II, v, 34, 1: Like an adder lurking in the weedes. ¶ *Ibid.*, III, xi, 28, 8–9: Like a discolourd snake, whose hidden snares Through the greene gras his long bright burnisht back declares.

Vergil, *Eclog.*, iii, 93: Latet anguis in herba (A chill snake lurks in the grass). ¶ Ovid, *Metam.*, xi, 775: Ecce latens herba coluber (Behold, a serpent hiding in the grass). ¶ Painter, *Palace of P.*, II, 247: Vnder the Grasse what lurking Serpent lieth. ¶ Stubbes, *Anat. of Abuses*, II, 7: Sub placidis herbis latitat coluber, vnder the pleasantest grasse, lurketh the venemoust adder. ¶ Greene, *Mamillia*, *Works*, II, 110: A snake in the grasse. ¶ Deloney, *Gentle Craft*, *Works*, 79: Supposing some Adder to lie lurking vnder the fair flowers.

Cf. Apperson, 583; W. G. Smith, 601; Stevenson, 2149:7; Tilley, S585.

705 A **SNAKE** IN ONE'S BOSOM

FQ, I, iv, 31, 3–4: In his bosome secretly there lay An hatefull snake. ¶ *Ibid.*, III, xi, 1, 1–3: O Hatefull hellish Snake, . . . in her bosome she thee long had nurst.

Petronius, *Satyricon*, 77: Tu viperam sub ala nutricas (You are nourishing a viper in your bosom). ¶ Erasmus, *Adagia*, 999B: Colubrum in sinu fovere (To nourish a snake in your bosom). ¶ Nashe, *Summers Last Will*, 1212–1213, *Works*, III, 272: In his bosome nurst A subtill snake. ¶ Deloney, *Thomas of Reading*, *Works*, 225: I will not nourish a snake in my bosome.

Cf. W. G. Smith, 600–601; Stevenson, 2148:8; Tilley, V68.

706 AS **SOFT** AS SILK

FQ, III, i, 65, 7: Her soft silken skin. ¶ *Ruines of T.*, 563: As soft as silke. ¶ *Muiopotmos*, 107: So silken soft. ¶ *Ibid.*, 362: Soft silken twyne.

Cf. Apperson, 585; Stevenson, 2155:8; Tilley, S449.

707 **SORROW** COMES UNSENT FOR

Shep. Cal., Maye, 152 153: Sorrowe ne neede be hastened on: For he will come, without calling anone.

Cf. Apperson, 589; W. G. Smith, 605; Stevenson, 2168:12; Tilley, S654.

708 THE CARE OF THE **SOUL** SHOULD COME BEFORE THE CARE OF THE BODY

View, 646: The care of the sowle should have bene preferred before the care of the bodye.

Publilius Syrus (1835), 970: Ulcera animi sananda magis, quam corporis (The wounds of the soul should be cured before those of the body).

Epictetus, *Doubtful Frag.*, 32: *Ψυχὴν σώματος ἀναγκαιότερον ἰᾶσθαι* (It is much more necessary to cure the soul than the body).

709 **SOWN** THICK, COME UP THIN

FQ, I, ix, 16, 9: True loves are often sown, but seldom grow on grownd.

Cf. Tilley, S692.

710 ONE MAN **SOWS**, ANOTHER MAN REAPS

Cf. no. 82: One beats the bush, another catches the bird

FQ, I, iv, 42, 4: Who reapes the harvest sowen by his foe.

New Testament: *John*, iv, 37: *ἐν γὰρ τούτῳ ὁ λόγος ἐστὶν ἀληθινὸς ὅτι ἄλλος ἐστὶν ὁ σπείρων καὶ ἄλλος ὁ θερίζων* (And herein is that saying true,

One soweth, and another reapeth). ¶ Erasmus, *Adagia*, 193E: Alii sementem faciunt, alii metent (Some sow, others reap).

Cf. Stevenson, 2178:7; Tilley, S691.

711 **SPARE** THE MAN, CONDEMN HIS VICES

FQ, V, xi, 17, 3–5: Deedes ought not be scand By th' authors manhood, nor the doers might, But by their trueth and by the causes right.

Publilius Syrus (1835), 648: Pacem cum hominibus, bellum cum vitiis habe (Be at peace with men, be at war with their vices). ¶ *Ibid.*, 1086: Res bona est, non extirpare sceleratos, sed scelera (Not the criminals, but their crimes, it is well to extirpate).

Seneca, *De Ira*, i, 16, 6–7: Bonus iudex damnat improbanda, non odit (The upright judge condemns the crime, but does not hate the criminal). ¶ Martial, *Epigr.*, x, 33, 10: Parcere personis, dicere de vitiis (To spare the person, to denounce the offence). ¶ Erasmus, *Enchiridion*, 64C: Irascere vitio, non homini (Be angry with the vice, not with the man).

Cf. Tilley, P238; C. G. Smith, 273.

712 IT IS NOBLE TO **SPARE** THE VANQUISHED

Cf. no. 365: To be able to do harm and not do it is noble

FQ, I, viii, 45, 7–8: "To doe her die," quoth Una, "were despight, And shame t'avenge so weake an enimy." ¶ *Ibid.*, II, viii, 51, 2–4: The conquerour nought cared him to slay, But casting wronges and all revenge behind, More glory thought to give life then decay. ¶ *Ibid.*, V, iii, 36, 9: It's punishment enough, that all his shame doe see.

Publilius Syrus (1934), 686: Satis est superare inimicum, nimium est perdere (It is enough to vanquish an enemy, more than enough to ruin him).

Statius, *Thebaidos*, vi, 816: Vincis, abi; pulchrum vitam donare minori (Leave the field, thou art victorious; it is noble to spare the vanquished).

Cf. C. G. Smith, 34.

713 FROM A LITTLE **SPARK** MAY COME A GREAT FIRE

FQ, I, ix, 8, 1–2: Sleeping sparkes . . . troubled once, into huge flames will grow.

Culman, 24: Parva scintilla contempta maximum excitat incendium (A little spark, neglected has caused a very great fire).

New Testament: *James*, iii, 5: ἰδοὺ ἡλίκον πῦρ ἡλίκην ὕλην ἀνάπτει (Behold, how great a matter a little fire kindleth)! ¶ Quintus Curtius, *Hist. Alex. Magni*, vi, 3, 11: Parva saepe scintilla contempta magnum excitavit incendium (Often to have ignored a tiny spark has aroused a great conflagration). ¶ Erasmus, *Adagia*, 911F: Ex minutissima scintillula gravissimum incendium (From the smallest spark comes the greatest fire).

Cf. Stevenson, 806:9; Tilley, S714; C. G. Smith, 274.

714 SHALL I **SPEAK** OR SHALL I BE SILENT?

Amoretti, xliii, 1: Shall I then silent be, or shall I speake?

Erasmus, *Moriae Encomium*, 429D: Eloquarne, an sileam (Shall I speak or be silent)?

Cf. Stevenson, 2349:3.

715 WHAT IT IS DISGRACEFUL TO DO, IT IS HARMFUL TO **SPEAK** OF

FQ, V, xi, 31, 9: Such loathly matter were small lust to speake, or thinke.

Culman, 12: Gravis culpa, tacenda loqui (It is a grievous fault to speak things that are not to be spoken). ¶ Publilius Syrus (1835), 812: Quod facere turpe est, dicere honestum ne puta (What it is disgraceful to do, think it no honor to speak of).

Cf. C. G. Smith, 276.

716 WHAT MUST BE SPENT, **SPEND** AT ONCE

View, 651: What must neede be spente as good spent at once.

Cato, *Disticha*, ii, 5: Fac sumptum propere, cum res desiderat ipsa (Make haste to spend when so the case desires).

717 WHAT WE **SPENT**, WE HAD; WHAT WE GAVE, WE HAVE; WHAT WE LEFT, WE LOST

Shep. Cal., Maye, 69–70: With them wends what they spent in cost, But what they left behind them is lost. ¶ *Ibid.*, Glosse, 86–88: That we spent, we had: That we gave, we have: That we lefte, we lost.

Cf. Apperson, 595; W. G. Smith, 613; Stevenson, 959:2; Tilley, S742.

718 TO RUN OUT OF **SQUARE**

FQ, V, Prol., 1, 7: The world is runne quite out of square. ¶ *Ibid.*, VII, vii, 52, 2: He some times so far runs out of square. ¶ *View*, 649: Through theyr other oversights, runne more out of square.

Udall, *Apoph. of Erasm.*, 80: Neither shall the sense be out of square. ¶ Warner, *Alb. Eng.*, IX, 52: Things, that of themselues be good, abuse brings out of square. ¶ Shakespeare, *Two Noble K.*, IV, iii, 106–107: Reduce what's now out of square in her.

719 WITH **ST. JOHN** (GEORGE) TO BORROW

View, 676: As Chaucer sayeth; St. John to *borrowe.*

Chaucer, *Complaint of Mars*, 9: With St. John to borowe. ¶ Chaucer, *Squire's T.*, 596: Seint John to borwe. ¶ Lydgate, *Complaint of the Black Knight*, 12, *Minor Poems* (E.E.T.S.), 383: With Saint Iohn to borowe. ¶ *Respublica* (E.E.T.S.), II, iii, 597: Than sing wee . . . "Saincte George the borowe."

Cf. W. G. Smith, 556–557; Stevenson, 947:1.

720 IT IS EASIER TO COUNT THE **STARS**

Cf. no. 675: It is easier to number the sands in the sea

FQ, IV, xi, 53, 1–2: More eath it were for mortall wight To . . . count the starres on hye. ¶ *Ibid.*, xii, 1, 5: More eath to tell the starres on hy.

Grange, *Golden Aphr.*, sig. D1: As easie as the numbring of the starres in the skies. ¶ Stubbes, *Anat. of Abuses* (N. Sh. S.), I, 77: I might with more facilitye number . . . the Starres in the skye.

721 BEWARE OF **STARTING** WHAT YOU MIGHT LATER REGRET

FQ, V, vii, 32, 9: Who shortly must repent that now so vainely bravest.

Publilius Syrus (1934), 125: Cave quicquam incipias quod paeniteat postea (Beware of starting what you may later regret).

722 IT IS HARD FOR A HUNGRY **STEED** TO STAY OUT OF A GREEN PASTURE

FQ, IV, viii, 29, 9: Hard for hungry steed t' abstaine from pleasant lare.

723 AS **STILL** AS A STAKE

Cf. no. 724: As still as a stone

FQ, V, iii, 34, 5: He stood as still as any stake.

Cursor M. (1300), 7526: He stood als still os stake. ¶ Gower, *Conf. Aman.*, VI, 190–192: I fro hire go Ne mai, bot as it were a stake, I stonde. ¶ Sidney, *Rem. for Love*, *Works*, II, 346: Then stood I still as any stocke.

Cf. Tilley, S809.

724 AS **STILL** AS A STONE

Cf. no. 723: As still as a stake

FQ, II, vi, 31, 9: Still he stood, as sencelesse stone.

Chaucer, *Troilus*, III, 699: Stille as stoon. ¶ Gower, *Conf. Aman.*, I, 1794: He lay stille as eny ston; cf. I, 2104; II, 874. ¶ Lydgate, *Minor Poems* (E.E.T.S.), 513: Domb and stille as ony stoon. ¶ *Beryn* (E.E.T.S.),

9*

653: Lay as styll as ony stone. ¶ *Thos. of Erceldoune* (E.E.T.S.), 233: Thomas stode styll as stone. ¶ Nashe, *Pierce P.*, *Works*, I, 209: Stands stone still.

Cf. Apperson, 602; Stevenson, 2215:11; Tilley, S879.

725 THE **STING** IS IN THE TAIL

FQ, I, i, 15, 2–4: Her huge long taile . . . was . . . Pointed with mortall sting. ¶ *Ibid.*, xi, 11, 1–9: His huge long tayle, wownd up in hundred foldes . . . And at the point two stinges in fixed arre, Both deadly sharp, that sharpest steele exceeden farr.

Cf. Tilley, S858.

726 AS HARD AS **STONE** (ROCK, FLINT)

Amoretti, xviii, 14: She as steele and flint doth still remayne. ¶ *Ibid.*, lvi, 9–10: Hard and obstinate, As is a rocke.

Cf. Apperson, 284; Stevenson, 1075:9; Tilley, S878.

727 **STOOP-GALLANT**

Shep. Cal., Feb., 90: Stoopegallaunt.

Cf. Spenser, *Shep. Cal.*, ed. by Herford (1925), pp. 100–101; *ibid.*, Renwick (1930), p. 185.

728 AFTER A **STORM** COMES A CALM

Cf. no. 107: After clouds, clear weather

Amoretti, lxii, 11–12: Stormes . . . turne to caulmes.

Culman, 16: Sequitur facile tempestatem serenitas (A calm follows a storm easily).

Lyly, *Euph. and His Eng.*, *Works*, II, 130: Fayre weather commeth after a foule storme. ¶ Harvey, *Letter-Book*, 43: After boisterus and bitter stormes there insuith a pleasaunt caulm.

Cf. Apperson, 604; W. G. Smith, 4; Tilley, S908; C. G. Smith, 278.

729 AS **STRAIGHT** AS A LINE

FQ, II, xi, 21, 6: Streight as line.

Cf. Apperson, 604; W. G. Smith, 624; Tilley, L303.

730 TO STRIVE TO TOUCH THE STARS AND STUMBLE OVER A **STRAW**

Shep. Cal., Julye, 99–100: He that strives to touch the starres Oft stombles at a strawe.

Greene, *Penelopes Web*, *Works*, V, 190: They which gaze at a Starre stumble at a stone. ¶ Greene, *Euphues His Censure to Phil.*, *Works*, VI, 250: Gaze not with the Astronomer so longe at the starres, that thou stumble at a stone. ¶ Greene, *Never Too Late*, *Works*, VIII, 180–181: I haue stared at a starre, but shall stumble at a stone. ¶ Greene, *Farewell to F.*, *Works*, IX, 248: In gazing at a starre you stumble at a stone. ¶ Lodge, *Rosalynde*, *Works*, I, 129: Staring at a star & stombling at a straw.

Cf. Tilley, S827.

731 THE **STREAM** (CURRENT, TIDE) STOPPED SWELLS THE HIGHER

FQ, II, iv, 11, 9: The bankes are overflowne, when stopped is the flood. ¶ *Ibid.*, III, vii, 34, 1–3: He that strives to stop a suddein flood, And in strong bancks his violence containe, Forceth it swell above his wonted mood.

Greene, *Tullies Love*, *Works*, VII, 144: Stop not then the streame, least it ouerflow; cf. VIII, 84. ¶ Sidney, *Arcadia*, *Works*, I, 253: Like a river the more swelling, the more his current is stopped; cf. I, 470. ¶ Deloney, *Gentle Craft*, *Works*, 73: A streame of water being stopt, ouerfloweth the bank; cf. *ibid.*, 151.

Cf. Tilley, S929.

732 **STRIFE** BEGETS STRIFE

FQ, IV, i, 25, 5–9: The seedes of evill wordes and factious deedes . . . Bring foorth an infinite increase, that breedes Tumultuous trouble and contentious jarre, The which most often end in bloudshed and in warre.

Culman, 7: Lis parit litem (Strife breeds strife).

Erasmus, *Adagia*, 693B: Lis litem ferit (Strife begets strife). ¶ Milton, *Sonnets*, xv, 10: For what can War but endless war still breed?

733 **STRIKE** WHILE THE IRON IS HOT

Lett. to Harvey, 44: Whiles the yron is hote, it is good striking.

Publilius Syrus (1835), 265: Ferrum, dum in igni candet, cudendum est tibi (You should hammer your iron when it is glowing hot).

Greene, *Arbasto*, *Works*, III, 224: Stryke while the Iron is hot; cf. V, 54, 88; VII, 66; VIII, 181. ¶ Lodge, *Rosalynde*, *Works*, I, 110: To strike while the yron was hote.

Cf. Tilley, I94; C. G. Smith, 279.

734 **STRIVE** (SWIM, STRUGGLE, ROW) NOT AGAINST THE STREAM

Cf. no. 669: It is best to run (drift, swim) with the stream

FQ, I, xii, 23, 3: To strive against the streame.

Ovid, *Rem. Amoris*, 121–122: Stultus . . . Pugnat in adversas ire natator aquas (He is a foolish swimmer who swims against the stream). ¶ Erasmus, *Adagia*, 748A: Contra torrentem niti (To strive against the stream). ¶ Foxe, *Acts and Mon.*, III, 720: To strive against the stream it availeth not. ¶ Greene, *Mamillia*, *Works*, II, 73: Striue not against the streame; cf. IV, 60; V, 62; VII, 73; VIII, 148; XIII, 337, 378. ¶ Harvey, *Marginalia*, 103: Yeeld to him, that cummith with maine force, and striue not against the streame.

Cf. Apperson, 606; W. G. Smith, 627; Stevenson, 2226:7; Tilley, S927.

735 AS **STRONG** AS A LION (HORSE)

Shep. Cal., Julye, 156: Stoute as steede of brasse. ¶ *FQ*, V, i, 20, 5: Strong as lyon in his lordly might.

Guy of Warwick (E.E.T.S.), 9587: As stowte as a lyon. ¶ Chaucer, *Troilus*, V, 830: Strong, and hardy as lyoun.

Cf. Apperson, 312; W. G. Smith, 627; Stevenson, 2228:10.

736 THE **STRONG** OFTEN NEED THE HELP OF THE WEAK

FQ, II, xi, 30, 1–2: So greatest and most glorious thing on ground May often need the helpe of weaker hand.

Sophocles, *Ajax*, 161: μέγας ὀρθοῖθ' ὑπὸ μικροτέρων (The great have need to be served by the little). ¶ Fuller, 4564: The great and the little have need of one another.

Cf. Apperson, 671; Stevenson, 1034:4; Tilley, W182.

737 TO **STUMBLE** AT THE THRESHOLD

Shep. Cal., Maye, 230: Chaunst to stomble at the threshold flore.

Erasmus, *Adagia*, 211E: In limine offendere (To stumble at the threshold); cf. *Colloquia Fam.*, 724D.

Cf. Stevenson, 2233:3; Tilley, T259.

738 A CHILD OFTEN **SUCKS** EVIL (VIRTUE) FROM THE NURSE'S MILK

Shep. Cal., Ded. Epist., 146–150: The last more shameful then both, that of their owne country and natural speach, which together with their nources milk they sucked, they have so base regard and bastard judgement. ¶ *Teares of the M.*, 261–262: Fed with Furies milke, for sustenaunce Of his weake infancie. ¶ *FQ*, IV, vii, 7, 9: But certes was with milke of wolves and tygres fed. ¶ *Ibid.*, VI, iv, 36, 7–9: Brave imps . . . fed with heavenly sap, That made them grow so high t' all honorable hap. ¶ *Ibid.*, VII, vi, 6, 9: And death, in stead of life, have sucked from our nurse. ¶ *View*, 638: They moreover drawe unto themselves, togither with theyr sucke, even the nature and disposition of theyr nurses.

Cicero, *Tusc. Disp.*, iii, i, 2: Ut paene cum lacte nutricis errorem suxisse videamur (So that it seems as if we drank in deception with our nurse's milk). ¶ Erasmus, *Adagia*, 283C: Cum lacte nutricis (With the nurse's milk). ¶ Erasmus, *Colloquia Fam.*, 773C: Iste malitiam cum lacte nutricis imbibit (He sucked in this ill humor with the nurse's milk). ¶ Painter, *Palace of P.*, III, 323: Sucked the same vertue oute of the Teates of Nourssеs Breasses. ¶ Guazzo, *Civ. Conv.*, *Works*, II, 47: The nurses milke is of such force, that the use thereof, maketh the childe take more after the Nurse, then the Mother which brought him into the world. ¶ Shakespeare, *Coriol.*, III, ii, 129: Thy valiantness was mine, thou suck'st it from me. ¶ Jonson, *The King's Entertainment at Welbeck*, 309–313, *Works*, VII, 802: Our *King* is going now to a great worke . . . to see his Native *Countrey*, and his Cradle, And fine those manners there, which he suck'd in with Nurses Milke, and Parents pietie!

Cf. Tilley, E198.

739 **SUFFERANCE** BRINGS ON MUCH YOU CANNOT SUFFER

FQ, II, iv, 34, 3–4: In their beginning they are weake and wan, But soone through suff'rance growe to fearefulle end. ¶ *Ibid.*, VI, v, 39, 7–9: Grievous paine . . . which the Blatant Beast Had given them, . . . through suffraunce sore increast.

Publilius Syrus (1934), 535: Patiendo multa venient quae nequeas pati (Sufferance will bring much you could not suffer).

740 HE THAT WALKS IN THE **SUN** WILL BE TANNED AT LAST

Shep. Cal., Ded. Epist., 45: How could it be . . . but that walking in the sonne . . . needes he mought be sunburnt. ¶ *Ibid.*, Maye, 267: With long traveile I am brent in the sonne.

Cicero, *De Oratore*, ii, 14, 60: Cum in sole ambulem, etiamsi aliam ob causam ambulem, fieri natura tamen, ut colorer (When walking in the sunshine, though perhaps taking the stroll for a different reason, the natural result is that I get sunburnt). ¶ Seneca, *Epist.*, cviii, 4: Qui in solem venit, licet non in hoc venerit, colorabitur (He that walks in the sun, though he walk not for that purpose, must needs become sunburnt).

Cf. Apperson, 609; Stevenson, 2244:4; Tilley, S972.

741 TO SING BEFORE DEATH, LIKE A **SWAN**

Shep. Cal., Oct., Glosse, 185–190: It is sayd of the learned that the swan, a little before hir death, singeth most pleasantly . . . As wel sayth the poete elsewhere in one of his sonetts. "The silver swanne doth sing before her dying day."

Erasmus, *Adagia*, 91F: Cantator cygnus funeris ipse sui (The swan sings at its own funeral).

Cf. Apperson, 612; W. G. Smith, 634; Stevenson, 2254:5; Tilley, S1028.

742 TO **SWEAR** BY ONE'S SWORD

FQ, III, x, 32, 7: By Sanglamort my sword . . . I sweare. ¶ *Ibid.*, V, viii, 14, 7: Swearing faith to either on his blade. ¶ *Ibid.*, VI, i, 43, 5–6: He made him sweare By his owne sword. ¶ *Ibid.*, vii, 13, 8: Swore by his sword. ¶ *View*, 634: They use commonly to sweare by theyr swoordes.

Langland, *Piers Plowm.*, A, I, 97: Dubbede knihtes, Dude hem swere on heor swerd. ¶ Shakespeare, *Much Ado*, IV, i, 276: By my sword, Beatrice, thou lovest me. ¶ Shakespeare, *Hamlet*, I, v, 147–148: We have sworn, my lord, already.—Indeed, upon my sword, indeed.

Cf. *FQ* (Variorum), V, 225.

743 A DRAM OF **SWEET** (MIRTH) IS WORTH A POUND OF SOUR (SORROW)

FQ, I, iii, 30, 4: A dram of sweete is worth a pound of sowre.

Trial of Treas. (1567), sig. A iii: A litle mirth is worth much sorow some say. ¶ Greene, *Never Too Late*, *Works*, VIII, 36: Buy forsooth a dram of pleasure with a pound of sorrowe. ¶ Clarke, 185: A dramme of mirth is worth a pound of sorrow.

Cf. Tilley, O86.

744 AS **SWEET** AS HONEY

FQ, II, iii, 24, 7: Sweete . . . like dropping honny. ¶ *Ibid.*, v, 33, 4: Sweet wordes, dropping like honny dew.

Cf. W. G. Smith, 635; Stevenson, 2259:1; Tilley, H544.

745 EVERY **SWEET** HAS ITS SOUR

Cf. no. 389: There is no honey without gall; no. 426: There is no joy without sorrow

FQ, I, iv, 46, 3–4: Litle sweet Oft tempred is . . . with muchell smart. ¶ *Astrophel*, 26: Sweet without sowre. ¶ *Amoretti*, xxvi, 9–10: So every sweet with soure is tempred still, That maketh it be coveted the more. ¶ *FQ*, VI, xi, 1, 8–9: A thousand sowres hath tempred with one sweet, To make it seeme more deare and dainty, as is meet.

Wilson, *Arte of Rhet.*, 30: The sweete hath his sower ioyned with him. ¶ Greene, *Morando*, *Works*, III, 101: Ech sweete hath his sower. ¶ Sidney, *Wooing-Stuffe*, *Works*, II, 340: Faint Amorist: what, do'st thou think . . . to devour A world of sweet, and tast no sour?

Cf. Clarke, 318.

746 TO LIVE BY THE **SWEET** OF OTHER MEN'S SWEAT

Mother Hub., 1152: The sweete of others sweating toyle.

Pettie, *Petite P.*, 250: You . . . live . . . by the sweete of other mens swet.

Cf. Apperson, 614; W. G. Smith, 636.

747 AS **SWIFT** AS A DEER

FQ, II, x, 7, 5: And flying fast as roebucke through the fen. ¶ *Ibid.*, xi, 23, 5: As swift . . . as chased stags. ¶ *Ibid.*, III, xi, 5, 8: Swift as any roe. ¶ *Ibid.*, VI, iv, 8, 3: For he was swift as any bucke in chace. ¶ *Ibid.*, VII, vi, 52, 4–5: From them fled more fast Then any deere.

Cf. Tilley, R158.

748 AS **SWIFT** AS A SWALLOW

Shep. Cal., Dec., 20: Like swallow swift I wandred here and there. ¶ *FQ*, II, vi, 5, 2: More swift then swallow. ¶ *Ibid.*, III, iv, 33, 5: As swifte as swallowes. ¶ *Ibid.*, V, i, 20, 4: Swift as swallow in her flight.

Greene, *A Quippe for an Upstart C.*, *Works*, XI, 214: As swift as a swallow.

Cf. Tilley, S1023.

749 AS **SWIFT** AS THE WIND

FQ, IV, vii, 18, 7: As swift as wind. ¶ *Ibid.*, V, vi, 7, 8: More swift then wind.

Cf. Stevenson, 2261:6; Tilley, W411.

750 AS **SWIFT** AS THOUGHT

Shep. Cal., Sept., 222: Swifter then thought.

Cf. Stevenson, 2262:2; Tilley, T240.

751 TO **SWIM** LIKE A FISH

FQ, V, ii, 13, 9: Could swim like to a fish.

Cf. Stevenson, 2262:5; Tilley, F328.

752 **TAG**, RAG, AND BOBTAIL

View, 662: They all came in, both tagge and ragge.

Cf. Apperson, 616; W. G. Smith, 638; Tilley, T10.

753 DO NOT MAKE A LONG **TALE** OUT OF NOTHING

Shep. Cal., Feb., 239–240: Tel it not forth: Here is a long tale, and little worth.

Guazzo, *Civ. Conv.*, *Works*, I, 133: According to the Proverbe, Make . . . of a matter of nothing, a long tale.

754 TOO MUCH **TALK** RESULTS IN WRONGDOING

FQ, VI, xi, 16, 2: They fall to strokes, the frute of too much talke.

Culman, 32: Garrulitas non est absque peccato (Overmuch talk is not without sin).

Cato, *Disticha*, ii, 11: Aduersus notum noli contendere verbis: lis minimis verbis interdum maxima crescit (In wordy war do not engage your friend; for trivial words in mighty strife may end).

755 IT IS HARD TO **TEACH** AN OLD HORSE (DOG) NEW TRICKS

FQ, III, viii, 26, 3: Hard is to teach an old horse amble trew.

Culman, 18: Canis antiquus catenae assuefieri non potest (An old dog cannot be wonted to a chain). ¶ Publilius Syrus (1835), 1105: Veterior canis catenis adsuefieri non potest (When the dog is too old you cannot get him used to the collar).

Erasmus, *Colloquia Fam.*, 662B: Vetulus canis non facile assuescit loro (An old dog will not be easily brought to wear the collar).

Cf. Tilley, D500, D501.

756 A WOMAN'S **TEAR** IS THE SAUCE OF MISCHIEF

FQ, VI, vi, 42, 3–9: To allure . . . fondlings . . . Into her trap . . . she could weepe and pray, And . . . Yet were . . . all her teares but water.

* Publilius Syrus (1934), 153: Didicere flere feminae in mendacium (Woman has learned the use of tears to deceive). ¶ *Ibid.*, 384: Muliebris lacrima condimentum est malitiae (A woman's tear is the sauce of mischief).

Cato, *Disticha*, iii, 20: Nam lachrymis struit insidias, du femina plorat (A weeping woman plots but to waylay).

Cf. Tilley, W638; C. G. Smith, 338.

757 A SAVAGE NATURE IS FED, NOT BROKEN, BY **TEARS**

FQ, VI, viii, 46, 5: The whyles she wayld, the more they [savages] did rejoyce.

Publilius Syrus (1934), 128: Crudelis lacrimis pascitur non frangitur (Tears gratify a savage nature: They do not break it down).

Cf. C. G. Smith, 285.

758 IN THE **TEARS** OF A HYPOCRITE IS CRAFT, NOT SORROW

FQ, I, v, 18, 4–6: A cruell craftie crocodile, . . . in false griefe hyding his harmefull guile, Doth weepe full sore, and sheddeth tender teares.

Publilius Syrus (1934), 536: Paratae lacrimae insidias non fletum indicant (The ready tear means treachery, not grief).

Lyly, *Euph. Anat. of Wit*, *Works*, I, 220: The Crocodile shrowdeth greatest treason vnder most pitifull teares.

Cf. W. G. Smith, 118; Tilley, C831.

759 WITH **TEARS** YOU CAN MELT IRON

Shep. Cal., June, 114: Teares would make the hardest flint to flowe.

Ovid, *Artis Amat.*, i, 659: Lacrimis adamanta movebis (With tears you can melt iron). ¶ Shakespeare, *3 Hen. VI*, III, i, 38: Tears will pierce into a marble heart.

760 TO SET ONE'S **TEETH** ON EDGE

Shep. Cal., Maye, 35–36: Ah, Piers! bene not thy teeth on edge, to thinke How great sport they gaynen with little swinck?

Cf. Tilley, T431.

761 BY **TELLING** OUR WOES WE OFTEN LESSEN THEM

Cf. no. 549: Misery without a voice is a hell; no. 349: Pent up grief will burst the heart

Shep. Cal., Sept., 17: Eche thing imparted is more eath to beare. ¶ *FQ*, I, ii, 34, 4: He oft finds med'cine who his griefe imparts. ¶ *Ibid.*, vii, 40, 9: Found never help, who never would his hurts impart. ¶ *Ibid.*, II, i, 46, 9: He oft finds present helpe, who does his griefe impart. ¶ *Ibid.*, IV, xii, 6, 3: Griefe may lessen being told.

Publilius Syrus (1835), 697: Poena allevatur tunc, ubi laxatur dolor (One suffers less, when one pours out his grief).

Greene, *Never Too Late*, *Works*, VIII, 85: A friend to reueale is a medcine to releeue: discouer thy griefe. ¶ *Stony. Pag.*, *Hesperia*, VII, 103–104: Many tymes th' impartinge of ones griefe vnto an other Eyther quite taketh yt away, or makes seeme farre lesser.

Cf. C. G. Smith, 277.

762 **TEMPERANCE** CONTRIBUTES MUCH TO HEALTH

FQ, II, iv, 33, 8–9: Sore have ye beene diseasd; But all your hurts may soone through temperance be easd. ¶ *Ibid.*, xi, 2, 9: Attempred goodly well for health and for delight.

Culman, 14: Modestia sanitati multum confert (Moderation contributes much to health).

763 HE IS MORE BUSY THAN HE HAS **THANKS** FOR HIS LABOR

Shep. Cal., Julye, 209: Thou medlest more then shall have thanke. ¶ *FQ*, II, ii, 36, 9: But of her love too lavish (litle have she thanck).

Cf. Tilley, T94.

764 AS **THICK** AS HAIL

Shep. Cal., March, 87: As thicke as it had hayled. ¶ *FQ*, IV, iii, 25, 5: As thicke as hayle. ¶ *Ibid.*, vi, 16, 5: As thicke as showre of hayle.

Cf. Stevenson, 2295:9; Tilley, H11.

765 TO RUN THROUGH **THICK** AND THIN

FQ, III, i, 17, 4–5: His tyreling jade he fiersly forth did push, Through thicke and thin. ¶ *Ibid.*, iv, 46, 1–3: Through thick and thin, . . . Those two gret champions did attonce pursew The fearefull damzell. ¶ *Ibid.*, vii, 23, 1–2: It forth she cald, and gave it streight in charge, Through thicke and thin her to poursew. ¶ *Ibid.*, VI, ii, 10, 2–4: His ladie . . . On her faire feet by his horse side did pas Through thicke and thin. ¶ *Ibid.*, vii, 44, 1–2: This was Disdaine, who led that ladies horse Through thick and thin.

Lydgate, *De Guil. Pilgr.* (1426), 22682: And, thorough thykke and thynne trace. ¶ Painter, *Palace of P.*, I, 345: Followeth his game in the thicket of a woode, rushing through thicke and thynne. ¶ Nashe, *Lenten Stuffe*, *Works*, III, 176: Spurre cutte through thicke and thinne.

Cf. Apperson, 623; W. G. Smith, 648; Stevenson, 2295:4; Tilley, T101.

766 ALL **THINGS** FIT NOT ALL MEN

FQ, III, i, 57, 1–3: Some fell to daunce, some fel to hazardry, Some to make love, some to meryment, As diverse witts to diverse things apply.

Cf. Stevenson, 1721:8; Tilley, T167.

767 THEY THAT **THINK** NO ILL ARE SOONEST BEGUILED

FQ, III, i, 54, 6: Who meanes no guile, be guiled soonest shall.

Publilius Syrus (1835), 577: Nimia simplicitas facile deprimitur dolis (Too much candor is easily duped).

Harvey, *Foure Lett.*, *Works*, I, 179: Poore credulitie sone beguiled.

¶ Cotgrave, *Dict.* (*s.v.* Deceu): He that things no hurt is soon deceived. ¶ *Ibid.*, (*s.v.* Penser): The harmlesse minded man is soone deceived.

Cf. Bacon, *Promus*, 1466, 1508; W. G. Smith, 650; Tilley, T221; C. G. Smith, 286.

768 NO ROSE WITHOUT A **THORN**

Amoretti, xxvi, 1: Sweet is the rose, but growes upon a brere.

Cf. W. G. Smith, 549; Stevenson, 2010:2; Tilley, R182.

769 **TIME** BRINGS THE TRUTH TO LIGHT

FQ, I, ix, 5, 9: Time . . . the truth to light should bring.

Culman, 27: Tempus ad lucem ducit veritatem (Time brings the truth to light).

Erasmus, *Adagia*, 528B: Veritatem tempus in lucem eruit (Time brings the truth to light). ¶ Greene, *Philomela*, *Works*, XI, 168: Time wil discouer any truth. ¶ *Ibid.*, 201: Time . . . is the reuealer of truth.

Cf. Tilley, T324; C. G. Smith, 288.

770 **TIME** CHANGES ALL THINGS

Cf. no. 95: All things change; no. 97: There are many kinds of change; no. 772: Time devours (consumes, wears out) all things

FQ, VII, vii, 48, 2–3; All things else that under heaven dwell, Are chaung'd of Time. ¶ *View*, 628: Time, woorking the alteration of all thinges.

Culman 9: Tempore omnia mutantur (All things are changed by time).

Lucretius, *De Rerum Natura*, v, 828–829: Mutat enim mundi naturam totius aetas ex alioque alius status excipere omnia debet (For time changes the nature of the whole universe, and one state of things must pass into another). ¶ Vergil, *Aeneid*, iii, 415: Tantum aevi longinqua valet mutare vetustas (Such vast change can length of time effect).

Cf. Stevenson, 2331:12.

771 **TIME** CURES ALL THINGS

Shep. Cal., Julye, 229–230: His hap was ill, But shall be bett in time. ¶ *Ruines of* R., vii, 13–14: For if that Time make ende of things so sure, It als will end the paine which I endure. ¶ *FQ*, IV, vii, 47, 6: Time for him should remedy provide. ¶ *Amoretti*, lvii, 14: Al my wounds wil heale in little space.

Publilius Syrus (1934), 467: Nihil non aut lenit aut domat diuturnitas (There's naught that time does not either soothe or quell).

Euripides, *Alcestis*, 1085: χρόνος μαλάξει (Time will bring healing). ¶ Menander, *Frag.*, 677K: πάντων ἰατρὸς τῶν ἀναγκαίων κακῶν χρόνος ἐστίν (Time is healer of all the necessary ills). ¶ Seneca, *Ad Marciam de Con.*, i, 6: Naturale remedium temporis (Nature's great healer, time). ¶ Chaucer, *Troilus*, V, 350: As tyme hem hurt, a tyme doth hem cure. ¶ Hawes, *Past. Pleas.*, 218: Do not I tyme, euery thynge aswage?

Cf. Stevenson, 2329:2–7; Tilley, T325; C. G. Smith, 289.

772 **TIME** DEVOURS (CONSUMES, WEARS OUT) ALL THINGS

Cf. no. 95: All things change; no. 770: Time changes all things

Shep. Cal., June, 38: Time in passing weares. ¶ *Ruines of T.*, 419–420: Vaine moniments of earthlie masse, Devour'd of Time, in time to nought doo passe. ¶ *Ibid.*, 556: Time doth greatest things to ruine bring. ¶ *Ruines of* R., iii, 8: The pray of Time, which all things doth devowre. ¶ *Amoretti*, lviii, 7: Devouring tyme. ¶ *FQ*, IV, ii, 33, 1–2: Wicked Time . . . all good thoughts doth waste, And workes of noblest wits to nought out weare. ¶ *Ibid.*, V, iv, 8, 1: Tract of time, that all things doth decay. ¶ *Ibid.*, VII, vii, 47, 5: Time on all doth pray.

Culman, 9: Tempus edax rerum (Time is a devourer of things).

Cato, *Collectio Monos.*, 67: Omne manu factum consumit longa vetustas (Long lapse of time consumes all handiwork). ¶ Ovid, *Metam.*, xv, 234: Tempus edax rerum (Time is the devourer of things). ¶ Painter, *Palace of P.*, II, 165: It is the property of tyme to consume all thinges.

Cf. Stevenson, 2327:5: Tilley, T326; C. G. Smith, 290.

773 **TIME** IS SWIFT-FOOTED

Mother Hub., 308–309: Time, flying with winges swift, Expired had the terme. ¶ *Daphnaïda*, 411–412: All times doo fly So fast away, and may not stayed bee. ¶ *Hymne of Heavenly L.*, 24: Flitting Time.

Culman, 8: Nihil fugacius tempore (Nothing is more fleeting than time). ¶ *Ibid.*, 9: Tempus celerrime aufugit (Time runs away very swiftly). ¶ *Ibid.*: Tempore nihil velocius (Nothing is swifter than time).

Vergil, *Georgics*, iii, 284: Sed fugit interea, fugit inreparabile tempus (Time is flying, flying beyond recall). ¶ Chaucer, *Clerk's T.*, 119: Ay fleeth the tyme; it nyl no man abyde. ¶ Erasmus, *Colloquia Fam.*, 650B: At aetas nunquam non defluit, sive dormias, sive vigiles (Time is always flying, sleeping or waking).

Cf. Apperson, 634; W. G. Smith, 659; Stevenson, 2322–2323; Tilley, T327; C. G. Smith, 292.

774 **TIME** IS THE NURSE OF HOPE

Mother Hub., 327: Times delay new hope of helpe still breeds.

Greene, *Perymedes*, *Works*, VII, 26: Time . . . is the nourse of hope.

775 **TIME** LOST (PAST) CANNOT BE RECALLED

Amoretti lxx, 14: None can call againe the passed time. ¶ *FQ*, IV, x, 14, 8–9: Time to steale, the threasure of mans day, Whose smallest minute lost no riches render may. ¶ *View*, 683: Time . . . being once loste will not be recovered.

Cicero, *De Sen.*, xix, 69: Horae quidem cedunt et dies et menses et anni, nec praeteritum tempus umquam revertitur (Hours and days, and months and years go by; the past returns no more). ¶ Ovid, *Artis Amat.*, iii, 64: Nec quae praeteriit, hora redire potest (The hour that has gone by cannot return). ¶ Ausonius, *Epigr.*, xxxiv, 4: Nec revocare potes, qui periere, dies (Nor canst thou call back the days that are gone). ¶ Greene, *Arbasto*, *Works*, III, 243: Time may be repented, but not recalled; cf. *Alcida*, *Works*, IX, 67. ¶ Lodge, *Rosalynde*, *Works*, I, 106: Time cannot bee recalde.

Cf. Apperson, 635; W. G. Smith, 660; Tilley, T332.

776 **TIME** TRIES TRUTH

FQ, IV, i, 54, 5: Till time the tryall of her truth expyred.

Tusser, *Husb.*, (E.D.S.), 220: Tyme it doth behoofe: Shall make of trouth, a perfit proofe. ¶ Pettie, *Petite P.*, 71: Tract of time shall shortly try for true. ¶ Lyly, *Euph. Anat.* of *Wit*, *Works*, I, Ep. Ded., 181: These thinges be true which experience tryeth. ¶ Greene, *Mamillia*, *Works*, II, 105: Time shall try all thinges true.

Cf. Tilley, T338.

777 TAKE **TIME** BY THE FORELOCK

Cf. no. 367: Make hay while the sun shines

FQ, II, iv, 4, 7–8: All behinde [Occasion's head] was bald, and worne away, That none thereof could ever taken hold. ¶ *Amoretti*, lxx, 7–8: Tell her the joyous time wil not be staid, Unlesse she doe him by the forelock take.

Greene, *Menaphon*, *Works*, VI, 105: Take opportunitie by his fore lockes. ¶ Delony, *Jack Newb.*, *Works*, 65: Take time by the forelocke. ¶ Jonson, *Cynthia's R.*, IV, v, 101, *Works*, IV, 129: Let vs then take our time by the fore-head.

Cf. Apperson, 635; W. G. Smith, 658; Stevenson, 2324:3; Tilley, T311.

778 **TIMES** CHANGE

FQ, VII, vii, 47, 6: Times do change and move continually.

Cato, *Ex Columbano*, 39: Tempora dum variant (Times change).

779 SO YOU **TOLD** ME

FQ, I, ii, 39, 6: As she me told. ¶ *Ibid.*, IV, xii, 27, 7: So he her told.

Cf. Stevenson, 1900:8; Tilley, T89.

780 THE **TONGUE** HAS RUINED MANY MEN

FQ, V, xii, 36, 3–5: Her cursed tongue . . . closely kils, Or cruelly does wound, whom so she wils. ¶ *Ibid.*, VI, i, 8, 8–9: With vile tongue and venemous intent He sore doth wound, and bite, and cruelly torment. ¶ *Ibid.*, vi, 12, 2–9: The Blatant Beast . . . his tongue doth whet Gainst all . . . to infest The noblest wights with notable defame: . . . he them spotted with reproch, or secrete shame. ¶ *Ibid.*, xii, 38, 4–5: His vile tongue . . . many had defamed, And many causelesse caused to be blamed.

Culman, 7: Lingua multos perdidit (The tongue has destroyed many men).

781 WITH **TOOTH** AND NAIL

FQ, VI, vi, 22, 5–6: With his teeth and nailes . . . Him rudely rent, and all to peeces tore. ¶ *Ibid.*, viii, 28, 6–7: With his nayles and teeth Gan him to hale, and teare, and scratch, and bite.

Cf. Apperson, 641; W. G. Smith, 200; Stevenson, 2352:11; Tilley, T422.

782 FROM **TOP** (HEAD) TO TOE (FOOT)

FQ, I, vii, 29, 6: From top to toe. ¶ *Ibid.*, II, i, 5, 9: From his head . . . to his feete. ¶ *Ibid.*, III, xii, 12, 1: From top to toe. ¶ *Dolefull Lay of Clorinda* (Variorum), 72: From head to feet.

Homer, *Iliad*, xvi, 640: ἐκ κεφαλῆς εἴλυτο διαμπερὲς ἐς πόδας ἄκρους (From his head to the very soles of his feet). ¶ Plautus, *Epidicus*, 623: Usque ab unguiculo ad capillum summumst (From her little finger tips to the topmost hair of her head). ¶ Erasmus, *Adagia*, 84A: A capite usque ad calcem (From head to foot); cf. 1077A. ¶ Hawes, *Past. Pleas.*, 145: Frome toppe to too. ¶ Skelton, *Magnyf.* (E.E.T.S.), 2364: From the fote to the crowne of the hede. ¶ Foxe, *Acts and Mon.*, I, 85: From top to toe; cf. IV, 198, 502. ¶ Harvey, *Letter-Book*, 102: From top to toe. ¶ Sidney, *Arcadia*, *Works*, I, 495: From toppe to the toe. ¶ Nashe, *Strange Newes*, *Works*, I, 295: From top to toe. ¶ Greene, *Vision*,

Works, XII, 227: From top to toe. ¶ Greene, *Looking-Glasse*, 2129-2130, *Works*, XIV, 92: From top to toe. ¶ Deloney, *Jack Newb.*, *Works*, 33: From top to toe.

Cf. Apperson, 125; Stevenson, 1096:2; Tilley, T436.

783 TO TURN **TOPSY-TURVY**

FQ, V, viii, 42, 4–5: All overthrowne to ground, Quite topside turvey. ¶ *View*, 655: Suddaynly turned topsy turvy.

Gascoigne, *Supposes*, III, ii, *Works*, I, 212: Turne it topsie turvie. ¶ Gascoigne, *Droome of Doomes Day*, *Works*, II, 221: Turned topsie turvey. ¶ Harvey, *Letter-Book*, 53: Al shuld be turnid topset tirvi; cf. *Pierces Super.*, *Works*, II, 131, 176. ¶ Greene, *Hist. of Orlando Furioso*, 438, *Works*, XIII, 135: Topsie-turuie turnd the bottome vp.

Cf. Stevenson, 2410:2; Tilley, T165.

784 AS A **TREE** FALLS, SO SHALL IT LIE

FQ, I, x, 41, 9: As the tree does fall, so lyes it ever low.

Cf. Apperson, 644; W. G. Smith, 402; Tilley, M64, T503.

785 **TRIAL** IS THE TRUEST TEST

FQ, I, xii, 3, 5: Which whenas trew by tryall he out fond. ¶ *Ibid.*, III, viii, 50, 5: Till triall doe more certeine truth bewray. ¶ *Ibid.*, IV, x, 1, 6: That I too true by triall have approved. ¶ *View*, 648: Trueth may be founde oute by tryalle.

Culman, 5: Experimento nihil certius (Nothing is more certain than trial).

Pindar, *Olympian Odes*, iv, 18: διάπειρά τοι βροτῶν ἔλεγχος (Trial is the true test of mortal men).

Cf. Stevenson, 2372:1.

786 **TROT** SIRE, TROT DAM, HOW SHOULD THE FOAL AMBLE?

FQ, VI, iii, 1, 6–7: Seldome seene, a trotting stalion get An ambling colt, that is his proper owne.

Cf. Apperson, 646; W. G. Smith, 212; Tilley, F408.

787 ANY DAY MAY BRING **TROUBLE**

View, 670: Troublous times may everye day bring foorth.

Old Testament: *Proverbs*, xxvii, 1: Boast not thyself of tomorrow; for thou knowest not what a day may bring forth. ¶ Seneca, *Troades*, 77: Nulla dies maerore caret (No day has been without its grief).

Cf. Clarke, 318; Apperson, 136; W. G. Smith, 131.

788 AS **TRUE** AS A TURTLE TO HER MATE

FQ, III, xi, 2, 9: As trew in love as turtle to her make. ¶ *Ibid.*, VI, viii, 33, 6: Never turtle truer to his make.

Greene, *Never Too Late*, *Works*, VIII, 65: As true as Turtles.

Cf. Apperson, 646; W. G. Smith, 671; Tilley, T624.

789 AS **TRUE** AS TOUCH

FQ, I, iii, 2, 5: True as touch.

Cf. Tilley, T446.

790 HASTY **TRUST** (BELIEF) IS OFTEN HARMFUL

FQ, I, vi, 12, 4: Harme to hasty trust ensu'th.

Ovid, *Heroides*, xvii, 39: Credulitas damno solet esse (Quick belief is wont to bring harm). ¶ Ovid, *Artis Amat.*, iii, 685: Nec cito credideris: quantum cito credere laedat (Do not believe hastily: what harm quick belief can do)! ¶ Lydgate, *Minor Poems* (E.E.T.S.) 477: Hasty credence hath causid gret hyndryng. ¶ Lydgate, *Fall of P.*, III, 4520: Hasti trust doth foolis ofte faille; cf. IV, 1057.

Cf. Stevenson, 162:16.

791 **TRUTH** IS ALWAYS ONE

FQ, V, ii, 48, 6: Truth is one, and right is ever one. ¶ *Ibid.*, xi, 56, 8: Truth is one in all.

Seneca, *Epist.*, lxxix, 18: Veritas in omnem partem sui eadem est (Truth is the same in every part). ¶ *Ibid.*, cii, 13: Veritatis una vis, una facies est (Truth has but one function and one likeness). ¶ Foxe, *Acts and Mon.*, VI, 280–281: The truth . . . remaineth always one, and like unto itself. ¶ Sidney, *Christ. Relig.*, *Works*, III, 282: Trueth can be but one.

792 **TRUTH** IS MIGHTY AND WILL PREVAIL

FQ, I, xii, 28, 7–8: Truth is strong, her rightfull cause to plead, And shall finde friends, if need requireth soe. ¶ *Ibid.*, III, i, 29, 8: Truth is strong.

Culman, 14: Nihil efficacius simplici veritate (Nothing is more effectual than plain truth).

Cicero, *Pro Caelio*, xxvi, 63: O magna vis veritatis . . . facile se per se ipsa defendat (How great is the power of truth . . . easily able to defend itself unaided)! ¶ Lucian, *Slander*, 11: *οὐδ' ἂν κατίσχυε τὴν πάντων ἰσχυροτέραν ἀλήθειαν* (And it would not prevail over truth, that is stronger than all else). ¶ Foxe, *Acts and Mon.*, VIII, 39: Noble anthem of victory, "Vicit verita," (The truth hath the upper hand). ¶ Fulwell, *Ars Adulandi* (1580), sig. E 4: Trueth in the ende shall preuayle. ¶ Harvey, *Pierces Super.*, *Works*, II, 162: If Truth be truth, that is, great and mightie, why should it not preuayle?

Cf. Apperson, 651; W. G. Smith, 675; Tilley, T579; C. G. Smith, 303.

793 AS FAR FROM THE **TRUTH** AS THE EAST IS FROM THE WEST

View, 632: Hath strayed from the trueth all the heavens wide (as they say).

Lyly, *Euph. and His Eng.*, *Works*, II, 118: As far from trueth, as the East from the West.

794 THE **TRUTH** OF A WORD DEPENDS ON HOW YOU UNDERSTAND IT

FQ, V, ii, 47, 7–9: And so likewise of words, the which be spoken, The eare must be the ballance, to decree And judge, whether with truth or falsehood they agree.

Publilius Syrus (1934), 712: Verbum omne refert in quam partem intellegas (For any word it matters how you understand it).

795 **TRY** (TRY YOUR FRIEND) BEFORE YOU TRUST

Amoretti, xlvii, 1–2: Trust not . . . Untill ye have . . . well tryde.

Publilius Syrus (1934), 134: Cave amicum credas nisi si quem probaveris (Beware of trusting anyone as a friend before you have tried him).

Cf. Apperson, 651; W. G. Smith, 675; Stevenson, 894:3, 2383:13; Tilley, T595; C. G. Smith, 306.

796 **TRY** (WEIGH) EVERYTHING THAT IS DOUBTFUL

FQ, III, xi, 24, 8–9: Rather let try extremities of chaunce, Then enterprised praise for dread to disavaunce. ¶ *Ibid.*, IV, i, 7, 5: Full many things so doubtfull to be wayd.

Culman, 5: Dubium quodcunque probato (Try everything that is doubtful).

Shakespeare, *Winter's T.*, I, ii, 257–259: It was my negligence, Not weighing well the end . . . To do a thing where I the issue doubted.

797 DON'T **TURN** BACK WHEN YOU ARE JUST AT THE GOAL

Cf. no. 146: No danger incurred, no danger repelled

FQ, IV, x, 17, 8–9: Unworthy they of grace, whom one deniall Excludes from fairest hope, withouten further triall. ¶ *Ibid.*, 53, 4–5: And folly seem'd to leave the thing undonne, Which with so strong attempt I had begonne.

Publilius Syrus (1835), 590: Noli reverti, ad finem ubi perveneris (Don't turn back when you are just at the goal). ¶ *Ibid.*, 845: Reflectere noli, ad terminum ubi perveneris (Don't turn back when you are just at the goal).

Sidney, *Arcadia*, *Works*, I, 154: Nothing is atchieved before it be throughlie attempted.

798 ONE GOOD **TURN** BEGETS (REPAYS, REQUIRES, DESERVES) ANOTHER

FQ, IV, i, 40, 5–9: Ye will me now with like good turne repay, And justifie my cause on yonder knight . . . do not dismay Your selfe for this; my selfe will for you fight, As ye have done for me.

Culman, 6: Gratia gratiam parit (One good turn begets another). ¶ *Ibid.*, 11: Beneficium semper beneficium provocat (One good turn always provokes another).

Erasmus, *Adagia*, 40E: Gratia gratiam parit (One good deed brings forth another).

Cf. Stevenson, 2400:6; Tilley, T616; C. G. Smith, 307.

799 TO **TURN** OVER A NEW LEAF

Mother Hub., 68: I meane to turne the next leafe of the booke.

Painter, *Palace of P.*, III, 248: You must turne ouer an other Leafe. ¶ Greene, *Menaphon*, *Works*, VI, 116: He thought to turne a new leafe.

¶ Nashe, *Pierce P.*, *Works*, I, 199: Let vs turne ouer a new leafe. ¶ Nashe, *Strange Newes*, *Works*, I, 276: Trip and goe, turne ouer a new leafe. ¶ Nashe, *Have with You*, *Works*, III, 30: I vow to turne a new leafe.

Cf. Apperson, 652; W. G. Smith, 676; Stevenson, 1374:1.

800 IN THE **TWINKLING** OF AN EYE

FQ, II, vii, 11, 4: In twinckling of an eye.

Cf. W. G. Smith, 678; Stevenson, 2402:3; Tilley, T635.

801 **TWO** HEADS ARE BETTER THAN ONE

Mother Hub., 82: Two is better than one head.

Erasmus, *Colloquia Fam.*, 824E: Plus vident oculi quam oculus (Two heads are better than one). ¶ Jonson, *For the Honour of Wales*, 92–93, *Works*, VII, 500: Two heads is better then one.

Cf. Apperson, 655; W. G. Smith, 680; Stevenson, 1096:1; Tilley, H281.

802 TO DO **TWO** THINGS AT ONCE IS TO DO NEITHER

Shep. Cal., Oct., 102: Unwisely weaves, that takes two webbes in hand.

Culman, 26: Qui simul duplex captat commodum, utroque frustretur (He that catches at a double profit at once, is deceived of both). ¶ Publilius Syrus (1835), 7: Ad duo festinans neutrum bene peregeris (To do two things at once is to do neither). ¶ *Ibid.*, 430: Lepores duo qui insequitur, is neutrum capit (One who chases two hares will catch neither).

Plautus, *Mostellaria*, 790–791: Heus tu, si voles verbum hoc cogitare, simul flare sorbereque haud factu facilest (Oh, sir! And you—just you consider the old proverb, please: "No easy task it is to blow and sip, together"); cf. Erasmus, *Colloquia Fam.*, 643D. ¶ Erasmus, *Adagia*, 790A: Duos insequens lepores, neutrum capit (In pursuing two hares a man catches neither).

Cf. Tilley, M318; C. G. Smith, 308.

803 **UNBID**, UNBLESSED

FQ, I, ix, 54, 5: Unbid, unblest.

804 **UNCOUTH**, UNKISSED (UNLOVED)

Shep. Cal., Ded. Epist., 1–12: UNCOUTHE, UNKISTE, sayde the olde famous poete Chaucer: . . . Which proverbe . . . served well Pandares purpose. ¶ *Ibid.*, 15–16: Uncouthe (as said Chaucer) is unkist, and unknown.

Culman, 6: Incognitum non amatur (A thing unknown is not loved).

Gower, *Conf. Aman.*, II, 467: For men sein unknowe unkest.

Cf. Apperson, 659; W. G. Smith, 683; Stevenson, 1311:3; Tilley, U14; C. G. Smith, 311.

805 **UNGIRT**, UNBLESSED

FQ, IV, v, 18, 7: *Ungirt unblest!*

Cf. Apperson, 659: W. G. Smith, 682; Tilley, U10.

806 THE **UNITED** SIDE WINS THE VICTORY

FQ, III, i, 66, 8–9: Joyning foot to foot, and syde to syde . . . in short space their foes they have quite terrifyde. ¶ *Ibid.*, IV, ii, 24, 6–7: Rather ought in friendship for her sake To joyne your force, their forces to repell. ¶ *Ibid.*, VI, v, 14, 7: Where singled forces faile, conjoynd may gaine.

* Publilius Syrus (1934), 4: Auxilia humilia firma consensus facit (United feeling makes strength out of humble aids). ¶ *Ibid.*, 327: Ibi semper est victoria ubi concordia est (Victory is ever there where union of hearts is).

Euripides, *Hecuba*, 884: *δεινὸν τὸ πλῆθος, σὺν δόλῳ τε δύσμαχον* (Mighty are numbers—joined with craft, resistless). ¶ Ovid, *Rem. Amoris*, 420: Quae non prosunt singula, multa iuvant (Things that avail not singly help when they are many).

Cf. Tilley, U11; C. G. Smith, 310.

807 **UNPITIED**, UNPLAINED

Daphnaïda, 79: Unpitied, unplained. ¶ *Astrophel*, 136: Unpitied, unplaynd.

Tasso, *Jer. Del.*, II, 16, 8: Unpitied, unrewarded.

808 **UNSUCCORED**, UNSOUGHT

FQ, , IV, viii, 51, 9: Unsuccour'd and unsought.

809 **UNWELCOMED**, UNSOUGHT

FQ, III, vii, 8, 4: Unwelcomed, unsought.

Tasso, *Jer. Del.*, XX, 90, 4: Uncalled, unsought.

810 SOON **UP**, SOON DOWN

Axiochus (Variorum), 219–220: Soone up, and sooner downe.

Rogers, *Naaman* (1642), 229: Soone up soone downe.

Cf. W. G. Smith, 604; Stevenson, 620:15.

811 TO LABOR IN **VAIN**

Cf. no. 441: To lose your labor

FQ, I, i, 55, 8: He saw his labour all was vaine. ¶ *Ibid.*, II, vii, 59, 1: The knight . . . seeing labour so in vaine. ¶ *Ibid.*, 61, 9: Lost his labour vaine and ydle industry. ¶ *Ibid.*, xii, 19, 7: Labour'd in vaine. ¶ *Ibid.*, III, x, 39, 9: We in vaine have toyld. ¶ *Ibid.*, IV, iii, 32, 5: Life and labour both in vaine to spend. ¶ *Ibid.*, VI, iv, 9, 1: When the salvage saw his labour vaine. ¶ *Ibid.*, xii, 32, 3: He had labourd long in vaine.

Old Testament: *Isaiah*, xlix, 4: Then I said, I have laboured in vain. ¶ *New Testament*: *Gal.*, iv, 11: *ὑμᾶς μή πως εἰκῇ κεκοπίακα εἰς ὑμᾶς* (I have bestowed upon you labour in vain). ¶ Gower, *Conf. Amant.*, III, 293: His labour was in veine.

Cf. Stevenson, 1334:8; Tilley, V5.

812 WHAT HAS **VANISHED** (BEEN DESTROYED) MAY BE LOOKED FOR BUT NEVER RECOVERED

FQ, IV, x, 13, 5–6: Some lost great hope unheedily, Which never they recover might againe. ¶ *Ibid.*, V, x, 26, 9: Who then can thinke their hedlong ruine to recure?

Publilius Syrus (1934), 568: Quod periit quaeri pote, reprendi non potest (What has vanished can be looked for but never recovered).

813 **VENUS** DELIGHTS IN REVELRY

FQ, III, vi, 22, 3–4: So my [Venus's] delight is all in joyfulnesse, In beds, in bowres, in banckets, and in feasts.

Erasmus, *Similia*, 587F: *Amor levatur cantu, corollis, osculis* (Venus delights in songs, in garlands, and in kisses). ¶ Northbrooke, *Treatise agst. Dicing*, 166: Loue is bred by reason of company, and cummunication with men; for among pleasures, feastings, laughing, dauncing, and voluptuousnesse, is the kingdom of Venus and Cupide. ¶ Shakespeare, *L. Lab. Lost*, IV, iii, 379–380: For revels, dances, masques, and merry hours Forerun fair Love, strewing her way with flowers. ¶ Lyly, *Woman in the Moone*, III, ii, 2–4, *Works*, III, 260: Ile [Venus] haue her wittie, quick, and amorous, Delight in reuels and in banqueting, Wanton discourses, musicke, and merrie songes. ¶ Marlowe, *Hero and L.*, I, 299–302: The rites In which Love's beauteous empress most delights, Are banquets, Doric music, mid-night revel, Plays, masques, and all that stern age counteth evil. ¶ Marston, *Pygmalion*, 134–135: Loves only empress Whose kingdom rests in wanton revelling.

Cf. Tilley and Ray, "Proverbs and Proverbial Allusions in Marlowe," *Mod. Lang. Notes*, L (1935), 354–355.

814 TO THE **VICTOR** BELONG THE SPOILS

FQ, I, vi, 5, 3–5: With greedy force he gan the fort assayle, Whereof he weend possessed soone to bee, And win rich spoile of ransackt chastitee. ¶ *View*, 612: All is the conquerours as Tully to Brutus sayth.

Aristotle, *Politics*, i, 2, 16: *τὰ κατὰ πόλεμον κρατούμενα τῶν κρατούντων εἶναί φασιν* (Things conquered in war are said to belong to their conquerors). ¶ Propertius, *Elegies*, iii, 4, 21: Praeda sit haec illis, quorum meruere labores (Be the spoil theirs whose toil has won it). ¶ Livy, *Hist.*, xxi, 13, 5: Cum omnia victoris sint (Since all things are the victor's).

Cf. Stevenson, 2200:6–7.

815 DO NOT TRIUMPH BEFORE THE **VICTORY**

FQ, IV, i, 50, 8–9: He woxe full blithe, as he had got thereby, And gan thereat to triumph without victorie.

Erasmus, *Adagia*, 283D: Ante victoriam encomium canis (You sing triumph before the victory).

Cf. Taverner, 59; Tilley, V50.

816 THE **VILLAIN** DELAYS HIS PUNISHMENT, HE DOES NOT ESCAPE IT

FQ, III, v, 14, 1–7: The villein sped himselfe so well . . . That shortly he from daunger was releast, . . . Yet not escaped from the dew reward of his bad deedes.

Publilius Syrus (1934), 526: Poenam moratur improbus, non praeterit (The villain delays his punishment, he does not escape it).

Sophocles, *Oedipus at Colonus*, 281: *μήπω γενέσθαι φωτὸς ἀνοσίου βροτῶν* (Never yet has a sinner escaped punishment). ¶ Tibullus, *Elegies*, i, 9, 3: Si quis primo periuria celat, sera tamen tactis poena venit pedibus (Even if at first we hide the perjury, yet in the end comes Punishment on noiseless feet).

Cf. Stevenson, 1919:2.

817 **VIRTUE** IS A MEAN

Cf. no. 523: Keep the golden mean in all things

Shep. Cal., Julye, 234: *In medio virtus.*

Aristotle, *N. Ethics*, ii, 6, 13: *μεσότης τις ἄρα ἐστὶν ἡ ἀρετή* (Virtue, therefore, is a mean state. ¶ *Ibid.*, ii, 9, 1: *ἡ ἀρετὴ ἡ ἠθικὴ μεσότης*

(Moral virtue is a mean). ¶ Horace, *Epist.*, i, 18, 9: Virtus est medium vitiorum (Virtue is a mean between vices). ¶ Seneca, *De Benef.*, ii, 16, 2: Cum sit ubique virtus modus (Since virtue is everywhere a mean). ¶ Chaucer, *Leg. Good Women*, 165: For vertu is the mene. ¶ Greene, *Carde of F.*, *Works*, IV, 77: Vertue alwayes consisteth between extremities.

Cf. Clarke, 3, 213; Tilley, V80.

818 **VIRTUE** IS ITS OWN REWARD

FQ, III, xii, 39, 5: Your vertue selfe her owne reward shall breed. ¶ *Ibid.*, V, xi, 17, 9: That is the vertue selfe, which her reward doth pay.

Ovid, *Ex Ponto*, ii, 3, 12: Virtutem pretium qui putet esse sui (Who considers virtue its own reward). ¶ Silius Italicus, *Punica*, xiii, 663: Ipsa quidem virtus sibimet pulcherrima merces (Virtue herself is her own fairest reward). ¶ Seneca, *Epist.*, lxxxi, 19: Virtutum omnium pretium in ipsis est (Reward for all the virtues lies in the virtues themselves). ¶ Claudian, *Panegyricus Dictus Manlio Theodoro Consuli*, xvii, 1: Ipsa quidem Virtus pretium sibi (Virtue is its own reward). ¶ Erasmus, *Colloquia Fam.*, 849A: Virtus ipsa sui pretium est (Virtue is its own reward). ¶ Erasmus, *Colloquia Fam.*, 858B: Ipsa virtus abunde magnum sui praemium est (Virtue is a sufficient reward for itself). ¶ Erasmus, *Institutio Principis Christiani*, 565E: Virtutem ipsam abunde magnum sui praemium esse (Surely virtue is its own reward). ¶ Sidney, *Arcadia*, *Works*, IV, 331: The Reward of vertue beeyng in yt self. ¶ Jonson, *Pleasure Reconciled to Virtue*, 329, *Works*, VII, 491: Vertue . . . being her own reward.

Cf. Apperson, 663; W. G. Smith, 687; Tilley, V81.

819 **VIRTUE** PROCEEDING FROM A BEAUTIFUL BODY IS VERY PLEASING

Amoretti, xxxix, 5–10: Sweet is thy vertue, as thy selfe sweet art. For when on me thou shinedst late in sadnesse, A melting pleasance ran through every part, And me revived with hart robbing gladnesse:

Whylest rapt with joy resembling heavenly madnes, My soule was ravisht quite, as in a traunce.

Culman, 20: Gratior est pulchro veniens e corpore virtus (Virtue proceeding from a fair body is very pleasing).

820 **VIRTUE** (INNOCENCE) PROVIDES ITS OWN LIGHT

FQ, I, i, 12, 9: Vertue gives her selfe light, through darkenesse for to wade.

Publilius Syrus (1934), 661: Suum sequitur lumen semper innocentia (Innocence ever follows her own light).

Cicero, *De Offic.*, i, 9, 30: Aequitas enim lucet ipsa per se (For righteousness shines with a brilliance of its own). ¶ Cicero, *Epist. ad Fam.*, vi, 1, 4: Ipsa virtus se sustenare posse videatur (Virtue seems able by herself to maintain her own ground). ¶ Ashley, *Of Honour* (Heltzel), 68: Vertue . . . shineth sufficiently of yt self. ¶ Milton, *Comus*, 373–374: Virtue could see to do what Virtue would By her own radiant light.

Cf. Tilley, I81.

821 NO POSSESSION IS GREATER THAN **VIRTUE**

FQ, III, Pro., 1, 1–2: Chastity, That fayrest vertue, far above the rest. ¶ *Ibid.*, V, iv, 9, 4–5: Vertue . . . the dowre that did delight. What better dowre can to a dame be hight?

Culman, 7: Mulieris dos pudicitia (Chastity is a woman's dowry). ¶ *Ibid.*, 10: Ampla satis forma pudicitia (Virtue is beauty sufficient enough). ¶ *Ibid.*, 17: Virtute nulla possessio major (No possession is greater than virtue).

Plutarch, *Lives*: *Solon*, vii, 1: *γὰρ ἀρετήν, ἧς κτῆμα μεῖζον οὐδὲν οὐδ' ἥδιον* (Virtue, the most valuable and pleasing possession in the world). ¶ Pettie, *Petite P.*, 124: Vertue and chastity is to bee preferred beefore worlde or wealth.

Cf. Stevenson, 2432:7; 324:1.

822 A **VOW** (PROMISE) IS A BOND

Cf. no. 630: Keep your promise

FQ, V, vii, 19, 7: The holy vow which me doth bind. ¶ *Ibid.*, VI, ii, 37, 5: I am bound by vow.

Harvey, *Pierces Super.*, *Works*, II, 72: Thinke promisse a bonde; cf. *A New Lett.*, *Works*, I, 270.

823 CIVIL **WAR** IS A DESTRUCTIVE EVIL

Visions of B., x, 9–10: Civill warres . . . made The whole worlds spoile.

Culman, 11: Bellum civile malum perniciosum (Civil war is a destructive evil).

824 THE END OF **WAR** IS UNCERTAIN

FQ, I, v, 11, 7: End of the doubtfull battaile. ¶ *Ibid.*, vi, 46, 4: Doubtfull battell. ¶ *Ibid.*, viii, 26, 3: The whole atchievement of this doubtfull warre. ¶ *Ibid.*, IV, iii, 28, 1–2: Thus did the battell varie to and fro, With diverse fortune doubtfull to be deemed. ¶ *Ibid.*, ix, 24, 8–9: This cruell conflict raised thereabout, Whose dangerous successe depended yet in dout. ¶ *Ibid.*, V, ii, 17, 1: Very doubtfull was the warres event.

Culman, 5: Belli exitus incertus (The end of war is uncertain). ¶ *Ibid.*, 5: Belli fortuna anceps (The fortune of war is doubtful).

Cicero, *Pro Milone*, xxi, 56: Incertos exitus pugnarum (The uncertainty of the issues of battle). ¶ Cicero, *Epist. ad Atticum*, vii, 3: Hic omnia facere omnes, ne armis decernatur; quorum exitus semper incerti (On our side we all do everything to avoid battle: you can never be sure of the issue of war). ¶ Vergil, *Aeneid*, iv, 603: Anceps pugnae fuerat fortuna (The issue of battle had been doubtful); cf. xii, 43.

Cf. Stevenson, 2447:2; Tilley, C223: C. G. Smith, 321.

825 TO BE **WARY** AND WISE

FQ, I, vii, 1, 1: What man so wise, what earthly witt so ware? ¶ *Ibid.*, viii, 7, 6: Wise and wary was that noble pere. ¶ *Ibid.*, 44, 6: To be wise, and ware of like agein. ¶ *Ibid.*, II, i, 4, 6: Wise and wary was the knight. ¶ *Ibid.*, v, 9, 6: Wary wise. ¶ *Ibid.*, vi, 26, 1: He was wise, and wary. ¶ *Ibid.*, vii, 64, 6: He was wary wise. ¶ *Ibid.*, IV, i, 17, 9: The warie wise.

Chaucer, *Rom. Rose*, 1258: Wys, and war. ¶ Chaucer, *Cant T.*, Gen. Prol., 309: A Sergeant of the Lawe, war and wys. ¶ Chaucer, *Shipman's T.*, 1555: This marchant, which that was ful war and wys. ¶ *Prov. of Wysdom* (Zupitza), 96: Be ware and wyse, and lye nought.

Cf. Apperson, 697; W. G. Smith, 718; Tilley, T291.

826 GOOD **WATCH** PREVENTS MISFORTUNE

Cf. no. 90: One can never be too cautious; no. 572: Neglect a danger, and it will take you by surprise

FQ, III, x, 3, 4–6: Yet warily he watcheth every way, By which he feareth evill happen may: So th'evill thinkes by watching to prevent.

Publilius Syrus (1934), 130: Caret periclo qui etiam cum est tutus cavet (He's free from danger who even in safety takes precaution). ¶ *Ibid.*, 555: Qui metuit calamitatem rarius accipit (One who dreads disaster rarely meets it). ¶ * *Ibid.* (1835), 61: Aspicere oportet, quicquid nolis perdere (Keep a sharp watch where you would not lose). ¶ *Ibid.*, 968: Ubi timetur, nil quod timeatur nascitur (When there is fear, nothing arises to be feared).

Cf. Tilley, W83; C. G. Smith, 322.

827 AS **WAVERING** (UNSTABLE) AS THE WIND

Shep. Cal., Dec., 126: All was blowne away of the wavering wynd. ¶ *FQ*, II, vi, 23, 5: The wind unstable . . . doth never stay. ¶ *Ibid.*, IV, ii, 5, 2: Alwaies flitting, as the wavering wind.

Pindar, *Pythian Odes*, iii, 104–105: ἄλλοτε δ' ἀλλοῖαι πνοαὶ ὑψιπετᾶν ἀνέμων (Changeful are the breezes of the winds that blow on high). Ovid, *Heroides*, xxi, 76: Stultum est venti de levitate queri (It is foolish to complain of fickle winds). ¶ Pettie, *Petite P.*, 190: Waver with the windes. ¶ *Ibid.*, 233: Wavereth with the wynd.

Cf. Apperson, 670; W. G. Smith, 695; Stevenson, 2514:13; Tilley, W412.

828 IN **WEAL** OR WOE

Cf. no. 829: There is no weal without woe

FQ, I, viii, 43, 1: In wele or woe. ¶ *Ibid.*, V, vi, 23, 9: Betide her wele or wo.

Chaucer, *Leg. Good Women*, 687: For wel or wo. ¶ Barclay, *Ship of F.*, I, 70: Wele nor wo. ¶ *Towneley Plays* (E.E.T.S.), IV, 125: Now in weyll, now in wo. ¶ *Tottel's Misc.*, I, 102: In weal, and wo. ¶ Milton, *Par. Lost*, IX, 133: Linked in weal or woe; cf. VIII, 638. ¶ Ray (1678), 351: Be it weal or be it wo.

829 THERE IS NO **WEAL** WITHOUT WOE

Cf. no. 426: There is no joy without sorrow; no. 828: In weal or woe

FQ, V, xi, 16, 3: Mongst wele some wo.

Cf. Tilley, W188.

830 LITTLE **WEALTH**, LITTLE CARE

Cf. no. 110: Much coin, much care; no. 631: Prosperity brings on anxieties

Shep. Cal., Maye, 110: Nought having, nought feared they to forgoe.

Greene, *Menaphon*, *Works*, VI, 48: In little wealth the least disquiet.

Cf. Apperson, 371; Tilley, W198.

831 THE GREATEST **WEALTH** IS CONTENTMENT WITH A LITTLE

Cf. no. 119: Happy is the man who is content with a little; no. 120: Happy is the man who is content with his own lot

FQ, VI, ix, 30, 5–6: Other, that hath litle, askes no more, But in that litle is both rich and wise.

Culman, 18: Dives est, qui nihil sibi desse putat (He is a rich man who thinks he wants nothing). ¶ Publilius Syrus (1835), 807: Quis plurimum habet? is qui omnium minimum cupit (Who has the greatest possessions? he who wants least).

Lucretius, *De Rerum Natura*, v, 1118–1119: Divitiae grandes homini sunt vivere parvo aequo animo (Man's greatest riches is to live on a little with contented mind). ¶ Northbrooke, *Treatise agst. Dicing*, 48: Seneca sayeth: *Diues est, non qui magis habet, sed qui minus cupit.* He is riche, not that hath much, but that coueteth least. ¶ Wodroephe, *Spared Houres* (1623), 480: He who is content in his poverty, is wonderfully rich. ¶ Ray, *Proverbs* (1670), 28: The greatest wealth, is contentment with a little.

Cf. Apperson, 112; W. G. Smith, 697; Stevenson, 414:7; Tilley, W194; C. G. Smith, 323.

832 TO MAKE FAIR **WEATHER**

FQ, IV, ii, 29, 3: Of all old dislikes they made faire weather.

Foxe, *Acts and Mon.*, VIII, 26: Every man caught him by the hand, and made fair weather of altogethers. ¶ Painter, *Palace of P.*, I, 352: To make faire weather of thinges.

Cf. Tilley, W221.

833 **WELLAND** SHALL DROWN ALL HOLLAND

FQ, IV, xi, 35, 1–3: The fatall Welland . . . if old sawes prove true (which God forbid) Shall drowne all Holland.

Cf. Taylor, 133; Tilley, W266.

834 AT THE **WELLHEAD** THE PUREST STREAMS ARISE

FQ, II, vii, 15, 7: At the well head the purest streames arise.

Cf. Stevenson, 2174:17.

835 A **WELL-PLANNED** PROJECT OFTEN FAILS

Muiopotmos, 320: But seldome seene, forejudgement proveth true.

Culman, 23: Non omnia veniunt, quae in animo statueris (All things do not befall which you purpose in your mind). ¶ *Ibid.*: Optime cogitata saepe pessime cedunt (Things devised for the best, ofttimes fall out for the worst). ¶ Publilius Syrus (1835), 77: Bene cogitata saepe ceciderunt male (A well-planned project often turns out ill). ¶ *Ibid.*, 607: Non omnia evenire, quae statuas, solent (Do not suppose everything will come to pass as you have arranged for it).

Sidney, *Poems*, *Works*, II, 216: Fore-accounting oft makes builders misse.

836 TO RUN AROUND LIKE A **WHEEL**

FQ, II, xii, 20, 6: Like to a restlesse wheele, still ronning round. ¶ *Ibid.*, III, vi, 33, 9: So like a wheele arownd they ronne. ¶ *Amoretti*, xviii, 1: The rolling wheele, that runneth often round.

Plutarch, *Moralia: Letter to Apollonius*, 103F: *τροχοῦ γὰρ περιστείχοντος* . . . (For the wheel goes round . . .).

837 AS GOOD NEVER A **WHIT** AS NEVER THE BETTER

View, 638: As good never a whitt as never the better.

Foxe, *Acts and Mon.*, II, 369: As our common saying goeth, "As good never a whit, as never the better"; cf. V, 728; VIII, 151. ¶ Harvey, *Foure Lett.*, *Works*, I, 230: As good neuer a whit, according to the prouerbe, as neuer the better; cf. *Letter-Book*, 25. ¶ Breton, *Wil of Wit*, *Works*, II, *c*, 60: As good never a whit, as never the better.

Cf. Apperson, 442; W. G. Smith, 448; Tilley, W314.

838 AS **WHITE** AS A LILY

Shep. Cal., Feb., 130: Dyed in lilly white. ¶ *FQ*, I, x, 13, 1: Araied ail in lilly white. ¶ *Ibid.*, xii, 22, 6–7: She did weare All lilly white. ¶ *Ibid.*, II, iii, 26, 4: All in a silken camus lylly whight. ¶ *Ibid.*, ix, 19, 1: In robe of lilly white. ¶ *Ibid.*, IV, x, 52, 4: All in lilly white arayd. ¶ *Ibid.*, xi, 49, 5: Phao lilly white. ¶ *Ibid.*, VI, x, 11, 8: Naked maidens lilly white.

Chaucer, *Sir Thopas*, 2057: As whit as is a lilye flour. ¶ Hawes, *Past. Pleas.*, 198: Whyte as ony lyly. ¶ Nashe, *Lenten Stuffe*, *Works*, III, 206: As lilly white as a Ladies marrying smocke.

Cf. Apperson, 680; Tilley, L296.

839 AS **WHITE** AS IVORY

Epithalamion, 172: Her forehead yvory white.

Greene, *Perymedes*, *Works*, VII, 77: As white as Iuory. ¶ Jonson, *Every Man in his Humour*, V, iii, 268–269, *Works*, III, 283: Saturne, sitting in an Ebon cloud, Disrobd his podex, white as iuorie; cf. V, v, 13, *Works*, III, 399. ¶ Jonson, *Volpone*, II, ii, 247, *Works*, V, 57: White, as iuory.

Cf. Apperson, 680; Tilley, I109.

840 AS **WHITE** AS MILK

Shep. Cal., Aprill, 96: A milkwhite lamb. ¶ *FQ*, I, i, 4, 9: A milkewhite lambe. ¶ *Ibid.*, III, i, 15, 2: Upon a milkwhite palfrey. ¶ *Ibid.*, vii, 30, 8: Milke-white palfreyes. ¶ *Ruines of T.*, 561: As white as anie milke. ¶ *FQ*, IV, xi, 49, 9: Milkewhite Galathaea. ¶ *Ibid.*, V, v, 2, 3: White as milke.

Lydgate, *Fall of P.*, I, 2670: Whit as mylk. ¶ Skelton, *Garl. of Laurell*, 797, *Works*, I, 393: Whyte as mylk. ¶ Sidney, *Arcadia*, *Works*, I, 346: As white as milke.

Cf. Apperson, 680; Tilley, M931.

841 AS **WHITE** AS SNOW

Cf. no. 843: Whiter than snow

Visions of the Worlds V., ii, 2: As white as driven snowe. ¶ *FQ*, I, viii, 30, 2: As white as snow. ¶ *Ibid.*, III, i, 63, 7: In her snow-white smocke.

Lydgate, *Fall of P.*, VI, 2142: Whiht as snouhe. ¶ Lyly, *Euph. and His Eng.*, *Works*, II, 18: A floure as white as snow. ¶ Greene, *Alcida*, *Works*, IX, 51: As white as snowe. ¶ Greene, *Repentance of Robert G.*, *Works*, XII, 168: As white as snow. ¶ Deloney, *Jack Newb.*, *Works*, 12: As white as the driuen snow; cf. *Gentle Craft*, 114.

Cf. Apperson, 681; Stevenson, 2488:1; Tilley, S591.

842 AS **WHITE** AS WHALE'S BONE

FQ, III, i, 15, 5: As white as whales bone.

Hawes, *Past. Pleas.*, 64: Whyte as whalles bone. ¶ *Tottel's Misc.*, I, 207: As white as whales bone.

Cf. Apperson, 680; Stevenson, 2487:8; Tilley, W279.

843 **WHITER** THAN SNOW

Cf. no. 841: As white as snow

FQ, I, i, 4, 2: Lowly asse more white then snow. ¶ *Ibid.*, III, v, 5, 6: Palfrey rydes more white then snow.

Sidney, *Arcadia*, *Works*, I, 218: More white then snow. ¶ *Ibid.*, 347: More white then whitest snowe.

Cf. Stevenson, 2487:4.

844 THE **WICKEDNESS** OF ONE OFTEN BECOMES THE CURSE OF ALL

FQ, III, ix, 2, 5: All are shamed by the fault of one.

Culman, 27: Saepe mali malefacta viri populus luit omnis (Oft times all the people suffer for a bad man's ill-doing). ¶ Publilius Syrus (1934), 404: Malitia unius cito fit male dictum omnium (The malice of one soon becomes the curse of all).

Cf. C. G. Smith, 326.

845 **WILL** HE, NILL HE

FQ, I, iii, 43, 7: Will or nill. ¶ *Ibid.*, IV, vii, 16, 6: Willed or nilled.

Seneca, *Epist.*, liii, 3: Vellet nollet (Willy-nilly); cf. cxvii, 4; *De Brev.*, viii, 5. ¶ Latimer, *Seven Serm.* (Arber), 175: Wil thei nill they. ¶ Foxe, *Acts and Mon.*, II, 119: Will they, nill they; cf. III, 363, 730; VIII, 556. ¶ Edwards, *Damon and P.*, 1506: Will I or nil I. ¶ Gascoigne, *Droome of Doomes Day*, *Works*, II, 261: Whether he will or nyll. ¶ Greene, *Mamillia*, *Works*, II, 86: Will you, nil you. ¶ Greene, *Carde of F.*, *Works*, IV, 90: Will she, nill she. ¶ Greene, *Menaphon*, *Works*, VI, 117: Wil they, nill they. ¶ Nashe, *Lenten Stuffe*, *Works*, III, 186: Will or nill hee.

Cf. Henderson, 271; Apperson, 688; W. G. Smith, 709; Tilley, W401.

846 THE **WILL** OF GOD IS GOOD

FQ, I, x, i, 9: All the good is Gods, both power and eke will.

Culman, 36: Voluntas Dei bona (The will of God is good).

847 WHAT **WILL** BE, SHALL BE

Cf. no. 178: The doom of destiny cannot be avoided; no. 570: The force of necessity is irresistible

Muiopotmos, 225–227: Whatso heavens in their secret doome Ordained have . . . must needs to issue come. *F.Q.*, IV, ii, 51, 8–9: What the Fates do once decree, Not all the gods can chaunge, nor Jove him self can free.

Cicero, *De Div.*, ii, 10, 25: Quod fore paratum est, id summum exsuperat Iovem (That which has been decreed by Fate to be Almighty Jove himself cannot prevent). ¶ Cicero, *De Fato*, vi, 13: Quidquid futurum sit id dicit fieri necesse esse (Whatever will be, he says, must necessarily happen). ¶ Jonson, *Epicoene*, V, iv, 106, *Works*, V, 266: An' it must it shall, sir, they say. ¶ O'Rahilly, no. 282: There is no escaping Fate.

Cf. Apperson, 560; W. G. Smith, 703; Tilley, M1331.

848 WHERE THERE'S A **WILL** THERE'S A WAY

FQ, I, vii, 41, 3–4: He, that never would, Could never: will to might gives greatest aid.

Publilius Syrus (1835), 801: Quid quisque possit, nisi tentando nesciet (No one knows what he can do till he tries).

Cf. Apperson, 687; W. G. Smith, 710; Tilley, W157.

849 TO THE **WILLING** THERE IS NO WRONG DONE

View, 624: To the willing there is noe wrong done.

Taylor, 95: Volenti non fit injuria (No injury is done to one who is willing).

Cf. Herbert Broom, *Legal Maxims* (Philadelphia, 1868), 204.

850 **WILLINGLY** DONE, EASILY DONE

FQ, I, ix, 47, 6–7: What then must needs be donne, Is it not better to doe willinglie?

Culman, 20: Jugum qui fert volens, leve efficit (He that willingly bears the yoke makes it light).

Erasmus, *Colloquia Fam.*, 734D: Nihil est difficile volenti (Nothing is hard to a willing mind).

Cf. Tilley, D407; C. G. Smith, 327.

851 TO **WIN** IT AND WEAR IT

FQ, IV, i, 47, 9: To win a willow bough, whilest other weares the bayes.

Cf. W. G. Smith, 711; Tilley, W408.

852 WHAT **WIND** BLEW YOU HITHER?

FQ, III, ii, 4, 5–6: What uncouth wind Brought her into those partes.

Greene, *Mirrour of Mod.*, *Works*, III, 15: I cannot but both muse and maruell what winde hath driuen you so sodeinlie into this coast. ¶ Greene, *Arbasto*, *Works*, III, 227: What strange wind should land me on this coast. ¶ Greene, *Pandosto*, *Works*, IV, 298: What wind had brought him thither. ¶ Greene, *Tullies Love*, *Works*, VII, 194: What winde hath driuen you into this coast? ¶ Greene, *Never Too Late*, *Works*, VIII, 147: What winde should driue him into the place.

Cf. Apperson, 690; W. G. Smith, 711–712; Stevenson, 2515:2; Tilley, W441.

853 WHILE **WIND** AND WEATHER SERVE

FQ, I, xii, 1, 9: Till mery wynd and weather call her thence away. ¶ *Ibid.*, II, xi, 4, 7–8: Let them pas, whiles winde and wether right Doe serve their turnes. ¶ *Ibid.*, xii, 87, 9: Let us hence depart, whilest wether serves and winde. ¶ *Virgils Gnat.*, 563: Did happie winde and weather entertaine. ¶ *FQ*, V, xii, 4, 5: The winde and weather served them so well.

Rolls of Parlt. (1455), V, 335: At the next Wynde and Wedder that wille serve theym. ¶ Sir E. Howard, *Orig. Lett.* (3rd Ser.), ed. Ellis, I, 150: If wynde and wedour will serve. ¶ Greene, *Carde of F.*, *Works*, IV, 138: As fast as winde and weather would serue them. ¶ Greene, *Perymedes*, *Works*, VII, 83: As soone as wynde and weather did serue.

854 **WINE** KINDLES COURAGE

FQ, I, v, 4, 5–7: They bring them wines . . . To kindle heat of corage privily.

Ovid, *Metam.*, xii, 242: Vina dabant animos (Wine gave them courage).

Cf. Stevenson, 2519:7; Tilley, W486.

855 GOOD **WINE** MAKES GOOD BLOOD

FQ, V, vii, 10, 3: Wine they say is blood.

Nashe, *Lenten Stuffe*, *Works*, III, 152: Giue me pure wine of it self, & that begets good bloud.

Cf. W. G. Smith, 257; Tilley, W461.

856 **WISDOM** (KNOWLEDGE) IS BETTER THAN RICHES

FQ, VI, Prol., 2, 3–4: Learnings threasures, Which doe all worldly riches farre excell.

Culman, 11: Cunctis opibus sapientia pretiosor (Wisdom is more precious than all riches).

Greene, *Never Too Late*, *Works*, VIII, 168: Wisedome is more precious than wealth.

Cf. Stevenson, 2537:10; Tilley, W526.

857 **WISDOM** IS WEALTH

FQ, VI, ix, 30, 7: Wisedome is most riches.

Culman, 9: Solus sapiens dives (The wise man is the only rich man). ¶ *Ibid.*, 26: Sapiens in se omnem habet substantiam (A wise man has all his wealth in himself).

Lucian, *The Dead Come to Life*, 35: *μόνον πλούσιον εἶναι τὸν σοφὸν* (Only the wise man is rich). ¶ Skelton, *Magnyf.* (E.E.T.S.), 4: Welth is of Wysdome. ¶ Lyly, *Euph. and His Eng.*, *Works*, II, 16: Wisedome is great wealth. ¶ Lodge, *Rosalynde*, *Works*, I, 17: Wit is great wealth. ¶ Nashe, *Lenten Stuffe*, *Works*, III, 213: There is no wisedome without wealth.

Cf. Stevenson, 2537:6; Tilley, W528.

858 A **WISE** MAN GROWS ANGRY SLOWLY

FQ, II, v, 21, 6–9: He was wise, Ne would with vaine occasions be inflam'd; . . . nothing could him to impatience entise. ¶ *Ibid.*, VI, i, 30, 7–9: He, that could his wrath full wisely guyde, Did well endure her womanish disdaine, And did him selfe from fraile impatience refraine.

Publilius Syrus (1934), 651: Sapiens locum dat requiescendi iniuriae (The wise man gives an injury room to settle down). ¶ *Ibid.*, 695: Tarde sed graviter sapiens [mens] irascitur (A wise man grows angry slowly but seriously).

859 FOR **WISE** MEN ALL THINGS ARE EASY

View, 609: Nothing soe hard but that, through wysedome, it may be mastred and subdued.

Seneca, *De Ira*, ii, 12, 3: Nihil est tam difficile et arduum quod non humana mens vincat et in familiaritatem perducat adsidua meditatio (Nothing is so hard and difficult that it cannot be conquered by the human intellect and be brought through persistent study into intimate acquaintance). ¶ Erasmus, *Adagia*, 675E: Omnia sapientibus facilia (All things are easy for wise men).

Cf. Taverner, 30, 45; Stevenson, 2536:4.

860 HE IS NOT **WISE** WHO COMMITS THE SAME ERROR TWICE

FQ, IV, i, 34, 7–9: Him wise I never held, That, having once escaped perill neare, Would afterwards afresh the sleeping evill reare.

Publilius Syrus (1835), 420: Lapsus semel, fit culpa, si iterum cecideris (An error repeated is a fault).

Harvey, *Marginalia*, 105: No wiseman offendith twice in on thing.

861 THE **WISE** MAN RULES EVEN OVER THE STARS

View, 609: The wyse man shall rule even over the starres.

Nashe, *Have with You*, *Works*, III, 124: *Sapies dominabitur astris* (The wise man will govern the stars). ¶ Greene, *Eupheus His Censure to Phil.*, *Works*, VI, 208: *Sapiens dominabitur astris*, a wise man may gouerne the starres; cf. *Mourning Garment*, *Works*, IX, 189. ¶ Bryskett, *Discourse of Civill Life* (1606), 172: The wise man ouer-ruleth the starres. ¶ Davies, *Commend. Poems*, *Works*, II, *m*, 4: Wisemen rule the Starres.

862 THERE IS NO **WISDOM** IN BEING WISE TOO LATE

Cf. no. 57: Beware of had I wist

FQ, III, iv, 37, 9: Deare wisedom bought too late.

Culman, 15: Re praeterita omnes sapimus (We are all wise when a thing is past). ¶ *Ibid.*, 24: Post factum plerumque magis sapimus (We are wise for the most part after a thing is done). ¶ Publilius Syrus (1934), 558: Qui cum dolet blanditur post tempus sapit (If a man takes to coaxing when he feels the smart, it is wisdom learned too late).

Cicero, *Epist. ad Fam.*, vii, 16, 1: Sero sapiunt (Man's wisdom comes too late). ¶ Erasmus, *Adagia*, 37F: Sero sapiunt Phryges (The Trojans became wise too late); cf. *Colloquia Fam.*, 885E.

Cf. Taverner, 3; W. G. Smith, 671.

863 WE ARE ALL MADE **WISER** BY LOSS

Shep. Cal., Sept., 68: Ah, fon! now by thy losse art taught.

Culman, 9: Quae nocent docent (The things which hurt us teach us). ¶ *Ibid.*, 12: Eruditiores efficimur omnes damno (We are all made wiser by loss).

Erasmus, *Adagia*, 39E: Quae nocent, docent (Things that are harmful teach).

Cf. C. G. Smith, 284.

864 WE ALL **WISH** THINGS FOR OURSELVES RATHER THAN FOR OTHERS

FQ, VI, viii, 41, 9: Each wisheth to him selfe and to the rest envyes.

Culman, 23: Omnes sibi melius esse malunt, quam alteri (All men wish better to themselves than to other men).

Terence, *Andria*, 426–427: Verum illud verbumst, volgo quod dici solet, omnis sibi malle melius esse quam alteri (It's a true saying you hear everywhere that every one sets his own good before his neighbor's). ¶ Erasmus, *Adagia*, 147A: Omnes sibi melius esse malunt quam alteri (All men have more consideration for themselves than for others).

Cf. Taverner, 15; Tilley, C251.

865 WHAT COMES BY **WISHING** IS NEVER TRULY OURS

FQ, III, i, 46, 9: Wishing it far off, his ydle wish doth lose.

* Publilius Syrus (1934), 1: Alienum est omne quicquid optando evenit (What comes by wishing is never truly ours).

866 THERE IS **WITCHCRAFT** IN FLATTERING WORDS

FQ, I, ix, 53, 2: Ne let vaine words bewitch thy manly hart.

* Publilius Syrus (1934), 251: Habet suum venenum blanda oratio (The wheedling speech contains its special poison).

Cato, *Disticha*, iii, 4: Sermones blandos blaesosque cavere memento (Beware of softly whispered flatteries).

Cf. Tilley, W588; C. G. Smith, 334.

867 THE FINEST **WITS** ARE SOONEST SUBJECT TO LOVE

FQ, II, ii, 26, 5–6: So Love does raine In stoutest minds. ¶ *Ibid.*, V, vi, 1, 8–9: For never yet was wight so well aware, But he at first or last was trapt in womens snare.

Painter, *Palace of P.*, III, 331: It is commonly seene, they which haue best vnderstandinge and knowledge, are soonest tangled in Loue.

Cf. Stevenson, 1485:9; Tilley, W576.

868 TO BE AT YOUR **WIT'S** END

FQ, II, xi, 44, 1: Nigh his wits end then woxe th' amazed knight.

Greene, *Spanish Masquerado*, *Works*, V, 263: At their wits end. ¶ Greene, *Vision*, *Works*, XII, 205: Therefore am I at my wits end. ¶ Nashe, *Christs Tears*, *Works*, II, 122: I am at my wits end.

Cf. Apperson, 699; W. G. Smith, 721; Stevenson, 2548:11; Tilley, W575.

869 OLD **WIVES'** TALES

View, 632: Old wives tales.

Plato, *Theaetetus*, 176B: γραῶν ὕθλος (Old wives' chatter). ¶ Cicero, *Tusc. Disp.*, i, 39, 93: Ineptiae paene aniles (Old wives' fables). ¶ Horace, *Sat.*, ii, 6, 77–78: Garrit anilis ex re fabellas (He rattles off old wives' tales much to the point). ¶ Erasmus, *Colloquia Fam.*, 892B: Sunt mendacia, fabulis plena anilibus (They are lies, full of old wives' tales). ¶ Lodge, *Rosalynde*, *Works*, I, 95: These are but olde wiues tales. ¶ Greene, *Groatsworth of Wit*, *Works*, XII, 119: An olde wiues tale.

Cf. Apperson, 465; W. G. Smith, 473; Stevenson, 2274:1; Tilley, W388.

870 WE BEGIN LIFE IN **WOE**, WE END IT IN MISERY

Cf. no. 552: Man is born to misery; no. 560: There is no mortal whom distress cannot reach

FQ, II, ii, 2, 8–9: Enter we Into this life with woe, and end with miseree!

Sidney, *Arcadia*, *Works*, I, 227: The man that feeling knowes, With cries first borne, the presage of his life.

Cf. Henderson, 239; Tilley, W889.

871 A **WOLF** IN SHEEP'S CLOTHING

Shep. Cal., Sept., 156–157: They [wolves] gang in more secrete wise, And with sheepes clothing doen hem disguise. ¶ *Ibid.*, 184–188: A wicked wolfe . . . Ycladde in clothing of seely sheepe. ¶ *Ibid.*, 206: The woolfe in his counterfect cote.

New Testament: *Matthew*, vii, 15: *Προσέχετε ἀπὸ τῶν ψευδοπροφητῶν, οἵτινες ἔρχονται πρὸς ὑμᾶς ἐν ἐνδύμασι προβάτων ἔσωθεν δέ εἰσιν λύκοι ἅρπαγες* (Beware of false prophets which come to you in sheep's clothing, but inwardly they are ravening wolves). ¶ Erasmus, *Colloquia Fam.*, 851A: Vulturi non dissimilis (He is a wolf in sheep's clothing). ¶ Guazzo, *Civ. Conv.*, *Works*, I, 137: A wolfe clothed in a sheepes skin.

¶ Gascoigne, *Glasse of Govt.*, IV, vii, *Works*, II, 71: Wolves do walke in wethers felles. ¶ Pettie, *Petite P.*, 124: Sutch raveninge wolves in sheepes cloathinge.

Cf. Henderson, 323; Apperson, 701; W. G. Smith, 723; Stevenson, 2555:2; Tilley, W614.

872 A **WOMAN** IS ALWAYS WAVERING AND INCONSTANT

FQ, III, ix, 6, 9: A womans will . . . is disposd to go astray. ¶ *Ibid.*, xii, 26, 3–4: There be phantasies In wavering wemens witt.

Culman, 6: Foeminae sunt inconstantes (Women are unconstant). ¶ *Ibid.*, 28: Varia & mutabilis semper foemina (A woman is always wavering and unconstant).

Vergil, *Aeneid*, iv, 569: Varium et mutabile semper femina (A fickle and changeable thing is woman ever). ¶ Seneca, *De Rem. Fortui.* (Palmer), 62–63: Nihil tam mobile quam foeminarum voluntas, nihil tam vagum (Nothing is so soon moved as a woman's will, nothing so unstable).

Cf. Tilley, W674; C. G. Smith, 337.

873 TO BE BORN OF **WOMAN**

FQ, VI, iii, 41, 9: He of woman was yborne.

Cf. Tilley, W637.

874 A MAN IS A FOOL WHO THINKS HE CAN CONTROL A **WOMAN'S** WILL

FQ, III, ix, 6, 7–9: Extremely mad the man I surely deeme, That weenes with watch and hard restraynt to stay A womans will, which is disposd to go astray.

* Publilius Syrus (1934), 217: Feminae naturam regere desperare est otium (To control a woman's nature is to abandon the hope of a quiet life).

Cf. Stevenson, 2583:7.

875 THE DRIEST **WOOD** IS SOONEST BURNT TO DUST

FQ, III, viii, 25, 5: The driest wood is soonest burnt to dust.

Greene, *Morando*, *Works*, III, 58: Drie sticks are soonest consumed with fire. ¶ Sidney, *Arcadia*, *Works*, I, 149: Old wood inflam'de, doth yeeld the bravest fire.

876 A **WORD** ONCE SPOKEN CAN (CANNOT) BE CALLED BACK

FQ, III, ii, 9, 1–2: The word gone out she backe againe would call, As her repenting so to have missayd.

Culman, 20: Facile volat verbum, tamen nunquam redit (A word quickly flies out, yet it never returns).

Horace, *Ars Poetica*, 390: Nescit vox missa reverti (A word once spoken cannot be recalled). ¶ Horace, *Epist.*, i, 18, 71: Semel emissum volat irrevocabile verbum (A word once spoken flies beyond recall). ¶ Plutarch, *Moralia*: *Ed. of Children*, 10F: *ῥηθὲν ἀναλαβεῖν ἀδύνατον* (The word spoken cannot possibly be recalled). ¶ Erasmus, *Colloquia Fam.*, 696F: Verba simul atque semel evolarint, non revolant (Words, when they are once out, cannot be called in again).

Cf. Stevenson, 2597:2; Tilley, W777; C. G. Smith, 339.

877 **WORDS** ARE BUT WIND

Shep. Cal., Oct., 36: Sike words bene wynd, and wasten soone in vayne. *Colin Clouts*, 716–717: Haughtie words . . . are like bladders blowen up with wynd. ¶ *FQ*, IV, v, 27, 7: He their words as wind esteemed light. ¶ *Ibid.*, VI, vi, 42, 9: Yet were her words but wynd.

Gower, *Conf. Aman.*, III, 2768: For word is wynd. ¶ Skelton, *Magnyf.* (E.E.T.S.), 578: Wordes be but wynde. ¶ Pettie, *Petite P.*, 231: Their wordes . . . bee but winde. ¶ Lyly, *Euph. and His Eng.*, *Works*, II, 221: The painted wordes were but winde. ¶ Greene, *Morando*, *Works*, III, 104: Wordes are but winde; cf. *Mamillia*, *Works*, II, 34, 99, 242. ¶ Harvey, *A New Lett.*, *Works*, I, 285: Wordes are winde.

Cf. Apperson, 710; W. G. Smith, 729; Stevenson, 2611:5; Tilley, W833.

878 **WORDS** ARE (SPEECH IS) THE IMAGE OF THE MIND

Cf. no. 375: What the heart thinks the tongue speaks

View, 638: Woordes are the Image of the mynd.

Culman, 16: Sermo character animi est (Speech is the character of the mind). ¶ *Ibid.*, 21: Mentis habitum sermonis cultus solet indicare (The manner of the speech is wont to show the disposition of the mind). ¶ Publilius Syrus (1835), 1092: Sermo imago animi est: vir qualis, talis est oratio (Speech is a mirror of the soul; as a man speaks, so is he).

Cf. Apperson, 594; W. G. Smith, 612; Tilley, S735; C. G. Smith, 214.

879 **WORDS** CUT DEEPER THAN SWORDS

FQ, IV, viii, 26, 9: Her spightfull words did pricke and wound the inner part. ¶ *Ibid.*, VI, vii, 49, 9: Words sharpely wound.

Culman, 24: Plures necat lingua, quam gladius (The tongue kills more than the sword).

Cf. W. G. Smith, 729; Tilley, W839; C. G. Smith, 341.

880 **WORDS** FRIGHTEN BABES

FQ, III, iv, 15, 3: Wordes fearen babes.

Sidney, *Arcadia*, *Works*, I, 468: Words . . . are but to feare babes.

881 MEN ARE PERSUADED BY GENTLE **WORDS**

FQ, IV, ix, 32, 9: With gentle words perswading them to friendly peace.

Culman, 11: Blandis verbis homines exorantur (Men are persuaded by good words).

Homer, *Iliad*, ix, 113: *δώροισίν τ' ἀγανοῖσιν ἔπεσσί τε μειλιχίοισι* (Persuade him with kindly gifts and gentle words). ¶ Lyly, *Euph. and His Eng.*, *Works*, II, 99: With faire wordes thou shalt yet perswade me.

Cf. Stevenson, 2608:8; 1781:13; C. G. Smith, 342.

882 NOT **WORTH** A PEA

Shep. Cal., Oct., 69: Nought worth a pease.

Cf. Apperson, 457; Tilley, P135.

883 IT IS FOOLISH TO CURE ONE **WOUND** AND MAKE MANY

FQ, III, v, 42, 1–2: O foolish physick, and unfruitfull paine, That heales up one and makes another wound!

Cf. Tilley, S647.

884 THE **WRATH** OF A KING IS ALWAYS DREADFUL

Muiopotmos, 15–16: Is there then Such rancour in the harts of mightie men? ¶ *FQ*, IV, viii, 1, 3–4: The displeasure of the mighty is Then death it selfe more dread and desperate.

Old Testament: *Proverbs*, xvi, 14: The wrath of a king is as messengers of death. ¶ Homer, *Iliad*, ii, 196: *θυμὸς δὲ μέγας ἐστὶ διοτρεφέων βασιλήων* (Great is the wrath of kings, cherished by Zeus); cf. Aristotle, *Rhet.*, ii, 2, 7. ¶ Seneca, *Medea*, 494: Gravis ira regum est semper (The anger of kings is always severe). ¶ Erasmus, *Colloquia Fam.*, 677F: Violenta res & impotens est regis animus concitatus, nec huc aut illuc duci potest, sed impetu suo fertur, velut oestro divino percitus (The wrath of a king is impetuous and unruly, and not to be led this way or that, but presses forward with a restless fury). ¶ Gascoigne, *Glasse of Govt.*, II, i, *Works*, II, 28: The kings indignation is the messenger of death.

885 WHERE **WRATH** IS JOINED WITH POWER THERE ARE THUNDERBOLTS

FQ, IV, iii, 15, 1–8: They both together fiercely met, As if that each ment other to devoure; . . . their powre They felt, . . . And fire did flash, like lightning after thunder.

* Publilius Syrus (1934), 214: Fulmen est ubi cum potestate habitat iracundia (It is thunder and lightning when anger dwells with power).

Cf. Tilley, W934.

886 IT IS **WRETCHED** TO LONG FOR DEATH, YET FAIL TO DIE

FQ, IV, vii, 11, 8–9: He in hell doth lie, That lives a loathed life, and wishing cannot die.

Publilius Syrus (1934), 556: Quam miserum est mortem cupere nec posse emori (How wretched to long for death, yet fail to die)!

887 IT IS NOT **WRONG** TO HARM ONE WHO HAS HARMED YOU

Cf. no. 586: Offenders should be punished

FQ, II, iv, 31, 5–6: She did first offend, She last should smart. ¶ *Ibid.*, VI, i, 26, 4–5: It is no blame To punish those that doe deserve the same.

Publilius Syrus (1934), 281: Impune pecces in eum qui peccat prior (You may safely offend against him who offends first).

Cf. C. G. Smith, 344.

888 THE **WRONG** NEVER BECOMES THE RIGHT

View, 650: Evill that is of it self evill will never become good.

Publilius Syrus (1835), 415: Jus omne supra omnem positum est injuriam (The right is ever beyond the reach of the wrong).

Taylor, 95: Quod initio vitiosum est non potest tractu temporis convalescere (What is wrong in its beginnings cannot be remedied by the passage of time).

Cf. Herbert Broom, *Legal Maxims* (Philadelphia, 1868), 136–141; W. G. Smith, 736; Stevenson, 1992:1.

889 THERE IS NO **WRONG** WITHOUT A REMEDY

FQ, II, i, 20, 5: All wrongs have mendes.

Draxe, 401, 1621 (*s.v.* Physicke): God hath provided a remedie for every disease. ¶ Fuller, 4879: There is a remedy for every thing, could we but hit upon it.

Cf. *Paradise of D. Dev.*, 210–211; Herbert Broom, *Legal Maxims* (Philadelphia, 1868), 147; Apperson, 527; W. G. Smith, 736.

890 **YIELD** A LITTLE AND GAIN MUCH

Cf. no. 891: To yield to the need of the time is no disgrace

FQ, V, xii, 19, 3–4: No shame to stoupe, ones head more high to reare, And, much to gaine, a litle for to yield. ¶ *Ibid.*, VI, xi, 6, 9: A little well is lent, that gaineth more withall.

* Publilius Syrus (1934), 64: Beneficia plura recipit qui scit reddere (He receives more benefits who knows how to yield).

Ovid, *Artis Amat.*, ii, 197: Cede repugnanti; cedendo victor abibis (Give way to your opponent; by yielding you will come off victorious). ¶ Cotgrave, *Dict.* (*s.v.* Recueiller): They that can yeeld will thriue.

891 TO **YIELD** TO THE NEED OF THE TIME IS NO DISGRACE

Cf. no. 890: Yield a little and gain much

FQ, III, iii, 52, 3–4: I deeme that counsel aye most fit, That of the time doth dew advauntage take. ¶ *Ibid.*, V, xi, 56, 3–4: To temporize is not from truth to swerve, Ne for advantage terme to entertaine, When as necessitie doth it constraine.

Culman, 17: Abjiciendus pudor quoties urget necessitas (Cause for shame is to be thrown away, as often as necessity constrains). ¶ *Ibid.*, 21: Inutilis est pudor, cum urget necessitas (Cause for shame is unprofitable when necessity compels). ¶ * Publilius Syrus (1934), 256: Honeste servit qui succumbit tempori (To yield to the need of the time is honorable service).

Plautus, *Asinaria*, 671: Quidvis egestas imperat (Need knows no shame).

Cf. C. G. Smith, 215.

892 **YOUTH**, SHOULD BE CONTROLLED BY REASON, NOT BY FORCE

Shep. Cal., Oct., 21–22: O what an honor is it, to restraine The lust of lawlesse youth with good advice!

Publilius Syrus (1934), 627: Ratione non vi vincenda adulescentia est (Youth must be mastered not by force but by reason).

BIBLIOGRAPHY

BIBLIOGRAPHY

With Explanation of Cue Titles
of Books Frequently Cited

Apperson, G. L. *English Proverbs and Proverbial Phrases*. London and Toronto: J. M. Dent and Sons, Ltd., 1929.

Bacon, Francis. *Promus of Formularies and Elegancies*. Illustrated and elucidated by passages from Shakespeare by Mrs. Henry Pott. London: Longmans, Green, and Co., 1883. Example of cue title with sample reference no.: Bacon, *Promus*, 357.

Baldwin, Thomas W. *William Shakspere's Small Latine & Lesse Greeke*. 2 vols. Urbana: University of Illinois Press, 1944.

Benham, Gurney. *Benham's Book of Quotations*. New and revised edition with supplement. London: George G. Harrap and Co., Ltd., 1948.

Bland, Robert, *Proverbs, Chiefly Taken from the Adagia of Erasmus, with Explanations*. 2 vols. London: Printed for T. Egerton, Military Library, Whitehall, 1814.

Bond, Donald F. "English Legal Proverbs," *Publications of the Modern Language Association of America*, 51 (1936), 921–935.

Brant, Sebastian. *Ship of Fools*. Translated by Alexander Barclay. 2 vols. Edinburgh: William Paterson; London. Henry Sotheran and Co., 1874.

Breton, Nicholas. *Works in Verse and Prose*. Edited by Alexander B. Grosart. Chertsey Worthies' Library. 2 vols. Edinburgh, 1879.

Burton, Robert, *Anatomy of Melancholy*. Everyman's Library. 3 vols. London: J. M. Dent and Sons, Ltd.; New York: E. P. Dutton and Co., Inc., 1932.

Camden, William. *Remains Concerning Britain*. London: John Russell Smith, 1870.

Cato, Dionysius. *Dicta Catonis*. Edited and translated by J. Wight Duff and Arnold M. Duff and included in their *Minor Latin Poets*. Loeb Classical Library. Cambridge, Mass.: Harvard University Press, 1934. *Collectio Distichorum Vulgaris*, pp. 592–596. *Catonis Disticha*, pp. 596–621. *Collectio Monostichorum*, pp. 624–629.

Cawdray, Robert. *Treasurie or Store-House of Similies.* London: Printed by Tho. Greede, 1600.

Cervantes, Miguel de. *Don Quixote.* Translated by Thomas Shelton. Library of English Classics. 3 vols. London: Macmillan and Co., Ltd., 1923.

Chaucer, Geoffrey. *Complete Works.* Edited by F. N. Robinson, Cambridge Edition. Boston: Houghton Mifflin Co., n. d.

Christy, Robert. *Proverbs, Maxims, and Phrases of All Ages.* 2 vols. in 1. New York: G. P. Putnam's Sons, 1904.

Clarke, John. *Paroemiologia Anglo-Latina in Usum Scholarum Concinnata. Or, Proverbs, English, and Latine.* Methodically disposed according to the commonplace heads in Erasmus his Adages. London, 1639.

Cotgrave, Randle. *Dictionarie of the French and English Tongues.* Whereunto is also annexed a most copious Dictionarie of the English set before the French by R. S. L. [Robert Sherwood Londoner]. London, 1632.

Culman, Leonard [Leonhardus Culmannus]. *Sententiae Pueriles, Anglo-Latinae.* Translated by Charles Hoole. Londini: Sumptibus Societatis Stationariorum, 1658. Example of cue title with sample page no.: Culman, 10.

Davies, John. *Complete Works of John Davies of Hereford.* For the first time collected and edited with memorial-introduction, notes, etc., by Alexander B. Grosart. Chertsey Worthies' Library. 2 vols. [Edinburgh]: Printed for private circulation [by T. and A. Constable], 1878.

Draxe, Thomas. *Treasurie of Ancient Adagies. Anglia Zeitschrift für Englische Philologie,* XLII (1918–1919), 361–424. Halle: Max Niemeyer.

Duschl, Joseph. *Das Sprichwort bei Lydgate.* Weiden: Buchdruckerei Ferdinand Nickl, 1912.

Erasmus, Desiderius. *Opera Omnia.* 10 vols. in II. Leyden, 1703–1706. Vol. I: *Epistolas, Similia,* and *Colloquia Familiaria.* Vol. II: *Adagia.* Vol. IV: *Moriae Encomium.* Vol. V: *Enchiridion.* Example of cue title with sample page no.: Erasmus, *Similia,* 588C., *Institutio Principis Christianini,* 591C.

——— *Familiar Colloquies.* Translated from the Latin by Nathan Bailey.

London: Hamilton, Adams, and Co.; Glasgow: Thomas D. Morison, 1877.

——— *Education of a Christian Prince.* Translated with an introduction on Erasmus and on ancient and medieval political thought by Lester K. Born. Columbia University Records of Civilization. New York: Columbia University Press, 1936.

Fergusson, David. *Scottish Proverbs.* From the original Print of 1641, together with a larger Manuscript Collection of about the same period hitherto unpublished. Edited by Erskine Beveridge. Scottish Text Society. Edinburgh and London: William Blackwood and Sons, 1924.

Foxe, John. *Acts and Monuments.* With a life and defense of the martyrologist by George Townsend. Third edition: revised and corrected with appendices, glossary, and indices. 8 vols. London: George Seeley, 32, Argyll Street, Regent Street, 1870.

Fuller, Thomas. *Gnomologia: Adagies and Proverbs; Wise Sentences and Witty Sayings, Ancient and Modern, Foreign and British.* London, 1732.

Gascoigne, George. *Complete Works.* Edited by John W. Cunliffe. Cambridge English Classics. 2 vols. Cambridge: Cambridge University Press, 1907–1910.

Golding, Arthur. *Shakespeare's Ovid: Translation of the Metamorphoses.* Edited by W. H. D. Rouse. King's Library. London: At the De La More Press, 1904.

Gorgeous Gallery of Gallant Inventions. Edited by Hyder E. Rollins. Cambridge, Mass.: Harvard University Press, 1926.

Gower, John. *English Works.* Edited from the manuscripts with introduction, notes, and glossary by G. C. Macaulay. 2 vols. Early English Text Society. London: Kegan Paul, Trench Trubner and Co., Ltd., 1900.

Greene, Robert. *Life and Complete Works in Prose and Verse.* For the first time collected and edited, with notes and illustrations, etc. by Alexander B. Grosart. Huth Library. 15 vols. Printed for private circulation only, 1881–1886.

Guazzo, Steeven. *Civile Conversation.* Translated by George Pettie and Barth. Young, with an introduction by Sir Edward Sullivan, Bart. Edited by Charles Whibley. Tudor Translations. Second Series.

2 vols. London: Constable and Co., Ltd.; New York: Alfred A. Knopf, 1925.

Handful of Pleasant Delights. By Clement Robinson and others. Edited by Hyder E. Rollins. Cambridge, Mass.: Harvard University Press, 1924.

Harvey, Gabriel. *Letter-Book,* A.D. 1573–1580. Edited from the original MS Sloane 93, in the British Museum, by Edward John Long Scott. Camden Society Publication. New Series, Vol. XXXIII. [Westminster], 1884.

——— *Marginalia.* Collected and edited by G. C. Moore Smith. Stratford-upon-Avon: Shakespeare Head Press, 1913.

——— *Works.* For the first time collected and edited with memoir, introduction, notes, etc. by Alexander B. Grosart. Huth Library. 3 vols. London: Printed for private circulation only, 1884–1885.

Hawes, Stephen. *Pastime of Pleasure: An Allegorical Poem.* Reprinted from the edition of 1555 for the Percy Society. London: T. Richards, 100, St. Martin's Lane, 1845.

Henderson, Alfred. *Latin Proverbs and Quotations,* with translations and parallel passages and a copious English index. London: Sampson Low, Son, and Marston, 1869.

Herbert, George. *Works in Prose and Verse.* Edited from the latest editions with memoir, explanatory notes, etc. Chandos Classics. London: Frederick Warne and Co., Ltd., n. d.

Heywood, John. *Dialogue of the Effectual Proverbs in the English Tongue Concerning Marriage.* Edited by John S. Farmer. London: Gibbings and Co., 1906.

Hislop, Alexander, *Proverbs of Scotland.* Collected and arranged, with notes, explanatory and illustrative, and a glossary. Glasgow: Porteous and Hislop, 41 West Nile Street, 1862.

Jones, Hugh Percy. *Dictionary of Foreign Phrases and Classical Quotations.* Edinburgh: John Grant, 1913.

Jonson, Ben. *Works.* Edited by C. H. Herford and Percy Simpson. 10 vols. Oxford: Clarendon Press, 1925–1947.

Kelly, James. *Complete Collection of Scotish Proverbs.* London, 1721.

Lodge, Thomas. *Complete Works.* Now first collected. . . . [Glasgow]: Vol. 1 printed for the Hunterian Club, 1883.

Lydgate, John. *Fall of Princes*. Edited by Henry Bergen. 4 parts (vols.). Washington: Carnegie Institution, 1923–1927.

Lyly, John. *Complete Works*. For the first time collected and edited from the earliest quartos with life, bibliography, etc. by R. Warwick Bond. 3 vols. Oxford: Clarendon Press, 1902.

MacDonald, T. D. *Gaelic Proverbs and Proverbial Sayings*. Stirling: Eneas MacKay, n. d.

Minor Latin Poets. Edited by J. Wight Duff and Arnold M. Duff. Loeb Classical Library. Cambridge, Mass.: Harvard University Press; London: William Heinemann, Ltd., 1934.

Montaigne, Michel de. *Essays*. Done into English by John Florio, 1603. With an introduction by George Saintsbury. 3 vols. London: David Nutt, 1892.

Nashe, Thomas. *Works*. Edited from the original texts by Ronald B. McKerrow. 5 vols. London: Sidgwick and Jackson, Ltd., 1910.

O'Rahilly, Thomas F. *A Miscellany of Irish Proverbs*. Dublin: Talbot Press, Ltd., 1922.

Otto, A. *Die Sprichwörter*. Leipzig: Druck und Verlag von B. G. Teubner, 1890.

Painter, William. *The Palace of Pleasure*. Done into English by William Painter. Edited by Joseph Jacobs. 3 vols. London: David Nutt, 1890.

Paradise of Dainty Devices. Edited by Hyder E. Rollins. Cambridge, Mass.: Harvard University Press, 1927.

Pettie, George. *Petite Pallace of Pettie His Pleasure*. Edited by Herbert Hartman. London: Oxford University Press, 1938.

Ray, [John]. *Collection of English Proverbs*. Cambridge, 1670; 2nd ed., 1678.

Representative English Comedies: From the Beginnings to Shakespeare. Edited by Charles Mills Gayley. New York: Macmillan Co., 1903.

Riley, Henry Thomas. *Dictionary of Latin and Greek Quotations, Proverbs, Maxims, and Mottos*. London: George Bell and Sons, 1880.

Rix, Herbert David. *Rhetoric in Spenser's Poetry*. Pennsylvania State College Studies, No. 7. State College, Pennsylvania, 1940.

Shakespeare, William. *Complete Works*. Edited by George Lyman Kittredge. Boston: Ginn and Co., 1936.

Sidney, Sir Philip. *Complete Works*. Edited by Albert Feuillerat. Cambridge English Classics. 4 vols. Cambridge: Cambridge University Press, 1912–1926.

Skeat, Walter W. *Early English Proverbs*. Oxford: Clarendon Press, 1910.

Skelton, John. *Poetical Works*. With notes by Alexander Dyce. 2 vols. London: T. Rodd, 1843.

——— *Magnyfycence*. Edited by Robert Lee Ramsay. Early English Text Society. London: K. Paul Trench, Trubner and Co., Limited 1906 (issued in 1908).

Smith, Charles G. *Spenser's Theory of Friendship*. Baltimore: Johns Hopkins Press, 1935.

——— *Shakespeare's Proverb Lore*. Cambridge, Mass.: Harvard University Press, 1963. Example of cue title with sample page no.: C. G. Smith, 1.

Smith, William George. *Oxford Dictionary of English Proverbs*. With an introduction by Janet E. Heseltine. Second edition, revised by Paul Harvey. Oxford: Clarendon Press, 1948. Example of cue title with sample page no.: W. G. Smith, 227.

Spenser, Edmund. *Works*. Edited by Edwin Greenlaw, Charles G. Osgood, F. M. Padelford, and Ray Heffner. A variorum edition. *The Faerie Queene*, 6 vols., 1932–1938; *Minor Poems*, 2 vols., 1943–1948; *Prose Works*, 1949. Baltimore: Johns Hopkins Press.

——— *Complete Poetical Works*. Edited by R. E. Neil Dodge. Cambridge Edition. Boston: Houghton Mifflin Co., n. d.

——— *Works*. Edited by R. Morris, with a memoir by John W. Hales. Globe Edition. London: Macmillan and Co., Ltd., 1929.

——— *Faerie Queene*. A New Edition with a Glossary, and Notes explanatory and critical by John Upton. 2 vols. London: Printed for J. and R. Tonson in the Strand, 1758.

——— *Complaints*. Edited by W. L. Renwick. London: Scholartis Press, 1928.

——— *Daphnaïda and Other Poems*. Edited by W. L. Renwick. London: Scholartis Press, 1929.

——— *Epithalamion*. Edited with an introduction and notes by Cortlandt Van Winkle. New York: F. S. Crofts and Co., 1926.

——— *Shepheards Calendar*. Edited by C. H. Herford. London: Macmillan and Co., Ltd., 1925.

——— *Shepherd's Calendar*. Edited by W. L. Renwick. London: Scholartis Press, 1930.

Stevenson, Burton. *Home Book of Proverbs, Maxims and Familiar Phrases.* New York: Macmillan Co., 1948. Example of cue title with sample page and reference no.: Stevenson, 516:2.

Syrus, Publilius. *Publilii Syri Sententiae.* Edited by R. A. H. Bickford-Smith. London: C. J. Clay and Sons, 1895.

——— *Sentences de Publius Syrus.* Traduction nouvelle par Jules Chenu. Paris: C. L. F. Panckoucke, 1835. Example of cue title with sample no. of a *sententia*: Publilius Syrus (1835), 229.

——— *Sententiae.* Edited and translated by J. Wight Duff and Arnold M. Duff and included in their *Minor Latin Poets.* Loeb Classical Library. Cambridge, Mass.: Harvard University Press, 1934. Example of cue title with sample no. of a *sententia*: Publilius Syrus (1934), 667.

Taverner, Richard. *Proverbs or Adages by Desiderius Erasmus.* Gathered out of the *Chiliades* and Englished by Richard Taverner, London, 1569. A facsimile reproduction with an Introduction by Dewitt T. Starnes. Gainsville, Florida: Scholar's Facsimiles and Reprints, 1956. Example of cue title with sample page no.: Taverner, 35.

Taylor, Archer. *The Proverb.* Cambridge, Mass.: Harvard University Press, 1931.

Tilley, Morris Palmer. *A Dictionary of the Proverbs in England in the Sixteenth and Seventeenth Centuries.* Ann Arbor: University of Michigan Press, 1950. Example of cue title with the no. of a proverb: Tilley, F693.

Tottel's Miscellany. Edited by Hyder E. Rollins. 2 vols. Cambridge, Mass.: Harvard University Press, 1928–1929.

Udall, Nicholas. *Apophthegmes of Erasmus.* Edited and illustrated with notes and parallel passages by Robert Roberts. Boston, Lincolnshire: Robert Roberts, 1877. Example of cue title with sample page and reference no.: Udall, *Apoph. of Erasm.*, 23:52.

Walz, Gotthard. *Das Sprichwort bei Gower.* Nordlingen: C. H. Beck'sche Buchdruckerei, 1907.

Warton, Thomas. *Observations on the "Faerie Queene" of Spenser.* London: Printed for R. and J. Dodsley and J. Fletcher, in the Turl, Oxford, 1754.

Werner, Jakob. *Lateinische Sprichwörter und Sinnsprüche des Mittelalters aus Handschriften Gesammelt.* Heidelberg: Carl Winters Universitätsbuchhandlung, 1912.

Whiting, Bartlett Jere. *Chaucer's Use of Proverbs.* Harvard Studies in Comparative Literature, Vol. XI. Cambridge, Mass.: Harvard University Press, 1934.

——— *Proverbs in the Earlier English Drama.* Harvard Studies in Comparative Literature. Vol. XIV. Cambridge, Mass.: Harvard University Press, 1938.

Wilson, Thomas. *Arte of Rhetorique.* Edited by G. H. Mair. Tudor and Stewart Library. Oxford: Clarendon Press, 1909.

Zupitza, Julius. *The Prouerbis of Wysdom*, *Archiv für das Studium der Neueren Sprachen und Litteraturen*, XC (1893), 241–268. Braunschweig: Druck und Verlag von Georg Westermann.

DISTRIBUTION INDEX TO THE PROVERB LORE QUOTED FROM SPENSER

DISTRIBUTION INDEX TO THE PROVERB LORE QUOTED FROM SPENSER

This distribution index lists Spenser's works in alphabetical order and shows under each title where the proverb lore quoted from Spenser occurs. The numbers in parentheses following the citations refer to the entry numbers in the "List of Spenser's Proverbs." The number in brackets at the end of each listing shows the total number of proverbs cited in that work.

FAERIE QUEENE, BOOK II

FAERIE QUEENE, BOOK III

FAERIE QUEENE, BOOK IV

FAERIE QUEENE, BOOK V

FAERIE QUEENE, BOOK VI

FAERIE QUEENE, BOOK VII

HYMNES IN HONOUR OF LOVE AND BEAUTIE

HYMNES OF HEAVENLY LOVE AND BEAUTIE

LETTERS TO HARVEY

MOTHER HUBBERD

MUIOPOTMOS

PROTHALAMION

RUINES OF ROME

108 (772); 108 (381); 109 (771); 109 (650); 110 (674); 110 (629); 111 (364); 112 (12); 112 (188); 113 (188); 114 (385); 114 (7). [12],

RUINES OF TIME

59 (337); 60 (387); 60 (79); 60 (12); 60 (533); 60 (441); 62 (95); 64 (426); 65 (463); 65 (772); 66 (613); 66 (653); 67 (687); 67 (706); 67 (772); 67 (840); 67 (11); 67 (427); 69 (171). [19]

SHEPHEARDES CALENDER

EPISTLE

5 (804); 5 (740); 6 (185); 6 (738); 6 (192). [5]

JANUARYE

10 (482). [1]

FEBRUARIE

11 (603); 11 (35); 12 (313); 12 (14); 12 (573); 12 (10); 12 (470); 12 (8); 12 (79); 12 (727); 13 (838); 13 (105); 14 (579); 14 (222); 14 (753); 14 (648); 14 (629); 14 (573); 14 (589); 15 (589). [20]

MARCH

16 (42); 16 (402); 16 (764); 16 (533); 17 (492); 17 (496); 17 (477). [7]

APRILL

19 (840); 20 (602); 20 (276); 22 (324). [4]

MAYE

23 (531); 23 (483); 23 (760); 23 (615); 23 (367); 23 (212); 24 (345); 24 (610); 24 (717); 24 (378); 24 (360); 24 (632); 24 (830); 24 (15); 24 (277); 25 (367); 25 (707); 25 (298); 25 (737); 26 (740); 26 (246); 27 (212); 27 (717). [23]

JUNE

29 (772); 29 (483); 29 (592); 29 (65); 30 (616); 30 (594); 30 (759). [7]

JULYE

32 (366); 32 (385); 33 (568); 33 (730); 33 (83); 33 (25); 33 (735); 33 (103); 34 (657); 34 (817); 34 (771); 34 (763); 34 (372); 34 (358); 36 (505). [15]

AUGUST

36 (578); 37 (103); 37 (672); 37 (487); 37 (83); 38 (530). [6]

SEPTEMBER

40 (1); 40 (761); 40 (107); 40 (349); 40 (663); 40 (94); 40 (132); 40 (863); 40 (108); 41 (76); 41 (36); 41 (433); 41 (684); 41 (871); 41 (44); 41 (626); 41 (474); 41 (454); 41 (871); 41 (230); 42 (871); 42 (25); 42 (268); 42 (290); 42 (750); 42 (619); 42 (652); 43 (619). [28]

OCTOBER

44 (82); 44 (238); 44 (892); 44 (25); 44 (47); 44 (877); 45 (882); 45 (479); 45 (802); 45 (620); 45 (142); 47 (741). [12]

NOVEMBER

48 (452); 50 (91); 50 (518); 50 (519); 51 (152); 51 (701); 52 (152). [7]

DECEMBER

53 (748); 53 (99); 54 (226); 54 (827); 54 (140); 55 (12); 56 (12). [7]

TEARES OF THE MUSES

71 (453); 72 (373); 72 (179); 72 (515); 72 (44); 72 (407); 72 (685); 73 (414); 74 (73); 74 (738); 74 (414); 76 (523); 76 (625); 76 (239); 77 (414); 77 (439); 77 (381); 78 (638); 78 (5). [19]

VIRGILS GNAT

80 (256); 80 (101); 81 (101); 81 (348); 82 (5); 83 (286); 83 (696); 83 (337); 83 (596); 83 (283); 84 (159); 84 (572); 84 (586); 84 (614); 86 (533); 87 (853); 87 (628); 87 (216). [18]

VISIONS OF BELLAY

125 (11); 125 (696); 125 (328); 125 (113); 127 (103); 127 (370); 127 (337); 127 (823); 128 (673). [9]

VISIONS OF PETRARCH

129 (447); 129 (271); 129 (12). [3]

VISIONS OF THE WORLDS VANITIE

123 (841); 123 (337); 123 (700); 124 (446); 125 (679); 125 (280). [6]

LATIN AND ENGLISH WORD INDEXES

LATIN WORD INDEX

This index contains the main words in all the *sententiae* quoted. The numbers refer to the entry numbers in the "List of Proverbs."

ENGLISH WORD INDEX

This is a catchword index to the proverb lore quoted from Spenser and to the translations of all the *sententiae* quoted. The numbers refer to the entry numbers in the "List of Spenser's Proverbs."